Circle the Wagons!

# Circle the Wagons!

## Attacks on Wagon Trains in History and Hollywood Films

GREGORY F. MICHNO *and*
SUSAN J. MICHNO

McFarland & Company, Inc., Publishers
*Jefferson, North Carolina*

*The present work is a reprint of the illustrated case bound edition of* Circle the Wagons!: Attacks on Wagon Trains in History and Hollywood Films, *first published in 2009 by McFarland.*

LIBRARY OF CONGRESS CATALOGUING-IN-PUBLICATION DATA

Michno, Gregory F., 1948–
Circle the wagons! : attacks on wagon trains in history and Hollywood films / Gregory F. Michno and Susan J. Michno.
p. cm.
Includes bibliographical references and index.

ISBN 978-1-4766-7236-6
softcover : acid free paper ∞

1. Frontier and pioneer life—West (U.S.)  2. Wagon trains—West (U.S.)—History—19th century.  3. Battles—West (U.S.)—History—19th century.  4. West (U.S.)—History—19th century.  5. Frontier and pioneer life—In motion pictures.  6. Wagon trains—In motion pictures.  7. Battles—In motion pictures.  8. West (U.S.)—In motion pictures.  9. Western films—History and criticism.  10. Historical films—United States—History and criticism.
I. Michno, Susan, 1947–  II. Title.
F596.M525   2018         978.'02—dc22                    2008041416

BRITISH LIBRARY CATALOGUING DATA ARE AVAILABLE

© 2009 Gregory F. Michno and Susan J. Michno. All rights reserved

*No part of this book may be reproduced or transmitted in any form or by any means, electronic or mechanical, including photocopying or recording, or by any information storage and retrieval system, without permission in writing from the publisher.*

Front cover: Poster of American Indians attacking covered wagons, Courier Litho. Co., Buffalo, New York, 1899 (Library of Congress)

Printed in the United States of America

*McFarland & Company, Inc., Publishers
Box 611, Jefferson, North Carolina 28640
www.mcfarlandpub.com*

# Table of Contents

*Preface* . . . . . . . . . . . . . . . . . . . . . . . . . . . . . . . . 1
*Introduction* . . . . . . . . . . . . . . . . . . . . . . . . . . . . 5

1. The Utter–Van Ornum Wagon Train . . . . . . . . . . . . . 11
2. The Bent and Towne-Tevis Wagon Trains . . . . . . . . . . 16
3. The Horn-Harris Wagon Train (*The Searchers, Ulzana's Raid*) . . . . 20
4. The Webster Wagon Train (*In the Days of the Pilgrims, The Missing*) . . . . . . . . . . . . . . . . . . . . . . . . . . . . 24
5. The Wilson Wagon Train (*The Comancheros, Comanche Station*) . . . . . . . . . . . . . . . . . . . . . . . 28
6. The Oatman Wagon Train (*The Unforgiven, Sioux Blood, White Comanche*) . . . . . . . . . . . . . . . . . . . . . . . . 33
7. The Ward-Masterson Wagon Train (*Soldier Blue, Rio Grande*) . . . . 38
8. The Fancher-Baker Wagon Train (*The Last Wagon, Dawn on the Great Divide*) . . . . . . . . . . . . . . . . . . . . . . . 44
9. The Shepherd and Miltimore Wagon Trains (*Fighting Caravans, The Painted Stallion*) . . . . . . . . . . . . . . . . . . . . . 49
10. The Box Wagon (*The Unforgiven*) . . . . . . . . . . . . . . . 56
11. The Rose-Baley Wagon Train . . . . . . . . . . . . . . . . . 63
12. The Sager Wagons (*Seven Alone*) . . . . . . . . . . . . . . . 65
13. The Morton-Marble Wagon Train (*The Forest Rose, The Half Breed, Two Rode Together*) . . . . . . . . . . . . . . . . . . 70
14. Anna Brewster Morgan (*Stolen Women, Captured Hearts*) . . . . . 78
15. The Fletcher Wagon Train (*Duel at Diablo, Fort Apache, Ulzana's Raid*) . . . . . . . . . . . . . . . . . . . . . . . . 83
16. The Smart and Adams Wagon Trains . . . . . . . . . . . . . 90
17. The Townsend Wagon Train (*The Big Trail*) . . . . . . . . . . 96
18. The Kelly-Larimer Wagon Train . . . . . . . . . . . . . . . 100

## Table of Contents

19. The Fisk Wagon Train (*Kentucky Rifle*) .................. 103
20. The Ake-Wadsworth Wagon Train (*The Outriders, How the West Was Won*) .................. 108
21. The Blinn-Buttles Wagon Train (*Little Big Man, The Searchers*) .................. 111
22. The Templeton, Kirkendall, and Floyd Wagon Trains (*Red River*) .................. 116
23. The Hayden, Crow, Blanchard, Snyder, and Baca Wagon Trains (*Two Mules for Sister Sara*) .................. 120
24. The Cooke and Custard Wagon Trains (*The Massacre, Chuka*) .... 126
25. The Lyman Wagon Train and Beecher Island (*The Plainsman, The Oregon Trail*) .................. 133
26. The Lyons, Shurly, Reel, and Hartz Wagon Trains (*Apache Rifles, Rio Grande, Broken Arrow, Hondo*) .................. 140
27. The Sawyers Wagon Train (*Wagon Tracks*) .................. 148
28. The Burrell-Foster Wagon Train (*The Red Raiders, Westward Ho the Wagons*) .................. 152
29. The German Wagon Train (*Rio Grande, Lonesome Dove, Last Train from Gun Hill*) .................. 157
30. Trail Deaths (*The Covered Wagon, The Big Trail, Westward the Women, How the West Was Won*) .................. 164
31. Stagecoach Attacks (*Stagecoach*) .................. 169
32. The Elm Creek Raid (*The Searchers*) .................. 175
33. Charles Goodnight and Oliver Loving (*Lonesome Dove*) ....... 182
34. *How the West Was Won* and *Into the West* .................. 189
35. Riding into the Sunset .................. 194

*Appendix A: The Wagon Train Movies* .................. 201
*Appendix B: Wagon Trains Referenced in This Study* .................. 214
*Chapter Notes* .................. 217
*Bibliography* .................. 224
*Index* .................. 231

# Preface

Historians are often most comfortable with an ordered, chronological progression in telling a story. Had this been purely a recapitulation of Indian attacks on western emigrant wagon trains, it would have begun with the 1829 attack on the Bent Wagon Train and ended with the 1876 attack on the Reel Wagon Train. The incidents would have been in temporal order, but the stories would have shifted from trail to trail. Another structural possibility is to sort the incidents geographically and tell the story of attacks on one trail before shifting to another. This would solve one problem, but play havoc with chronology.

Neither of the above schemes worked adequately, however, when comparing the wagon train attacks to cinematic depictions. There were too many overlaps. With substantial numbers of western movies depicting actual events, and actual events reprised on film, a list of attack episodes in relation to analogous films and films in relation to attacks would have resulted in much repetition. What is left is a hybrid, where attack incidents are gathered temporally or geographically as economically as possible, and linked to the films that warrant comparisons. Thus, the chapter titles generally contain the name of a wagon train(s), plus the name of the film(s) it is being compared with. Nevertheless, there remains some repetition, since so many western films contained elements of actual incidents.

The wagon train episodes in this study are not all-inclusive; there are more incidents excluded here simply due to space limitations. We have focused on most of the major events, which should illustrate the widespread nature of the attacks and what kind of a job Hollywood and historians have done in telling the stories. Since historians tend to focus on the Oregon Trail, as perhaps the most famous of the old overland trails, a map is provided to show the other trails and the extensive areas where attacks occurred — virtually across the length and breadth of the West. There was danger on every road. Discussions that omit the Bozeman, Santa Fe, or Butterfield trails, for instance, will not result in valid conclusions.

In Appendix A, one will find a filmography that includes movies in which wagon trains played some importance. Movie plots are briefly noted if they were not discussed in the main text. Appendix B is a chronological list of wagons trains discussed in the book, along with numbers of wagons, people, and casualties, when known.

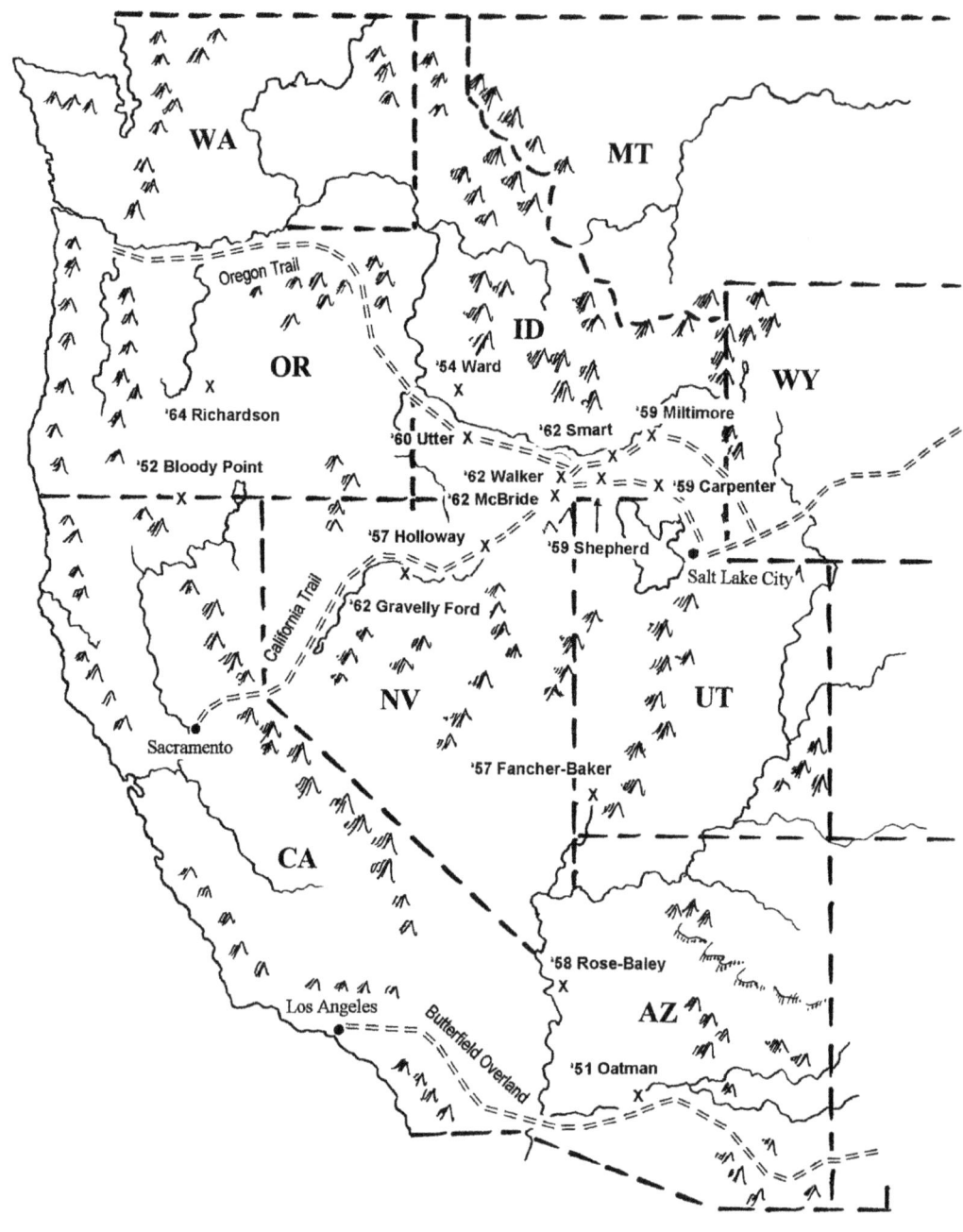

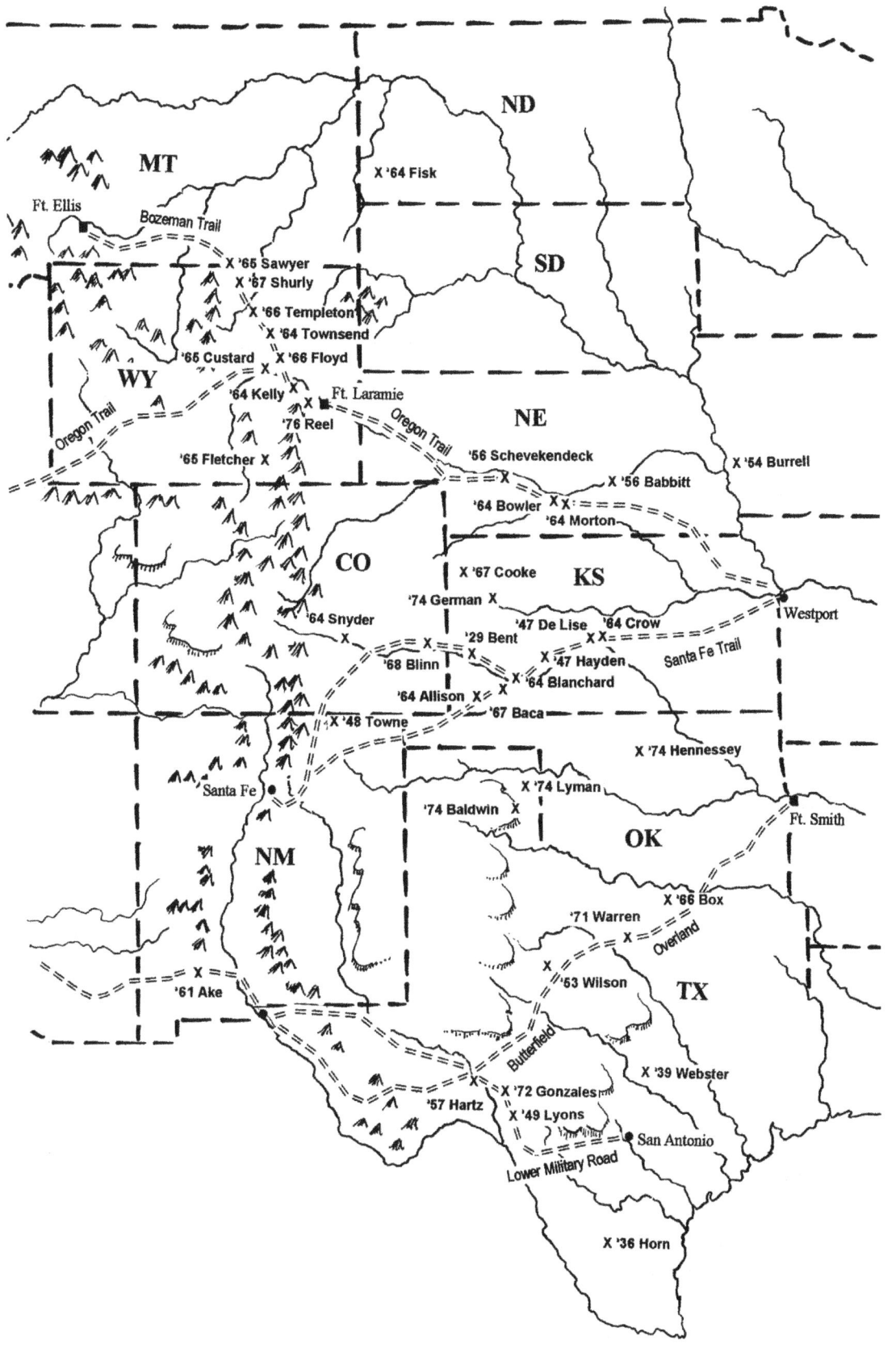

# *Introduction*

A battle has been raging between movies and history, or rather among filmgoers, critics, and historians. It is said that Americans "learn" more about history from films than they do from books, and the lessons learned are wrong. Most of us have cherished memories of films and television programs we saw as children and teenagers; those cinematic visions during our formative years seem to stand out sharply from the haze of the past. Those of us growing up in the middle decades of the 20th Century experienced a number of things in common that influenced us to a lesser or greater extent. Exposure to defining events helps shape generations, and at times there are tangible boundaries that form generations into distinct blocks. The 76 million people born between 1946 and 1964, representing about one-third of the United States' population at the time, were the Baby Boom generation.[1]

Concurrent events shaped the Boomer cohort. Their parents had great expectations; there was a recent military victory in World War Two, the times were prosperous, and people had faith in the future. Millions of children kicked the market into an orgy of buying and selling, from diapers, toys, bicycles, and clothes to washers, dryers, refrigerators, bigger cars, and new homes in the suburbs. Generations have a mood and a shared experience. The single event perhaps most responsible for tying the boomers together was the development of television. The Boomers watched Howdy Doody, Mickey Mouse, and Walt Disney, and TV ads sold them Hula Hoops, Silly Putty, Slinkys, and Barbie dolls. But perhaps the defining experience of the Boomer children occurred in 1955 when Walt Disney introduced Davy Crockett to the masses. Almost overnight, every child had to have a coonskin cap, a powder horn, and an "Old Betsy" rifle. The Crockett phenomenon spawned the "Frontierland" that became a staple of the Disney amusement parks. The "West" was alive and well and a part of our consciousness.

Television shaped the Boomers' image of the West. Arguably, it is likely that the Wild West was always the sustaining fantasy of American children, at least those growing up before the 1970s. Although the conflict with the Indians in the East lasted longer, the most recent conflicts took place in the trans–Mississippi West, and it was usually the images of mounted, war-bonneted warriors of the plains that captured childhood imaginations and drew the majority of the moviemaking media's attention. Thus, the films and episodes of the westward migration beyond the Mississippi will be our focus. Because battles between the U.S. Army and the Indians received the great majority of coverage on film and in print, we will concentrate instead on the civilian–Indian conflicts and a staple of so many movies and serials: the wagon trains.

Television catered to our perceptions of the past. Among the Boomers' first heroes was Hopalong Cassidy; and by 1950 the children wore $40 million worth of his black outfits and six-shooters. Singing cowboys Gene Autry and Roy Rogers were next; and then lawmen like Wyatt Earp, and gentlemen rogues like the Cisco Kid, helped sell $283 million worth of toy guns, boots, chaps, and lassos between 1955 and 1959. Action and adventure series increased on TV from 10 percent of all programs in 1953 to 50 percent in 1960. When movies and drama were added into the mix they accounted for about 80 percent of prime-time shows.

There were about 500 Western movies produced in the 1950s, and almost as many episodes of TV series Westerns. With *Cheyenne* (1955–63), *Maverick* (1957–62), *Gunsmoke* (1955–75), *Wagon Train* (1957–65), *Rawhide* (1959–62), *The Rifleman* (1958–63), *Have Gun, Will Travel* (1957–63), *Laramie* (1959–63) *Bonanza* (1959–73), *The Rebel* (1959–61), *Sugarfoot* (1957–61), *Cimarron City* (1958–60) and *Bat Masterson* (1958–61), to name a few, by the late 1950s, television cowboys ruled the airwaves.[2]

The Boomers witnessed history through television, but they were not the only generation to watch the mythic past on the screen. The GI Generation, born between 1901 and 1924, and the Silent Generation, born between 1925 and 1942, saw much of their history at the theater.[3] The GI cohort, who later won World War II for the Allies and is sometimes called the "greatest generation," saw the first Western films ever made, and the first cowboys of the silent screen — Bronco Billy Anderson and William S. Hart. They watched train robberies, covered wagons, stagecoach chases, Indian attacks, and damsels in distress, with the situations inevitably saved by the likes of Tom Mix, Ken Maynard, Hoot Gibson, Douglas Fairbanks, Tim McCoy, George O'Brien, Harry Carey, Buck Jones, and Bob Steele.

With the advent of the talkies in the late 1920s, some silent stars faded away, some crossed over, and many new ones appeared. By the 1930s, the older "GIs" and the younger "Silents" could witness the American West through the exploits of six-gun cowboys like Johnny Mack Brown, Wallace Beery, Bill Elliott, Bob Livingston, Tom Keene, Bob Baker, Tex Ritter, Joel McRae, Randolph Scott, Gary Cooper, and, of course, John Wayne. Before the birth of the Boomers, the two preceding generations watched the popular Western epics of the 1940s, with stars such as Errol Flynn, Clark Gable, Joseph Cotton, Montgomery Clift, Gilbert Roland, Rod Cameron, William Holden, Gregory Peck, Tyrone Power, and Henry Fonda.

The 1950s witnessed the end of the "B" Western. One by one they dropped in the dust. Johnny Mack Brown, Rex Allen, Whip Wilson, Tim Holt, Bill Elliott, Charles Starrett, Monte Hale, Roy Rogers, and Gene Autry were gone by 1954. But more epic "A" Westerns, still generally holding to the traditional code of behavior, took their place. The Boomers could still get their horse opera fill by watching, Rogers, Allen, Autry, and Boyd, who had successfully made the switch to television, continue to ride, shoot, and save the day. Add to them the Lone Ranger and Wild Bill Hickok, and it was blissfully apparent to the suburban Boomers that all was right with the world.[4]

The actors changed but the message was similar. It was our manifest destiny to follow the setting sun. The "enemies" preventing the migration were sometimes Mexicans or white bandits, but almost always Indians. They attacked pioneers in covered wagons. They attacked stagecoaches, freighters, cattlemen, ranchers, settlers, Pony Express riders, railroads, and forts. Soldiers chased, fought, and killed Indians. There were nearly endless chains of raids and retaliations. The frontiersman, soldier, and cowboy were agents through which Americans would achieve their destiny. Many people lost their homelands. Many were killed. It was not the most sanguine story, but it happened. The "West" was a violent time and place. By the end of the 20th Century, three generations of Americans had watched their history on the movie or television screen. But how good a job did the actors and actresses, writers, producers, and directors do? Were they telling us the truth? Did their productions echo history or fabricate it?

A recent revisionist interpretation makes an assertion that may surprise the average American: the wild Western frontier was not wild. The "Wild West" was, in fact, quite a mild and ordinary time and place. The image of the West that we have come to know is said to be simply a creation of the media. The dangers of the Western migrations and the Indian wars are nothing more than figments of the imaginations of the novelists and filmmakers. The history we think we know is a lie.

One of the spokesmen for the debunkers is former Secretary of the Interior Stuart L. Udall, who grew up in the new state of Arizona—ironically, by far the bloodiest state in terms of Indian fights and casualties.[5] Udall contends that "the blood and guns images" of the West are not true, and "the West as a whole was not a region driven by excessive violence." He then incongruously declares that western violence can be found in "the massacres and wanton killing of Indians by units of the United States Army."[6]

Udall's views are echoed by a number of historians. At a roundtable discussion at the 1999 Western History Association conference, Udall stated that all the presenters shared a similar belief: violence was not a principal factor in the development of the West. They had an agenda. According to Robert R. Dykstra, the shootings at Columbine High School in Colorado left historians with a political task: to de-escalate violence by de-emphasizing violent history. Frontier violence, said Dykstra, was all a hoax.[7]

Other presenters blamed today's violence on the movies, said that our national character was not influenced by the frontier, denied the seminal foundation myth of Frederick Jackson Turner, and said that to rectify matters it might be necessary to confront organizations that promote gun ownership. They pronounced that something must be done to counteract our gun culture and its inherent violence. In one respect, the clarion has a familiar ring. Social scientists were blaming TV violence for the increase in juvenile delinquency in the 1950s. Then again, Socrates bewailed the increasing violence of the teenagers in ancient Greece.

Admittedly, every generation rewrites its history, but must it be altered at such a price? The distortion of our past—the attempt to sweep the facts under a rug of obfuscation for some imagined collective good—is not what we should expect from historians in a democracy.

Warfare and violence happened. They need not be glorified, but they can't be denied. Historians have an obligation to present the truth, but when they alter or hide the truth because they have become self-appointed guardians and censors with their own political agendas, they become lesser specimens than the members of the media that they malign. The media folks are in the entertainment business; they are not weighed down with the burden that honest historians must carry.

One of the staples of the Western movie was the Indian attack on the wagon train. It is seen in countless films and television programs. Hollywood shows us that the western trek was fraught with peril, but there are historians who tell us that it was not dangerous to travel the great overland trails. Travel on the California-Oregon Trail, for instance, is depicted as a walk in the park. Udall says that it is a "myth that emigrants in wagon trains faced ever-present threat of attack" by Indians. Merrill Mattes presents an excellent account of the western migrations up to 1866, as does John Unruh, who makes use of Mattes but stops his study at 1860. According to them, about 200,000 people used the California-Oregon Trail from 1850 to 1860, and Indians killed about 316 emigrants. The selective location and time period distort the true picture, for there were many more years, many more trails, and many more casualties. An 1860 guidebook to the Pike's Peak region in Colorado touted the "perfectly safe" California-Oregon Trail, as opposed to the Santa Fe Trail, which was "notoriously unsafe for travellers."[8]

There are numerous statements from a number of historians, all denying or diminishing the Indian menace to emigrants and wagon trains. Speaking only of the Oregon Trail, Mattes says that Indian attacks on wagon trains "rarely happened except in later dime novels and television programs." Mattes also says, "Cases of actual kidnapping from wagon trains along the Platte ... are not recorded." He asserts, "Although Indian attacks on stagecoaches have long been a staple of Western fiction, authentic instances of such attacks are rare." Mattes makes more statements concerning wagon travel, concluding that "until the 1860s there are almost no documented cases of Indians attacking a civilian wagon train, and even then they were rare."[9]

Naturally, it is easier for an historian to "prove" westward migration was safe when omitting data from the Santa Fe Trail. John Faragher, in his study of families on the Overland Trail, echoes Mattes and Unruh. He incorrectly states that in the 1840s and early 1850s "there were no war parties directed at emigrants." Besides that, Faragher says, there was little to worry about even during times of increased conflict, because "most people got through with little or no difficulty."[10]

George R. Stewart was one of the first historians to disparage the idea that Indians attacked wagon trains. In his 1962 book, Stewart wrote that he included no stories about "the Beleaguered Wagon Train" because "I have never found it so recorded in the authentic sources." Stewart was skeptical it ever happened because he didn't believe Indians would do it. "Why," Stewart rhetorically asked himself, "should he go galloping around in that silly and hopeless fashion, exposing himself and his pony to rifle fire from men in a sheltered position?"[11] Because Stewart found no incidents within his limited temporal and geographical framework, and apparently didn't dig deeply enough into the records, he found no examples. But they did occur — many times — as we shall soon see.

John Unruh, who is often cited as an expert on the western migrations, also used Stewart's study, which he claimed "punctures the colorful myth of beleaguered emigrants surrounded by attacking Indians galloping about the encircled wagons." Unruh believed that mass media' "preoccupation with Indian depredations ... resulted in radical distortion of the historical record." He stated that one "fact" was clear: "The actual dangers of the overland venture have been considerably misrepresented by the myth-makers."[12]

Glenda Riley joined in to say that the media have overemphasized Indian fights and violent confrontations between the races. She says that women's diaries showed the female emigrants liked the Indians and sympathized with them, and that Indians and white women were not adversaries. Lillian Schlissel, in her study of women on the overland trails, held much the same sentiment. To expose this distortion one needs only to read what some female travelers said about their experiences. We can probably imagine what white female captives of the Indians would have said to 21st Century historians who trivialized their experiences.[13]

In a different vein, author Sandra Myres disparages the reliability of women's reminiscences and diaries, but similarly concludes, "Even during the height of hostilities between army and Indians, immigrant trains were rarely harassed." She also affirms that "Contrary to the modern mass media's portrayal of the beleaguered wagon train surrounded by hundreds of screaming savages armed with rifles and fire arrows, such attacks simply did not take place, particularly among the Plains tribes."[14]

It is easy to see where Myres got her ideas; she cited Unruh, who cited Stewart. One author who started another such chain of error was Robert Munkres. In his 1968 article he studied the Oregon Trail, also within a limited time and place framework, and concluded that emigrants faced little danger from Indians, and that wagon trains of reasonable size and discipline "were almost always safe from open Indian attack."[15]

In a more recent survey of American western history, Richard White tells us that "the major danger to western migrants in folklore — Indian attack — was rare." White men disguised as Indians "were responsible for atrocities," and there was "a relative paucity of Indian attacks on western immigrants." It should be no surprise to find that White cites Faragher and Unruh. In yet another history of the American West, authors Faragher and Robert Hine cite Faragher and White; and, in addition, they cite Michael Bellesisles and Dee Brown, who lent their own brand of history to the mix.[16]

One of the more recent studies of the Western migration, by Michael Tate, follows in the same footsteps. Tate tells us that "the trail experience never reached the level of violence commonly depicted in later literary and cinematic portrayals." He refers to Unruh, Riley, Schlissel, and Munkres, and says his study confirms their findings that "Indian attacks upon wagon trains have been greatly exaggerated."[17]

Thus, an historiographical "trail of tears" proliferates. One historian makes an inaccurate statement, and, like a broken record, historians down the line pick up the error and reiterate it again and again within an apparent circle of friends; the initial incorrect declaration thus becomes an established fact simply by repetition. Still, there would probably not be all this reiteration if the parroted interpretations did not mesh with personal agendas. But all is fair, apparently, in the quest to prove our West was mild, and that our myths of soldiers, Indians, pioneers, and covered wagons are primarily a fallacious creation of the media.

There is one major problem with the above authors' contentions that Indians rarely attacked wagon trains—they are plainly, simply, irrevocably wrong.

If contemporary historians are not giving us an accurate picture of our past, can we trust the movies to faithfully represent our history? Were three generations of movie fans duped by Hollywood?

It is a major contention of this book that art imitates life, and the horse still remains in front of the cart. The media did not create the past—it followed and echoed it. Films helped make the West a part of our myth and culture—but without the historical West the films would not have been possible. Moviemakers only elaborated on a theme of national origins already intrinsic in our very foundations. Despite the protestations that movies about the West have little basis in reality, Hollywood has done a commendable job in depicting actual events—at least in the first half of the 20th Century. In some instances we find that Hollywood has produced more accurate history than have a number of historians.

The usual introductory caveats must be inserted here. This is a story about Indian attacks on wagon trains. The details are graphic. Yes, we are aware that white soldiers and civilians also participated in atrocities against Indian tribes, and those episodes have been detailed in numerous books and movies over the past 50 years. The very real trail danger that emigrants faced from Indians, in contrast, is a feature that has been whitewashed during the same half-century.

Join us in an evaluation of movie history and reality. As Hondo Lane (John Wayne in *Hondo*, 1953) called out to the teamsters lashing their horses and driving the train away from the pursuing Apaches, "Circle the wagons!"

# 1

## The Utter–Van Ornum Wagon Train

### Idaho, September 1860

The sun broke above the eastern horizon on the Snake River Plain, the start of a clear, warm day. There would be no time to rest and ponder the red sky at morning, however, for this Sunday, 9 September 1860, would be a good day to make some time. The emigrants had already been on the roads for months, but still had more than 600 miles to go to reach the end of the trail in Oregon. The leader of the wagon train, Elijah P. Utter, had guided this group of emigrants all the way from Geneva, Wisconsin. Two weeks earlier they were at old Fort Hall, a popular stopping place on the trail. There they met soldiers, men of the 2nd Dragoons under Lt. Col. Marshall S. Howe. The dragoons spent much of the summer escorting emigrants along the dangerous Snake River Road and were looking forward to returning to Fort Douglas in Utah Territory. Howe assigned 22 soldiers to escort them as far west as Raft River, and then they would be on their own. Six more soldiers who had recently mustered out of the service decided to join the wagon train.

There had been Indian trouble in the area previously. The Ward Train was almost wiped out in 1854, farther west on the same road. In 1857 emigrant trains were attacked in what is today Nevada and Utah. In 1858, Indians drove the Mormons out of Fort Lemhi, north of Fort Hall. In 1859, a train was attacked at Cold Springs, and the Miltimore Train was attacked just 25 miles southwest of Fort Hall. Shoshones or Bannocks had been the Indians involved in those incidents. In 1860, Paiutes attacked Pony Express riders and stations along the California Branch of the Overland Trail, but so far this year no attacks were reported on trains along the Oregon Branch.

With the addition of the six soldiers, the Utter party now numbered 44 souls. There were eight wagons, about 100 cattle, and several horses. The Utter family consisted of Elijah, his wife Abagel, and ten children, including three from her previous marriage, Emeline, Christopher, and Elizabeth Trimble. The Van Ornum family consisted of Alexis and his wife Abigail, and their five children, Marcus, Eliza, Reuben, Lucinda, and Minerva. The Myers family included Joseph and Mary and their children, Isabella, Margaret, Harriet, Carolyn, and Eugene, plus Joseph's brother John. Daniel and Elizabeth Chase rode with their three children, Daniel Jr., Albert, and Mary. A number of single men were along: Jacob and Joseph Reith, brothers in their twenties, Judson Cressy, Samuel Gleason, Lewis Lawson, Goodsel Munson, and the ex-soldiers, Charles Chaffee, Charles Kishnell, Theodore Murdoch, Charles Schaumberg, Henry Snyder, and William Utley.

Beyond Raft River, when the army escort turned back, the discharged soldiers took over as guards. After a few days of uneventful travel the train arrived at Salmon Falls, a popular fishing site. The Indians there were surly. At Three Island Crossing, Utter and Van Ornum decided they would stay on the south bank of the river to save time, and by 8 September they had reached a point near the junction of Castle Creek and the Snake River. The next morning they were up before dawn, and by seven o'clock the wagons' tongues and axles creaked and groaned in the bone-dry air, once more heading west.

If anyone, after months of hard travel, had any remaining romantic allusions about the western trek, their idyll was shattered that morning. A dust cloud on the horizon announced that someone was approaching. Utter stood on the seat of his wagon and gazed to the west. They were Indians! Utter ordered the wagons to form a tight circle and placed the stock inside, then waited. Within a few minutes a large band of Bannocks rode up, whooping and firing their guns. They did not charge the wagons, and Utter did not know if they meant to attack them or try to stampede the stock. In any case, the cattle were secured, and the determined emigrants put up a stout front. After an hour the Bannocks waved a white cloth to signal that they wanted to parley. They indicated they were hungry, and the wary emigrants decided that if they fed them they would let them move on in peace. The Indians were admitted to the circle and breakfasted, under the suspicious eyes of the emigrants, who kept their weapons handy. After filling their bellies, the Indians indicated they meant them no harm, and they were free to travel on down toward the river to water their stock. The pioneers were not convinced. When the Bannocks left, Utter moved the wagons out, but led them uphill, keeping on the main road.

The charade ended when Utter moved the wagons away from the river. The Bannocks charged in again, shouting their war cries and firing arrows into the cattle and bullets into the wagons. Utter called for them to circle once more, but while doing so, the lead driver, Lewis Lawson, caught a bullet and tumbled off dead. Ex-soldier William Utley was mortally wounded and died soon after. The emigrants, desperately trying to control the frightened animals and

Near Castle Butte, Idaho, site of the initial attack on the Utter–Van Ornum wagons.

careening wagons, managed to close ranks, but as the last wagon pulled into place, another ex-soldier, Charles Kishnell, was shot and killed. The emigrants shot back as well as they could from within the dubious protection of their wagon corral. They kept up a solid fire for the rest of the day. It was said that 13-year-old Charles Utter shot five Indians. Joseph Myers believed they were good marksmen and said it was death for an Indian to show his head. He claimed that they killed 25 to 30 warriors.

The claim was likely an exaggeration, for the Bannocks showed no sign of being hurt or of going away. They besieged the train all Sunday night and kept it up on Monday morning. Soon the red sun rose in the sky and the soaring temperatures and lack of water made the youngest children wail with thirst. They all needed water, but the river was about 400 yards away. They were 34 hours without water, and by late afternoon they could take it no longer. They abandoned four wagons with a considerable amount of supplies in them, hoping the Indians would be satisfied with the plunder, then hitched up the remaining four wagons and made a dash for the river.

It didn't work. As soon as they broke their protective corral the Bannocks ignored the abandoned wagons and attacked again. John Meyers was shot dead, and a few others were hit. The four remaining ex-soldiers, Chaffee, Murdoch, Schaumberg, and Snyder, who were riding in front as point men, galloped away at full speed. The two Reith brothers, although afoot, threw their empty weapons away and ran after the ex-soldiers. The remaining emigrants, left to fend for themselves, ran headlong for the river.

Judson Cressy was killed in the melee. Elijah Utter, holding one-year-old Susan, was shot down as he ran. Abagel rushed back to him, and her children followed close behind her. Emeline Trimble pleaded with her mother not to go back, but she would not listen. Emeline snatched up little Susan and left them. Abagel was murdered next to Elijah, as were four of her children, Mary, Emma, Wesley, and Abby. As the sun set that evening, only 27 people out of the original 44 were left hiding in the brush near the Snake River.

They spent a horrible night, expecting to be killed, watching the fires from the burning wagons, and hearing the yells from the triumphant Bannocks. The warriors were temporarily satiated, however; for, after celebrating for a few hours, they gathered all the property they could carry, rounded up the cattle and horses, and moved off into the night. The white survivors only had a few weapons and bullets left. Worse, they only had one loaf of bread and a few corncakes for food. They traveled west along the river, moving at night and hiding by day. A few Indians harassed them, but they were kept at bay. After four days the Indians disappeared, and the survivors began traveling by day. After about ten days they arrived at the Owyhee River junction with the Snake. They were so tired and hungry that they decided to make shelters of willow branches and wait for someone to rescue them. Surely, they hoped, other wagon trains would be coming along the trail. But there were no other wagons. They were the last of the season.

Their only hope for succor would be in the four ex-soldiers and two Reith Brothers who fled during the attack. The six men headed northwest toward Fort Walla Walla, 250 miles away. But would they help? They must have realized that in abandoning their comrades they would be seen as dastardly cowards. In addition, Charles Chaffee had not mustered out of the service, he deserted; and he was not about to walk into an army post. The six men argued and split up. Murdoch, Schaumberg, and Snyder made it as far as the John Day River in northeastern Oregon, where Indians caught and killed two of them. Only Snyder escaped, later to be found by a settler, half-starved and on the edge of madness.

Meanwhile, Goodsel Munson and nine-year-old Christopher Trimble, the two strongest survivors at the camp on the Owyhee, began to walk for help. By great luck they came upon the camp of Chaffee and the Reiths, about 25 miles further down the Snake River. That night

Chaffee killed his horse. They divided up the meat and sent young Trimble back alone with a large share for the starving survivors. The four men continued on, but Chaffee and Munson dropped out 40 miles farther, near the mouth of Burnt River. Chaffee was later caught, convicted of desertion, and hanged. On 2 October, the Reiths made it to the Umatilla Indian Agency. The first rescue parties searched but found no one.

Back in the survivors' camp, Trimble returned with the meat, but it was soon devoured. Young Trimble left camp, found a band of Shoshones and managed to explain their predicament. The Indians returned several times with food, but each time demanded more for payment. When one of the survivors mentioned the word "soldiers" the Indians became suspicious and angry. They rode off with Trimble and killed him; the brave young boy who had been instrumental in keeping the remaining emigrants alive, was gone. At that point some of the survivors decided they would have to get away or they would all be killed. The Van Ornum family, Sam Gleason, and Charles and Henry Utter began walking west. Ten others stayed behind. Near the Snake River, just beyond Farewell Bend, the Indians caught up with Van Ornum's group, attacked, and killed six people.

On 9 October word reached Fort Dalles, and Capt. Frederick T. Dent, 9th Infantry, took 100 mounted infantry and dragoons and, with Jacob Reith as guide, headed back down the trail. Dent sent an advance detachment of 40 dragoons under Lt. Marcus A. Reno, who would have his day of infamy 16 years later during the Battle of the Little Bighorn. On the 19th Reno found Munson and Chaffee, naked and starving, on Burnt River. Reno left most of his men in camp on Burnt River where the town of Huntington now stands, and continued to the Malheur River. Finding nothing, he returned to within two miles of camp when he spotted fresh tracks. Hurrying on, he discovered a ghastly scene, with six stripped, mutilated bodies gleaming in the moonlight. Reno had found the remains of six of the ten who had split off from the rest back on the Owyhee. They appeared to have been dead about five days. Three had their throats slashed, and others were pierced with arrows. Abigail Van Ornum had been whipped, scalped, and raped. Reno followed children's footprints to the banks of the Snake River, but the four of them, Reuben, Eliza, Minerva, and Lucinda Van Ornum, ranging in age from eight to 14, were gone.

Little is known of their fate. The oldest girl, Lucinda, was said to have killed two Bannock women while trying to escape, and the warriors killed her. The two other girls either wandered off and were lost, or died of starvation; travelers claimed to have seen them at various times, being led around by the Indians with collars on their necks. It was even reported that Indians sold two of the children to the Mormons. Only Reuben was recovered, two years later, by the efforts of his uncle, Zachias Van Ornum, and the army.

The remaining ten emigrants slowly died of starvation. Joseph Myers later said in the November 24 *Oregon City Argus*: "We ate weeds, grass, and anything at all we could find.... Finally one of the children died; we cut it up and ate — and so on until we had eaten three of them. The mother helped eat her own children...."

"We became almost frantic," Emeline Trimble wrote years later in her 1892 booklet, "Left by the Indians." "Food we must have, but how should we get it? Then an idea took possession of our minds which we could not mention to each other, so horrid, so revolting to even think of, but the awful madness of hunger was upon us, and we cooked and ate the bodies of each of the poor children, first sister Libbie, then Mr. Chase's little boys...."

Captain Dent finally found the survivors' camp on 27 October. Dent and Capt. Andrew J. Smith, 1st Dragoons, witnessed the horrible scene. Said Smith: "They were in deplorable condition, quite naked and starved, having subsisted on berries, and, as a last resort, on the remains of one of their own party who had died some days previous." The soldiers arrived with clothing and food just before the survivors were about to dine on recently deceased one-year-old Susan.

## 1. The Utter–Van Ornum Wagon Train

Only 14 members of the Utter–Van Ornum Wagon Train ever reached the trail's end in Oregon: all seven members of the Myers family, Elizabeth Chase and her daughter Mary, the Reiths, Munson, Snyder, and Emeline Trimble. They all could testify to the very real dangers of migrating west in covered wagons. Although their final fate was extremely tragic, their experience was not exclusive.[1]

The story of the Utter–Van Ornum Wagon Train had almost all the ingredients a novelist or filmmaker could desire to construct a rip-roaring adventure story: families, quests, Indians, soldiers, danger, drama, betrayal, treachery, bravery, pathos, captivity, rescue, and even cannibalism! The more famous Donner Party was not the only group having to partake of human flesh in order to survive a journey across the continent. The Utter–Van Ornum Party was perhaps the archetype of "hard luck" caravans on the Western journey. Even so, its story is comparatively unknown, except by a handful of historians and buffs. Although it may be an epitome, it was not unique. Indians attacked wagon trains all across the West, as well as civilian and army freight wagons, stagecoaches, and even railroad trains. White women and children were captured, and forts were assaulted. It happened in the movies and it happened in reality. Hollywood, in the first half of the 20th century, depicted those events in literally thousands of films, and captured the essence of the story more accurately than it did in the second half of the century. Hollywood in the first half of the century did a better job depicting the essence of American history than many historians do today.

# 2

## The Bent and Towne-Tevis Wagon Trains

### Kansas, August 1829; Colorado, June 1848

One of the earliest Indian attacks on a wagon train in the trans–Mississippi West occurred along the Santa Fe Trail in what is today southwestern Kansas. The Santa Fe Trail in the 1820s and 1830s has been virtually ignored by a number of historians who seek to downplay violence and danger on the western trails. Of course it is easier to "prove" a point by framing the study area in a time and place that will support a desired conclusion. When we look beyond selected years on a limited portion of only one trail, the results may be surprising—but surprising only to some historians, and not to Hollywood. The trail and trade route between points in Missouri and Santa Fe had only been in operation a few years before attacks began. Just who "started" it is debatable.

William Becknell, out of Franklin, Missouri, took pack mules to Santa Fe in 1821, and the next year he inaugurated use of the first wagons on the trail. Mules and horses pulled the first wagons—oxen not coming into vogue until the 1830s. The mules and horses were a bit faster, but they wore out more easily, were not as strong as oxen, and were a much greater temptation to the Indians. Almost from the first day, traders and travelers realized that they had to corral the wagons and livestock at night to prevent theft of their animals. The Indians, particularly the Pawnee in the early years, and the Kiowa and Comanche later, coveted the horses and mules. They wanted the animals, and cared little if the men protecting them lived or died—at least at first.

Although theft was common in the early years, it was not until 1828 that the first serious rounds of killings began. Two young traders returning to Missouri, Daniel Monroe and Robert McNees, strayed from their train in what is now northeastern New Mexico. Indians killed them. Their companions took revenge on the next Indians they met, killing five of them along the Cimarron River. The Indians, probably Comanches, retaliated by stealing nearly one thousand head of livestock. A short time later, Comanches attacked a train and killed the wagonmaster, John Means. The survivors fled in the night and buried what goods they carried with them, plus some silver they had mined, on Chouteau's Island in the Arkansas River.

The attacks led to an expedition in the summer of 1829 by Capt. Bennet Riley, 6th Infantry, who took 200 soldiers from Fort Leavenworth to protect traders along the trail. The train Riley escorted was captained by 29-year-old Charles Bent, who, with brother William, had not yet built their famous fort on the Arkansas River. Charles and William, and brothers David and William Waldo, were taking a train of about 38 wagons and 79 men west. Traveling with them were a number of survivors who had buried their goods on Chouteau's Island the year before.

Bent and Waldo were perturbed that Riley's wagons were drawn by oxen, which would slow them all down.

At Chouteau's Island, the traders tried to convince Riley to escort them all the way to Santa Fe, but south of the Arkansas was Mexican territory, and Riley could not cross. He said he would wait there until early October for the caravan to return, and escort it the rest of the way back. Unfortunately, it was in Mexican territory, south of the river on the Cimarron Cut-off, that most of the trouble had been happening.

On 10 July, Bent's train left Riley behind and crossed the river. Riley had given them a last warning, as if the trail-savvy traders needed Riley's advice. Nevertheless, Riley suggested they stick together and stay within one hundred yards of their wagons before sending out a hunting party. The traders didn't listen.

Only six miles from the crossing, Indians jumped the train. The heavy sand had slowed the wagons to a crawl, and they were stretched out nearly a mile. To guard against surprise, Bent had sent out about 16 men to the front and flanks to give warning of Indians. The Indians obliged and charged after the scouts. William Bent, riding a black mule, kicked the animal into a run back toward the wagons. He made it. Warriors caught Samuel C. Lamme and killed and scalped him. Charles Bent joined William, and the two rushed toward the Indians, trying to bluff them and slow them down while the train had time to circle up. The tactic stalled the Indians for enough time. The men of the train corralled and began to dig rifle pits. About 50 warriors charged, but split around the train as the defenders began firing. They circled around the wagons, leaning behind their ponies' necks and firing from underneath, but pulled away when the traders brought into play a small cannon. From a safer range the warriors taunted the defenders by waving Lamme's bloody scalp. Several volunteers broke out of the circle to ride back to Captain Riley for help. By nightfall, Riley was hauling his infantry, wagons, and slow oxen through the same deep sand, coming to the "rescue." The next dawn the Indians saw the soldiers approaching and simply melted away. They had killed a man and stolen some animals, and were content for the time being.

While most of the men of Bent's train pleaded with Riley to go on with them, the rest had had enough and wanted to return east. Riley accompanied the wagons west for another two days before halting, insisting he could not penetrate any further into Mexican territory without causing an incident. Riley would not let some of Bent's men join up with him, and the rest were shamed into continuing on to Santa Fe. William Waldo said they had a horrible trip, constantly on guard, exhausted, and unable to sleep more than three or four hours a day. A party of Mexican buffalo hunters joined them, and they traveled together for mutual protection. Word of their plight reached Taos, and not until frontiersman and trapper Ewing Young joined them, with the likes of Kit Carson and 95 mountain men, did the merchants of Bent's train feel comparatively safe.[1]

Although Bent's Train suffered no more attacks on that route, the Santa Fe Trail never was completely safe from Indian attack. A westbound merchant train left Missouri for Santa Fe in May 1848. Among the traders were Preston Beck, Sam Wethered, Elliott Lee, Thomas O. Boggs, H. O'Neil, Peter Joseph de Tevis, and Smith Towne. They stayed together up to the Middle Crossing of the Arkansas. There, most of the party took the Dry Route, but Lee, Towne, Tevis, and about 12 others took the Mountain Route.

At Bent's Fort they were joined by Charles Towne (Smith's brother), the mixed-blood Pascual Riviere, nicknamed Blackhawk, a Delaware named Little Beaver, a man named Piles, and frontiersman, trader, and guide Lucien Maxwell. Charles Towne, Blackhawk, Maxwell, and several others had been attacked while trying to cross the usual route over Raton Pass just a week earlier, and they decided to try a cut-off to avoid the Indians that might still lie in wait for them. In the party were six- and four-year-old Mary and James Tharp, the children of William Tharp, a trader who had been killed by Indians the year before. The traders, friends of William Tharp, were taking the children to their grandparents in Taos when their mother in Pueblo was either unwilling or unable to care for them any longer.

They left Bent's Fort about 16 June and headed for Manco Burro Pass, which Charles Towne described as "a perfectly easy route" through the mountains. At noon on 19 June they stopped for lunch in a little valley at the top of the pass at 8,430 feet in elevation, and just inside the Colorado line about a dozen miles southeast of present-day Trinidad. While the stock was put out to graze and they sat down to eat, about 150 Jicarilla Apaches, possibly aided by Utes, jumped them. The Indians ran off the animals and swept by the camp, firing as they went. The defenders drove them away, but the Indians returned and fired the grass. The flames failed to drive the defenders out.

After a four-hour fight, one was killed and five were wounded, and they decided they had to break out of the circle and climb the mountain walls. As they broke out, Elliott Lee was hit in the hand and thigh, but continued on with the walking wounded. Charles Towne was hit in the thigh, but the bullet broke his leg, and, said Lee, he "was left to the mercy of the Indians."[2]

By nightfall, eight were wounded, but they seemed to have escaped. They traveled through the night, and at daylight they covered themselves with dirt and rocks to ward off the cold and hide from Apache searchers. Lee's wound slowed him down, and the party left him behind. He walked and crawled toward Taos, eating some food he found in an abandoned Indian camp. On the seventh day he met up with a small party of miners, one of whom was Thomas Boggs, who had taken the Dry Route when the original train split up at Middle Crossing, and was now on his way to Taos instead of Santa Fe. They stopped in Mora, where Lee recuperated for a time before making his way to Taos.

Four of the party were killed: Charles Towne, Jose Cortez, Jose Carnuel, and Pascual Riv-

Manco Burro Pass, site of the June 1848 attack on the Towne-Tevis wagon train.

iere. Of the rest, only Tevis was not wounded, and he went ahead for help. Dick Wootton guided 40 soldiers to bring the rest of them in to Taos, much the worse for wear. In Taos, Andres Fernandez died of his wounds. Mary and James Tharp never made it. They were captured early in the escape attempt, and word of their capture was not reported at first. About three months later, Taos merchants ransomed them back for $160, but Mary Tharp died shortly afterwards. The attack resulted in increased military activity against the Jicarillas, and Manco Burro Pass was rarely ever used again.[3]

Attacks on wagon trains such as these along the Santa Fe route began a decade or two before a number of historians even begin their studies of trail hostilities on the Oregon route. Some trail wisdom was already coming into play: never take a cut-off. And the Indians and wagon trains were beginning to produce grist for Hollywood's first classic screenplays.

# 3

# The Horn-Harris Wagon Train
# (*The Searchers, Ulzana's Raid*)

## Texas, April 1836

Some of the first wagon train attacks did not take place on any of the established trails. One of the earliest against an Anglo emigrant wagon train in the trans–Mississippi West occurred in Texas in 1836, shortly after the Battle of the Alamo. Besides being one of the earliest episodes, it was somewhat unique in that the train attacked was going "backwards." Defying the stereotypical image of a progression of emigrants heading east to west, the Horn Train consisted of emigrants who had experienced the West and found it much too dangerous, as well as deficient in a number of amenities that could be had in the "civilized" East. These emigrants were attacked while heading east, out of the Wild West.

A major player in the story, Sarah Ann Horn, was born in Huntington, England, in 1809, the youngest of ten children of the Newton family. She was 18 years old in October 1827 when she married John Horn. They had two sons, John, born in 1828, and Joseph, born in 1829. John Horn was a London merchant, but talk of cheap land in America enticed them, and they sailed for New York in July 1833. Having heard of Dr. John Charles Beales and his proposed colony in Coahuila-Texas, the Horns joined a group of emigrants and sailed south.

The party of 59 emigrants left Copano Bay, near present-day Bayside, Texas, in January 1834. They headed to the Rio Grande near present-day Eagle Pass, then north to Las Moras Creek, reaching the selected site on 16 March. They named the new town Dolores. Almost from the first day the colony was plagued with problems: the soil was not productive without irrigation, the creek was too small, the site was too remote, the colonists were not experienced in town-building, and the land company tried to regulate their daily activities. A clique of Germans argued with Beales, and some of them abandoned the colony after the first year.[1]

Beales tried to bring in more colonists, but only three families and 15 men arrived. Finally, fearful of Indians and the Mexican Army, the colonists called it quits. The Horns wanted to pull out with four other families and a number of young men, but Sarah and John were sick and unable to travel. The missed opportunity meant disaster.

The colony broke apart in early March 1836. Some headed northeast to try and join up with Sam Houston's Army, while others traveled back toward Copano Bay. John Horn and family formed a small party with the Harris Family and nine other men. They wanted to reach Matamoros and catch a ship for England, leaving the God-forsaken wilderness far behind. They pulled out 8 March 1836, two days after the fall of the Alamo.[2]

The little band feared Mexican forces along the Rio Grande, so they roughly followed the course of the Nueces River. On 4 April they stopped at a lake, which was probably southwest of today's Tilden, Texas. Little is known about the Harris Family. Mrs. Harris was not from England, and joined up with the expedition in the States. Sarah Horn was caring for Mrs. Harris's three-month-old baby girl because of her condition, which Sarah called "broken breasts."

While dressing the baby, which was probably the only child born in Dolores, Sarah saw Indians riding toward their camp. She ran to her husband, but he said there was no danger. Seconds later, Peneteka Comanches attacked, shooting an arrow into the chest of a man standing next to Sarah. A warrior clubbed John Horn to the ground, crushing his skull. They took Sarah and the children to the wagon, where Sarah gave Mrs. Harris back her child. The Indians made short work of the men and then took the women and children to their camp. The captives were stripped and given nothing to eat or drink: That night, Harris and Horn were bound together with a rope, unable to do anything but listen to their children crying.

The next day, the thirsty and hungry baby cried piteously. Sarah, who could speak a little Spanish, asked for some flour to make the baby something to eat. A warrior grabbed the little girl and threw her high into the air. Said Sarah, "This barbarous act having been repeated three times, its sufferings were at an end." An Indian hung the baby's body on a mule's saddlehorn, but the women refused to ride until he removed the corpse.[3]

The next day, to the surprise of the two white women, Mr. Harris and a young German were brought in. They had survived their wounds and were placed nearby so the women could watch them die. Sarah said that Mr. Harris "cast an agonizing look at his dear wife and myself, but he uttered not a word." The men were shot dead on the spot.

When the Indians were 30 miles from Matamoros they attacked and killed a small number of Texans, then raided a Mexican's ranch and killed the entire family. Joseph was badly hurt when he fell from a mule, and his cuts became infested with maggots. He lay in the dirt at night, crying in pain and begging for water, but received no succor. Sarah could not stand seeing her children tortured. She said she would rather see them dead than suffer more.

The Indians raided another ranch, but two warriors were wounded. A posse chased them, and they abandoned the area. About 18 April they passed the site of the initial attack on the wagon train, and Sarah noted the parched and blackened bodies still lying in the sun. When the Indians divided into smaller groups, Horn and Harris were separated, but Joseph still remained near his mother. They traveled steadily for two months. At one river crossing, Joseph again fell off a mule, but instead of anyone helping him, an angry warrior struck him with his lance, severely cutting him below the eye and knocking him back into the river. Joseph finally reached shore, and Sarah gave the warrior a verbal tongue-lashing in Spanish. The warrior's response was to make Joseph travel on foot the rest of the day, and Sarah was cruelly whipped that night. The punishment, however, "had no terrors for a miserable wretch like me," she said. The strokes of the whip "seemed to me of no more weight than a feather. Indeed, I felt recreant to mortal existence, and my soul, desperate with the tantalized affections of a wife and mother, would fain have preferred the most cruel death to life such as mine."[4]

The abuse never stopped, it only waxed and waned. In June the Indian bands met up, and Sarah Horn briefly saw Mrs. Harris, who she described as appearing "barely to exist." After several more days' travel, they split up again, and this time Mrs. Harris and the two boys went off with different groups. Sarah was alone and despondent. She had a new master, and another mistress she described as "an utter stranger to the feelings of humanity." The woman beat her, but this time Sarah took a different tack. Because of what she had "witnessed of savage courage in contact with unresisting and inferior numbers, that they were the most dastardly cowards," Sarah decided she would fight. When her Indian mistress hurled an object at her head, Sarah picked it up and threw it back, "and I found that I fared much better for it."[5]

Sarah Horn and Mrs. Harris met occasionally, and Sarah was worried. As bad as her

Burt Lancaster and soldiers are ambushed by the Apaches in *Ulzana's Raid* (Universal, 1972), which illustrated the true nature of Indian war and contrasted with several liberal, cliché-ridden films of the decade.

treatment was, she believed it worse for Harris. "[H]er sufferings were greater than mine.... We mingled our tears as she exhibited to me the marks of savage brutality, which she will bear in her person to the grave."[6]

Sarah saw her children only a few times over the ensuing months. In June 1837, Comancheros—generally Hispanics who acted as middlemen between businessmen, traders, and the Indians—visited the Comanche camp at the headwaters of the Canadian River. Through the efforts of American merchant William Donaho, the Comancheros bought Mrs. Harris. Sarah was glad that Mrs. Harris "was released from her sufferings," but now she felt even more alone, and keenly felt "the truth of the saying that 'misery loves company.'" In her despondency, Sarah pondered that "the God of Heaven only knows why, and how it is, that I am still alive."[7]

Mrs. Harris ended up in Missouri. With no husband, children, or close relatives, she had nearly completed her odyssey. She had relatives in Texas, but because of the shame of her captivity, she did not want to go there. She chose to live with some distant kin near Boonville, Missouri, but soon died of the ravages and abuse she suffered while a prisoner.[8]

Back in New Mexico Territory, Sarah Ann Horn was prisoner for another year before being purchased from the Indians. Her son, John, had frozen to death, and Joseph was taken away with another band. She had a premonition of her fate: "Time shall roll on, and soon my hopes and fears shall be hushed in the silence of death." On 22 August 1838, she joined a wagon train and headed east. Her premonition of an early death proved correct. She died in Missouri in 1839.[9]

The extremely harsh treatment of many women captives, as illustrated in the Horn-Harris incident, happened many other times. Raiding warriors almost always killed the men and older boys, and captured the women and younger children. Films have depicted the rough treatment women received. In one of the most famous and most analyzed films, John Ford's *The Searchers* (1956), we learn the result of Indian captivity on white women who were rescued after living with the Indians. Ethan Edwards (John Wayne) and Martin Pawley (Jeffrey Hunter) see the women sitting on the floor, one of them playing with a doll, appearing half-crazy. Ethan says to Pawley that "They were white — once."

In *Ulzana's Raid* (Universal 1972), Apaches under Ulzana (Joaquin Martinez) raid the Riordan Ranch. They hang Mr. Riordan upside down on a fence and burn him to death, and then abuse and gang rape Mrs. Riordan (Dran Hamilton). When scout McIntosh (Burt Lancaster) and the soldiers find her, she is nearly dead and mentally unglued. That evening she wades in a muddy pond trying to scrub her shame away.

"I have to wash it off," she moans. But when "It won't come off" she tries to drown herself. The idealist Lt. Garnett DeBuin (Bruce Davison) begins to have second thoughts about the Indian as a noble, innocent child of the forest.

Of course not all Indian captives later went insane, but neither did one have to be taken prisoner to experience a mental breakdown. An attack and a massacre will certainly be enough to tip the scales for some unfortunate individuals. One such occurrence took place near Humboldt Wells in present-day Nevada. At dawn on 13 August 1857, a band of Paiutes attacked the Holloway Wagons, a small train with only ten emigrants, while camped near the head of the Humboldt River. The seven men, two women, and a baby never had a chance. While sitting around a breakfast campfire, the emigrants were hit by a volley of arrows and bullets coming from a nearby bank of willows. Several were hit. Only one man managed to get his gun and fire a few shots before he was wounded. He fled to the riverbank and hid in the bushes. Two more wounded men escaped.

The Indians charged in and killed one man who lay sick and was too weak to defend himself. Mrs. Holloway was sleeping in a tent in her nightgown. She tried to run, holding her two-year-old daughter, but an arrow struck her and she fell. A warrior pulled the arrow from her flesh and jabbed it again and again into her, to make sure she was dead. She was not. She remained conscious long enough to see an Indian take the toddler by its feet and swing her head against a wagon wheel. Mrs. Holloway fainted as she was scalped, and the Indians left her for dead. The Indians began looting the wagons and driving off the stock, when another train pulled into view, scaring them off. In their haste to get away, they dropped the scalp. Mrs. Holloway's husband and child were among the dead. About the only thing she recovered from the disaster was her scalp. She took it and had a wig made from it, and a photograph of her wearing the wig has survived. The photo lasted longer than she did. Scarred by her wounds and haunted by the recurring nightmares of the massacre, Mrs. Holloway lost her mind.[10]

# 4

# The Webster Wagon Train
## (*In the Days of the Pilgrims, The Missing*)
### Texas, October 1839

John Webster left Virginia for Texas in 1837, seeking land, good soil, and a milder climate. The Flesher and Stillwell Families joined the Websters on their journey down the Ohio River and Mississippi River to New Orleans. From there they took a ship across the Gulf of Mexico to Texas, and eventually trekked to Bastrop on the Colorado River. They stayed there about two years before Webster purchased military land up north near the San Gabriel River. With typical pioneering spirit, the families moved on.

Accompanying John Webster was his wife, Dolly (age 32), and their children, Booker (10), and Patsy (3). The Stillwell, Flesher, and Morton families joined them, along with eight young men seeking new lands on the frontier. The two-wagon ox-train left on 27 September 1839. They passed Austin and in a few days were between the forks of the San Gabriel. Unknown to them, Comanches were watching from atop Pilot Knob. Near the North Fork, two of the young men saw Indians ahead and raced back to alert the rest. Some wanted to retreat, but others said "that they would rather die, than go back and be laughed at as cowards."[1]

After much argument, however, they all agreed to go back; but it was too late. They traveled all night, but on the morning of 1 October they reached a narrow prairie with thick timber along both sides. Sixteen Comanches suddenly attacked them from the rear. There were 13 mounted men in the Webster train, and they charged after the Indians, firing and hitting two. It was only a ruse, however, for about 150 Comanches attacked the front of the train. Old Indian-fighter Benjamin Reese encouraged the settlers. He had them turn the oxen loose and pull the wagons together. The Indians charged by on horseback, and the whites fired as they circled, but few were hit. A Mexican in the Webster party tried to escape but made it only 50 yards before being killed.

Mr. Morton was hit next, then Perry Reese. John Webster took a ball in the chest and went down, then Mr. Baylor and Mr. Bezely. Nelson Flesher, Dolly Webster's nephew, fell with a gunshot to the thigh. Warriors ran up to John Webster and were about to scalp him when one shouted, "Blanco, blanco!" apparently reluctant to take his full head of white hair. Stillwell was killed, but being bald, the Indians only took his wig. Dolly Webster was wounded. In a short while, only Silsby and Hicks were still fighting, but they too went down. Only Dolly, Booker, and Patsy were still alive. Dolly watched the warriors scalp and mutilate the dead, and then she swooned.[2]

The Comanches plundered the wagons, seemingly very interested in the gold watches and looking glasses, but they discarded more than $1,300 in specie. Dolly revived as warriors were stripping off her clothes; she resisted and was beaten. The warrior who claimed her dragged her off by the hair. The Indians traveled west to their village where the Indian women took turns beating her.

When the Comanches pulled out they separated Dolly from her children. She was forced to walk, while women rode by and poked her with lances and shoved bloody scalps in her face. The women were the worst, Dolly said: "Their treatment to me was cruel in the extreme." In late October they gathered in a large encampment on the headwaters of the Colorado. There, Dolly met more unfortunate captives. One of them, Matilda Lockhart, who had been with the Indians for more than a year, gave Dolly advice as to how she should behave to prevent so many beatings.[3]

In early November, Dolly had the good fortune to meet Booker and Patsy. They talked about escape. When the Indian women saw them conversing, they "fell upon and beat us most unmercifully, and ran off and left us." Dolly quickly made up her mind. She grabbed the children by the hands and ran, hoping to find a white settlement. Scratched by mesquite, tired, thirsty, and hungry, with nothing but pecans to eat, the three traveled for nearly two weeks. By the last of November they had passed the mouth of the San Saba, but Booker was so sick he couldn't travel. Dolly's hopes soared when she saw a party of men dressed in "English costume," but they proved to be a band of Mexicans, Caddoes, and runaway slaves. The Websters were prisoners again.

"Here sleep the victims of the Webster Massacre." Davis Cemetery, Leander, Texas.

In early January 1840 they met up with the same Comanches Webster had escaped from. The Comanches traded one mule for Booker, and a week later Dolly's old Comanche "master" traded a horse for her and Patsy. The chief and his wife tied Dolly down outside the tipi and placed Patsy inside between them. Dolly got loose and picked up a gun with the intention of killing him and clubbing his wife with the empty rifle. "But," she said, "my heart failed me." On 10 January they were all back in the Comanche camp.[4]

In mid–February the camp moved to the upper Frio River. The Indian women located a number of beehives on a rocky ledge, and not wanting to be stung, they tied Mrs. Webster to a long rope and lowered her down the cliff face. As Dolly dangled nearly 100 feet above the canyon floor, she attempted to get the honey, only to be stung profusely. The angry women hauled her back up, and, said Dolly, "beat me cruelly" and "burned nearly all my hair off my head."

Unable to fight back, Dolly thought of a stratagem. "I knew they were very superstitious," she said. With another captive as an interpreter, she told them "that if they did kill me, I would rise the next day with the sun, and come back and burn them all up." Strangely enough, the threat made them desist.[5]

In March, the Indians moved near San Antonio and traded another captive for ammunition.

But when the Indians took in Matilda Lockhart, burned and disfigured from the abuse she had suffered, the situation erupted in the Council House Fight of 19 March 1840. Meanwhile, Dolly's mental and physical condition had deteriorated to the point that she could wait no longer.

The night of 15 March, Dolly took Patsy by the hand and headed for a dense thicket in the direction she hoped to find San Antonio. A short way from the village she came upon a friendly Caddo who spoke English. He said that if the Comanches caught her again they would kill her. Dolly told him, "I would rather die than to live the way I did," and continued on into the gloom. It rained all night. They found the remains of a freshly killed deer and ate it. On the third day the weather turned frigid, and Dolly was colder than she had ever been in her life. She thought Patsy would freeze to death.

They walked on, passing several bands of Indians, but always avoided being seen. They found the carcass of a dead horse and ate the putrefied marrow from its bones. Likewise, a dead deer sustained them the next day, and then prickly pears. After 13 days the emaciated mother and daughter were about to give up, but Dolly had a vision that if she could just keep going a little farther, she would be saved. On the afternoon of 28 March she saw a house.

Out of nowhere, two Mexicans found them and took them in, giving them water and food. A man rode up and asked if she was Mrs. Webster. She replied in the affirmative. It had been nine days since the Council House fight and Matilda Lockhart's rescue, and Matilda had informed the authorities that other captives were in the area.[6]

Dolly and Patsy were cared for by several ladies. "The stench of the poor woman's clothes was so dreadful," said Mary Maverick, "that Mrs. Jacques fainted away." Dolly was reunited with Booker on 4 April when the Comanches brought in a few more captives to exchange for Indian prisoners captured in the Council House fight. "Booker Webster's head was shaved," said Maverick, "and he was painted in Indian style." Booker informed them of the murders of many of the other captives. He said the Indians took the American prisoners "and roasted and butchered them to death with horrible cruelties." Only he and one girl were spared because they had previously been adopted into the tribe.

The townsfolk collected $490 for the Websters, plus, said Dolly, "clothes enough to last us a year." In two months Dolly Webster went to Austin, where she met President Mirabeau Lamar, who congratulated her on regaining her freedom. With no relatives in Texas, the Websters made their way back to Virginia.[7]

With plenty of historical examples to draw from, the capture and abuse of prisoners by the Indians has been a staple of films almost since day one. A few of the earliest movies released by Edison depicted some Indians' apparent penchant for torture. In 1908, a Vitagraph film, *In the Days of the Pilgrims*, echoed the theme, where a pioneer and his daughter are captured and taken to an Indian village. Like Dolly Webster, the movie heroine dreams of killing the chief, and finally follows through, tomahawking the chief before she is rescued. Another historical incident involved Nelson Lee, captured and held by the Indians for about two years until an opportunity presented itself in 1858, when he hatcheted a Comanche chief and escaped.

A century later there are very few movies that attempt to depict the horrible treatment that could be meted out to women captives. In *The Missing* (2004), Maggie Gilkeson (Cate Blanchett) is alone with her daughters in a wilderness cabin. Lily Gilkeson (Evan Rachel Wood) is captured by Apaches, led by an evil shaman, and has to be rescued by her long-lost grandfather, Samuel Jones (Tommy Lee Jones). The film graphically depicts what fate could be in store for young female captives, but it goes awry in intimating that the abuse was likely the result of one demonic witchdoctor's madness, when such cruelty was legion in surviving women's captivity narratives. There are many other real-life incidents that document the abuse of captives.

The Websters' experience, along with that of Horn and Harris, illustrate the dangers of travel along routes other than the Oregon Trail. Many studies have been conducted, by the likes of historians Munkres, Mattes, Unruh, Faragher, Riley, Myres, and Tate, that concentrated on the Oregon Trail and drew conclusions that traveling west wasn't a dangerous proposition in regards to Indian attacks. Two major reasons they came to this conclusion, however, was that they selected only one route and limited their time frames. People did not travel only on one road and only during specific years. When we broaden the perspective in space and time, we see that travel in the West in the 19th century was fraught with danger. Hollywood has depicted that fact more aptly than some historians.[8]

# 5

# The Wilson Wagon Train
## (*The Comancheros, Comanche Station*)

### Texas, September 1853

Jane Smith was born on 12 June 1837, in Alton, Illinois, one of five sisters and five brothers. In the mid–1840s, William Smith and Jane Cox Smith packed up the family and moved to Missouri, but in a short time wanderlust and news of the greener pastures in Texas prompted them to move again. They settled in Lamar County, near Paris, Texas, where the green pastures proved harsh. Three of the Smith boys died, and in 1852 Mr. and Mrs. Smith died within a day of each other. The eldest Smith brother, a Texas Ranger, came home to care for his orphaned siblings. After securing homes for them with different neighbors, he was taking four-year-old Ellen to live with an aunt when he caught a fever and died. By early 1853, Jane had lived with several neighbors and believed the way to get out of her unfortunate circumstances was to wed. In February 1853, Jane (age 15) married James Wilson, a 19-year-old starting his own farm.[1]

Farming didn't work. Hearing stories of California gold, the Wilsons joined a party of emigrants, which included James's father and James's three younger brothers. In Hunt County they formed a 22-wagon company, all under command of Henry Hickman. The 52 men, 12 women, and several children left on 6 April 1853, heading for El Paso. They trailed west to Forts Belknap, Phantom Hill, and Chadbourne, southwest to the Pecos, then upriver to the New Mexico border where they left the river and turned west. On 1 June, near the Guadalupe Mountains, Mescalero Apaches attacked the train and stole 19 cattle. Six men rode out after the raiders but were repulsed. The depleted train eventually reached El Paso.

A number of men did not get along with wagon boss Hickman and left the company to join another train. James Wilson and family, and five other men, waited for a month, but thieves stole most of their property. They decided to return home.

In late July the little caravan retraced its tracks. On 1 August they were near the Guadalupe Mountains when Mescaleros attacked them again. James Wilson and his father had gone only a short distance from the wagons when, Jane said, "they fell into the hands of the Indians. I saw them no more after this. I was told that they had been murdered.... I found myself thus bereaved and destitute, in a land of strangers." Jane and her three brothers-in-law turned around again and hurried back to El Paso. On 8 September a small party under a Mr. Hart, consisting of four other Americans, one of them a discharged soldier, and one Mexican, was heading east. Jane and the Wilson boys joined them. They crossed west Texas without molestation, but a few days' journey west of Fort Phantom Hill some men of the train ran off with some of the stock. Hart took the eldest Wilson boy (age 14) and rode off after the thieves. Jane, the two youngest Wilson boys, and the Mexican tried to keep up. The discharged soldier fell behind and disappeared.

## 5. The Wilson Wagon Train

Ruins of Fort Phantom Hill, Texas, where Jane Wilson was heading when attacked.

Hart never returned. Jane kept going, and about noon the next day, southwest of present-day Abilene, about 15 Comanches appeared in front of them. The Mexican left the wagon and went ahead, trying to show he was friendly, while the mules, hearing the war cries, began to run. One of them fell and dragged the wagon to a halt. The Indians were upon them in an instant. Jane saw them bring the Mexican in, strip him, tie him up, and shoot him in the back. Another warrior stabbed and scalped him, dropped the scalp into the Mexican's hat, and put the bloody mess on his own head. "I was stupefied with horror as I gazed on this spectacle," Jane said, "and supposed that my turn would come next."[2]

The Comanches and their captives headed northeast. The first night the Indians took Jane's clothes, "except barely enough to cover my person." One Indian took George Wilson (12). A Mexican, once taken captive himself and now riding as a Comanche warrior, claimed Meredith (7). Another warrior claimed Jane. That night she watched them stretch and dry the scalp of the Mexican who had been her traveling companion.

Starting out the next day, George and Meredith were painted to look like young Comanches, and given their own bows and arrows and horses to ride. They appeared to enjoy the adventure. Jane was treated cruelly; warriors cut off her long hair and decorated their own hair with hers. The hot sun beat down on her nearly bald head and burned it severely. Every day was rife with what Jane termed "repeated acts of inhumanity towards me."

After 12 days they met two warriors and a woman. Up to that point, Jane said, "my sufferings had been so severe as to take from me all desire to live." She thought she might now receive some compassion from another female, but the woman treated her worse than the men did, beating her with whips and sticks. Jane believed the Indians were well aware that she was about eight months pregnant, and hoped the physical abuse would make her lose the baby.

In camp, Jane "was obliged to work like a slave," carrying large loads of wood on her bare back, which was cut so badly that the blood trickled down her legs. She was forced to chase stock through the briars until her feet were torn to ribbons. Jane could never work as fast as the Indians ordered, and for punishment she was whipped, stoned, or "knocked down and stamped upon by the ferocious chief." Jane hated her captors. She often contemplated killing her "inhuman masters," particularly the chief, and "thought if I could only cut him to pieces I could die contented." When murder was not immediately on her mind, death was. "Every indignity was offered to my person which the imagination can conceive," she said. "Nothing could soften them into pity, and I ardently desired death that my torments might come to an end."[3]

Since Jane could only walk slowly, the Indians pointed her in the right direction and sent her out ahead every morning, catching up to her later. About 25 days after her capture, they sent Jane out early, as per the routine, but this time she was determined to escape. Instead of plodding along, once she got out of sight she ran off in a different direction as fast as her weary body would go. When she could go no further, she hid in some bushes. The next day she saw the tracks where the Indians had searched for her. She was free, but she was alone in the wilderness, probably somewhere either in present-day western Oklahoma or the eastern Texas Panhandle.

Jane shook off her despair, found a little grove and built a brush shelter. She ate hackberries and drank at a nearby spring. It was late October, and the weather grew cold and rainy. Wolves came near at night, but she frightened them away. On the twelfth day after her escape, New Mexican Comancheros discovered her. Immediately discerning her predicament, they took her along and gave her clothing, a blanket, and a burro to ride. In a few days they saw Indians, and the Comancheros hid Jane while they went to parley. They said they would return that night, but they did not.

In the morning Jane found Juan Jose, one of the Comancheros. He told her she must remain hidden while they negotiated with the Comanches. Jane hid in a grass-covered ravine all day until Juan brought her some bread and told her to be patient. Jane waited, and heard Comanches calling out in the distance. Juan returned to her again that night with more food and water. This time he told her she must stay hidden for another week, as they must move on for a time and could not take her, or the Indians would know. Jane watched them all disappear, and with them went all her hopes of rescue.[4]

The next day she went to the abandoned campsite and found a log that was still burning. Using it, and adding fuel to the flames, she was able to keep warm. She took shelter at night in a hollow cottonwood stump. Jane was once more ready to give up, but eight days later the Comancheros finally returned. "I was so overjoyed," she said, "that I rushed toward them unmindful of briars and sore feet." Juan gave her a horse to ride and they headed west, reaching the village of Pecos in late November 1853. There she met Capt. James H. Carleton of the 1st Dragoons, and received women's clothing from some of the army wives. Raymond Meriwether, son of New Mexico Territorial Governor David Meriwether, escorted Jane Wilson to Santa Fe. Governor Meriwether said, "On her arrival she presented the most pitiful spectacle I had ever seen. She was in rags, emaciated, and her mind somewhat disordered." Jane gave birth to a stillborn child, and was taken care of by several American and Mexican ladies.[5]

Jane worried about her two brothers-in-law, wanting the authorities to rescue them. She believed no one had known about the attack on their party, but she was mistaken. There was a survivor from their wagon train, either another Mexican teamster or the discharged soldier. Friendly Comanches found the wounded man, shot in the shoulder, and brought him in to Fort Phantom Hill. The rescued man told the story to Capt. Henry H. Sibley, 2nd Dragoons, in command at Phantom Hill, and the Captain sent out two patrols to pursue the Indians. They never could pick up a trail. On 8 October Sibley wrote to Texas Indian Agent Robert S. Neighbors, telling him what happened and asking for ransom money to buy back the captives.[6]

Neighbors did all he could. Friendly Delawares and Caddoes went to various Comanche bands trying to purchase the captives, but they learned that the Indians had already sold the two boys, one to a band in the north, and the other to a Chickasaw trader named Brown. On 13 December, 1853, Governor Meriwether wrote to Texas Governor Elisha M. Pease, saying that Jane Wilson was in Santa Fe, that he had sent out traders to purchase the Wilson boys, and asking if Pease would help. Pease passed the news along to Robert Neighbors, and the agent answered that he already had searchers out looking for them.

The boys were finally recovered in March 1854. George was brought in to Fort Arbuckle, Indian Territory, and placed in the care of Major Humphreys. A Kickapoo named Johnson recovered Meredith, the younger brother, and brought him to the fort, where Capt. Seneca G. Simmons, 7th Infantry, took him in.[7]

Governor Meriwether paid $50 to Jane Wilson's rescuers and spent $300 for her care. Jane was finally sent home in the spring of 1854. She told her story to a correspondent from the Santa Fe *Weekly Gazette*, and the narrative was reprinted in other newspapers, such as the New York *Commercial Advertiser*. Rochester, New York, bookseller Dellon M. Dewey printed Jane's story in 1854, and two years later it appeared in John Frost's anthology *Indian Battles, Captivities and Adventures*. Jane told her story in the hope of spreading the news to facilitate the release of her brothers-in-law. She probably never even knew the story was reprinted, that Dewey printed a booklet, or that Frost included it in his collection. She made no money from publicizing her sufferings, and faded out of history like so many of her fellow captives.[8]

Wilson's story is another one illustrating the very real threat faced by travelers, and not only on the over-studied Oregon Trail, but on what was to become the Butterfield Overland in Texas. Again there is harsh treatment of a female captive, but an added twist to the plot is the appearance of rescuing Comancheros — in somewhat similar circumstances as in the recovery of Sarah Horn. The Comancheros were usually New Mexican Hispanics who traded with the Comanche and Kiowa, generally guns and ammunition for horses and mules. The trade was usually harmful to everyone except those who made money off the deal: the Comancheros, the Indians, and the New Mexican suppliers (but you would never convince one of the rescued captives that the Comancheros were a menace). The U.S. Army tried to stop the illicit trade but was unsuccessful for many years. By 1865, Brig. Gen. James H. Carleton allowed some traders to operate for the purpose of liberating captives, while unlicensed traders were likely to be convicted in Texas but acquitted in New Mexico.[9]

The 1961 movie *The Comancheros* highlighted this operation, with Texas Ranger "hero" Jake Cutter (John Wayne) and his sidekick Paul Regret (Stuart Whitman) breaking up the lucrative business. In this film, however, the Comancheros are depicted as nearly all evil, with character actor Jack Elam, as Horseface, typical of the gang members. They have few redeeming qualities, and their main joys in life apparently are to set up an empire of drinking, brawling barbarians, and to unleash a swarm of Indians armed with Winchesters against the unsuspecting frontier. Nothing is mentioned about their humanitarian rescues of human captives (albeit for rewards).

A more "civilized" Comanchero, of sorts, is Jefferson Cody (Randolph Scott) in Budd Boetticher's *Comanche Station* (1960). Cody, because he has experienced first-hand the loss of a wife to marauding Indians, spends his days seeking out hostile bands to buy back any white captives he can find. His "good" Comanchero-like persona is motivated by compassion rather than profit.

Cody recovers white captive Nancy Lowe (Nancy Gates) through his own money and effort, but there remains the underlying question of why Nancy's own husband, John Lowe (Dyke Johnson), did not personally search for her. A complication occurs when Ben Lane (Claude Akins) and his gang learn that there is a reward for the rescued woman. They plan to steal the woman from Cody and turn her in for the money.

Randolph Scott safely returns Nancy Gates to her son, P. Holland, in *Comanche Station* (Ranown Productions, 1960).

The inevitable showdown and gun battle occurs, but Cody wins in the end. In the final scenes he returns Mrs. Lowe to her husband. With the husband, wife, and son reunited, Cody learns why Mr. Lowe did not search for his wife: he is blind. In the days of the classic Westerns, and in historical reality, there had to be a very good reason why a man would not search for a wife who was a prisoner of the Indians.

# 6

# The Oatman Wagon Train
## (*The Unforgiven, Sioux Blood, White Comanche*)

### Arizona, March 1851

In many Western films, and in many historical instances, it was thought that the threat of Indian attack on a large, well-defended wagon train was minimal, for there was safety in numbers. The assumption was incorrect, as we shall read of later; however, danger did increase as the number of emigrants banding together decreased. When the travelers included but one family and one wagon, it was the proverbial recipe for disaster.

Royse Oatman was a hard-luck farmer and businessman. After failing in several endeavors in Pennsylvania and Illinois, and injuring himself on his farm near Fulton, Illinois, Royse decided to head west. He answered the call of Mormon Rev. James Brewster to establish a new Zion near the junction of the Gila and Colorado Rivers in what was then New Mexico Territory (now Arizona). Royse and Mary Ann Sperry Oatman, with their seven children, Lucy (age 17), Lorenzo (16), Olive Ann (14), Royse Jr. (10), Mary Ann (7), Charity Ann (4), and Roland (1), left Illinois in 1850 to rendezvous with the gathering colony in Independence, Missouri. There were about 90 emigrants, including the Oatman, Thompson, Mateer, Brewster, Goodale, Lane, Wheeling, Wilder, and Brimhall families. On 5 August 1850, with about 25 wagons and 200 head of cattle, they set out on the Santa Fe Trail.[1]

Disagreements over religious practices and resting on the Sabbath threatened to tear them apart. The group split up near Santa Fe, with 32 emigrants under Brewster taking the northern route, and the Oatman contingent of about 20 people and eight wagons taking the southern route. The road dipped into Mexico, then northwest to Tubac. The year was ending as the slow-moving caravan pulled into Tucson and rested for one month.[2]

The Mexican inhabitants convinced most of the party that the road ahead was too dangerous, but the Oatman, Kelly, and Wilder families moved on. By mid–February they had crossed a 90-mile desert and got as far as the Maricopa and Pima villages. The cattle were weak and provisions were low. Kelly and Wilder elected to stay, but Oatman was determined to go on alone. In mid–March Royse dragged his family across the desert, following the nearly dry Gila River. Only one yoke of oxen and two cows were left, and they were too poor to pull the two wagons uphill. Seven days out of the Pima village, a Dr. Le Conte and his guide rode past and promised that he would send help once he got to Yuma. About 90 miles east of Yuma, Royse and his family struggled across the uncommonly rain-swollen Gila, made their way to a sandy island where the team became mired, and camped for the night.[3]

In a windstorm that night the family huddled around a small fire and talked about Indians. Some said they would run if Indians appeared, and others said they would stand and fight. Olive said, "I will not be taken by these miserable brutes. I will fight as long as I can, and if I see I am about to be taken, I will kill myself. I do not care to die, but it would be worse than death to me to be taken a captive among them."[4]

The next day, 19 March, the Oatmans continued across the Gila, then ascended a mesa about 200 feet above the river. The pull was hard and they unloaded the wagons to make it easier for the oxen. Royse was overcome with gloom. He sank down near the wagon and groaned, "Mother, mother, in the name of God, I know that something dreadful is about to happen!"[5]

They rested, ate, and, when the sun was setting, began to move on, hoping to make a few miles in the cooler evening. Then Lorenzo looked back and saw Indians approaching. There were 19 Yavapais, armed with bows, arrows, and clubs. Royse tried to put up a bold front, spoke to them in Spanish, and asked them to sit down. The Indians wanted tobacco and food. Royse said he had little, and by giving it to them, he would condemn his own children to starvation. They demanded food nevertheless. Royse gave them bread, but it was not enough.

The warriors sprang upon the defenseless family with war clubs. They crushed Royse's skull. Mrs. Oatman jumped from the wagon and grabbed little Roland. Warriors knocked her down and beat both of them to death. A warrior grabbed Olive and yanked her away from the wagon; she fainted. An Indian clubbed Lorenzo in the head, knocking him to the ground. Another grabbed Lucy by the hair and pulled her to the ground while several of them smashed her face until she was unrecognizable. Charity was killed with one blow. Royse Jr. stood in shock, while an Indian came up and beat him to death. Mary Ann was standing alone, holding a rope attached to the lead oxen. She dropped the rope and covered her face with her hands. A huge warrior picked her up and carried her away.[6]

Indians took Lorenzo's hat and shoes, dragged him to the edge of an embankment, and threw him 20 feet to the bottom. Incredibly, the next day he regained consciousness. His face was beaten and bruised, part of his scalp was gone, and he could not open his eyes because of the dried, clotted blood. He crawled to the Gila River, drank, and bathed his wounds. After resting, Lorenzo stumbled upriver for two days. On the third day he saw wagons approaching; they were the Kelly and Wilder families. He told them what had happened, and they all turned around and hurried back to the Pima village. Kelly, Wilder, and a number of Pimas went to the massacre site to bury the bodies. Two weeks later they joined another party of white men heading west, took Lorenzo along, and finally made it to Yuma.[7]

The Yavapais took Olive and Mary north across the desert, amusing themselves by threatening Mary with death to the extent that she would run screaming into Olive's arms. Their bare feet were cut and torn from the rocks and cactus. Olive said that when they camped that night "Food was offered me, but how could I eat to prolong a life I now loathed. I felt neither sensations of hunger nor a desire to live." She wanted to kill herself, but that would leave Mary alone.

When they reached a village about 100 miles away, the Indians tied the girls in the center of a clearing and danced around them, striking them and spitting in their faces, putting on what Olive called a display "of their barbarity, cruelty, and obscenity." When the ordeal was over, Olive and Mary settled into their new lives as slaves. The Indian women were the cruelest, giving them the hardest tasks and beating them at the least provocation. Many a day Mary would entreat her sister: "How long, O how long, dear Olive, must we stay here; can we never get away? Do you not think they intend to kill us?" Olive had little hope, but she encouraged Mary, and they both prayed daily that they would somehow be delivered.[8]

It was in early 1852 when a band of Mojaves bought the girls for two horses, three blankets, some vegetables and beads. They traveled north for 11 days to the Mojave village on the Colorado River. Here the girls worked in the fields, planting and raising wheat, corn, melons,

Oatman Flat, on the Gila River, Arizona, near the site of the March 1851 attack on the Oatman Wagons.

and vegetables. Concerned that the girls might escape, and to facilitate in their identification and make them ashamed to go back to the whites, the Mojaves tattooed the girls' faces. Olive pleaded for them to desist, but to no avail. The painful process left their chins decorated with blue-black markings.

The summer of 1853 was especially dry, the crops failed, and Mary could not work as fast as the Indians required. They beat her more and fed her less. With the approach of winter, Olive and Mary got little or nothing, and in early 1854 Mary wasted away and died. The Mojaves wanted to burn her body, but Olive would not hear of it, and was finally allowed to bury her.[9]

Olive was astonished when, in February 1856, a Yuma Indian arrived in the village with a message from the soldiers at Fort Yuma demanding her release. The long-delayed rescue attempt came as a result of Lorenzo's efforts, plus the help of a Mr. Grinnell. Lorenzo had gone to California where he sought help from the newspapers, the governor, and the Indian Department. He even joined a prospecting party that searched the area in 1855, but he could learn nothing about the captive white girls. At Fort Yuma, Grinnell, a carpenter, heard the story and questioned Indians and emigrants about the girls. When the Yuma Indian Francisco talked to Grinnell about the captives, Grinnell said that the whites would make war upon the Indians if the girls were not released. Grinnell took him to the fort, and Francisco explained that if the soldiers would give him four blankets and some beads, he would bring the girls in.

Francisco arrived at the Mojave village and made his proposal, but the Mojaves insisted Olive was an Indian taken from a distant tribe. The council continued into the next day, when Olive finally blurted out who she was and pleaded to be rescued. The Mojaves wanted to kill them both, but Francisco talked fast, threatened, and finally succeeded in gaining her release. In February 1856 Francisco turned Olive over to Grinnell at Fort Yuma.[10]

Olive received clothing, food, and care, but she was an emotional and physical wreck. Lorenzo learned of her rescue and rode from Los Angeles to get her. They stayed for a time with the Thompsons, one of the families that started out on the journey with them. Susan Thompson Lewis, who had been a friend of Olive and Lucy Oatman on the trip, learned much of Olive's ordeal. She described Olive as a "grieving, unsatisfied woman" who left behind two mixed-blood children with the Mojaves, and who "shook one's belief in civilization."

Olive later wrote a letter to Robert Kelly, a single man who accompanied them through most of their journey. The letter belies the fiction espoused by some contemporary historians that Indian captivity for white women was generally a benign or a good experience. To Kelly, Olive wrote that she felt much better,

> since I have risen from the dead and landed once more in a sivilized world ... the events of the past five years of my life has been misery and dispare I have been A slave to those fiends that committed the bloody masicree to toile and worke for them that had the blood of then that ware near and dear to me stained up under thare hands that driven the happy smiles from my brow and bediewed my life with tears. It seems like a dream to me to look back and see what I had ben thrue and just now waking up.[11] [original spelling and punctuation preserved]

Lorenzo and Olive collaborated with Royal B. Stratton to publish their story, and Stratton arranged for them to accompany him back East. They took a steamship by way of Panama, and arrived in New York in March 1858. Olive lived with her father's relatives near Rochester, and attended school in Albany. When Olive was 28 she married John B. Fairchild. They moved to Michigan for seven years and then relocated to Sherman, Texas. Olive stayed in close contact with Lorenzo for the remainder of their lives. Lorenzo died in Red Cloud, Nebraska, on 8 October 1901. Olive died in Texas on 20 March 1903.[12]

During Olive Oatman's five-year captivity she had an Indian "husband" and bore him two children—not an uncommon experience for white women captives in the West. Her experience was merely one instance of many. Lucinda Eubank, captured in August 1864 along the Little Blue River in Nebraska, was pregnant by her captor, a Lakota named Blackfoot. After Lucinda was rescued, she confided to another woman that she would never let the unborn child see the light of day. Elizabeth Ann Fitzpatrick, captured in the Comanche and Kiowa raid on Elm Creek, Texas, in October 1864, was raped and abused; after her rescue she delivered a stillborn child. Anna Morgan gave birth to a half-Indian son after her recovery, and her husband made life hell for her. One of the most famous of the white captives to have mixed-blood children was Cynthia Ann Parker, captured at Parker's Fort, Texas, in 1836. Cynthia Ann was not "rescued" until 1860, and by then she had at least three children with her Comanche husband; one of them, Quanah, became a famous chief. It may have been easier on Olive that she left her children behind and did not try to integrate them into an intolerant white world.[13]

The difficulty for a mixed-blood child living in either world was expressed early in the silent film era. Where "half-breeds" were usually portrayed as treacherous, *The Barrier of Blood* (Ammex, 1913) sympathetically portrays a young mixed-blood man trapped between two worlds and unable to marry the woman he loves. From the other side, *Bear Hunt Romance* (Pathé, 1911) explores the dilemma of an Indian woman who loves a white man. In *Blazing Arrows* (Western Pictures, 1922) the hero, John Strong/Sky Fire (Lester Cuneo), doesn't believe he can marry his sweetheart because he thinks he is part Indian. The conundrum is fully resolved when he learns both his parents were white.

The social tensions inherent in mixed-race love and marriage was a subject fully explored during the silent film era—perhaps surprisingly, given the contemporary impression that filmmakers and society as a whole were prudish nearly a century ago.[14]

The problem of whites raising a mixed-blood child, or worse yet, a full-blooded Indian child (at least when the neighbors find out), is shown in John Huston's *The Unforgiven* (United Artists, 1960). In a study of racism, Rachel Zachary (Audrey Hepburn), not looking much like an Indian, is an orphaned Kiowa girl raised by the white Zachary Family. Her own "brother," Cash (Audie Murphy), is one of the most bigoted of all, reacting violently when he learns his "sister" is an Indian. He wants her out of the house, refusing to live with a "red-hide Nigger." The only semblance of decency is evidenced by the adoptive mother, Matilda (Lillian Gish), and brothers Ben (Burt Lancaster) and Andy (Doug McClure), who try to protect her from their racist neighbors. Rachel, who has secretly loved Ben all her life, believes, erroneously, that she will never have him as a husband when she discovers she is a Kiowa.

Variations on the storyline were seen in the silent era — for instance, in *Sioux Blood* (MGM, 1929), adapted from a story by Harry Sinclair Drago. Two brothers were separated as children; Indian raiders captured one, who became known as Lone Eagle (Robert Frazer), while the other, Flood (Tim McCoy), was raised by whites. Flood meets Barbara Ingram (Ena Gragory) and learns that the Sioux have taken her father prisoner. They both volunteer themselves as hostages to free the father but learn too late that the old man has already been killed. Flood is about to be burned at the stake, but first he has a hand-to-hand fight with Chief Lone Eagle, leading to their fortuitous discovery that they are brothers. Learning that he is white, Lone Eagle helps them escape, and they all reach the safety of a white town.

Similar storylines were used several times, including in *White Comanche* (1968), a comparatively low-budget film with washed-out color, by International Producers Corporation. Joseph Cotton plays Sheriff Logan, and Rossana Yani is dancehall girl "Kelly," who is captured in a stagecoach raid and raped by Notah, a mixed-blood son of a white father and Comanche mother. Pre–*Star Trek* William Shatner plays the dual role as the "bad" twin, Notah, and his "good" brother, Johnny Moon. (The idea of the good and bad lookalike brothers was used many times, including in *End of the Rope* [Aywon, 1923], and all may have been influenced by Alexander Dumas' 1841 novel *The Corsican Brothers*.) Both sons were raised by the Comanches, but Moon says neither the whites nor Indians really wanted them. As they grow to manhood, the evil Notah prefers to remain with the Indians, while the somewhat more civilized Johnny Moon opts for the white lifestyle. Notah raids a white miners' camp and kills everyone. One Comanche is wounded and Notah kills him, it being his policy to leave no sick or wounded behind. The mixed-blood is shown to be worse than the real Comanches, who tire of his viciousness. Notah's constant raids and killings get his twin in trouble through mistaken identity, and Moon insists that they fight it out once and for all. In the end, Moon wins the duel and Notah is burned on an Indian funeral pyre. One researcher claims that white boys who spent much time with the Indians "had a reputation for being crueler to their fellow Anglos than the Indians were." If so, then Notah in *White Comanche* is a historically accurate character.[15]

# 7

# The Ward-Masterson Wagon Train
# (*Soldier Blue, Rio Grande*)

## Idaho, August 1854

The attack on the Utter-Van Ornum Wagon train in 1860 was not the first massacre of emigrants in what is now Idaho. Six years earlier an attack occurred that was perhaps more barbarous than that perpetrated on the Utters and Van Ornums. The treatment meted out to the white victims was, arguably, worse than Hollywood has ever dared to show onscreen.

Although emigration was less in 1854 than in the previous five years, there were still about 10,000 people who made the trek to Oregon or California. One large train left Missouri in April. It consisted of a multitude of families, but the person who emerged as the leader was Alexander Scott Yantis of Johnson County, Missouri. The Yantis family included Mr. Yantis, his wife, and nine sons and daughters. The Perry Family of Garden Grove, Iowa, joined them, and included Walter G. Perry, Harriet Perry, and their four children, along with a 19-year-old teamster, Empson Cantrell. The Lake Family included George and Elizabeth, and their three children. The Kirkland Family included Moses and Nancy Pipes Kirkland, their daughter Elizabeth, who was married to William Andrew Cox, and several children and young men, totaling 13. Harvey Jones and his wife Eliza Jane later joined the train, as did David A. Neely, his wife, and two sons.

The largest group of wagons belonged to the Ward and Masterson Families, also from Missouri. Members included Alexander Ward (age 41), and his wife Margaret R. Masterson Ward (37) and children, Mary E., Robert G., William M., Newton Jasper, Edward L., Flora A., Susan F., and Francis, the baby. Another child, Thomas C. Ward (4), may have died before they started, or died along the way. Elizabeth Masterson White (30) and her son George (8) were going to join husband and father William White, who was already in Oregon. James Alfred Masterson and his wife Vilinda Campbell Masterson (16), and Robert Masterson, James's brother, traveled in a separate wagon. Charles Adams and Dr. Thomas Adams, from Michigan, joined them, as did William Babcock, a lawyer from Vermont, and Samuel Mulligan. Brothers John and Rudolph Schultz, of Wisconsin, joined them on the trail.[1]

When everyone was traveling together, the train numbered about 65 people and a dozen wagons, but they did not always stick together. Moving in jumps and halts, the families rode and walked across the plains and into the mountains, always jockeying for a better position or a better path, or to be out of someone else's dust or closer to water. At old Fort Hall on the Snake River the train crossed over to take the Jeffrey's Cut-off on the north side of the Snake River and split into three sections. The Indians had burned the grass to starve the emigrants' cattle, and the emigrants felt it would be wiser to divide the train to give the livestock a better chance to find forage. As they crossed the Camas Prairie, Yantis pulled out ahead, Ward was in the middle, and Perry fell behind. Yantis arrived at the Boise River on 16 August. The Perrys brought up the rear, camping at what is probably today's Wild Horse Creek, near Hill City, Idaho, the night of 18 August.

The next morning the Perry-Kirkland Wagons traveled about one hour when they saw Indians approach. Mariah Kirkland was riding in advance of the train, but when her horse spooked and became unmanageable, she dismounted and tried to lead it back. When the horse bolted, Mariah ran and arrived safely back at the wagons. The Indians got her horse. They approached, halted the train, and begged for some whiskey. When the emigrants indicated they had no whiskey, the sullen warriors rode to the rear of the train. There they met three men driving their few cattle and horses. Walter Perry figured they could use a few more horses and tried to trade a pistol for a pony, but the bargaining soon broke down in angry words. As the emigrants tried to leave, the Indians shot two of the men. Walter Perry took a bullet through the right lung and George Lake collapsed with the words "I am a dead man."[2]

The emigrants retaliated. Moses Kirkland fired his revolver, wounding one Indian, and his son fired his shotgun at another. The Indians retreated to a safer area, and both sides kept up a long-range fire. Empson Cantrell was shot through the abdomen, nearly always a fatal wound, but still held his position and returned fire. The surviving men held off the Indians for several hours, but with Lake dead and Perry and Cantrell dying, they realized that they would have to try a different tack. The emigrants hoped that the Indians really wanted their horses, and if they would give them up, the Indians would go away. Moses Kirkland called for a truce and managed to convey that they would give up their horses if the Indians would leave them alone. Eight-year-old Mary Perry did not think the whites put up a good fight. She later said, "They acted very cowardly, showing no disposition to fight the Indians, but willing to get off at any terms, which they did by motioning to the Indians to some five head of horses, which were a short distance from the wagons; they were taken by them and the firing ceased."[3]

When the Indians rode away with the horses, the Perry-Kirkland parties hurried on, trying to catch up to the rest of the train, no doubt figuring there would be better protection in numbers. The section ahead of them, however, fared much worse than they did.

Moving faster than the rest, Alex Yantis traveled along the Boise River, where on 19 August Indians stole a cow from Harvey Jones. On 20 August the party was at the Canyon Crossing of the Boise River, near today's Caldwell, Idaho.

The Ward Train had fallen about 12 miles behind Yantis. Around noon on 20 August the Ward Train pulled off the road on the south side of the Boise River about 25 miles above its mouth, to have lunch and let the livestock graze. A little earlier two white men and three Indians rode up and asked to trade for some of Ward's horses, but there was no deal. While the train nooned, Robert Ward (age 16) was guarding the stock when the three Indians suddenly reappeared and drove off a horse. Robert ran in with the warning, and the Ward-Masterson Party hurriedly hitched their wagons and returned to the trail. No sooner had they strung out than the Indians surrounded them, and they quickly circled the wagons and prepared for an attack. The Indians charged as the last wagon was pulled into place. Estimates of attacking Shoshones varied greatly from 30 to 200.

Charlie Adams was shot through the shoulder in the first assault. One Indian was killed, and the others retreated to the brush and continued their barrage from cover. Alexander Ward, Robert Ward, Dr. Adams, Babcock, Mulligan, and the unnamed driver of White's wagon fought doggedly from under the wagon beds and behind the wheels, while the two Schultz brothers cowered in their wagon. The emigrants held the hostiles off for two hours, but one by one the men were all picked off, and when the defensive fire noticeably slackened, the Indians rushed the wagons. They yanked the two German brothers from their hiding place and slaughtered them.

Most of the women and children were huddled in one large wagon. William Ward (15) and Newton Ward (13) viewed their position as hopeless.

"Let's run into the brush and hide," William said, and the two boys sprinted away. While running, William was skewered with an arrow through his right side and fell unconscious. Indians rode their horses over him. Newton was shot in the right side and went down. As he tried to crawl away, a warrior struck him a glancing blow on the head with a club, knocking him senseless.

At the same time the attack was occurring, Alexander Yantis, David Neely, Harvey Jones, a young man named Ames or Amen, and three others were about a dozen miles ahead, but backtracking in search of missing stock. They encountered one wagon belonging to James A. Masterson, his wife, and brother, who had pulled out ahead of the rest early in the morning and had not stopped to eat. Yantis suspected trouble and recommended he catch up to the train ahead. Yantis and the searchers stopped to rest at Canyon Crossing about two in the afternoon, when they spotted far-off wagons. Yantis and Neely rode over, but as they neared the wagons they realized the train was under attack. They returned, marshaled the other searchers, and rushed back to the scene of battle. When they got there they saw the Indians already driving two of the wagons away, down the hill and into the willows. Said Harvey Jones:

> We rode up within rifle shot of the wagons in the bushes. An Indian rode out of the bushes towards us in a very daring manner. Mr. Yantis dropped behind some bushes and slipped up close to the Indian before the Indian saw him. He shot at the Indian. The Indian appeared to be severely wounded, wheeled his horse and dashed into the bushes.[4]

In the brief encounter, young Ames was shot dead. Three of the searchers retreated out of range of danger and stopped; three others continued to fight. Soon the Indians realized the rescue party was too insignificant in number to pose a threat, and rode off with their spoils, allowing Yantis, Neely, and Jones to approach the corral. Newton Ward had regained consciousness and remained hidden in the brush until he was sure the voices he heard were from white men. He stumbled out of hiding, and the three men helped him up on a horse. It appeared that everyone was dead or taken by the Indians, and Yantis decided to hurry to Fort Boise, alert the soldiers, and gather enough men to go after the women and children, in the hope they were still alive.

Yantis overtook James Masterson about dark, and they settled Newton into a bed in their wagon. Newton was Masterson's nephew. They looked back east and saw an eerie glow in the sky; the deserted wagons were ablaze! They then hastened west and overtook the rest of Yantis's train about two in the morning. They arrived at Fort Boise the evening of the twenty-first. Alexander Yantis sent a message to two large wagon trains ahead to inform them of the attack and request help to rescue the women and children. John T. Noble, John Colgate Bell, Orlando Humason, and fifteen other men formed a rescue party. A mixed-blood Indian guide, Tabbaboo, joined in the search. They left for the massacre site on 22 August.

Upon arrival near a charred wagon, they found the bodies of Alexander Ward, Robert Ward, Samuel Mulligan, Charles Adams, William Babcock, and one of the Schultz Brothers. A half mile beyond, four more victims were discovered in the brush: Dr. Adams, the other Schultz, the driver of White's wagon, and Ames. One hundred yards farther they discovered Mary E. Ward's body. The 17-year-old had been shot in the head, bruises and teeth marks were evident on her left cheek, and a piece of iron protruded from her genitals, evidence of a brutal death.

Further on was another burned wagon, with the charred remains of two dogs. Fifty yards beyond were three more burned wagons, and 600 yards farther was Elizabeth Masterson White. Her head had been beaten to a "perfect jelly," and her body was stripped and scalped. They found a sixth wagon in the thick undergrowth a half mile away. Thirty yards from this, on the

Memorial marker for the August 1854 Ward-Masterson Massacre, near Caldwell, Idaho.

north shore of the Boise River, they discovered a deserted Indian camp containing the bodies of the pregnant Margaret Ward and three children. Margaret's body was stripped, raped, cut extensively, and bruised; scars on her body showed that she had been burned with hot pieces of iron, and her face bore the deep wound of a tomahawk near the right temple, probably the death blow. Indian Agent R. R. Thompson later reported, "Several parts of the limbs were picked up some distance from the fire." The children, Flora Ward (7), Susan Ward (3), and the Ward baby had been held by their hair and roasted alive in front of Margaret. It was later revealed that the Indian women had performed these atrocities. The searchers could not find Edward Ward (11), George White (9), or William Ward. They were uncertain if another child, Thomas C. Ward (4), was among the missing. All together, 19 people were killed, wounded, or missing.[5]

William Ward lay unconscious in the brush during the night. On 21 August, he awoke and began walking and crawling toward the Boise River, with an arrow still protruding from his side. Too weak to cross the river, he stumbled along the south side, thus missing the rescue party that was traveling along the north bank. He found herbs and berries to eat, and made it to Henry Isaacs's Ferry by Fort Boise on the 25th, where some men removed the arrow and fed him. The Yantis train had already moved on, taking the wounded Newton Ward with them and assuming he was the only survivor. Nez Perce messengers caught up to Yantis on Burnt River in Oregon, with a note that William was alive and would be sent along later. Mrs. Isaacs cared for William for a week and arranged for him to accompany another train. Because he still had to lie flat in a wagon, they charged him a dollar a day.[6]

In 1854, Maj. Granville O. Haller, 4th Infantry, captured two Indian participants of the Ward massacre, and they revealed the fate of Edward Ward and George White. The Indians said, "One of those boys they had carried off died and the other took on so that they killed him." They survived a month or less after the massacre.

William Ward did not meet up with his brother Newton until several months later. Newton went to the Willamette Valley near Eugene, Oregon, with his uncle, William Masterson, arriving in October. William did not arrive until December. Newton lived for ten years, near Salem, with James H. Ward, a member of one branch of his father's large, extended family. Although young for soldiering, both boys joined and fought with the Oregon Infantry in the Yakima War of 1855. Both of them died in 1925.[7]

Although Hollywood has given us many films of Indian attacks on wagon trains, it has never graphically depicted atrocities of the sort that were committed upon the Wards and Mastersons. In the first half-century of films, whites would die onscreen, but usually in a nearly bloodless collapse, or occasionally with an arrow shown awkwardly protruding from the unfortunate victim. After-battle tortures, rapes, and other atrocities were absent. Instead, in a rather perverse reversal, movies in the latter half of the 20th century began depicting white soldiers as villains. Where filmmakers with some sense of decorum once avoided showing Indian atrocities, they later seemed to relish depicting white depravities.

One prime example was *Soldier Blue* (Avco Embassy, 1970). It is argued that director Ralph Nelson wanted to make a statement against the Vietnam War and atrocities that were coming to light, such as the killing of Vietnamese civilians at My Lai. As an "all-purpose metaphor for the oppressed," he would use American Indians as victims, and show them graphically massacred at the 1864 fight at Sand Creek. The Cheyennes are only seen a couple of times during the film — once at the beginning when they attack the paymaster's wagons, and once at the end when a Cheyenne village is destroyed. In between, the movie is essentially a blossoming love story between Honus Grant (Peter Strauss) and Cresta (Candace Bergen).

Cresta was once a captive of the Cheyennes, but after two years she returns to the white world. Cresta has learned many nasty habits, including unabashedly displaying bodily functions and stealing from the dead — a characterization that seems out of line with the sympathy the director supposedly wanted to elicit for the Indians he sought to portray as more civilized than the whites. It is also puzzling that Cresta voluntarily returns to a people she once escaped from; but, in any case, they welcome her with open arms. The final massacre scene, which really has nothing to do with the rest of the movie, is simply a gratuitous show of violence, as the "mad" Colonel Iverson (John Anderson) sends his men to slaughter, rape, and pillage.

In a similar vein, Arthur Penn's *Little Big Man* (1970) has a graphic massacre scene in which the "mad" Lieutenant Colonel Custer destroys a Cheyenne village on the Washita, indiscriminately killing men, women, and children alike.

In *The Searchers*, John Ford would never show slaughtered whites; we never see Aaron Edwards (Walter Coy), Martha Edwards (Dorothy Jordan), or Ben Edwards's (Robert Lyden) corpses — the sight is left to the audiences' imagination. Likewise, Ford does not show the horrible things that the Indians had done to the captive Lucy Edwards (Pippa Scott); but the horror is evident on her Uncle Ethan's face.

Lucy could have been the fictional counterpart of Mary or Margaret Ward, but Hollywood, at least at one time, had the decency not to show us the details. In *Rio Grande* (Republic 1950), Ford also conceals the bodies of the Indians' victims. Apaches steal a couple of wagons with white women and children. When the soldiers catch up, they find the wreck of one wagon, with only the bonnet of Mrs. Bell lying in the mud in mute testimony as to what probably happened to her.

What Hollywood in the 1950s would not show of Indians doing to whites, it seemed to revel in a reverse role only a decade or so later. Indian massacres of whites were very real occurrences on the frontier. Today that fact is often forgotten, denied, or whitewashed. One alleged historian and film critic has contended that incidents of Indians massacring whites were nearly all exaggerations; therefore, traumatic westerns showing white captives are counter-realistic

## 7. The Ward-Masterson Wagon Train

43

U.S. soldiers are depicted as barbarians in the finale of *Soldier Blue* (Avco Embassy, 1970), supposedly based on the 1864 Sand Creek "Massacre."

and counter-historical, and whenever massacres of settlers are depicted, they really are sly reversals of what were white massacres of Indians.[8]

Hollywood, at least in its earlier years, had a better grasp of American History than do some contemporary historians. It understood that Indians did attack and slaughter white emigrants, although it depicted the massacres with restraint. So far in the 21st century, a film graphically depicting the things Indians did to the Wards and Mastersons has not been made; if whites were the perpetrators, perhaps this would be another story.

# 8

# The Fancher-Baker Wagon Train
## (*The Last Wagon, Dawn on the Great Divide*)
### Utah, September 1857

One of the larger and most well-organized wagon trains to cross the continent was gathering in Arkansas in the early months of 1857. Alexander Fancher and John T. Baker were not heading to California for gold, but for the lucrative cattle market. The two men had been planning the trek for two years, and were including only the most respectable, "sober, hard-working, plain folks" they could find (which included the Mitchells, Millers, Dunlaps, and Camerons). The group was perhaps the most well-stocked and supplied of any that went west. The 140 emigrants and 40 wagons that rolled out on 7 May also included about 1,000 cattle, and stashed aboard the wagons was about $100,000 in gold coins and currency.

Not following the more heavily traveled paths, the train moved across northwest Arkansas and the northeast corner of Indian Territory (Oklahoma), and followed the Arkansas River to Bent's Fort and Pueblo. It went north along the east face of the Rockies and took the Cherokee Trail across the Laramie Plains, then west to Fort Bridger. In Salt Lake City in early August, a heretofore nearly uneventful trip began to turn ugly.

The political situation had gotten worse, with Brigham Young and his disciples ranting against the Gentiles crossing their land, and the interfering U.S. Government sticking its nose into matters Young considered none of its business. As the U.S. threatened to send an army to bring order, the Mormons swore they would defend their lands and lives against any invaders. The Fancher-Baker train pulled into this highly charged atmosphere. Where Mormons once gladly sold supplies to emigrants for a tidy profit, now they would not lift a finger to help and directly shunned the emigrants. It was reported that some of the rebuffed travelers, in turn, made flagrant anti–Mormon remarks; and when Mormons refused to sell them food, the emigrants threatened to return with the military to punish the Saints.

As Fancher headed down along the Wasatch Mountains, Young wrote to Elder Jacob Hamblin, 250 miles south at Mountain Meadows, that he must convince the Indians "that they have either got to help us or the United States will kill us both." Orders went out to church leaders across southern Utah to prohibit the emigrants from getting through. John D. Lee, a leading, zealous disciple of Young, living in Harmony, got the word. He believed he had "the direct command of Brigham Young" to exterminate the emigrants.

The harried and shunned Fancher-Baker train entered Mountain Meadows, a welcoming valley with wood, water, and grass about 30 miles southwest of Cedar City. After the hostility they had faced from the Mormons, it was with some sense of relief when they reached the oasis to rest for a few days before crossing the harsh deserts to the west. Uncharacteristically, Fancher let his guard down, failing to post sentries, failing to encompass the fresh spring of water within the campsite, and neglecting to circle the wagons in a defensive position.

At dawn on Monday, 7 September, as several early-risers began preparing breakfast, shots and shrieks erupted from the rocks and hills all around them. Within moments, a few children and seven men were shot down, and many more were wounded, including John Baker and Alexander Fancher, the latter taking a bullet through the throat. Fancher's nephew Matt (age 25) took over, calling for them to belatedly circle the wagons. They hastily dug trenches to sink the wagons down near their axletrees and threw up mounds of earth in front. The women dragged the dead and wounded into the center. More than 50 children ran and screamed, adding even more confusion to the scene.

There was no close-up assault, however; and only sporadic firing continued throughout the day. The spring was about 100 yards outside of the wagon circle, and all the cattle grazing in a valley beyond were taken. The siege continued through Wednesday. More wounded had died, and the smell of decaying bodies of humans and horses became unbearable. The lack of water was the worst. In despair, the emigrants sent two little girls, dressed in bright white clothes and carrying buckets, to the spring. Both were shot dead.

That night, William Aden and another man called the Dutchman slipped quietly out of the circle, leading their horses and hoping to find help. Several miles away they saw a campfire and stopped, thinking that it was from another emigrant party coming behind them. It was a party of Mormons. Aden dismounted and explained about the assault, but one of the men walked over to him and shot him in the chest. The Dutchman wheeled on his horse and escaped, but not before being wounded. He got back to the besieged train and told what happened. Finally, the emigrants realized the extent of the forces they were fighting. They had assumed about 200 Paiutes were assailing them; there were indeed Paiutes there, under Moquetas and Big Bill, but their main adversaries were the Mormons.

On Thursday night, three more men tried to ride out for help, this time to California, but the Mormons caught and killed them all. On Friday morning, John D. Lee, William Bateman, and a few others rode out with a white flag and an American flag. Hoping this would be their salvation, the emigrants eagerly listened to Lee's offer of help. Lee explained that the Indians wanted to kill them all, but he would try to save them and get them back to Cedar City — but first they would have to give up all their weapons and surrender. The train leader, Matt Fancher, and the badly wounded John Baker saw no alternative but to give up. The dying Alex Fancher, however, in a delirious fever, said, "Good God no, Matt!"

They didn't listen and they surrendered. Lee ordered the emigrant men, women, and children to divide into three groups. The women and children were led away first, and were a half mile away from the men; each male had his own Mormon guard. As the women pulled out of view into a low swale, a Mormon, probably John Lee, called out, "Halt! Do your duty!" With that, the Mormons turned and sliced the throats of their prisoners or shot them down if they survived the knife attack. At the sounds of the shooting, the women realized they had been tricked, and tried to run, but other Mormons began to systematically slaughter them as well. Some of the women and older girls, including Ruth (age 14) and Rachel (16) Dunlap, were raped before they were killed. There may have been Paiutes present, but almost all of the killing was directed and done by the Mormons. One band of Shivwits Paiutes witnessed the fighting from the hills, but they were said to have abandoned the area soon after.

The massacre sputtered out when there were no more victims. It took only minutes to kill 121 people; 17 of the youngest children were spared — those thought to be under the age of innocence, about eight years old, and who would not remember the day's horror. The children were divided up among several Mormon families. Some were old enough to remember — and they did. The Mormons confiscated property amounting to $70,000. It took 20 years to catch and

Mountain Meadows, Utah, site of the September 1857 massacre of the Fancher-Baker wagon train.

convict John D. Lee of the murders—and only after the Mormons gave him up as a sacrifice to save the scores of others who were just as guilty. He was executed on 23 March, 1877.[1]

One of the key factors leading to the Mountain Meadows Massacre was the emigrants' lack of vigilance. Fancher and Baker had ably organized and led the train three-fourths of the way through their journey, taking daily and nightly precautions during the march across the Great Plains. When they finally relaxed their guard, disaster struck. Fancher did not circle his wagons, set out sentries, or camp with a water supply within easy access.

A similar situation was played out in the movie *The Last Wagon* (Fox, 1956). Directed by Delmer Daves, the film depicts a small wagon train heading west through dangerous Apache country. Joining up with it is racist and tyrant Sheriff Bull Harper (George Mathews), with his prisoner Comanche Todd (Richard Widmark), who lived 20 years with the Indians. Todd is chained to a wagon wheel and refused food and water by the vicious sheriff, while the people of the train are divided as to whether to humanely succor him or see him suffer as a murderous white renegade.

One night the train is camped, stretched out along a wooded trail in the mountains, with no water source nearby, while a lone young guard decides to go for a moonlight swim with five others back at the river a few miles from camp. Of course, the Apaches attack and wipe out the train, killing all except Todd, who somehow survives being rolled off a cliff still chained to his wagon-wheel prison. When the six people return near dawn, they find the devastation and learn that if they want to survive, they will have to depend on Todd. However, while three of them, including young Billy (Tommy Rettig), believe Todd is their salvation, the other three, including a young man named Ridge (Nick Adams), do not trust Todd and would rather see him die chained to the wheel. They finally agree to set Todd free, and after they salvage parts from the wrecked train to assemble one last wagon, he guides them to safety. Near the climax of the film, when they discover that the Indians may overwhelm them, Todd tells the young men—who

## 8. The Fancher-Baker Wagon Train

Renegade Richard Widmark is chained to a wagon wheel in *The Last Wagon* (Fox, 1956). A few of the emigrants, including Felicia Farr and Tommy Rettig, believe he should be set free, while others want him to die.

have only one gun and three bullets left after Ridge stupidly wastes the ammunition shooting at a rattlesnake — that they must save the last three bullets for the three young women. Preventing women from falling into the hands of the Indians and "a fate worse than death" was a major concern on the frontier. At the finale, they find a small squad of soldiers with two supply wagons loaded with ammunition. When the Apaches are massing for an attack, Lieutenant Kelly (James Drury) calls out, "Circle the wagons!" and they rig up a dynamite surprise for the Indians. Todd fires a flaming arrow into the powder just as the Indians approach, blowing up the wagons and allowing the soldiers and emigrants to escape.

Like the Fancher-Baker train, *The Last Wagon* emigrants learned the hard way the importance of circling up for defense. The majority of the emigrant trains suffered no attacks. When they did occur, however, the results were often disastrous.

Another movie theme mirrored in the fate of the Fancher-Baker train was the involvement of white men disguised as Indians. That the Mormons played that game is evident. Several of the children who were not killed because they were supposedly too young to remember, recalled the events clearly. Little Kit Carson Fancher talked to a reporter two years after the massacre. "My father was killed by the Indians," he said. "When they washed their faces they were white men."[2]

A similar discovery was made by Alex Kirby (Steve Clark) after being wounded in an "Indian" attack on a wagon train in *Dawn on the Great Divide* (Monogram, 1942). Buck Roberts (Buck Jones) and Sandy Hopkins (Raymond Hatton) are scouts, leading a wagon train of emigrants and supplies west. Unfortunately, there is an organized band of crooked white men who are trying to monopolize all the commercial routes for themselves, and will go to any length to prevent other interests from cutting in on their deal.

Jim Corkle (Harry Woods), the head bad man, even has a band of cutthroats who disguise themselves as Indians to attack emigrants and freighters who are intruding on his little kingdom. Kirby and Jack Carson (Rex Bell) warn the approaching train. They have just parleyed with the Indians and learned that whites, not Indians, were involved in the recent attacks. Buck and Sandy come up with a not-too-bright stratagem: if Indians attack, they will split the wagons, with the emigrants taking one path and the supply wagons another — the idea being that the Indians will chase the supply wagons, because that's what they are really after. Buck and most of the armed men will stay hidden in the supply wagons to give the Indians a deadly surprise.

A subplot of the film illustrates another peril that pioneers had to contend with: on the road, a lone woman gives birth to a baby but dies in the process. A childless couple take in the infant, and the train moves on. Similar incidents happened in reality and will be discussed later.

*Dawn on the Great Divide* (Monogram, 1942) was Buck Jones' last film. It was released just after he died in the fire at the Cocoanut Grove in Boston on 28 November, 1942, which killed 492 people.

When the "Indians" finally attack, the wagon train splits and runs, but contrary to plan, the Indians go after the emigrants, eventually killing or mortally wounding all of them. After the massacre, Kirby regains consciousness lying next to a dead assailant, and when he examines the body, he lifts the man's wig to find out that he is white. He gets the confirming information back to Buck with the supply wagons before he dies. After Buck learns of the disaster, he makes the understatement of the movie: "Splittin' the train wasn't such a good idea."

When Corkle's men once again attack the supply trains while camped at Beaver Lake, this time they do run into Buck's armed men who are hiding under the wagon covers waiting for them. The bad guys are killed or captured, and Corkle's little empire comes crashing down.

# 9

# The Shepherd and Miltimore Wagon Trains
## (*Fighting Caravans, The Painted Stallion*)

### Idaho, July and August 1859

There were a few other attacks on wagon trains where whites may have been involved. They occurred in what would become Idaho, in 1859. The cause of the first attack is disputed. The Salt Lake City *Deseret News* reported that several Flatheads approached an emigrant train to trade, but were fired upon and two of them killed. The Flatheads supposedly appealed to the Shoshones for help, and a combined force attacked the next unfortunate train that came by. Another version has it that a small, unnamed train was camped on the Hudspeth Cut-off several miles west of Twin Springs, when Shoshones came by and asked for something to eat. They received some bread, but upon leaving, they shot a Mr. Hall in the heart and stole 11 cattle and horses. In either case, the Shepherd Train was the next on the scene.

Ferguson Shepherd (age 36) was captain of a small train of about 20 people, all from Howard County, Missouri, and heading for California. The attacked party came down out of the mountains back to Twin Springs, warned Shepherd not to leave because of the danger ahead, and pleaded with him to help regain their stolen livestock. Shepherd, for whatever reasons, thought it best that he keep his party moving, and they pulled out at seven A.M. on 27 July. As they ascended the mountains, they looked back to see Indians attacking the other trains camped at Twin Springs; but they hurried on, figuring the trouble was behind them. They got a few miles farther when one of the horses collapsed. As the men looked the animal over, trying to determine what ailed it, the Shoshones caught up to them.

One of their first bullets killed Ferguson Shepherd. War whoops echoed from the rocks all around them, and bullets and arrows came flying. William Diggs, Clayborn F. Rains, and William Shepherd were killed next, and James D. Wright was mortally wounded. The rest of the men tried to fight back, but Ignatious M. Smith was hit, and a bullet struck Mrs. Wright in the back while she was leaning out, trying to secure the wagon gate. With that, most of the other male defenders fled — George Avery, James Ward, George Parson, and J. McGuire took the remaining horses and rode away.

Mrs. Bettie Diggs Shepherd estimated that the fight lasted about three-quarters of an hour before the 50 Indians, who did not rush them, seemed to back off a bit. The survivors got out of the wagons and began winding their way out of the mountains back toward Twin Springs. Mrs. Annie Shepherd, who was described as "very delicate," became too weak to carry her baby, and the wounded Ignatious Smith carried the eight-month-old until he became too weak to proceed. The three of them hid in the brush until they could regain their strength.

A few miles down the trail, Townsend Wright rode up on a mule. He had been taking care

Cold Springs Canyon, Idaho, near the site of the July 1859 attack on the Shepherd Wagon Train.

of his wounded brother, but realized he could do no more; he cut a mule loose from the harness and rode back. He let Bettie Shepherd ride the animal. The four men who had fled the attack early reached Twin Springs and warned the Skaggs train — the one that had been attacked early that morning — as well as the Fairbanks, Pierce, and Hereford trains that pulled in later in the morning. The combined groups, now about 200 men and 52 wagons, circled up for the night. At dusk, Annie Shepherd wandered in. Said Bettie Shepherd, "She was almost an insane woman. When she came in sight of the camp, she was fired upon for an Indian." Five men went out to find the baby she abandoned, but darkness and Indians forced them back.

The next morning the entire train moved out. Incredibly, they found Annie Shepherd's baby — bruised, scratched, and severely burned by the sun, but still alive. They also found the wounded Mrs. James Wright, holding her 18-month-old child and hiding under a wagon along with her fatally wounded husband. Little Joe Wright (age 5) was trying to take care of his parents. When the Indians had come they took the Wright girl and slammed her against a rock, breaking her thigh. They ransacked the wagons, stole 34 head of stock and rode away. For some reason they did not kill the Wrights. The trains moved on, burying the bodies at nightfall in one grave along Sublett Creek. James Wright died nine days later. Dr. Anton W. Tjader commented that the little Wright girl "was partly deranged for some time after so cruel a treatment."

The possibility that there were white men with the attacking Indians was first mentioned by Maj. Isaac Lynde, 7th Infantry, who had spoken to some of the survivors. "The people state that they recognized at least three white men, painted and dressed as Indians, in the attacking party," Lynde reported. There was no further verification, but the story spread through the territories that white men were leading Indian attacks on wagon trains.[1]

Another attack the month after the Shepherd incident also resulted in reports that white men were involved. On 20 August, a train of 20 emigrants and five wagons from Iowa and Missouri, under Milton Carpenter, passed a trader's camp on Utah Territory's northern border. After they rode on, an Indian stopped to ask the trader, a man named Porter, if the emigrants had any powder and lead. Getting a negative answer, the warrior left to inform his friends, and only a short time later a band of about 60 Shoshone fired on Carpenter's train.

A. L. Root of Iowa was killed, and three other men were badly wounded. The emigrants fled five miles back to Porter's, while the Indians plundered and burned the wagons, and stole 68 head of livestock. The wagonless and destitute survivors hooked up with several other trains and continued their journey.

Another train, under Edwin A. Miltimore, suffered a worse fate 11 days later. Edwin (age 55) was from Vermont, and his wife, Catherine Dean (44), was from New York. Their ten children were born in different states as the family forever moved westward, hoping for a better life, like so many other families of the time. What they thought were the last children were born in Illinois and Iowa, but the Miltimores were still not done — a baby girl was born on the road, somewhere in present Nebraska. Although Edwin Miltimore was captain, Milton Harrington, his son-in-law, was the train's organizer. Even though he made adequate preparations for the 19 travelers, the bad weather, poor grass, swollen streams, and large number of stock they brought kept them moving at a slow pace. West of South Pass a couple of men convinced them to take Lander's Cut-off, said to have better grass and water, and to be less traveled. Lorenza Suberr, who was traveling with the Miltimores to that point, recalled several strangers talking, with one of them saying, "Ain't I glad that the party [the Miltimores] have taken that road." Lorenza didn't know the gist of the conversation at the time, but later came to believe "that harm was intended to them."

Had the strangers meant them harm, they would probably have struck somewhere along Lander's Route, but the Miltimores reached Fort Hall safely and rejoined the main Oregon Trail. On 31 August, 1859, the train was about 25 miles west of Fort Hall, in the vicinity of today's American Falls. It was there that disaster struck — aided, perhaps, by the mistake of letting the wagons became separated. Since the cattle were lagging behind, Edwin dropped back with two wagons, and had James Miltimore (age 18) and Myron Kline go back to round up the strays. Two Miltimore boys, George (20) and Alonzo (16), went duck hunting. Milton Harrington, who had married Miltimore's daughter Fanny, had moved ahead to camp, along with another young couple, Alfred Hill and his wife and child.

The two rear wagons had just begun rolling when three men rode up. Charles N. Miltimore (12), who was driving the last wagon, later recalled that they were Indians "or white men disguised as Indians." One of the men rode up to Charles and asked, "Where are you going?"

"To California," Charles answered.

"No you ain't," the man responded in English.

They rode only a sort distance when they came to a fork. "There are no tracks going this way," one rider pointed out.

"Take the other road," another rider ordered Miltimore. Charles remembered that they "spoke good English," and that the one who talked to him had light brown hair, and the others wore beards. With the wagons turned off on a side path, 15 or more riders suddenly charged at them, whooping and shooting. Most of the attackers were Indians, probably Shoshones under Pagaeh and Sowwich. One of the three men who had been riding along with the wagons turned and shot Edwin Miltimore dead. Several volleys tore into the lead wagon, and Catherine died, along with William (11), Mary Ellen (5), and the baby girl.

Charles jumped down from his wagon and ran toward the other wagons; the bullets flew around him, one going through his hat, but he escaped. George and Alonzo heard the firing and came up, but they saw that they were badly outnumbered and remained hidden in the bushes. The raiders caught James Miltimore and Myron Kline among the cattle and killed them also.

In the lead wagons, Milton Harrington heard the shooting and rode back with a few men, coming upon Charles with a few raiders at his heels. When they saw Harrington and a few armed men approaching, the attackers turned back. Charles stammered out the news that everyone else was dead, and they all hurried to the lead wagons to set up a defense. The marauders soon came in full force, and the emigrants retreated into the rough breaks along the Snake River. Harrington and Nathan Titus fired at a warrior who approached closer than the rest and killed him. By then it was dark, and the survivors grabbed what they could carry and carefully picked their path along the shore, heading downriver. Throughout the night they could hear hollering back on the bluff tops.

By forced marching the next morning they caught up to Alfred Hill's wagon and found George and Alonzo Miltimore, who arrived just before they did. The harried emigrants hurried west for three days before running into a small government train near Raft River, under Lt. Henry B. Livingston, 2nd Dragoons, with seven soldiers and a guide. Livingston escorted them east to Major Lynde's camp on Bear River. As he did after the Shepherd Massacre, Lynde sent soldiers to the scene of the Miltimore attack. The bodies they found were horribly mutilated and scalped. Little Mary Ellen's legs and ears were cut off, and her eyes gouged out.

The survivors stayed at Camp Floyd, Utah Territory, during the winter, working what odd jobs they could find. The next summer, Milton Harrington and his wife Fanny took the surviving Miltimore children with them as they all traveled back to settle in Wisconsin—the farmlands of the Midwest (only about 50 miles from Milwaukee) apparently being quite wild enough for them for the rest of their lives.

What the people of the Shepherd and Miltimore wagon trains learned was that the trek West was clearly fraught with many perils, and savage brutality was not exclusive to any one race.[2]

The concept of emigrants facing dangers from whites as well as Indians was featured in *Fighting Caravans* (Paramount, 1931). The movie had a somewhat similar storyline to *The Big Trail*, which came out the previous year, and both owed much to the silent classic *Covered Wagon* (1923). Given "A" status, with star Gary Cooper in the lead role, *Fighting Caravans* did better at the box office than *The Big Trail*, although it did a poorer job depicting wagon train travel.

Clint Belmet (Gary Cooper) is saved from going to jail by pretending he is married to Felice (Lily Damita). To stay out of more trouble, he joins his saddlemates Bill Jackson (Ernest Torrence) and Jim Bridger (Tully Marshall) in leading a wagon train of emigrants and freighters from Missouri to California. The year is 1861, and the film depicts the Union soldiers leaving the West to head back to the East to fight in the Civil War. With less soldiers around, it supposedly will be open season on the emigrants for the Indians and white villains.

As the train arrives in dangerous country, wagon boss Couch (Roy Stewart) announces, "Let's curl up our wagons and bed down here for the night." White villain Lee Murdock (Fred Kohler), who is traveling with the train to better direct its destruction, convinces Couch not to stop there but to hurry up to get through Indian country as fast as possible. The train splits up, with Murdock insisting that one party of 18 wagons is large enough for safety. Of course, the Indians attack. Kiowas and Comanches, assisted by Murdock, surprise the train while it is crossing a river. In the chaos, Murdock kills Jim Bridger, and a warrior kills Bill Jackson; but before he dies, Jackson shoots down Murdock. Clint Belmet rescues Felice and ends the attack by blowing up a dynamite wagon in the river. In the end, Clint gives up scouting to marry Felice.

A remake of *Fighting Caravans* appeared in 1934, as *Wagon Wheels*, with Randolph Scott as Clint Belmet. A few minor changes placed the events in 1844; the score includes more songs, such as "Onward Christian Soldiers" and "Wagon Wheels"; and the story adds a little boy named Sonny Wellington (Billy Lee), who takes joy in stinging attacking Indians with stones from his

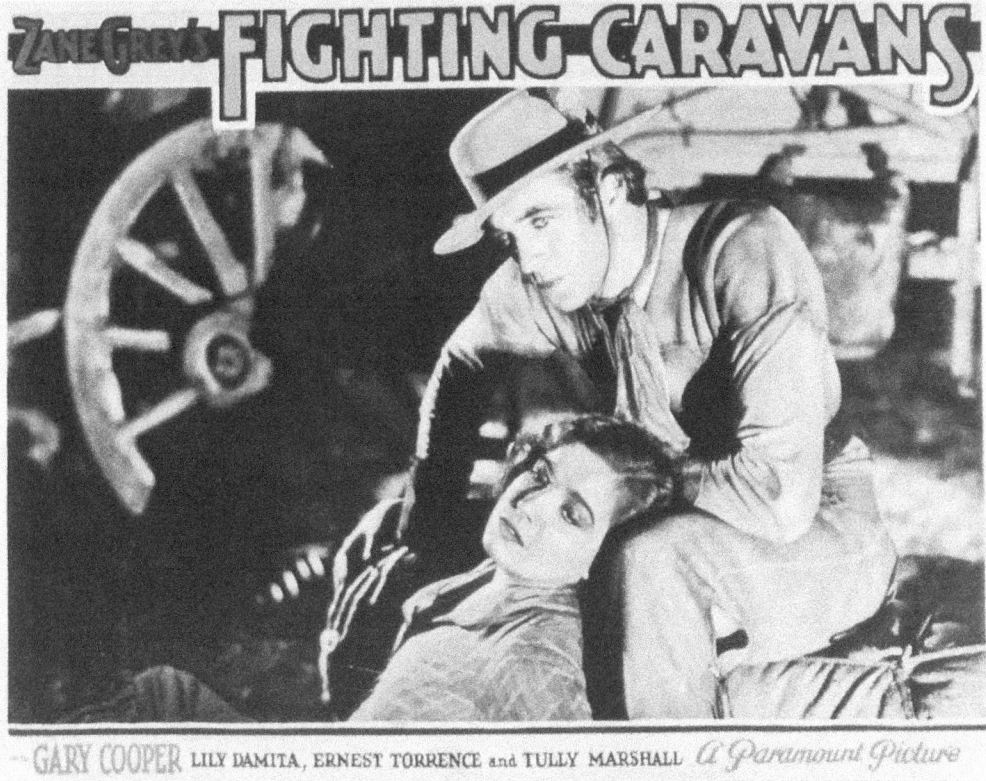

Lily Damita and Gary Cooper form the love interest in *Fighting Caravans* (Paramount, 1931), another epic in the mold of *The Covered Wagon* and *The Big Trail*. Some unused footage was later inserted into its 1934 remake, *Wagon Wheels*.

slingshot. The white villain this time is Ken Murdock (Monte Blue). Clint again blows up a wagon in the river to end the Indian attack and ends up marrying the girl, Nancy Wellington (Gail Patrick).

A passel of white villains appear in *The Painted Stallion* (1937). Republic studios made 66 serials between 1936 and 1955, and this 12-chapter offering was one of the better ones.[3] The plot, set in the 1820s, was certainly unusual. Walter Jamison (Hoot Gibson) is taking a wagon train west from Independence, Missouri, to Santa Fe to begin a trading enterprise. He is accompanied by U.S. envoy Clark Stuart (Ray "Crash" Corrigan), with credentials to negotiate a trade agreement with the Mexican government. The deposed Spanish-appointed governor, Dupray (LeRoy Mason), is determined that nothing will stop him from keeping his lucrative commercial hold; he plans to destroy the wagon train before the new governor arrives. The train will be a tough nut, however, for among its members are Jim Bowie (Hal Taliarerro); a young Christopher Carson (Sammy McKim), who receives his moniker "Kit" from envoy Stuart; and even Davy Crockett (Jack Perrin), who joins up later.

Dupray's minions, led by Zamorro (Duncan Renaldo), and including gang member Bull Smith (Charles King), incite the Comanches to attack the train during its journey. The Indians are willing to comply. "Form a circle!" yells Captain Jamison, and the 40-odd wagons link up in an almost perfect loop on the prairie, while the Indians ride around, killing some of the freighters, but taking more damage themselves. Even young "Kit" shoots his first Indian.

The Indian attack is thwarted, but the screen caption later informs us that "even worse

were the white renegades...." Dupray sends his men out to do the job, and Zamorro leads the white outlaws, some of whom have infiltrated the train, in a series of attempts to destroy it. The white renegades try especially hard to kill the envoy Stuart—trying to drown him in a swollen river crossing, chasing him in a "death leap" over a cliff, dropping him through a trap door in a cave, shooting at him while he's locked in a closet, and any number of other implausible scenarios. The villains divert the wagons through the wrong mountain pass, dynamite a cliff to start an avalanche, fire on the train from ambush, steal the ammunition wagon and blow it to pieces, attempt to capture the real governor before he arrives, set the governor's Santa Fe residence on fire, and cause a rockslide to try to kill rescuers from the wagon train who have come to save the captured Stuart, Bowie, and Crockett.

The number and variety of traps and miraculous escapes are typical of the serial westerns, but the most unusual twist comes from a mysterious blond woman who rides a painted stallion and repeatedly saves the wagon train with her "whistling arrows" of unerring accuracy. The "blond goddess," we learn from the new governor after the villains are foiled and he is safely installed in office, was a white girl who survived a wagon train massacre and was raised by the Comanches. The Indians worshipped her, and she dedicated her life to keeping peace. The rider of the stallion (Julia Thayer) appears time and again, saving Stuart on several occasions, and killing Zamorro in the end. Her horse is just as remarkable, leaping great rocky chasms, kicking in a jailhouse door to rescue Stuart, fighting and whipping Zamorro's horse in single combat, and driving Dupray to the edge of a cliff where he is finally shot by Captain Jamison. Stuart and the blond rider get together at the end, and presumably all is well.

Movies like *The Big Trail, Fighting Caravans, Dawn on the Great Divide, The Oregon Trail* (1939), and *The Painted Stallion* featured white villains causing most of the problems for wagon trains. It did happen, but not nearly to the extent that Hollywood depicted. Scores of pictures in the 1930s and 1940s used white badmen as a plot staple, possibly more than they used Indians. Although there are many historical details in error in *The Painted Stallion* (such as the combatants using double action revolvers in the 1820s), the film was never represented as factually portraying any single historical incident. It did correctly show that there were dangers from whites as well as Indians on the trails heading west—a fact that almost every moviegoer in the first half of the 20th century understood as true, but that some historians and filmmakers have since forgotten or disregarded.

*The Painted Stallion* featured a dedication, captioned in every chapter: "To the heroes of yesterday! Those pioneers who braved the perilous trek westward, defeated a hostile wilderness, and blazed a glorious trail across the pages of history!" A one-dimensional paean perhaps, but it's arguably more accurate than today's politically correct denial that anything good ever came out of the westward march.

***Opposite:*** *The Painted Stallion* (Republic, 1937) was a serial Western focusing on a wagon train heading to Santa Fe which is beset by a number of perils and usually saved by a blond Comanche "goddess" riding her painted pony.

# 10

## The Box Wagon
## (*The Unforgiven*)

### Texas, August 1866

The film *The Last Wagon* included a scene where the men, Todd (Richard Widmark), Ridge (Nick Adams), and Clint (Ray Stricklin), were prepared to kill the women, Jenny (Felicia Farr), Jolie (Susan Kohner), and Valinda (Stephanie Griffin), to save them from capture. In *Ulzana's Raid* (Universal, 1972), keeping the last bullet for suicide was not only an option, it became a reality when, as the Apaches attack, a soldier shoots Mrs. Rukeyser (Gladys Holland) in the forehead, then places the gun barrel into his mouth and pulls the trigger.

It was not a Hollywood fabrication. The idea was widespread on the Western frontier, given the fate suffered by many captured women; and although few, if any, women were ever shot to prevent their capture, the fear that brought about contemplating such an act was very real. Arguably the most famous soldier from Western history, George Armstrong Custer, was one of the chief protagonists in disseminating the idea. The incident that helped shape his attitude began with an Indian attack on a lone wagon of white travelers.

In August of 1866, the Kiowa sub-chief Satanta, characterized as middle-aged, brawny, partial to hard liquor, and violent, led a war party of Kiowas from Kansas to Texas. As they crossed the West Fork of the Trinity River they came to Elm Creek in Cooke County, a few miles from Gainesville, and spotted a wagon traveling along the road.[1]

The unsuspecting victims were the Box family. Mary Matthews was born in Gibson County, Tennessee, in 1824. Her family moved to Texas in 1832. In 1842, at age 18, she married James Box. They lived in Titus County and Hopkins County, where most of the children were born. James Box was a Union man, and when the Civil War began in 1861, he moved his family far out on the frontier in Montague County because he did not want to join the Confederacy. The Boxes lived a precarious existence on the frontier, where Union sympathizers were scorned and feared, and even hanged for their sympathies.[2]

The Boxes survived the war and hoped to live their lives in peace, but it was not to be. In June 1866, one of James's brothers was deathly ill, and another lost a leg in a farming accident. The Boxes went to Hopkins County to help them out. On 10 August, stocked up with household goods and leather hides, they started back to Montague County. It rained for much of the five-day journey, and during the melancholy trip James Box declared that he had a premonition that he would never get home. On 15 August, only about three miles from their cabin at Head of Elm (now Saint Jo, Texas), James spotted someone moving along a hill and assumed it was his neighbor.[3]

"I wish that man would come down to us," James told Mary, "so that I could borrow his horse for our jaded one, and then we could get home faster."

## 10. The Box Wagon

When Mary looked in the direction he pointed, she said, "Why, there are three or four of them."

"They are Indians," James realized, and added, "we are gone." Turning to his 17-year-old daughter, he said, "Margaret — get my six-shooter, quick!"[4]

Before she could retrieve the pistol, Satanta and 23 Kiowas were upon them. One of them shot an arrow into James's chest, and he fell backwards into the wagon. He sat up, yanked the arrow free, took the pistol and fired. Another arrow hit him in the head, this time knocking him out of the wagon. Somehow, James Box rose again and stumbled to the far side of the wagon before he fell dead. The warriors were on him, scalping him twice and cutting open his jaw. A Kiowa grabbed Mrs. Box by the hair and pulled her out of the wagon. The screaming younger girls, Josephine (13) and Ida (7), were tied to ponies. Margaret broke free and ran to her dead father, holding tight to him until the Indians pulled her away. After the Indians had stolen everything from the wagon, they tied Mrs. Box and Margaret to horses and rode off at a gallop. Mrs. Box held baby Laura while on horseback.[5]

Kiowa Chief Satanta led several wagon train attacks and was known to have blown a bugle, imitating cavalry calls.

Charlie Grant, Bill Grant, John Loving, and Zeke Huffman, who had just ridden atop Wheeler's Mound, about one-quarter mile from the road, witnessed the attack. The men were unarmed and watched in horror, unable to do anything to help. They rode to Charlie Grant's father's home for arms and reinforcements. They returned that night, with another man named Cherry, and a one-armed black man, "Old Jack Loring." Leather hides and the wagon's contents were scattered over the prairie, and they found feathers and broom weeds stuck to Box's bloody body. The next day a larger posse formed, including Jim Coursey, Dan Brunson, and Captain Brunson. For many days they followed the trail into Indian Territory. There they discovered Laura's battered body, then gave up and returned home.[6]

The Indians traveled north for two weeks. Margaret ripped off pieces of her dress from time to time, hoping that pursuers would spot them. Instead, the warriors saw what she was doing and tore the remaining clothing from her body. Whenever they stopped to rest, Mary and Margaret were repeatedly raped. On the eleventh day, Mary Box accidentally dropped little Laura as they rode. Laura was badly injured, and the crying irritated the warriors. Laura was either on the threshold of death or had just expired when an Indian grabbed her from Mary's arms, threw her against a tree in a rocky ravine, and left her behind. The rescue posse got to that point before turning around.

The Kiowas rode on. Warriors would not allow Mrs. Box to drink, and her tongue swelled in her mouth. One of her daughters took off her slipper as they crossed a stream and filled it with water to give to her mother. Mrs. Box managed to drink most of it before a warrior saw her and knocked it from her hands. Then they beat the girl almost to death. After reaching the main village near the Arkansas River, the Boxes were together for four days. Each night the mother and three girls occupied one shelter—the one where the scalp of James Box was hung. A dance was held, and the spoils and prisoners were divided up. Mary was separated from her children and taken to another camp about six miles away. She was beaten, abused, and enslaved from dawn to dusk.[7]

"I had to pack wood and water," Mary said. "When I delayed they would hit and beat me and even the squaws would knock me down. I was very sick while with the Indians, notwithstanding they would beat me. It was a terrible life."[8]

Margaret, described as "a beautiful girl just ripening into womanhood," fell into the hands of a chief who forced her "to become the victim of his brutal lust"; but when he tired of her he sold her to another Indian for two horses. This Indian sexually used her until he traded her to a third Indian, who used her and passed her on. The Kiowas subjected Josephine to the same cruelties and outrages.[9] Ida was too young to be sexually abused, but she spent much of the time alone and crying uncontrollably. Occasionally she would see her mother when the bands camped near each other, and she tried to run to her. Her behavior so enraged her captors that they stuck her bare feet into a campfire "until every portion of the cuticle was burned therefrom." With charred feet, she could not run. Months later her feet were not fully healed. When rescued she had almost forgotten English.[10]

It is unlikely that any of them would have survived a long captivity with such treatment. Comparatively speaking, they were fortunate that the Indians realized that they had more to gain by selling them than by keeping them as slaves and concubines. Indians had been taking captives for decades, and the white men always gave money or supplies to get them back. Eager to turn a profit, Satanta rode to Fort Larned to talk to Maj. Cuvier Grover, 3rd U.S. Infantry. Satanta told Grover that they had gone to Texas "to make peace with the whites there, but had been received in a hostile manner and, in consequence, had taken the captives." Now, however, Satanta was ready to give them up. Grover told him he must wait until he could contact Agent I. C. Taylor to learn what disposition he wanted of the captives. Taylor left Fort Zarah and rode to Larned, meeting Satanta there on 12 September. Satanta proposed to give up the captives, Taylor said, "providing I would pay him liberally for them." Instead, Taylor angrily asked if Satanta had forgotten the Little Arkansas Treaty in which the Indians promised not to take any more prisoners. He told the Kiowa "that he knew perfectly well that it was in violation of the treaty." Taylor said he "would not pay him one dollar for them" but that he must bring them all to the fort, deliver them to Grover, and wait until their agent, Jesse Leavenworth, arrived to settle the matter with them. Satanta asked Taylor for ten days to talk over the proposition in council, and he would return with an answer. Taylor agreed.[11]

Instead, Satanta rode southwest to Fort Dodge, met Capt. Andrew Sheridan, 3rd U.S. Infantry, and made a similar offer. Sheridan sent Lt. Gustave A. Hesselberger, an interpreter, and two soldiers, Lee Herron and John McLaurie, to the Indian camp to negotiate for the prisoners. In the village, Satanta refused to give up the prisoners without a suitable ransom. They negotiated and finally agreed on a combination of money and supplies of about $2,800 in value. The Kiowas demanded powder and lead, but Hesselberger insisted he would be unable to get that for them. Hesselberger's party quickly returned to Fort Dodge, procured the ransom, and rode back to the village. That evening, the lieutenant paid cash to the two Indians who owned the two eldest girls to prevent "a repetition of indignities to which ... they had been continually subjected." The next morning, Hesselberger took Margaret and Josephine back to Fort Dodge.[12]

Lee Herron, one of the enlisted men who took the ransom goods to the Indian camp, recalled Margaret and Josephine were "a pitiful looking sight." He stated, "The eldest daughter gave birth to a half-breed a short time after their rescue."[13] A few days later, Indians brought Mary and Ida in, and they were given additional blankets and provisions. Gen. William T. Sherman, on an inspection tour, arrived at Fort Dodge shortly after the affair and instructed Captain Sheridan that he was not to purchase any other captives from the Indians. The Boxes had been rescued just in time.[14]

When Agent Taylor learned of Satanta's duplicity, and that the military was contradicting his instructions, he wrote to Commissioner of Indian Affairs D. N. Cooley. Taylor demanded to know who authorized Sheridan to pay the ransom money. He called the attention of the department "to the fact that every prisoner purchased from the Indians amounts to the same as granting them a license to go and commit the same overt act." Taylor insisted it was time that "the strong arm of the government" brought the Indians to their senses.[15]

Lieutenant Hesselberger escorted the Boxes to Fort Leavenworth in November. They stopped at Fort Riley on the way and met Lt. Col. George A. Custer and his wife Elizabeth. Both of them commented on the Boxes' horrible condition. For Libbie, it was a revelation:

> I could not find any language to repeat what the poor mother and eldest daughter told me of their horrible sufferings during the year of their captivity. I had not been long away from a home where my parents not only shielded me from all sorrow and trouble, but guarded me from even tales of misery which would have made a spot on the sun of a most radiant girlhood.[16]

George and Libbie both heard Mary say that the Indians dashed Laura's brains out against a tree, that they raped and abused the mother and the oldest girls, and that Ida's feet were severely burned.[17] Said Libbie: "Their melancholy was most heart-rending, for even their release from captivity would not bring them back to the husband and father so dear to them, or put in the maternal arms two innocent infants that had been murdered."[18] From what Libbie learned from Margaret, she came to believe that Indian captivity truly "was worse than death." In his book *My Life on the Plains*, Custer wrote, "Far better would it have been had the remaining members of the family met their death in the first attack." Describing what happened to Margaret, he concluded that she "was exposed to a fate infinitely more dreadful than death itself."[19] Initially, one of the chiefs, "robbing her of that which was more precious than life, and forcing her to become the victim of his brutal lust, bartered her in return for two horses to another chief." The girl was passed from one captor to another, "undergoing a life so horribly brutal that, when meeting her upon release from captivity, one could only wonder how a young girl, nurtured in civilization and possessed of the natural refinement and delicacy of thought which she exhibited, could have survived such degrading treatment."[20]

The story of the Boxes' ordeal made a lasting impression on the Custers, and it was one of the reasons that he later ordered his trusted officers that if it ever became inevitable that Libbie would fall into the hands of the Indians, they were to shoot her dead first. Libbie wrote in *Boots and Saddles*:

> My danger in connection with the Indians was two fold. I was in peril from death or capture by the savages, and liable to be killed by my own friends to prevent my capture.... While I knew that I was defended by strong hands and brave hearts the thought of the double danger always flashed into my mind when we were in jeopardy.[21]

The first time Libbie nearly realized her worst nightmare was in June of 1867 (see Chapter 24). Another time was in 1874 at Fort Abraham Lincoln in present-day North Dakota when the Indians threatened the garrison while the majority of the regiment was absent from the fort. The women gathered in the Custer house. Libbie stated, "I do not think the actual fear of death was thought of so much as the all-absorbing terror of capture."[22] They seriously discussed their options of committing suicide or killing each other if the Indians got into the fort.

George Armstrong Custer, Thomas W. Custer, and Elizabeth Custer. The general and his wife played a part in propagating the frontier tenet that one should always "keep the last bullet for yourself."

The Box killings and captures were significant incidents leading Custer and, later, many other officers to issue orders that their wives were to be killed to prevent them from falling into the clutches of hostile Indians.[23] The Box incident was a contributing factor that led to Gen. Winfield S. Hancock's expedition to the Kansas plains in 1867, which in turn developed into the Sheridan-Custer winter campaign of 1868, leading to the Battle of the Washita (depicted in the 1970 film *Little Big Man*). The Indians killed two white captives at the Washita, Clara and

Willie Blinn, whose story is described in Chapter 21. Custer was able to rescue two others, Sarah White and Anna Morgan, the following spring.

As for the Boxes, with no money and few relatives to assist them, they stayed at Fort Leavenworth for some time before returning to Texas. Little is known about their subsequent lives. Ida, perhaps because of her burned and infected feet, died shortly thereafter. Josephine reportedly married a man named Crowe, while Margaret, apparently surviving her traumatic experience, married Dan Brunson, a childhood sweetheart and one of her would-be rescuers.[24] Mrs. Mary Matthews Box married Captain Brunson, the father of Dan Brunson.[25]

The Box family became unwilling players in a small incident of the Indian Wars that blossomed into a drama of unintended consequences. The Boxes and the Custers became catalysts in the development of the frontier tenet: "When fighting Indians, keep the last bullet for yourself."[26]

The fact that Indians were involved in the captive trade is well illustrated by the Box incident. Satanta first brought the Boxes near Fort Larned and tried to negotiate for their sale with Agent I. C. Taylor. Taylor rebuffed him, citing the Little Arkansas Treaty in which the chiefs promised to take no more captives. The agent, frustrated and angry that the chiefs continued to disregard their promises, wrote that the Indians "boastfully say that stealing white women is more of a lucrative business than stealing horses."[27]

That very conception was developed in Alan Le May's novel *The Unforgiven*, and later onscreen in the movie version. The storyline begins with a party of white settlers who attack a Kiowa village and kill most of the inhabitants. Tired of the killing, William Zachary takes an orphaned baby Kiowa girl to raise as his own daughter. Besides his wife Matilda (Lillian Gish) and his oldest son Ben (Burt Lancaster), few, if any, people know the secret. Years later a mysterious, half-crazy stranger, Abe Kelsey (Joseph Wiseman, who later played Dr. No), shows up to reveal the secret, thus turning neighboring families against each other and causing a rift in the Zachary family

The Kiowa Lost Bird (Carlos Rivas) shows up at the Zachary Ranch demanding the return of his sister, whose white name is Rachel (Audrey Hepburn). Ben, now head of the family, refuses to give her back, and the Kiowas take their revenge by attacking local families as they go about their business. They kill Charlie Rawlins (Albert Salmi), who has just been betrothed to Rachel, thus antagonizing Charlie's parents, Zeb (Charles Bickford) and Hagar Rawlins (June Walker). When the neighbors realize that the Kiowa attacks are a result of Ben's refusal to give up Rachel, and that she is a full-blooded Kiowa, their friendship turns to hatred, sparking virulent comments (among them one from Mrs. Rawlins, who calls Rachel a "Kiowa squaw" and the Indians "red Niggers every one").

Before Rachel learns she is a Kiowa, she wonders why the Indians are seeking her. "Why would they want to buy me?" she asks her mother.

"Because you're a girl, my pretty," Mrs. Zachary answers. "Horses and women are all the same to a Kiowa, to be bought or traded."

The line and sentiment, which in the 21st century generally will be interpreted as racist, is an accurate representation of how a significant number of Plains Indians, many blossoming capitalists among them, viewed white females and livestock — as commodities to be bought and sold.

When Rachel learns she is not really white, she is devastated and wants to go to her real brother to save all the whites further trouble. Ben and Andy Zachary (Doug McClure), and Mrs. Zachary, are determined to keep her in her adoptive home. Brother Cash Zachary (Audie Murphy), who hates Indians, cannot stay in the same household and leaves. The climax arrives when Lost Bird and his warriors attack the ranch to forcibly take Rachel back to the tribe. Ben gives his mother a pistol to use on herself, "just in case." In the resulting fight, the Kiowas burn the house, kill Mrs. Zachary, and force the last three defenders into the root cellar.[28]

**John Saxon and Burt Lancaster are rivals for Audrey Hepburn, an orphan Kiowa girl raised by a white family, in *The Unforgiven* (United Artists, 1960).**

Hearing gunfire from the Rawlins Ranch, Cash has a change of heart and rides to the rescue, arriving in time to help Ben and Andy kill the last of the Kiowas—all but one. Lost Bird enters the burning house and tries to take Rachel, but instead of returning with him, she shoots him with a pistol. Rachel, now knowing the truth of her situation, is free to marry Ben, who has loved her all of his life but was prevented from showing his affection because of the façade he had to maintain. The three brothers and Rachel stand outside of the burnt ranch at the end, watching a flock of geese in the sky.

The racism that *The Unforgiven* portrays was a real part of many frontier settlers' lives—but so was the ethnocentrism of many Indian tribes; and it was a fact that they took captives not only to replace lost tribal members, but, as Agent Taylor said in 1866, because trafficking in white women was "a lucrative business."

# 11

## The Rose-Baley Wagon Train

### Arizona, August 1858

The families who made up the Rose-Baley train came from southern Iowa and northern Missouri. Most of them made their separate ways to eastern Kansas, where they joined up for convenience and safety's sake. After the news of the horrible fate of the Fancher Train in Utah, they hoped to avoid trouble by taking the southern route to California. In addition to the Roses and Baleys, other families included the Browns, Bentners, Udells, Daleys, Hollands, Hedgpeths, and Joneses, plus a number of employees. All told, there were about 92 people, with 34 adult males. The combined trains set out on the Santa Fe Trail in mid–May 1858.

Reaching Albuquerque in late June, they heard of a new route, Beale's Wagon Road, newly opened and supposedly safer and shorter than the established route farther south along the border. Although touted by the army and the citizens of Albuquerque, the road was unproven, and there would be no other trains in advance of them that they might follow or seek help from. Regardless, only the Udells voted against taking it. The train pulled out on 26 June after hiring Jose M. Savedra, who had guided several expeditions through the territory, including Edward F. Beale's earlier in the year. Despite Savedra's credentials, the route had little game and less water, and he had little luck in finding waterholes.

By the time they got to what is now western Arizona, they had been traveling during the cooler nights with the wagons strung out so as not to overtax the scarce water sources. On 27 August they reached the rough Sitgreaves Pass in the Black Mountains. There had been little Indian trouble—only a few troublesome Hualapais who shot a few arrows at them and stole some cattle. They had heard that the Mojaves were friendly, probably not realizing that they were also the same Indians who had held Olive and Mary Ann Oatman captive. While some of the less exhausted families rode west for the Colorado River, the remainder rested at the pass.

Near the river, Mojaves confronted portions of the Rose and Baley families and demanded to know what the whites were doing there. Although assured that they were just passing through, the Indians did not trust them and became impudent. One warrior grabbed Mrs. Rose's breast, and she ran screaming back to the wagon. Leonard Rose, anxious not to start a fight, held his anger in check. Other Indians approached the Alpha Brown wagon. When Mrs. Brown asked if she could get some water, they offered her some, but only if she would give them her dress. Others indicated that they would like to take her boy with them. Alpha Brown returned to chase them off, but the incident proved ominous.

During the next few days, more emigrants made the ride down from Sitgreaves Pass, and more Mojaves appeared to threaten those gathered on the east side of the Colorado River. When the emigrants began to chop down cottonwoods to build rafts, the Indians thought they were beginning to build cabins. About two in the afternoon of 30 August, the Mojaves struck. Sallie Fox, the 13-year-old stepdaughter of Alpha Brown, was climbing on the wheel of a wagon when she noticed some Indians sneaking through the underbrush on their hands and knees.

"The Indians are coming, and they will kill us all!" she cried out.

The warning was just in time. The men, who were taking a short siesta, grabbed their weapons and met the Indian charge head-on. Robbed of a total surprise, the Mojaves made a half-hearted attack and then went after easier targets. Alpha Brown, Ed Akey, and Lee Griffin were caught near the river building the raft. Akey and Griffin made a run for the camp. Akey had his pistol out and shot two Indians, but Griffin took two arrows in his arm. At the edge of the wagon circle an arrow caught Akey just below the left collarbone. Brown mounted his horse and tried to ride for the wagons, but a volley of arrows struck him. His horse carried him to the camp, where he dropped off dead. Back at the wagon corral, about 25 men remained to fight off about 300 warriors. Thankfully, the Indians were armed only with bows and arrows, and did not make a concentrated attack. They worked their way around the perimeter and fired whenever a target presented itself, wounding about one dozen emigrants, including Sallie Fox, Elizabeth Jones, William R. Baley, Tom Hedgpeth, and L. J. Rose. The fight at the wagons ended when Gillum Baley, who had been in the Illinois Militia during the Black Hawk War in 1832, carefully aimed his rifle at a man who appeared to be the chief. His shot hit the mark, and the chief, possibly Jose, crumpled dead to the ground. The shot seemed to stop the action.

Not so lucky was the Bentner family, who had left the mountain camp the night before—disregarding the protests of William Krug and some of the Baleys, who insisted that they wait and travel together. Mr. Bentner wanted to hurry to the river. The Mojaves caught his family of seven before it could get to safety. They killed Mr. and Mrs. Bentner and all five of their children. The body of the oldest girl, 18 years of age, was later found stripped, with her face horribly mutilated. The other bodies were never found. At the river corral the emigrants could see the Mojaves waving the fresh scalps from a pole.

With the chief's death, the Indians seemed content to run off the livestock and retire for the night. They had lost about 17 warriors. The emigrants, shocked at the day's action, voted to retrace their steps all the way back to Albuquerque. The road was long and hard. With the loss of most of their animals, many wagons and much property had to be abandoned. The few waterholes they found on their outbound journey seemed to have dried up, and the game was gone. Only by luckily running into a few other wagon trains that were following in their wake, and who agreed to turn back to Albuquerque with them, did the remnants of the Rose-Baley train survive. The last of them struggled back on 13 November, two and one-half months after being attacked.[1]

Because of the first disaster on the Beale Road, later emigrants seldom used the route. Historians who seek to downplay Indian attacks on emigrants almost wholly ignore the dangers of little-used routes such as Beale's Road because by limiting the geographic scope, it is easier to "prove" a thesis. Although historians generally ignored Beale's Road in Arizona, filmmakers found the area north of Beale's Road on the Arizona-Utah border a terrific place to make movies.

Hollywood didn't "discover" Monument Valley; the persistent local homesteaders and ranchers Harry and Mike Goulding convinced it to shoot a movie there. In 1938, Harry Goulding sat around in the United Artists office long enough until someone consented to listen to his idea. When director John Ford and producer Walter Wanger saw Harry's photographs of the area, they were intrigued and questioned him about the area's potential. Harry always answered "yes" to all of their questions, whether he was positive or not. When Ford and Wanger told Harry to get back to Monument Valley and get ready for about 100 movie personnel in about three days, he was stunned. They wrote him a check right then.

"Oh, by the way, what's the name of this picture?" Harry asked.

"*Stagecoach*," Ford answered, and the rest, as they say, is history.[2]

# 12

# The Sager Wagons
## (*Seven Alone*)

### 1844

Heinrich (Henry) Sager was born in 1805 in Loudon County, Virginia. Naomi Carny was born in Virginia in 1807, the daughter of a Baptist minister. They married in May 1830, lived in Ohio for a time, and moved to Missouri in 1838. Henry had a farm in Platte County and was a jack-of-all-trades able to build anything that was needed, from a spinning wheel to a coffin. His shop was quite popular. Naomi did fine needlework and gave Sunday school lessons to the children.

In 1843 the talk of the town was of missionary Marcus Whitman, who had led a group of emigrants over the Rocky Mountains to the Oregon country. Henry was restless, and Naomi had heard of Oregon's healthy climate, so they made plans to raise their family in the idyllic Willamette Valley. In April 1844, the Sagers packed up their belongings and their children, John Carny (age 13), Francisco "Frank" (12), Catherine (9), Elizabeth Marie (7), Matilda Jane (5), and Hannah Louise (3), and joined a wagon train. The large group consisted of more than 700 pioneers in three trains under Cornelius Gilliam, John Thorp, and Nathaniel Ford. The Sagers joined the company of William Shaw (Gilliam's brother-in-law). They left on 19 May, 1844, with the Sager's wagon one of the last two bringing up the rear.[1]

On the night of 21 May, Sac Indians raided the encampment and stole more than 800 cattle, nearly the entire herd. The next day, however, a posse under Gilliam recovered all but six of the stock. On 31 May, on the South Fork of the Nemaha River near present-day Seneca, Kansas, Naomi gave birth to Rosanna. Naomi was ill for two days following the birth, and the train remained camped while she regained her strength.

On 7 June they camped in a driving rainstorm by the North Fork Black Vermillion River. With little luck keeping warm and dry, Naomi and Henry became ill. On 15 June, with the river still flooding, the company had to retreat almost a day's travel to escape the river's wrath.[2]

Not until early July did the train reach the Platte River, where they saw massive herds of buffalo, and the emigrants spent a few days hunting and curing meat for the remainder of the trip. On the afternoon of 1 August, Catherine attempted to jump down from the wagon as it rolled along, a feat the children had perfected, but an ax handle snagged her dress and caused her to fall beneath the wagon wheels. Her left leg was shattered. Henry Sager set her broken leg, and Dr. Theopolis Degen, a German surgeon traveling with the train, approved his skillful repair. Catherine was restricted to the wagon for the remainder of the journey. The train reached Fort Laramie that night.

Traveling beyond Laramie, John, Frank, and Henry became ill with "camp fever" (probably typhoid fever). The two boys recovered, but Mr. Sager died on 28 August, after pleading with Captain Shaw to see that his family reached Oregon. Henry Sager was buried along the west bank of the Green River in present-day southwestern Wyoming. Dr. Degen had been driving the wagon when Henry was taken ill, and he told Naomi he would see they got to the Willamette Valley.[3]

Tragically, Naomi began to manifest symptoms of typhoid, including fever and delirium. During one of her sane moments she said her farewells to her children and asked Dr. Degen and Captain Shaw to see them to the Whitman Mission. Naomi Sager died 25 September and was buried at Pilgrim Springs, mid-way between Salmon Falls and the Three Island Crossing of the Snake River.

Dr. Degen, and William Shaw and his wife Sally, cared for the children. The baby was passed among the women of the train, who acted as wet nurses for the infant. As the group approached the Snake River at Three Island, Captain Shaw decided to ease the burden of the Sager's ox team by reducing their wagon to a two-wheeled cart. He condensed their belongings and sold off what was unnecessary.

In mid–October they arrived at Grande Ronde, where one of the Sager girls walked too close to the campfire, causing her dress to burst into flames. Dr. Degen extinguished the flames, saving her life but badly burning his hands. Soon afterwards, Captain Shaw heard crying one night and discovered that little Hannah had climbed from the wagon; unable to get back in, she was nearly frozen. He placed her in bed between Dr. Degen and her brother John, where the body warmth revived her.[4]

After crossing the Blue Mountains, Captain Shaw rode to the Whitman Mission at Waiilatpu, about 25 miles upstream from Fort Walla Walla, to see if the Whitmans would take the Sager children. In early November, Dr. Degen took the six oldest children in their two-wheeled cart to their new home at Waiilatpu. Baby Rosanna remained in the train with a wet nurse and was brought to the mission a week later. Marcus and Narcissa Whitman decided to adopt all the children. In Oregon City, on 3 June, 1845, Whitman became the children's legal guardian.[5]

The tragic story of the Sagers was told in the film *Seven Alone* (1974), albeit with a much more heroic portrayal of the children and a much happier ending. Henry Sager (Dewey Martin) is depicted as a stern father, particularly hard on his oldest son, John, who he whips many times at the slightest provocation. Naomi Sager (Anne Collings) is the mother who somehow looks too young and fresh for a pioneer woman who has borne seven children and worked for years at the drudgery of maintaining a farm. She tells Henry time and again that she will never move to Oregon, but in the next scene they are in a wagon train heading west.

While on the trail, John Sager is whipped again by his father and runs away, only to have an Indian steal his clothes. Later, Indians attack the lone Sager Wagon that has dropped behind to look for John. They are saved by Henry, who fights a duel with a warrior and kills him, but not before taking a knife wound. They are assisted in the nick of time by none other than Kit Carson (Dean Smith), who just happens to be wandering by. Actually, in the summer of 1844 Carson was just finishing a year of exploring with John C. Frémont and had gone down to Bent's Fort in southern Colorado and then to Taos. He was never near the Oregon Trail while the Sagers were passing through. In the movie, Catherine Sager (Debbie van Orden) has her leg broken when she falls beneath a wagon wheel, which did occur in reality. The movie also depicts the deaths of Henry and Naomi Sager, he of blood poisoning from the knife wound, and she from what was called "black dysentery." In the film, John Sager renames baby Rosanna "Henrietta Naomi Sager" in honor of the dead parents. John actually did request the name change, but it was legalized by the Whitmans the following spring when the girls were baptized at the Mission.

After the wagon train arrives at Fort Hall, the movie begins to rapidly diverge from reality.

***Seven Alone*** (Doty-Dayton Releasing, 1974) was billed as a true story, but the real story of the Sager Children was much more tragic than could be shown in a family movie.

Whereas Dr. Degen and the Shaw family took care of the Sager children, and Degen took them all the way to the Whitman Mission, the movie shows John Sager disliking the doctor and wanting nothing to do with him. Dr. Dutch (Aldo Ray) is portrayed as a buffoon who can barely take care of himself, let alone heal the sick. As the people of the wagon train debate whether or not to send the children back to Ohio, John is determined to lead the family to Oregon and build a home, just as he had promised his mother.

Whitman Mission near Walla Walla, Washington, site of the November 1847 massacre.

The seven children, five of them played by brothers and sisters of the Petersen Family, sneak out one night and head into the wilderness, meeting friendly Indians who give them food and nurse the baby. Unfortunately, the Indians leave them behind, and the children are forced to continue alone. Winter approaches, snow falls, and the seven are on the verge of freezing and starvation when John pushes on alone and miraculously finds his way to the Whitman Mission. The other six are rescued. The film fades out with a picture of an idyllic meadow in Oregon, and the audience assumes the children all eventually reach there, build the home their parents dreamed of, and live happily ever after.

*Seven Alone* was made as a family movie. The actual ending of the Sager story could not very well have been told in a family format. The seven children were at the Whitman Mission in November 1847 when the Cayuse Indians began massacring people after a measles epidemic killed both whites and Indians alike. When Indians tomahawked Marcus Whitman in the head, John Sager, now 16, tried to shoot his pistol at the assailants; they held him down and killed him. The next day Indians flushed Frank Sager out of hiding and killed him. About one dozen whites died in the initial frenzy. For the surviving girls and women, the next month was a time of abuse and rape. Mary Smith (age 15) and Susan Kimble (16) were taken as Indian "wives," and Esther Lorinda Bewley (22) was raped almost daily. An Indian tried to take Catherine Sager, now 13, as a "wife," but she staunchly resisted, insisting that she was not yet old enough.

Years later, Catherine wrote:

> In giving a history I have had to touch upon a delicate subject — one that I have always avoided in conversation, namely, the treatment of the young women by the Indians.... I have not related many things.... I think it never before appeared upon the annals of American history where female captives were treated with like brutality. We were subject to continual insult while we stayed with them, harassed by fear and exposed to their ill treatment.[6]

In early December, Hannah Louise, now six, died from the measles, as did Helen Mar Meek (age 10), daughter of the famous trapper and scout Joe Meek. On 19 December, 1847, Peter Skene Ogden of the Hudson Bay Company finally bought the remaining 49 captives, and the four surviving Sager girls finally made it to Oregon. They never found the home they had sought;

they were all shifted among several families, some kind and some cruel. The youngest, Henrietta, married Morgan Kees, joined a traveling circus, and was shot dead by mistake in 1870, (the recipient of a bullet meant for her husband). Catherine married Clark Pringle and died in 1910. Elizabeth, who had lived with six families, married William Fletcher and died in 1925. Matilda married three times and died in 1928, the last of the Sager children.[7]

Hollywood, in this instance, used actual incidents to tell a story that, in the end, contained both accuracies and inaccuracies. A happy ending suited Hollywood this time. It probably never would dare to depict the truly horrible ordeals the Sager children experienced.

# 13

## The Morton-Marble Wagon Train (*The Forest Rose, The Half Breed, Two Rode Together*)

### Nebraska, August 1864

Nancy Fletcher was born in Indiana in 1845. The family moved to Sidney, Iowa, four years later. Nancy married Thomas Frank Morton in 1860 when she was only 15 years old. In the span of four years they had two children, Charlotte Ann and Samuel Thomas.[1] Mother and children contracted measles in the spring of 1863; Nancy survived, but both children died. In August 1864, after a long grieving period, Nancy decided to join her husband, her brother William, and her cousin John Fletcher on their last freighting trip of the season.

Unbeknownst to them, the well-traveled Oregon Trail they were about to take was to become the focal point of shocking Indian raids, where more than 70 white travelers and homesteaders were killed within a few-week span. The unsuspecting victims rode into the thick of it. The wagon train consisted of Morton's three wagons, Michael Kelly's six wagons and his six teamsters, and William Marble's three wagons, including James Smith and his wife, Charles Iliff, Mr. St. Clair, and Marble's son Danny. They spent the night of 7 August camped east of Plum Creek, on the south side of the Platte about 30 miles west of Fort Kearny.[2]

That same night, Mart Bowler, wagonmaster of a 26-wagon bull train owned by freight contractors Byram and Howe, was camped four miles west of Plum Creek. Bowler's men were up early the next morning rounding up strays when the Indians attacked. Fourteen-year-old Will Gay, on his first job, was out farthest from the camp and was first to see the charging warriors. He fired his pistol five times in the direction of the chasing Indians, all the while galloping his mule back to the camp. The racing warriors followed him right into the circle.

Gay's warning shots had alerted the bullwhackers, allowing enough time for them to get their weapons. Bullets flew every which way among the wagons, and when two warriors were hit, the rest of them broke out of the corral and joined the others, circling around and shooting from a safer distance. The fighting only lasted several minutes. Suddenly the attackers pulled back. Apparently there was a better target a bit farther to the east.

That same morning Nancy Morton climbed into her wagon and took the reins so her husband could rest after having spent several hours on guard duty. Lt. Joseph Bone, 7th Iowa Cavalry, was nearby at the Thomas Ranch, on his way to muster out of the army, when he spied Indians descending the bluffs to the southeast. A crescent shaped formation of about 100 Indians thundered down upon the Morton-Marble wagons, engulfing the doomed target with a cacophony of bloodcurdling war cries and gunfire. The wagons scattered, some toward the bluffs and others toward the river. The defenders, armed only with pistols, were little threat to the Indians. From Plum Creek Station, Bone telegraphed for help from Col. Samuel Summers at Fort Kearny: "Send [a] company of men here as quick as God can send them. One hundred Indians in sight firing on ox train."[3]

There would be no last-minute rescue. Nancy realized the horsemen were Indians, and she alerted Frank. As he pulled the wagon off toward the bluffs, Nancy swung over the side but was struck by the wagon wheel and broke several ribs. The last words she heard from her husband were, "O my dear, where are you going?" Her brother and cousin both stood in the grass ahead, firing at the warriors as they circled. Within minutes almost everyone was slain. Mrs. Smith escaped into the reeds by the river while Nancy Morton, wounded by two arrows, and Danny Marble, were captured. "Those killed were all scalped in my presence," Nancy said.[4]

Nancy Fletcher Morton was 19 years old when captured from her wagon train in 1864 (courtesy Nebraska State Historical Society).

An old warrior beat Nancy with a whip when she refused to ride with him. Warriors threatened to kill her, but she told them, "I would rather die than to be led into captivity." Nevertheless, they forced her onto a pony. The carnage was horrible, with the wagons wrecked, the freight scattered and plundered, and human bodies and dead horses strewn about. An Indian, who Nancy thought was named Red Cloud, forced her to ride behind him, while Big Bear took Danny Marble. Many of the Cheyennes were Dog Soldiers under Bull Bear. They frequently threatened the captives with death.[5]

Colonel Summers arrived at ten that night, much too late to catch the Indians. He discovered Mrs. Smith hiding in a field and in a state of shock. The next morning the soldiers buried 11 men in a mass grave, and two others where they had been killed farther down the road. The bodies were stripped, scalped, and full of arrows. Some had their eyes gouged out, and others had their tongues cut out. Some had their private parts cut off and stuffed into their gaping mouths.[6]

Nancy Morton and Danny Marble were gone. The Indians stopped at noon to rest and eat. Danny Marble ran to Nancy for comfort, and with good sense he concluded, "Let's do what they want and then they won't kill us." Then they sat down and cried. A man who Nancy described as a "swarthy Frenchman" helped remove the two arrows still protruding from her side. Later, Big Crow, who would be one of Nancy's main tormentors, rubbed her brother's bloody scalp in her face. In camp that evening, Danny became so sick that he thought he would die. Nancy tried to sooth him and said, "Surely God would rescue us from their demon hands."

The second night, after another long day of riding, the warriors performed a war dance around a pole decorated with human scalps. Nancy thought she would be killed; she survived, but her unborn baby did not. "I suffered terribly," she said. "I had a miscarriage on account of

Plum Creek Massacre site, Nebraska, August 1864.

my severe and ill treatment, and my eyes went blind." Indian women beat and kicked her. Danny Marble knew his father was killed, and he acted as if Nancy Morton was his mother. She provided what comfort she could, but, overwhelmed with their situation and in a moment of despair, she proclaimed she wanted to die. The alarmed boy protested, "Then I will be left all alone!" A group of drunken braves began to hurl spears at the boy, and Nancy told them to stop and leave him alone, for, "He is my papoose."[7]

A short time later, Nancy learned that she had partners in misery. The other captives were Lucinda Eubank (age 23), her children Isabelle (3) and Willie (6 months), Laura Roper (16), and Ambrose Asher (7). They were taken along the Little Blue River in Nebraska, on 7 August, as part of the same large raid that resulted in the massacre along Plum Creek. All the captives were treated harshly. Four of them were later recovered by Maj. Edward Wynkoop in September 1864 and taken to Denver: Laura Roper, Isabelle Eubank, Ambrose Asher, and Danny Marble.

Danny was characterized as perceptive, creative, and talkative. Mentally, the boy seemed to have withstood his captivity, but he was not well physically. A short time after he reached Denver he was struck down by typhoid fever. He was sent to Camp Weld military hospital under Dr. A. A. Smith, Assistant Surgeon of the 1st Colorado. Smith treated Danny as well as he could, but the boy died on 9 November. The army neglected to notify his mother. It was not until December 1864 that Ann Marble received a letter informing her of her son's death. Laura Roper corresponded with Ann Marble, and on 7 January, 1865, she wrote, "Hope your wish will come true that every one of the Indians will be extinguished.... Poor little Dan wish he was alive.... Keep up good spirits you will meet him in heaven."[8]

The three remaining captives were still with the Cheyennes, and both women were breaking down mentally and physically from the ordeal. For six months Nancy Morton was "subject to their passions and lusts, and the most brutal treatment that mortal being could be subjected

Four captives rescued in September 1864: Ambrose Asher, Laura Roper, Isabelle Eubank, and Danny Marble (courtesy Nebraska State Historical Society).

to." At one time she became so despondent she tried to hang herself from a tipi pole, but her captor caught her and hauled her down.[9]

In January 1865 two traders bought Nancy for $2,154 worth of goods. In February Nancy left Fort Laramie in a wagon train for Fort Kearny. They stopped at Plum Creek to allow her time for reflection. At last, in March 1865, Nancy arrived at her parents' home in Sidney, Iowa. "Oh, the joy that reigned supreme in the family is almost indescribable," she said. "It seemed to me like I had arose from the dead, and had awakened and found myself in Paradise." Nancy married George Stevens in November 1865 and had four children during the succeeding years. She died in 1912 at 67 years of age.[10]

Isabelle Eubank suffered great emotional and physical trauma as a captive, resulting in sleeplessness, nightmares, and bizarre behavior. The damaged waif was passed among the Denver townsfolk. One family changed her name to Mary. The frail little girl, with poor health and emotional problems, died on 18 March, 1865.[11]

Lucinda Eubank suffered more acutely than the other two adult captives, for she resisted more and did not cooperate with the Indians. She was beaten, abused, passed among the warriors, and was not recovered until May 1865. On her trip east, the wagons stopped at Camp Rankin near the ruins of Julesburg. There she met a Mr. Davenport, who had ridden from Denver with news of Isabelle's death. Mrs. Noble Wade, camp laundress, extended her home and hospitality to Lucinda and Willie while they awaited an eastbound stage. Lucinda told Mrs. Wade she was pregnant with Blackfoot's child, the Indian who had kept her and abused her the longest, and she swore that the unborn child would never see the light of day. Lucinda never elaborated, but she either aborted the child or killed or otherwise disposed of it in some manner shortly after its birth. Although she later married two more times, she never had any more children. She died in 1913, and Willie died in 1925.[12]

Lucinda's ordeal was real. A similar story was portrayed on film as early as 1912, in *The Forest Rose*, based on a novel by Emerson Bennett. Rose (Marguerite Snow) is captured and tortured in what one researcher called "a disturbing but pointless portrayal of bloodthirsty Indians."[13] Disturbing probably, but historical reality is not pointless. The fictional Rose also confides to her rescuer and potential suitor that after her experience she can no longer marry or bear children with any man. Rose is a near image of Lucinda.

Contrary to false impressions one might have about Victorian or Progressive era taboos concerning "delicate" subjects, there were many early films that portrayed the trials of attempted mixed marriages or cross-racial rape. In *The Half Breed* (Triangle 1916), Lo Dorman (Douglas Fairbanks) is the mixed-blood son of an Indian mother raped by a white man. After he is born his mother commits suicide. Lo is raised by an old Indian and is rejected by white society. In the years between 1908 and 1922 there were 18 films produced with the words "Half Breed" in the titles.[14]

Lucinda Eubank's solution to having an Indian's child was abortion or murder. Other captives with children resulting from rapes chose to keep and raise them. Given the stigma placed on interracial children at that time, those decisions may have been even tougher in the long run — for the children as well as the mothers. Ethan Edwards's pronouncement in *The Searchers* that freed ex-captives "were white — once" was an accurate depiction of a mindset shared by many in the mid–19th century.

Although frontier-dwellers understood the horrific experience that could befall captives of the Indians, a number of authors of the late 20th and early 21st century have obvious biases in favor of the Indians and against the white settlers and the U.S. Army. The historical trend is to tread softly on events that might offend ethnic groups, but truth cannot be suppressed, nor history altered, for the gratification of any group.[15]

Today's trends extend beyond indictment of the military; in the current politically correct way of reporting Indian behavior in the 19th century, even acts of hostage taking are distorted or denied. A recent example can be seen in *Halfbreed*, a biography of George Bent, in which the anti-settler, anti-military prejudice is evident. Morton, Eubank, and Roper wrote or told of their ordeals with the Cheyennes, which entailed beatings, rapes, and tortures, but the authors shift blame away from that tribe and sugarcoat the women's experiences.

Laura Roper told the Marysville, Kansas, *Advocate Democrat* that she recalled one time when a "squaw" dressed her and combed her hair. The authors used that one statement as being representative of the women's experience. In that same recollection, however, Roper also stated, "The squaws jumped on me and pulled my hair and beat me until I began to think my time had come." The authors' portrayal is deceitful.

In *Halfbreed* we find similar comments about Nancy Morton when the author states that she had suffered hardships "but had not suffered sexual abuse." The claim is preposterous. Morton clearly said, "I was subject to their passions and lusts, and the most brutal treatment that mortal being could be subjected to." She also said that "she suffered from all the abuse and indignity that could be practiced toward her not only by one Indian, but by many."[16]

Unfortunately for a number of people who survived captivity, returning to the white world may not have been much of an improvement. Such an experience was demonstrated in *Two Rode Together* (Ford-Shpetner/Columbia, 1961). A wagon train full of settlers who have had their children stolen by the Indians over the past years rolls into the fort to plead for help in recovering their family members. A cynical marshal, Guthrie McCabe (James Stewart), and Lt. Jim Gary (Richard Widmark), have the task of going to Comanche Quanah Parker (Henry Brandon) to try to buy back the captives. McCabe and Gary meet Marty Purcell (Shirley Jones), whose brother Steve (David Kent) was taken a dozen years ago. McCabe tries to tell Marty that recovering him now would be useless, for he was probably a Comanche warrior by now and would

## 13. The Morton-Marble Wagon Train

James Stewart and Richard Widmark argue about the efficacy of rescuing white captives held by the Indians in *Two Rode Together* (Ford-Shpetner/Columbia, 1961).

rape her if he had a chance. Nevertheless, she blames herself for his capture and still wants him back.

The wagons are full of grieving parents with the forlorn hope of having their loved ones restored. At least one of them, Harry J. Wringle (Willis Bouchey), is as cynical as McCabe. He makes a deal with McCabe to buy back any boy of about the right age, just to appease his wife, who, he claims, will never know the difference anyway. In the Comanche camp, McCabe and Gary meet Quanah, and explain that they have brought rifles, knives, and ammunition to purchase captives. They find Freda Knudsen (Regina Carrol), now the wife of a Comanche warrior and the mother of several of his children, and figure she is too far "gone" to be recovered. They find Hannah Clegg (Mae Marsh), the wife of the Rev. Henry Clegg (Ford Rainey), and mother of two young men, Ortho (Harry Carey, Jr.) and Greeley (Ken Curtis), who are "mentally challenged" and have previously given Lieutenant Gary fits, even fighting him over claims to "their girlfriend," Marty Purcell. When Gary talks in private to Hannah, now an aged crone, she tells him it is too late for her to go back.

"Do you want to be listed as dead?" Gary asks.

"I am dead," Hannah replies.

Quanah is somewhat reluctant to sell the captives, particularly a young, pretty, Mexican woman, Elena de la Madriaga (Linda Cristal), who has been the "wife" of a fierce warrior, Stone Calf (Woody Strode), for the past few years. Yet the shiny new repeating rifles are too great a temptation, and Quanah, the budding entrepreneur, sells two captives, Elena and a teenaged boy, Running Wolf (David Kent). Stone Calf returns to find his wife gone, but McCabe kills him when he tries to take her back.

At the wagon train, McCabe and Gary bring back the two captives. Elena has no family there and believes she would rather be with the Indians because the white women shun her and gossip behind her back. No one really knows who Running Wolf's parents are. They all see, however, how untamed the boy is, and they have to tie him up to restrain him. Harry Wringle wants no part of his wildness and backs out of the deal he made with McCabe. No one will claim the boy until Mr. William McCandless (Cliff Lyons) and his wife Mary (Jeanette Nolan) take him. Mary believes he is their lost son, Toby, and tries to smother him with kindness. When she makes the mistake of cutting him loose from his bonds, he grabs the knife and kills her.

The settlers are outraged, and many come to believe that it was a mistake to bring back any of the captives. They grab Running Wolf to hang him. In the scuffle, they knock over a music box, now in the care of Marty Purcell, who previously told Lieutenant Gary that it once belonged to her brother and how much he loved listening to its simple melody. When the music box falls open and begins playing, the boy dives for it.

"Mine! Mine!" he cries, before the settlers drag him away to string him up to the nearest tree. Marty, Jim Gary, and the audience finally learn that Running Wolf is Steve Purcell.

Elena's experience is not quite as tragic. She and McCabe go to a dance at the fort, but McCabe can't dance and none of the officers will dance with Elena. The officers' wives either won't speak to her or ask her what it was like to be a Comanche squaw. Finally, McCabe loudly chastises the officers and tells them that Elena was treated better by the Comanches. Elena decides to leave the territory and head to California where no one knows her past. McCabe hops on the stage with her and they head into the sunset.

It was not easy for recovered female captives, and it was only a little better for males. Had the fictional Running Wolf–Steve Purcell lived, he would have found it nearly as difficult to readjust. The true-life experiences of several ex-captives illustrate what the situation could be like. Rudolph Fischer, taken in Texas in 1865, did not return to Fort Sill until 1877, after many of the Comanches already surrendered. Rudolph went back to his parents for less than a year, but returned to his Indian family for a "visit" and stayed for 22 more years.

Indians captured Adolph Korn from his parents' farm in Texas in 1870. He was treated roughly, but eventually adjusted to his new life and became a warrior. Adolph was recovered at Fort Sill two years later. He was at times sullen and wild, and appeared unhappy, but he never tried to run away back to the Indians. He was never successful in any endeavors, never married, and was always a loner. In his last years he was a hermit, living in a cave in the Texas Hill Country.

Clinton and Jefferson Smith were captured near San Antonio in February 1871. The Comanches later sold Jeff to the Apaches, and both boys learned the ways of the warrior. They were hellions, fighting and raiding with their respective tribes. Clint was recovered in 1872 and returned to Texas with Adolph Korn. Jeff was recovered in 1873. Although shy and apparently unhappy at first, both brothers adjusted back into white society and lived productive lives.

Herman and Willie Lehmann were captured by Apaches from their home in Mason County, Texas, in May 1870. From Fort McKavett, a squad of 9th Cavalry "buffalo soldiers" picked up the Indian trail and chased them. During the scramble, the warrior who had Willie riding behind him threw the eight-year-old from his horse in his mad dash to get away. Willie thus missed his prolonged tutorial on becoming an Indian warrior. Herman, however, after a rough introduction, became a willing student. Over the next several years, Herman, riding with the Apaches first, and then later the Comanches, raided settlers, stole cattle, fought against the Texas Rangers, and killed. Herman finally returned home in 1878, at the age of 19, after many of the other bands had surrendered. He never adjusted well to white society. He tried manual labor and cattle-raising, and even ran a saloon (but he drank up all his profits).

Although readjustment was tough for some male captives, most of them quickly fit in, got on with their lives, and never went back to the Indians. In the West, freed female captives were even less inclined to want to live out their lives with the Indians. Although Hollywood has somewhat accurately depicted the rough treatment of captives, it has created a false impression that many captives wanted to return to their captors.[17]

# 14

## Anna Brewster Morgan
## (*Stolen Women, Captured Hearts*)

### Kansas, October 1868

Unlike Lucinda Eubank, some ex-captives who had been raped chose to keep their mixed-blood children and so faced another ordeal trying to fit back into the white world. A classic example was Anna Brewster, who was born in New Jersey in 1844 and moved to Ottawa County, Kansas, in 1867 to help her brother Daniel run a farm. Anna Brewster, said to be "a beautiful young woman with blue eyes and thick lustrous hair of yellow hue," married James S. Morgan in September 1868.[1]

Anna moved to his cabin near present Delphos, just a few miles from her brother's place. They had only been married a few weeks when, on 13 October, 1868, James went out to work in the field of his neighbor, David Mortimer. It was a damp, foggy morning, and Morgan figured it would be too wet for Indians to effectively use their bows, so he left his gun at home. He did not realize the Indians had been armed for years, and had gotten a new supply of weapons from Agent Edward Wynkoop just two months earlier. That morning Morgan spied several Lakotas coming at him through the cornfield.[2]

One warrior fired a bullet into his hip, and his horses bolted. James stumbled into the high corn, reached the Solomon River, and swam across to hide in the willows. The Indians went after the horses, and Morgan crawled to a neighbor for help.

Some of the horses ran back to the Morgan cabin where Anna saw them and assumed James was hurt. She strapped on a revolver, mounted one horse, led the other one, and headed to where he was working. As she rode in the tall grass near the river, warriors sprang up, grabbed the bridle and knocked her unconscious with a club. When she came to, she was "in a strange country among the hills, bound tight to my horse."[3]

That night Anna Morgan was gang raped. The days blended together, and a week or more of travel brought them to the headwaters of the Republican. About one month after her abduction, Anna Morgan was traded to the Cheyennes and joined a camp with another white captive, Sarah White, who had been taken two months earlier about 25 miles north of where Anna was captured.

Anna said the women worked, doing "menial service such as carrying wood from the creek for the more favored squaws." Sarah and Anna tried to cooperate to gain the Indians' confidence. All the while, said Anna, "we were laying by a supply of dried buffalo meat so we could escape for civilization the first opportunity presented." One day they crept past the guards, found a trail and "traveled for dear life." They walked at night and hid in the day. One night they saw a light in the distance and hoped it was Fort Dodge, but the next morning they made an ill-advised move in the daylight and the Indians caught them. "I fought hard and said I would not go back," said Anna. "But they took me by main force and whipped me and bound me onto the pony."[4]

The women were beaten and placed under more restrictions. The village moved to the upper Washita in Indian Territory, just downstream from the camp of Black Kettle, which Custer attacked on 27 November, 1868. When the soldiers charged, the Indians killed two other white captives, Clara and Willie Blinn. Fortunately for White and Morgan, the village they were in escaped, and they were not murdered.

Strangely enough, after Custer's destruction of Black Kettle's village, the women's treatment improved. Perhaps the Indians realized that the soldiers might strike them someday, or that they would eventually have to return the captives, and it might be easier on them if they were treated better. Soon after, an Indian "proposed" to Anna Morgan. "I married him," she said, "thereby choosing the least of two evils and never expecting to see a white person again." The warrior brought her small gifts, and the Indian women treated her more kindly.

Troops searched for the Indians through the winter of 1869. Lt. Col. Horace Moore, 19th Kansas, said the men were weary of the long marches and short rations, but when they thought "of Mrs. Blinn and her little boy, [and] of the hundred murders in Kansas," they tightened their belts and marched on. The Indians evaded the soldiers until March 1869 when detachments of Custer's 7th Cavalry and the 19th Kansas Cavalry caught up to Stone Forehead's Cheyenne village on Sweetwater Creek.

Marching with the 19th Kansas was Dan Brewster. He had been looking for his sister since her capture, not unlike the quest Martin Pawley (Jeffrey Hunter) undertook for his sister in *The Searchers*. Dan Brewster caught up with Custer at Camp Supply, Indian Territory, in a scene similar to Ethan Edwards (John Wayne) and Pawley's arrival at a military camp in *The Searchers*. Brewster explained his situation to Custer, stating that he required no horse, weapon, or pay, but only wished to search for his sister. Custer put him on the payroll as a substitute teamster. Later, Custer wrote that Brewster "displayed more genuine courage, perseverance, and physical endurance, and a greater degree of true brotherly love and devotion, than I have ever seen combined in one person."[5]

Custer took Cheyenne hostages from Stone Forehead's camp to force them to return the two white women. Late in the afternoon on 19 March, the white captives were put on one pony and sent toward Custer's camp. Custer and other officers watched through field glasses as they approached. Dan Brewster stood by his side. Custer described one of the women as being short and heavy and the other as tall and slender.

"The last one must be my sister"; Brewster interjected, "she is quite tall. Let me go and meet them, this anxiety is more than I can endure." Custer would not allow it, fearing that if one of them was his sister, the sight of her might provoke him into taking revenge on the nearest Indian. Custer sent a few officers ahead, but Brewster could not restrain himself and ran forward. Lt. Col. Moore was one of the first on the scene. Before Brewster could reach them he took the older woman by the hand and asked if she was Mrs. Morgan. She said she was, and then introduced the other as Miss White.

"Are we free now?" Anna asked. Moore said yes. She asked, "Where is my husband?" Moore said he was wounded and recovering. Her next question was, "Where is my brother?" Moore told her he was in camp, but the situation was soon revealed when Brewster came running up to her.[6]

When the women reached the soldiers' camp a cheer went up, and Custer said there were many tears shed at the reunion. The women wore government flour sacks, Indian leggings, and moccasins, and one of the first things Custer heard Dan Brewster say was, "Sister, do take those hateful things off." Fortunately, Custer had a female cook in camp, and she was able to spare some extra clothing for the women.

Most of the soldiers were completely satisfied at having rescued them without a fight, yet there were those in the 19th Kansas who were disappointed because they had enlisted specifically to fight the Indians who had been devastating their state. Sarah White and Anna Brewster Morgan had been rescued without an attack that would have cost many lives. The military so outnumbered the Cheyennes on this occasion that had they attacked, they would certainly have had a greater victory than at the Washita. Custer, however, weighed his options and chose to negotiate for the release of the women. He successfully rescued them without loss of life and without paying a ransom, showing that he could learn from experience, and that he was a diplomat and negotiator as well as a proven fighter.[7]

The women were very much the worse for wear. David L. Spotts, a private in Company L, 19th Kansas, said one of them (Morgan) "appeared to be 50 years old, although she was less than 25. She was stooped, pale, and haggard, looking as if she had been compelled to do more than she was able." She wore several "kinds of material, pieces of tents and blankets, all worn out and sewed together with strings." Of Miss White, Spotts said she was dressed about the same and was pale, but was "younger looking and did not show the hard usage."[8]

Custer said that the women told of such "cruelties, and enormous indignities that it is surprising that civilized beings could endure it and still survive." In his book, he wrote, "There was much in their story not appropriate for these pages." His wife Elizabeth later penned: "The young faces of the two, who not a year before were bright, happy women, were now worn with privation and exposure, and haggard with the terrible insults of their captors, too dreadful to be chronicled here." Writing about Mrs. Morgan, David Spots said, "It is impossible to imagine the mental agony and physical torture endured."[9]

Many years later Anna Morgan told her story to a neighbor, Emily Harrison. Harrison printed the story in a 1907 article, which presents a different picture of the devastating experience of her captivity. As Mrs. Harrison told it, when Anna was rescued, she heard that "there were two white men in the camp, [and] I did not care to see them. I was surprised to see my own brother walk into the tent." Harrison also said that Anna told her, "After I came back, the road seemed rough, and I often wished they had never found me."[10]

Anna went back to her husband, but her life would never be the same. James Morgan resented the fact that Anna had become an Indian's "wife." The situation deteriorated when Anna gave birth to a half–Indian son. She named him Ira Arthur and insisted "that the babe's blood was as pure as any of the rest of my children." James, however, did not think so, and their marriage became more strained.

About a year later, some 7th Cavalry officers rode by the Morgan place. They noticed a half–Indian boy playing in the yard, knocked on the door, and, much to their surprise, recognized Anna Morgan. They talked for a few minutes and learned that all was not well. Her husband, instead of trying to help her "forget the misery through which she had passed," often upbraided her as if she were responsible for her misfortunes. Perhaps James's anger was calmed somewhat after the child died at the age of 17 months.[11]

Anna lived with James Morgan until 1880, when she finally left him. He sued and obtained a divorce by her consent. Journalists came to her door asking for her to tell her story, but she would not do it. She considered it a disgrace. In 1893 Anna wrote to a friend that "rather than the world should know what I have been forced to endure, I would rather live the remaining days of my life in poverty than have these dreadful facts known."

In another letter, Anna wrote:

> My life received a blight at that time [her capture] which will go with me to the grave. Life has been worth nothing to me since then. Do not mention my husband to me. He reproached me times without number for my misfortune, for having been a helpless victim to the atrocities of the wild savages…. They say, each cloud has a silver lining, but that has not turned to me yet.

Anna never found the silver lining. By 1900 she was placed in the Kansas Insane Asylum in Topeka. Perhaps the condition was hereditary, but certainly the anguish, physical, and mental stress she was under for decades must have contributed to her condition. Anna Brewster Morgan died in the asylum on 11 July, 1902.[12]

As some historians misrepresented Laura Roper and Nancy Morton's experience with the Indians, others distorted Anna Morgan's, portraying her captivity as a picnic and asserting that she was well-treated. Five years after Anna died, Emily Harrison, as previously mentioned, printed a story of Anna's captivity in which she said that one of the Indians Anna "married" treated her kindly, and that her road after her return to civilization was so rough she often wished she had never been found. Even if Harrison's rendition is correct, it is less of an endorsement of Indian treatment than it is an indictment of an intolerant white society.

One historian cited none of the abundant sources to the contrary, but took Harrison's version and used it to show that captives had it good living with the Cheyennes. He also claimed that Anna's situation "was not the first time a captive had expressed longings to return to the People [Cheyennes] after being taken from them." Tellingly, however, he offered no other examples. His biases are even more glaring when he writes of the Cheyenne treatment of the German family children, captured by Cheyennes in 1874 (see Chapter 29).[13]

With historians promoting such tall tales, it is little wonder that the politically correct film media of the late 20th century would have a difficult time distinguishing fact from fiction. *Stolen Women, Captured Hearts*, a 1997 made-for-TV movie, is a prime example. It is romantic fiction, pure and simple—a 90-minute soap opera. The problem is, it claims to be "based on a true story." The opening captions place it in 1868, when Custer has just destroyed an Indian village and the Indians are seeking revenge. The set-up provides a ready-made reason for the Indians to raid wagon trains and cabins. Unfortunately for the audience, the history is already twisted, for the Indians were raiding, capturing, and killing in Kansas long before Custer attacked the Cheyenne village on the Washita. They were marauding while Custer was off active duty serving out his court-martial sentence. In 1868 Custer attacked the village in retaliation for the Indian raids—he was not the cause of their raids.

After the film opens with a complete 180-degree reversal of the actual cause-and-effect, the precedent is set for the continued demolition of historical events. In the opening action, Sioux attack a wagon train. Warriors are about to kill two women, but one of the braves, Tokalah (Michael Greyeyes), stops them, for he has seen one of the women before—Anna Brewster (Janine Turner)—in a vision, clutching a bible. The women safely reach Fort Hays. Anna, at the behest of her brother, the Rev. Dan Brewster (Ted Shackelford), is betrothed to farmer Dan Morgan (Patrick Bergin). She marries him, but he proves to be far too inexperienced at love for Anna's tastes.

Indians, led by Tokalah, raid the Morgan Cabin and capture Anna and her friend, Sarah White (Jean Louisa Kelly). The women resist but realize it is hopeless. After a time, Sarah still refuses to become "Indianized," but Anna is finding her new life pleasant, especially because she has fallen for Tokalah. All the while, a mixed-blood boy, Cetah (William Lightning), helps indoctrinate Anna into an Indian frame of mind by telling her he is the son of a soldier who kidnapped his Indian mother, raped her, brutalized her, and whored her out to the troops until she died. Cetah ran away to join the Indians. Cetah also teaches Tokalah to learn handy English phrases, such as "White man is son-of-a-bitch." In the meantime, Lt. Col. George Custer (William Shockley), assisted by soldiers under Captain Farnsworth (Dennis Weaver), Dan Brewster, and Dan Morgan, are searching for the captives.

At one point, Sarah convinces Anna to escape. They try but are caught. Sarah is devastated, but when Tokalah seizes Anna again, she says, "I was so afraid you wouldn't come after me." That night they finally make love, and Anna learns how much better at it Tokalah is than her husband.

Custer and the troops approach, marching not to the tune of "Garryowen" or "The Girl I Left Behind Me," but to the "British Grenadiers." Custer meets with the Indians and demands the women's return. Tokalah agrees to give back Sarah but not Anna. Morgan, listening in at the council, realizes that the Indian has "lain" with Anna, and wants to kill him. He is restrained. Custer says he will hold Chief Luta (Saginaw Grant) until both women are returned. The next day, warriors attack Custer's camp, but they are repulsed and Tokalah is badly wounded.

In the village, the Indians release Sarah. Anna cares for Tokalah and believes he is dying. She says she will return to him again in another vision. She rides to Custer and gives herself up for the release of Chief Luta.

Some time later Anna is back in the cabin with husband Dan Morgan. She is unhappy but making the best of it. Sarah visits her and, with a change of heart, realizes how happy Anna was with the Indians. Sarah suggests Anna run away back to them. One night Morgan asks Anna to sleep with him again, for they have not done so since her return. He blamed the "damn savages" for ruining her. Anna sleeps with Morgan. The next morning he wakes to find her gone. Anna takes the horse and rides to the Indian village, which is destroyed. She assumes everyone is dead, but lo, she sees Tokalah chanting on a hilltop. She runs to him. He thinks he is seeing the vision she promised, and they live happily ever after.

*Stolen Women* is nothing like the true story it purports to be based on. The real incidents in 1868 were tragic. The tragedy of the 1997 film is that many people will see it and believe it was true.

In the 1960s, about 30 years before *Stolen Women*, a tide of change was already ushering in a "new" depiction of Indian-white relations. *The Talisman* (a.k.a. *The Savage American*, Mars Productions, 1966) opens after a wagon train massacre, with only one Cheyenne warrior (Ned Romero) and one white woman (Linda Hawkins) left alive. The warrior intends to kill her, but he interprets a bird circling above as a sign that he must spare her life. Terrified at first, the woman comes to trust the warrior after he builds a fire and feeds her.

He is determined to take her back to her own people, and fights enemy Crow Indians, winter weather, and bear attacks to get her home. They fall in love. On the way, they meet five mountain men, and they realize that the five whites will probably be able to get the woman home more easily than the warrior. Before he goes he gives the woman his amulet for protection.

Of course, the white frontiersmen are vicious curs, and before the night is over they have her staked out on the ground preparing to rape her. One man has some decency and tries to stop them, but they kill him, rape her, and leave her to die.

Having second thoughts, the warrior returns the next day to find her still alive, but senseless, limbs still spread-eagled and staked out. He gives her to the care of two old Shoshone women and tracks down the remaining mountain men, torturing and killing them one by one. Thus, the vengeance is meted out to the evil white frontiersmen.

With such stories being shown to movie audiences for upwards of five decades, it is no wonder that so many Americans have developed a guilty conscience, seeing their ancestors as savages and denigrating their country's past achievements. Propagating and perpetuating self-hatred is not one of Hollywood's stellar achievements; it was destructive for Indians and it is destructive for whites. The caricature of most Indians being sly, murdering "redskins" is just as historically incorrect as characterizations of most frontiersmen as filthy, lascivious louts.

# 15

# The Fletcher Wagon Train
(*Duel at Diablo, Fort Apache, Ulzana's Raid*)

## Wyoming, July 1865

Most of the historians who have studied the emigrants on the Oregon and Overland Trails through Nebraska and Wyoming have understated the violence and the number of wagon train attacks. Michael Tate, in one of the more recent studies, has opted to narrow his focus on the central route, covering only the years of 1840 to 1870, which omits all the other years and trails. As a result, his conclusions are similarly narrow: wagon train travel was comparatively safe from Indian attack. Tate only finds eight events "that somewhat fit the notion of 'massacre,'" and concludes the trail experience was never as violent as "depicted in later literary and cinematic portrayals."[1] This study references more actual violent attacks than there are films portraying them.

Even in the narrow scope of Tate's study on the central routes, he has overlooked several attacks. A few of them occurred right on the main route along the Platte River. The attacks were the result of tragic mistakes that led to innocent parties suffering. In August 1856, a war party of Cheyennes, looking for their Pawnee enemies, flagged down a Salt Lake mail coach to beg for tobacco. The driver, believing he was being attacked, fired his pistol and sped away, reaching Fort Kearny with an arrow in his arm. Capt. George H. Steuart, with a detachment of 1st Cavalrymen, went in pursuit of the Cheyennes. Downriver from the fort, Steuart charged into about 80 warriors camped near Wood River. The Indians, believing they had done no wrong, were unprepared for the fight and fled after having six men killed and ten wounded.

Steuart's attack led to a series of raids by the vengeful Indians. They found their first victims on the Council Bluffs Road about 33 miles northeast of Fort Kearny. The small four-wagon train carried emigrants on their way to Utah and included Almon W. Babbitt, the Secretary of Utah Territory and delegate to Congress. The Cheyennes hit the camped train on the night of 25 August, killed two men and one child, wounded a man, and carried off Mrs. Wilson, the mother of the slain child. They killed Mrs. Wilson when she could not ride fast enough to keep up with them. On 30 August, Cheyennes attacked an emigrant party at Cottonwood Springs, 80 miles west of Fort Kearny. They killed Mrs. William Schevekendeck and carried off her four-year-old boy. On 6 September, Cheyennes attacked a Mormon train returning east and killed two men, one woman and one child, and captured another woman.

Although Almon Babbitt's train was recently attacked, he apparently had not learned his lesson. On 2 September, he and two other men left Fort Kearny in a carriage bound for Salt Lake City, refusing Capt. Henry W. Wharton's advice to wait for an army escort. The Cheyennes found them on the 5th or 6th of September, and quickly killed them. Their three bodies were found on 26 September, on the north side of the Platte River by O'Fallon's Bluff, near present-day Hershey, Nebraska.²

Another attack that Tate omitted, and one whose circumstances have been incorrectly reported by historians for years, was the attack on the Fletcher Wagons. Jasper Fletcher was born in Derbyshire, England, and came to America in 1861, settling in Illinois. He had a good income as a coal-mining engineer and received more money from his father, coming to America with about 21,000 English pounds. Fletcher decided to move to California in 1865.

Mr. Fletcher bought two wagons and three horses to pull his goods, which included tea, tobacco, bacon, sugar, and two feather beds. His family consisted of his wife, Mary Ann, and children, Amanda (age 13), William (11), Jasper Jr. (6), Oscar D. (5), and Elizabeth (3). Amanda and her three brothers were born in England, and Lizzie was born in Illinois.

They were very well off compared to most emigrant families. Jasper owned six new suits of clothes, two overcoats, and two sets of carpenter's tools. Mary Ann had velvet and silk dresses, and a shawl that cost 100 pounds. They bought an additional $500 worth of provisions in Rock Island. Leaving on 10 May, 1865, they went to Davenport and Omaha, then along the Platte to Fort Kearny. They took the road down the South Platte to what Amanda Fletcher called "Jewel Station" (Julesburg), and then the cut-off toward Denver, where they rested on a creek for two weeks. Continuing northwest into the Laramie Basin, the train had grown to 75 wagons and 300 people—certainly, they believed, a large enough group to deter Indian attack.

The Fletchers were never very friendly with the other families and kept slightly ahead of the main group. On Monday, the last day of July, they stopped for dinner just east of Rock Creek Station, about 25 miles east of Fort Halleck. There was a toll bridge over the fast-running creek. Joe Bush built the station in 1860 and lived there with his Indian wife.³

Jasper Fletcher had never seen an Indian in his life before nearly 300 Cheyennes and Arapahos rode down out of the mountains and attacked. Mary Ann, Amanda, and Lizzie had strolled closer to the creek, about 300 yards from the wagons. Warriors cut them off, killed Mary Ann, threw Amanda and Lizzie on their ponies, and took them across the bridge and part way up the hillside. An arrow hit Jasper in the right wrist, but he and his boys escaped to the east where they met up with the main wagon train. Amanda watched the Indians plunder their wagons and set them aflame.

Packed among the contents was a green sheet-iron moneybox. Amanda knew it well. She was in charge of its safety and had counted the money many times. Inside were 17,000 English-pound notes and 3,000 in gold sovereigns. The family had discussed taking so much money with them, but American money fluctuated in value, and they figured the English pound was good and the gold better. "Their money was good anyplace," Amanda said.⁴

The warriors, many from Sand Hill's band of Cheyennes, took Lizzie from Amanda on the first day. Minimic, who was once involved in trying to free hostages Laura Roper and Nancy Morton from Black Kettle, was Amanda's captor. They separated from the main party and wandered down into Kansas. Amanda turned 14 years old on 19 August, a birthday she dejectedly kept to herself. As they traveled, Indians showed her the money they had stolen from her father and asked her to count it for them. Minimic alone had about 2,400 English pounds. The Indians first used their stolen money when they bought sugar, coffee, flour, and blankets from William Bent. The Indians gave the money to Amanda to count to make sure it was correct, and she passed it to Bent. After doing business, the Indians moved on.

Several days later, Charles Hanger, a partner in the firm of Hanger & Morris, and working under the auspices of Agent I. C. Taylor, rode into a nearby Arapaho camp on Bluff Creek about 40 miles southeast of Fort Dodge. He traded with the Arapahos for a few days, then packed up and moved to the Cheyenne camps, where he found about 4,000 Indians there for a council.

"I visited a camp of Cheyenne dog soldiers in February," Hanger said, "and found among

## 15. The Fletcher Wagon Train

Rock Creek, Wyoming, near the site of the July 1865 attack on the Fletcher Wagons.

them a captive white girl, aged about fourteen years." Minimic paid Hanger for supplies with the money stolen from Mr. Fletcher, and he noticed Amanda counting the money. He knew that he must try to buy her, but Minimic wanted a high price. Since Hanger had just made plenty of money, he met Minimic's demand of $1,665.

"I did the trade that bought Mrs. [Fletcher] Cook at the time," Hanger later deposed. Jasper Fletcher's money had served some good purpose. The next morning, Hanger sent Amanda with one of the mixed-blood Poisal Brothers back to the Arapaho camp, where Captain Gordon escorted her to Fort Dodge and then to Fort Larned, where she was "given in charge of Major [Edward] Wynkoop the Indian agent at the post."[5]

Amanda was sent to Davenport, Iowa, where her father had acquaintances who agreed to take her in. Mr. Fletcher, then in Salt Lake City, did not have the money to send for her. At first, Jasper and Amanda assumed little Elizabeth had been killed, but they doggedly kept seeking information. They heard rumors that she might still be held captive, and wrote to Lt. Col. George A. Custer at Fort Riley, Kansas, to ask him for help. Custer wrote to Amanda on 27 January, 1867, saying that he had news that a little white girl was being held by the Cheyenne Cut Nose. Lt. Owen Hale and guide Will Comstock had seen her on the Smoky Hill River, 250 miles west of Fort Riley. Custer told Amanda that Comstock believed the child could be ransomed for a couple of horses. Jasper, unfortunately, did not have enough money to buy a horse.[6]

When, in the late winter of 1867, Lieutenant Colonel Custer heard that the military had in their possession a boy belonging to the Cheyennes, he wrote to Gen. Winfield S. Hancock that it would be a good strategy to trade the boy for Elizabeth Fletcher. The government, however, in a fit of penitence after Sand Creek, thought it best not to further antagonize the Indians. Custer's trade proposition failed and Lizzie was never recovered.

Cut Nose frequently came in to the stage stations to trade, and was often accompanied by the captive. Custer never saw her, but reports reached him that she was a beautiful girl from four to seven years old, with fair complexion, blue eyes, and silver-gold hair. Cut Nose was said to have given her the name "Little Silver Hair," and would not sell her. When the fighting began in the spring of 1867, Custer heard no more about her.[7]

Amanda later married, and spent many years searching for her sister and seeking compensation for her family's losses, but to no avail. Lizzie was gone, and the government denied her claims. In a fit of frustration, Amanda stated, "No amount the government would allow could ever repay me for my sufferings while a prisoner with the Indians." Amanda's ordeal was sugarcoated by historians George Hyde and Peter Powell, both stating that she was well-treated by her captors. The tribulations experienced by Amanda Fletcher and many other captives are unknown to, or dismissed by, Michael Tate. While discussing the capture and abuse of Jenssine Grundvig, taken along the central route in September 1865, Tate claims such an event "was so seldom recorded along the trail that it was statistically irrelevant."[8] We would hope that Mr. Tate never experiences such an "irrelevant" episode.

Before Hollywood went "politically correct" it did a much better job of depicting some women's ordeals than did several historians. Apparently no white person ever learned the final fate of Lizzie Fletcher. She may have been killed, died of abuse, exposure, starvation, or disease; she may have wanted to return; she may have contently lived out her life with the Indians; possibly she was torn between options.

The latter scenario is depicted in *Duel at Diablo* (United Artists, 1966). In the film, director Ralph Nelson gives us a hint of the bloodshed he was willing to depict four years later in his gory *Soldier Blue*. *Duel*'s storyline is basic: a party must get a wagon train of explosives safely through Apache country to Fort Concho. More substance arises in the subplots, which include scout Jess Remsberg (James Garner) searching for the killer of his Indian wife; Lt. Scott McAllister (Bill Travers) trying to lead 25 green troopers in what he considers a suicide mission; and Willard Grange (Dennis Weaver) both loving and hating his wife Ellen (Bibi Andersson), who has been reluctantly rescued from Apache captivity.

One of director Nelson's objectives was to depict the harmful effects of racism, but he missed another chance to get in a dig at white society when he cast black actor Sidney Poitier as ex-soldier Toller, who was once a sergeant in a white cavalry regiment — something that was never permitted in a white regiment on the Western frontier. Toller, now a civilian and making a living by catching and breaking wild horses to sell to the U.S. Cavalry, also joins the train as one of the few men who might be able to safely guide them to Fort Concho.

The tension is thick between Will Grange and Ellen. Jess Remsburg, who rescues Ellen from the Apaches, brings her back to the home where she is not wanted. Will despises her because she has been the "wife" of an Apache, and he makes life hell for her. In addition, Ellen is ostracized by the townsfolk, who either shun her or try to assault her. Once more, Jess has to fight to rescue Ellen, this time from a gang of white hoodlums who figure that since she already has been "used" by the Apaches, a little more such activity wouldn't do her any harm.

Fed up with her treatment by the whites, Ellen flees back to the Apaches to be with her mixed-blood infant, a child that she never told Will about. In the Indian village Ellen learns that Chata (John Hoyt) blames her for the death of his own boy.

"You're going to kill me," Ellen says.

"No," Chata responds. "You will be alive when I bury you in the grave of my son."

He vows to exact this vengeance when he and his warriors return from wiping out the wagon train. The Indian women beat her in the meantime. Ellen is truly caught between two worlds. And, yet again, she is "saved" by scout Jess Remsberg, who brings her and her child back to the wagon train to find her husband Will Grange, a freighter who has joined in the trek to Concho. There, Will learns for the first time that his wife not only lived with the Apaches but bore a child, angrily calling the baby "a half-breed bastard."

The Indians attack the wagons and kill about half the troopers, driving the remainder of the train into Diablo Canyon, the only place that has a waterhole. Scout Remsberg breaks out to go to Concho for help, plus to get revenge, for it is there he believes his wife's killer resides— in the person of the town marshal John Crawford (Clay Dean). The two men fight, and just before Jess is about to kill the marshal, he learns that it was not Crawford who killed his wife but Will Grange, the man Jess had tried several times to help.

Jess rides back to Diablo Canyon with the cavalry, hopefully in time to rescue the trapped survivors, who are being picked off one by one by well-aimed Apache arrows. Lieutenant McAllister is hit several times and dies of his wounds. There are only a few left, including Toller, who somehow manages to keep pristinely clean in his fancy white suit while the others are torn, ragged, and begrimed. At this point Will incongruously offers his pistol to Ellen, who is to keep the last two bullets for herself and the baby. Even more oddly, Ellen accepts it; but she uses it not on herself but on Apaches who have broken into their circle. Later that night, Apaches sneak into the perimeter and capture Will, dragging him a short distance away to torture him. During the following day his screams of agony serve to further unnerve the survivors and remind them of their likely fate.

But not so. Jess and the cavalry arrive just in the nick of time, surrounding Chata and forcing him to surrender. Ellen and the baby, Toller, and a few others are saved. Jess is still determined to take revenge on Will Grange for killing his wife. Heading out to find the murderer, Jess sees Will, tied upside down to a wagon wheel, slowly being roasted over an open fire—and still alive. We see Will's half-charred arm reaching out while he pleads for Jess to kill him. Jess places his pistol in Will's burned hand. The shot is fired, and Will comes to his end—apparently director Nelson's idea of a fitting reward for a racist.

As we have seen, the ordeal that Ellen Grange went through had its historical antecedents. Women experienced harsh captivities and sometimes harsh re-assimilations back into white society. What Hollywood occasionally overemphasized was the frequency with which white female captives shunned white society and wanted to return to the Indians, as shown in *Duel at Diablo* and *Soldier Blue*. For every movie Ellen or Cresta who preferred Indian life, there were many more women who were only too glad to be back in the white world, wanting nothing to do with the Indians again. For the few who exaggerated their sexual abuse to perhaps make their stories more attractive to a potential publisher, there were likely many more who were raped but denied it. A study of this, *A Fate Worse Than Death*, illustrates these points. While some studies of Eastern captivities indicate that nearly one-third of female captives preferred to remain with the Indians, in the West the situation was very different: only one female captured in the seven to fifteen-year-old age group of the study wanted to return to the Indians. That girl was Cynthia Ann Parker, who was taken in 1836 when ten years old, spent 24 years with the Comanches, and had a husband and three children. "Rescued" in 1860, she wanted to return to her Indian family but was not allowed to. That one instance is often cited as proving that freed female captives preferred to return to the Indians. The contention is nonsense.[9]

Other movie characters met a similar fate as that of Will Grange in *Duel at Diablo*. In *Fort Apache* (RKO, 1948) Lt. Michael S. O'Rourke (John Agar), who has been out riding with the lieutenant colonel's daughter, Philadelphia Thursday (Shirley Temple), finds the smoldering ruins of some burned wagons. Back at the fort he reports to Lt. Col. Owen Thursday (Henry Fonda): "The trail wagons, sir. Burned. Two troopers, Barry and Williams, dead. Spread-eagled on the wheels. Roasted."

"My daughter saw that?" asks the angry Thursday. The graphics of the situation are not shown onscreen, however—that sort of detail came later.

In *Ulzana's Raid* (1972) the Apaches capture settler Willie Rukeyser (Karl Swenson) alive. They tie him to a tree in a sitting position, with his legs spread open and staked down. When

**In a scene with actual historical antecedents, Dennis Weaver is about to be burned to death on a wagon wheel in *Duel at Diablo* (United Artists, 1966).**

the soldiers later find him, they find the ashes of a fire that burned out his crotch. His dead dog's tail has been stuffed into his mouth. (Even the movies of the 1970s could not show what some warriors put in dead victims' mouths.)

The movie tortures have historical antecedents. In April 1872, Comanches attacked the Anastacio Gonzales Wagon Train at Howard's Well, 20 miles southeast of Fort Lancaster, Texas. They quickly killed most of the men, and lashed the survivors to wagon wheels where they soaked them with kerosene and burned them to death. Among the train passengers were Marcela Sera, her baby, and her elderly mother. The Indians killed the baby and captured Sera and her mother.

In July 1874, Wagonmaster Patrick Hennessey and three drivers were taking wagons with supplies to feed the Kiowas and Comanches at Fort Sill when they were attacked by a band of Cheyennes. All four men were killed and mutilated. Hennessey, for whom Hennessey, Oklahoma, is named, was chained to a wagon wheel, partially buried in his own oats and corn, and roasted alive.

One of the most infamous incidents occurred in May 1871 on the Salt Creek Prairie near present-day Loving, Texas. About 150 Kiowas and Comanches, under the Kiowa prophet Mamanti, waited on the trail between Forts Griffin and Richardson for their victims. On 18 May, Gen. William T. Sherman, Inspector Randolph Marcy, and a small escort rode past the watchful eyes of the Indians. They would have been wiped out, except Mamanti had a vision that told him he should attack the second group that went by. Later that afternoon a train of ten wagons

## 15. The Fletcher Wagon Train

**Salt Creek Prairie, Texas, site of the May 1871 attack on the Warren Wagon Train.**

belonging to the freight company of Warren & DuBose rode by. Wagonmaster Nathan Long was in charge of the train carrying supplies to Fort Griffin. The quickness of the attack did not leave enough time for Long to fully form up in a circle. Three teamsters were killed in the first rush, but the others fought back valiantly, killing or wounding three warriors. Another teamster went down, and seven broke out, running for Cox Mountain to the east; two were killed and the other five were wounded but escaped.

The Indians concentrated on the men left at the wagons. The Kiowa, Hau-tau, ran to a wagon and claimed it as his own, but the tarp rose and Sam Elliott shot him in the face, tearing off his jaw. The enraged warriors rushed Elliott, dragged him out, chained him to a wagon wheel, built a fire, and rolled the end of the wagon over it. When Elliott screamed too much, the mortally wounded Kiowa beat out his teeth with the butt of his knife and then cut out his tongue.

Col. Ranald S. Mackenzie rode to the scene after one teamster made it to Fort Richardson with the story of the attack. His patrol buried seven men, five of them with their heads split open, and all mutilated. Elliott, Mackenzie wrote, was "chained to a wagon wheel and burnt in many places to a crisp." Sherman, when he learned of his close brush with death and the severity of the attack, finally agreed to turn loose his cavalry to chase the raiding Indians onto their heretofore sacrosanct reservation in Indian Territory.[10]

When it comes to depicting violence in the Old West, Hollywood can be more accurate than some historians would like to admit.

# 16

## The Smart and Adams Wagon Trains

### Idaho, August 1862

The Oregon and California Trails were among the most dangerous emigrant routes in the 1850s and 1860s. One of the earliest attacks in that section took place on the Applegate Trail. Applegate's route branched off from the main California Trail southwest of present-day Winnemucca, Nevada. It headed northwest across the barren Black Rock Desert, through High Rock Canyon, across Surprise Valley and Fandango Pass in northeast California, and into Oregon. The emigrants, after crossing many miles of waterless desert and bare rocks, probably breathed a sigh of relief as they entered a more watered, timbered, and seemingly hospitable country in southwest Oregon.

The one advantage of traveling a barren route was that it was less frequented by Indians, who preferred the same amenities of friendly climate and terrain as did the emigrants. It is possible that the emigrant train, whose leaders' names have been lost to history, may have let its guard down. In any event, the Modocs, angry at the travelers coming through their territory, struck back at the unfortunate emigrants in September 1852. At a place since called Bloody Point, almost on the California-Oregon border, the trail pinched between a rocky lava bluff and the shore of Tule Lake. It was there the Modocs struck. Without warning, they descended on the train and slaughtered 62 emigrants. Only one man escaped. Two young girls, ages 12 and 14, were taken captive to eventually become the wives of their captors. Little else is known about the tragic episode.[1]

Farther east and ten years later on the California Trail, the travel proved no safer.

In September 1862, another unnamed emigrant party was moving along the Humboldt River in north central Nevada. The four families had joined together for mutual protection and had taken the Hastings Cut-off. The hard road had left them in dire need of recuperation, and they remained three weeks at Charles Stebbins's trading post in Ruby Valley. Their numbers, depending on the source, were between 13 and 23, including five children. One of the children, a girl of ten, became attached to Mr. and Mrs. Stebbins, as well as to a Paiute woman named Maggie who worked for Stebbins. They tried to talk the family into leaving the girl with them, to no avail.

The emigrants finally continued on their journey; Maggie followed behind. Several days later when they had joined the main California Trail, Paiutes or Shoshones jumped them near Palisades Canyon east of Gravelly Ford, a good crossing place of the Humboldt River. The entire party was wiped out except for the ten-year-old girl. Maggie had gotten word that Indians might try to attack the party, and when the rumor proved true, she rushed in during the chaos, snatched the girl away and escaped. As she tried to get back to Ruby Valley, warriors caught up with her.

They beat Maggie senseless, took the child, tied her to a stake in the ground, committed "a nameless outrage upon her," and stabbed her to death. Maggie later regained consciousness and made her way back to Stebbins's store to tell the news.

Stebbins sent word to the military and, with several other men, searched for the girl. They found her body, with "open, dead eyes staring," and buried her. Nevada Governor James W. Nye received word and, in a 15 September communication, asked Gen. George Wright for troops to be stationed from the Humboldt River to Ruby Valley, for, he said, "There has been some bloody work there within a few days." He requested that a portion of Col. Patrick E. Connor's California soldiers, then on their way to Salt Lake City, be halted in the Gravelly Ford area until the year's emigration had passed. The soldiers, under Maj. Edward McGarry, later took their revenge upon the Indians of the area.[2]

The people of the Smart Train and Adams Train were not taking cut-offs. They had not taken the Hudspeth Trail like the Shepherds, or the Lander Trail like the Miltimores, and they were among

Pioneer grave above Gravelly Ford, Nevada, vicinity of several Indian attacks on wagon trains.

many other wagons, probably believing that there was safety in numbers. Although there were many wagons, the families were stretched out along six miles of trail, and the Indians apparently did not read the books that said large wagon trains were immune from attack.

On 8 August, 1862, Indians jumped the 11-wagon Smith Train from Warren Country, Iowa, killing five emigrants and stealing their 16 horses. The wandering survivors eventually made it to a Mormon settlement.

In the same area the next day, about 150 Shoshones and Bannocks fell upon four wagon trains strung out along the Oregon Trail along the Snake River from American Falls west to Massacre Rocks. The rocks were a massive lava formation near the Snake, two miles west of a gully through which the trail passed. Pocatello, a Shoshone leader, had decided emigrants and their wagon trains could no longer cross his lands.[3]

Pocatello's warriors first hit the Smart Train, consisting of 25 men, a few women, and 11 wagons, about one-half mile east of the rocks. The terrain was very broken and rocky, and without warning the Indians struck the last wagon, trailing about 300 yards to the rear. They emerged from a ravine on the south and shot arrows at the two men in the wagon. Three arrows pierced one of the men. Undeterred, they lashed the animals forward until one of the animals was struck and the wagon toppled over. The men ran up to the next wagon, leaving the remaining horses, and dodging arrows and bullets as they ran. Captain Andrew J. Hunter issued orders for the men to circle the wagons, ready their arms, and defend the train.

The emigrants responded immediately, although most had never fought Indians before. The raiders rode around the wagons, fired, yelled out their most ferocious war whoops, and struck fear into the emigrants. Warriors rode up one of the ravines nearest the wagons, dismounted, and crept through the thick sagebrush until they were a stone's throw away. A rifle shot rang out and Captain Hunter was struck in the neck. He muttered a few words and died.

The warriors saw Hunter fall, gave out another whoop, and increased their fire. Although the wagons were in a rough circle, there was a ridge of higher ground about 50 yards away, and the defenders raced for the new position. Bullets cut the sleeves of A. J. Cassady's coat and shirt but didn't break the skin. He was congratulating himself on his luck when another bullet smashed into his hip, causing a serious, but not mortal, wound. The emigrants continued to fire whenever they caught sight of the Indians, but hit few, if any. The warriors rode with great expertise, turning their horses quickly, at one moment sitting upright and the next flattening themselves against their horses' backs. The scene of circling Indians was later played out in scores of Western movies.

The emigrants, regardless of the Indians' attempts to inspire fear, warmed to the situation and adopted their own form of bravado: after they fired a volley they would swing their hats and howl defiantly at the Indians. The battle raged for two hours before the Indians withdrew, taking two mules and plunder from the toppled wagon. The emigrants, who had initially halted while five men went down the bluffs to the Snake River to fish, moved on to a safer camp less than a mile away, awaiting the return of the fishermen and hoping they had not been killed. The five fishermen were discovered and chased, but the warriors only caught and killed one of them, Massimo Lippi, whose body was recovered three days later.[4]

The Shoshones may have broken off the fight because another train was coming into view, and from 75 to 100 warriors rode two miles east to where the Adams Wagon Train was rolling along. Captain George W. Adams, hearing distant gunfire, quickly circled his 13 wagons, and the men prepared a defense. The Indians rode toward the corral, circling and shooting, much as they had done against the Smart Train.[5]

The air was filled with their war whoops as they shot their weapons, circled, withdrew to reload, and repeated the assault. Adams's people, however, either had less gumption than those of the Smart Train, or saw a chance to escape when the warriors pulled back. They fled their wagons, hoping the Indians would plunder their belongings and not chase after them. The Indians didn't behave as expected, however. They ran off the stock and stripped the wagons bare, but they also chased down the running emigrants. In the stampede they killed George Adams (the captain's son), Charles Bullwinkel, and George Shepard, and badly wounded Captain Adams's daughter Elizabeth.

Charles Bullwinkel had originally been traveling with the Kennedy Train, the next one in line four miles to the east. Bullwinkel left the larger train on 25 July at the crossing of the Green River. Although traveling alone for much of the time, he finally joined up with Adams on 9 August and probably felt some relief to be with another train again. Regardless, Bullwinkel's time had come. The Indians shot him eight times. Bullwinkel's dog, growling and snapping at the attackers, proved its loyalty by staying with its master to the end. Warriors had to put four bullets into the dog to stop it. The Indians stole $6,000 from Bullwinkel, plus four choice horses.[6]

The Indians pulled away at night, and the Kennedy Train pulled up and joined the remains of Adams's train, forming a corral of 86 wagons. On Sunday, 10 August, Captain John K. Kennedy auctioned off some effects of the dead of the two trains to provide for those who survived. A trunk of fine books and some paper were among the auctioned items.

In the morning, 40 well-armed, mounted men, led by Kennedy, headed out to look for the Indians and recover the stolen stock. Five miles to the south they found the Indian camp, where

Massacre Rocks, Idaho, near the site of the August 1862 attack on the Smart and Adams wagon trains.

300 Indians waited for them. Kennedy's pursuit soon turned into a flight for life. The Indians had many firearms, and their first attack caused three-fourths of Kennedy's men to flee. A running battle ensued, with the Indians chasing various scattered parties from three to eight miles. Captain Kennedy attempted to rally the men but quickly lost three men killed and a few wounded. They believed they had killed six Indians and some ponies. Kennedy and a handful of his men fell back to a ten-wagon ox train they found on the road and attempted to stand off the Indians. One man volunteered to ride for help to the main Kennedy Train. Reinforcements, led by Captain Bristol, of about 30 more men went to Kennedy's aid. During the fight, Kennedy was mortally wounded, shot through his side above the hipbone. The dead included M. O. Tappl, Thomas Paul, and George Teaser; the latter was also scalped. Two missing and assumed dead were William Mottes and Thomas Newman.

When the Indians chased them back to the river, they found that another train, Captain Wilson's, had come up and added 46 more wagons to the defense. Sixteen men formed a search party to look for the two missing men, but with no success. The next morning, another search party of 100 men formed up to resume the search, but the dying Captain Kennedy advised against taking a chance on losing more men.[7]

There were now more than 180 wagons assembled on the plain south of the Snake River, and the Indians wisely ended their attacks. The combined trains moved on. Nine men would recover from their wounds: James Crawford, Thomas J. Adams, Thomas Bradford, John Walker, A. J. Cassady, E. A. Sullivan, John Miller, John Patterson, Ephraim Taylor, and Giovanni Benvenuti. The morning of the 11th, John Kennedy appeared to be improving, but he suddenly took a turn for the worse and died that same evening. Young Elizabeth Adams also died that day, bringing the total emigrant fatalities to ten. On 12 August, Elizabeth Adams was buried in a wagon box along the trail.[8]

The combined trains traveled on together in a line that stretched almost three miles. They rolled to the Raft River and set up camp on the west bank. At this point the roads split, one for Oregon and Washington, and another for California. The Kennedy Train took the road to Oregon, while the remnants of the Smart and Adams trains, along with the Thompson, Newburn, and Wilson trains, a total of 111 wagons and 200 men, took the road to California. On 14 August, while traveling through a canyon, they discovered the remains of a wagon and three dead men who had been buried in shallow graves about two or three weeks before. The head and face of one corpse was sticking out of the ground, while another's legs protruded, and a third had hands and arms uncovered. After viewing this sight, Jane Gould wrote in her diary, "I wish all the Indians in Christendom were exterminated."[9]

Early in the pre-dawn of 15 August, on the upper Raft River in the vicinity of some notable formations that would come to be called the City of Rocks, the emigrants were camped in a precarious spot surrounded by mountain walls when everyone was startled by gunfire and Indian war whoops. Now in overall command, Captain Walker yelled out, "Come on you red devils." The emigrants, becoming experts at the drill, hurriedly took quilts, feather beds, and mattresses to stuff into all the exposed spots between the circled wagons. The shots came from some willow trees near the stock corral. The half-hearted attack was soon over, however, and no emigrants were injured. The morning light revealed that rifle balls had passed through three of the Thompson Wagons' covers, and an arrow was found in the corral. Captain Walker cautiously sent scouts ahead and posted guards in advance, to the side, and to the rear of the train. A half-mile down the road, about ten Indians were spotted riding in the direction of the last night's camp, but they steered clear of the emigrants. There were no more attacks, and the train made it safely to California.[10]

Although the reconstituted Walker Train made it through the City of Rocks, near present-day Almo, Idaho, another party passing through one month later was not as fortunate. The small train of 15 men under Charles McBride and John Andrews was returning from California to the States. On 12 September, 1862, they were camped near City of Rocks near the Utah Territory border. Leaving early in the morning, they heard the lowing of cattle, saw smoke from campfires, and assumed there was an emigrant train ahead of them. Instead, they rode into a village of Shoshones and Bannocks. At first the Indians appeared friendly, and the men tried to purchase cattle from them. The negotiations broke off when the Indians told them they must bring all their men into the village and they would sell them all the beef they wanted. Suspecting treachery, the white travelers bypassed the village and moved on. Suddenly, about 40 warriors fired on the wagons from ambush.

McBride and Andrews kept the train rolling, firing as they rode, and the fighting stretched on intermittently for 20 miles. Finally they took refuge behind rocks along Cassia Creek near Raft River. They drove the Indians off, but not before losing six men killed and two wounded. With their horses stolen or killed, the nine survivors crept away in the moonlight. After five days without food, they barely made it to the Mormon settlements at Box Elder.[11]

From this series of attacks on the Oregon Trail it is clear that Indians would attack trains of almost any size. No one was safe. An interesting sidelight of these attacks stems from the incident wherein Charles Bullwinkel's dog stayed with him to the end. The tale of the faithful dog has been part of many Western films, from the silent era on.[12]

A television series that ran from 1954 to 1959, *The Adventures of Rin Tin Tin*, carried on this storyline. In many episodes, Rusty (Lee Aaker), a boy raised by the army after Indians killed his parents, is saved by Sgt. Biff O'Hara (Joe Sawyer) or Lt. Rip Masters (James Brown). Usually, rescue comes after Rusty's dog, Rin Tin Tin, runs back to Fort Apache to give warning.

Such a premise seems rather far-fetched, one would suppose. Strangely enough, however, it did happen. In the 1850s and early 1860s, the Navajos in northeastern Arizona were determined

## 16. The Smart and Adams Wagon Trains

**Near City of Rocks, Idaho, site of the September 1862 attack on the McBride-Andrews Train.**

to drive out the army and force the abandonment of Fort Defiance. At sunrise on 17 January, 1860, about 250 Navajos under Chief Huero attacked a wagon train and the post's beef herd at Cienega Amarilla (Yellow Swamp) near Black Creek, about eight miles south of the fort.

The warriors surprised four soldiers on a wood-cutting detail about 400 yards outside the corral; three were immediately cut down, but the fourth escaped. The Indians swept on toward the cattle, but the herd guard of 35 enlisted men from detachments of Companies B, C, E, and G, 3rd Infantry, held off the attackers. The Navajos made two determined charges. Two Indians were shot off their horses, and the rest could not get closer than 125 yards to the corral. Sergeant Gable of Company C tied a message for help around his dog's neck and sent it running to the fort.

About noon, a friendly Indian approached Fort Defiance with news of the fighting. Officers were skeptical until Gable's dog remarkably trotted in just then with the message. Meanwhile, more Navajos attacked a lumber detail in the mountains near the fort, and word of its predicament also came in. Capt. Oliver L. Shepherd, 3rd Infantry, took 50 men and headed out for the lumber camp, while Lt. Alexander N. Shipley and Lt. Silas Kendrick took 25 men south to Cienega Amarilla.

While the relief parties marched out, Huero's warriors attacked a mule train heading for the fort, severely wounding a teamster and killing one of the soldier escorts. By the time the rescuers arrived, the Navajos were gone. Lieutenant Kendrick counted 130 arrows protruding from the bodies of the three soldiers caught outside the corral, but the rest of the wood detail and herd guard were saved—all thanks to Sergeant Gable's dog. Unfortunately, the name of the canine hero was not recorded.[13]

# 17

# The Townsend Wagon Train (*The Big Trail*)

## Wyoming, July 1864

It appears that the standard tale that Indians never attacked large wagon trains, and that there was safety in numbers, didn't always stand the test of actual historical experience. Certainly there was more danger when traveling alone or in small parties, but a large number of wagons didn't guarantee immunity. The Shoshones and Bannocks hit the Smart and Adams trains, which were part of a larger group but were stretched thin at the time. They did not bother the entire assemblage when it consisted of about 180 wagons, yet they made a half-hearted attack on the 111-wagon section under Captain Walker.

How large a train would Indians venture to attack? The answer was found on the Bozeman Trail in 1864. John M. Bozeman was among the first to use the trail that would take his name, when, in 1862 and 1863 he took a route between the North Platte River in present Wyoming, and the Bannack and Virginia City mines in present Montana, along the east side of the Big Horn Mountains. In 1864 Bozeman was recruiting wagons along the North Platte, encouraging travelers to take his route as the shortest road to the mines—shortest, but not necessarily safest.

During the last days of June a great number of emigrants gathered near Richard's Bridge on the North Platte River, deciding whether to continue on the Oregon Trail, take Jim Bridger's Road to the Montana mines along the west side of the Big Horns, or Bozeman's route on the east side. Many of them chose Bozeman's route and moved north. On 1 July they were camped 30 miles north on Salt Creek, waiting for more wagons to come up to form a stronger party. Since Bozeman had already gone with the first train that season, the travelers elected officers and scouts to take them through: Captain A. A. Townsend, and guides John Boyer and Raphael Gallegos.

The train, the third of the season, consisted of emigrants mainly from Wisconsin, Illinois, and Iowa. Benjamin W. Ryan kept a detailed diary of the trip, and recorded that on 3 July they were ready to go, with a full train of 150 wagons, 375 men, 36 women, 56 children, 636 oxen, 79 horses, 10 mules, and 194 cows. The businesslike Ryan calculated that if all the men used every available weapon they carried, they could shoot 1,641 times without reloading—which ought to have been plenty to ward off any Indian attack.[1]

The guides led them down the alkaline, nearly dry Salt Creek. They reached good water at the Powder River on 5 July, crossed to the north bank, moved upstream three miles and camped. There they rested one day. On the morning of the 7th they pulled out but went only two miles before they corralled and had breakfast. A dust cloud announced approaching Indians, and the guides rode out to see what they wanted. The Indians, mostly Cheyennes led by Spotted Cow, said they were out searching for Crows, but demanded that the emigrants feed them and then turn the train around and return to the North Platte. The Indians ate, but grew quite belligerent regardless. Meanwhile, six suspicious emigrants, including Dr. Henry N. Crepin, T. J. Brundage, E. Butterfield, and Asher Newby, rode back over the trail to look for a man named Mills who had rode off earlier toward the first camp to look for a stray cow. The Indians left, and Captain Townsend began moving the wagons up the trail.

The six riders got about two miles east of the corralled train when they heard a shot; about 40 warriors were coming. Crepin tried to veer off toward the river, but the warriors countered his move and forced him back to the others. When the Indians got closer they fired but missed. The emigrants paused to fire a round, and then charged directly into the warriors, hoping to break through to the wagons. The wagons were hastily circled again on a flat next to the river, just above the mouth of the South Fork Powder and on the opposite side. Several men were stationed on a hilltop overlooking the corral, which proved to be a strategically sound move, for they could keep the Indians at a distance with their shooting.[2]

In their dash to break through to the wagons, Asher Newby, who had been a Confederate captain under John Hunt Morgan, was hit by an arrow in the back and fell from his horse. Other emigrants came out of the corral to fire at the pursuing Indians, while Brundage rode back to get the wounded Newby. The steel pointed arrow had gone three inches into his backbone and struck his left lung. Dr. Crepin attempted to remove the arrow but failed, while an army doctor named Hall succeeded in extracting it.

The Indians set fire to the surrounding prairie, but the men advanced in a ring around the wagons while the women and children helped dig a trench around the corral and carried buckets of water from the river to wet down the area. The emigrants, with long-range rifles, kept the Indians at bay. Even so, a man named A. Warren was hit in the bowels and died the next morning. At approximately 11 A.M., 15 warriors climbed down the bluffs and went north about one and a half miles where they encountered and killed Frank Hudelmeyer, who had foolishly left the train early in the morning to go hunting. After the Indians departed, some of the emigrants discovered his body, skewered by eleven arrows and a ball that had passed through his brain. The Indians kept up the siege until three in the afternoon. Townsend then crossed the wagons to the south side of the Powder, moved two miles upstream and camped for the night.

In addition to Warren, Mills was also killed. The next emigrants coming through in the Coffinbury Train found Mills's scalp hanging on a bush, and his horse and cow. They took the scalp to Virginia City, where Mills's brother identified it. One more man was missing and presumed killed. The seriously wounded Newby recovered. The Indians were probably Northern Cheyennes and Oglalas. The emigrants believed they had killed about 12 Indians, as well as wounding several more.[3]

That the Indians would confront and attack a train of 150 wagons and 467 people may have been a shock to the emigrants, who had been told that they needed to gather in large numbers for safety. The Indians' audacious action proved, once again, that Hollywood was not fabricating a tale when it depicted such scenes.

One of the earlier movies to include an attack on a large train was *The Big Trail* (Fox, 1930). Raoul Walsh directed the epic Western and, on the recommendation of John Ford, cast a relatively unknown actor, John Wayne, in the lead role as scout Breck Coleman. The film was shot in an early widescreen process called Grandeur, which still looks remarkable today. There are wagons and emigrants galore, with a supporting cast of hundreds of cattle, horses, dogs, chickens, and goats. The people behave realistically, doing daily chores, cooking, washing, repairing, and readying for the great journey, which will take the first wagon train to Oregon. Unfortunately, the movie did not do well at the box office, probably due to the Great Depression, which turned moviegoers' attentions to comedies rather than a serious epic about nation building. Wayne fell into the relative obscurity of the "B" Western until rescued in 1939 by John Ford, who cast him as the lead in *Stagecoach*.

The storyline of *The Big Trail* follows a great train of emigrants through its trials and tribulations as it breaks a new trail to Oregon. Breck Coleman is the scout who agrees to guide the train, but only because he believes the killers of his best friend are in the company. Indeed, the villains are the wagon boss, played by the dirty "he-grizzley" Red Flack (Tyrone Power Sr.), and his henchman Lopez (Charles Stevens). Coleman and Flack both know that one of them will have to die in the end, and they play a deadly cat-and-mouse game with each other throughout the trip.

Breck and Ruth Cameron (Marguerite Churchill), a pretty, unmarried young woman making the westward trek with her younger brother and sister, have a love-hate relationship. Ruth is torn between loving Breck because of his courteousness, good looks, and manliness, and hating him because his profession means he must kill when necessary. In one scene, a confused Breck says to himself, "Zeke always told me women were damn funny," which was notable because the taboo word "damn" was used onscreen in 1930, nine years before Clark Gable shocked audiences by using it in the final scenes of *Gone with the Wind*.

Bill Thorp (Ian Keith), a Louisiana gambler, tries to win Ruth's affections with his promises of marriage and lies of his owning a large plantation. Thorp takes up with Flack, and the two plot to kill Breck; but instead it is Thorp who is killed by Zeke (Tully Marshall), Breck's sidekick.

The wagon train crosses the prairie, journeys through a forest of huge trees, crosses a desert, and winds its way over mountains, all with the attendant snowstorms, rainstorms, swollen rivers, mud, dirt and dust. In a dramatic, but unrealistic, scene, the wagons are shown being winched and roped down a nearly vertical cliff. The episode was undoubtedly included to echo the story of emigrants using a windlass to lower wagons down a bluff at the North Platte River, near present-day Lewellen, Nebraska. The place was known as Windlass Hill, but whether emigrants really used the device is still debated. In any case, the Windlass Hill slope is much more gradual and practical for wagons than the cliffs in the movie—had any sane wagon boss come upon such a precipice, he certainly would have taken a hundred-mile detour rather than attempt the cliffs.

Of course, the film had to have its obligatory Indian attack. In a mountain valley, hundreds of Indians, said to be Cheyennes, charge at the wagons. Breck shouts out, "Corral! Corral!" and the train rapidly circles up in a large defensive perimeter. The movie emigrants stuff barrels, mattresses, and bedding in between the wagons to plug the gaps, just as the real emigrants in Walker's wagon train did during the Indian attack near City of Rocks. In one panoramic shot of the wagon circle there appears to be at least 50 corralled wagons. Before they left on their journey there was talk among the emigrants that they must gather up as many wagons as they could, because more wagons meant greater safety. Even so, they were attacked. The real folks of the Townsend Train waited on Salt Creek with the same idea in mind, and with the same result. Indians attacked whenever numbers and circumstances dictated a chance of success. A small train was undoubtedly at greater risk, but the story that Indians would not attack a large wagon train is false.

After two charges and riding in several circles around the wagon train, the Indians are beaten off. The emigrants bury the dead, which, judging by the number of mounds and crosses, appear to be about a dozen—certainly not an exaggeration when compared to historical instances. One woman leaves a doll on a little girl's grave, and they move on.

Near the end of the journey the emigrants are caught in the high mountain snows, and there is talk of turning back. Breck gives them his best Manifest Destiny speech:

The epic film *The Big Trail* (Fox, 1930), although a box office failure, was one of the best to show realistic sequences of a huge wagon train struggling with terrain and weather while crossing the continent.

> We can't turn back! We're blazing a trail that started in England. Not even the storms of the sea could turn back the first settlers. And they carried it on further. They blazed it on through the wilderness of Kentucky. Famine, hunger, not even massacres could stop them. And now we picked up the trail again. And nothing can stop us! Not even the snows of winter, nor the peaks of the highest mountain. We're building a nation and we got to suffer! No great trail was ever built without hardship. And you got to fight! That's right. And when you stop fighting, that's death. What are you going to do, lay down and die? Not in a thousand years! You're going on with me!

The story ends when they reach Oregon. Breck has fulfilled his promise to lead them across the country, but now he must kill Flack and Lopez.

"But, you can't do this awful thing," Ruth pleads with Breck.

"Frontier Justice," he replies.

Breck goes on to find Lopez frozen to death in the snow, and he ends Flack's life with one of the knife throws he is famous for. He returns to the sunny valley where Ruth and the other settlers have built their cabins, and they presumably live happily ever after.

*The Big Trail*, although not a box office success, did realistically depict the trials of an overland journey, right down to the circling Indian attack on a large wagon train. Hollywood, in its early years, although sometimes getting the details wrong, understood the concept.

# 18

## The Kelly-Larimer Wagon Train
### Wyoming, July 1864

Several days after the Townsend Train was attacked, Indians hit another party of emigrants on the Oregon Trail about 80 miles away. The train members were mostly from eastern Kansas, although Fanny Wiggins Kelly was born in Canada in 1845. She and her husband, Josiah H. Kelly, lived near Geneva for several years in what Fanny called a "pleasant prairie home" until Josiah's health failed. Hoping that a change of climate would help, Josiah packed up his family to move to Montana, at that time called Idaho Territory. They left in May 1864 for what Fanny called "the golden hills of Idaho." In the wagons were Josiah and Fanny Kelly; Mary Hurley (age 5), who was Fanny's niece and adopted daughter; Franklin, their Negro servant; Andrew Sullivan, Josiah's hired driver; and Gardner Wakefield. During the next couple of weeks Andrew Sharp, Mr. Taylor, William J. Larimer and his wife Sarah, and their son Frank (8) joined them. The emigrants made it safely to Fort Laramie, where they were assured that the road was safe and the Indians were friendly.[1]

Although a few other wagons joined up, the Kellys and Larimers preferred to travel in a small group since they could make better progress. Fanny Kelly tried to ease Mary's fear of Indians, telling her they were civil and harmless. Unfortunately, their idyll was shattered on 12 July as they dipped into a ravine and crossed Little Box Elder Creek, about four miles beyond LaPrele Station, where more than 200 Lakotas swept down on the train. Josiah thought they should defend themselves, but, considering the odds, Fanny and Sarah insisted on appeasement. The Indians swarmed around them, professing friendship. One Indian who spoke broken English introduced himself as "Ottawa." He said he was a good Indian, and told them they only wanted food and supplies. They expressed an interest in Josiah's best horse, and Josiah gave it to them. The emigrants fed the Indians; but with supper over, so was the charade, and the warriors turned on them and began the slaughter.

Mr. Kelly and Mr. Larimer were wounded but escaped. Wakefield was shot down and mortally wounded. Franklin was hit many times. Sharp went down a few feet from Fanny, and Taylor was shot in the forehead. The Indians plundered the wagons, taking what they wanted and destroying the rest. Sharp's wife later claimed they lost $1,005 in property. Warriors threw Fanny from the wagon, injuring her legs. Fanny begged a warrior not to kill her and Mary. They took Fanny, Sarah Larimer, and the two children captive.[2]

A lone wagon approached from behind, and the warriors went after it. They shot and killed a rider in front of the wagon; and the man driving spun the vehicle around, gave the reins to his wife, and fired at the pursuing warriors as the woman whipped the horses back to the main wagon train to the east.

Josiah and Andy hid for a time, and then ran for the other train. They spread the alarm, but were disappointed when the train leader chose to corral the wagons and wait for help.

At the attack scene, Sarah Larimer was distraught, saying, "The men have all escaped and left us to the mercy of the savages." Fanny thought it was better than being killed, because they might still be rescued. She put on a brave front, but admitted, "Those hours of misery can never be forgotten."[3]

That evening the Indians headed north. In the darkness, Fanny let Mary slip off the horse they were riding, with instructions to make her way along the creek to the main trail. The scheme seemed to work, and soon Fanny tried the same trick. She slid off her horse and crouched on the ground, but Indians following behind found and beat her. She told them Mary had fallen off and she was trying to find her. They put Fanny back on the horse and said they would find the girl in the morning. Some Indians did find Mary, but they killed and scalped her, and left her body on the trail.

Fanny Kelly, taken from a wagon train in Wyoming in July 1864 (courtesy Kansas State Historical Society).

When Josiah finally got the other emigrant train to move forward the next day, they rescued Mr. Larimer, who had hidden in the bushes all night, and buried the bodies of the lone rider, Mr. Sharp, Mr. Taylor, and Franklin. Franklin's legs had been pinned together by an arrow and his skull was crushed. Mr. Wakefield was discovered alive in some brush about a mile from the scene of the attack. He'd been hit by three arrows, and in the interim had attempted to remove them, succeeding only in breaking the shafts and leaving the steel points embedded in his body. Sullenly, they moved on to Deer Creek Station at present-day Glenrock, Wyoming, and reported the attack. A telegraph message was sent to Fort Laramie, and Col. William O. Collins, 11th Ohio Cavalry, ordered a pursuit. Josiah Kelly accompanied the soldiers, but the chase resulted in little else than the death of Lt. John R. Brown of Company E, 11th Ohio. Fanny Kelly was gone.[4]

Surprisingly, on the second night after the wagon train attack, while the Indians made their first camp, the Larimers escaped. Fanny had been tied up for the night because of her previous escape attempt; and before they were separated, Sarah made Fanny promise not to leave her. Instead, Sarah and Frank Larimer crept away in the darkness, leaving Fanny behind. After four days of wandering, tired and hungry, they stumbled onto Deer Creek Station and were reunited with William Larimer, who was there recovering from his wound. When he could travel again, they gave up the idea of going to Montana and returned to Kansas.[5]

Lakotas took Fanny north to the Tongue River. Along the way, as in the story of Hansel and Gretel, she tore up bits of paper, hoping to leave a trail for any would-be rescuers. Incredibly,

Little Box Elder Creek, Wyoming, near the site of the July 1864 attack on the Kelly-Larimer wagons.

one of her notes was found 12 years later by Lt. James H. Bradley, 7th Infantry. Bradley was on a scout for Col. John Gibbon in the preliminary stages of the campaign that resulted in the Battle of the Little Bighorn. On 21 May, 1876, he found an Indian burial scaffold near the junction of the Rosebud and Yellowstone Rivers. Among the items buried with the warrior was a paper signed by Fanny Kelly that concluded, "I am compelled to do their bidding." This convinced Bradley that Fanny was forced into a "worse fate than death!"[6]

The Indians, with Kelly in tow, moved north of the Black Hills. In late July 1864 they reached a large village near the badlands east of the Little Missouri, and near a prominence called Killdeer Mountain. There, on 28 July, Brig. Gen. Alfred Sully and 2,200 soldiers attacked about 3,000 warriors in what was one of the largest battles of all the Indian wars. By the day's end, Sully forced the Indians to flee to the west, taking Fanny with them. After Sully turned back to the Missouri River to re-supply, the Indians moved into what is now southwestern North Dakota. On the horizon they spotted another wagon train coming from the east, crossing their land in a place where they had never seen any wagon trains before.

# 19

## The Fisk Wagon Train (*Kentucky Rifle*)

### North Dakota, September 1864

Discoveries of gold in what is now Idaho and Montana led to opening new trails to the mines, of which John Bozeman's was one. Not all emigrants and gold seekers, however, trekked along the Oregon Trail before branching off to the north. Residents of the upper Great Lakes States, Minnesota and Iowa sought a shorter route to the mines. They wanted to go directly across the Dakotas, but were deterred by thousands of hostile Sioux. Minnesota citizens finally prevailed upon the government to provide money for an escort. Capt. James Liberty Fisk, using his political connections, was given orders to organize, equip, and conduct an escort for an emigrant train going from Minnesota to Fort Benton on the Missouri. Fisk took trains across in 1862 and 1863, traveling along the left bank of the Missouri. In 1864, new discoveries of precious metals led to even more emigrants and fortune-seekers looking for a shortcut to the promised land.

Once again, Captain Fisk was selected to lead the latest "Montana and Idaho Expedition." Taking advantage of the soldier movements across the plains during the current Dakota War, Fisk left Fort Ridgely in Minnesota and took a more southerly route than in the previous two years, striking the Missouri River at Fort Rice. Serious trouble was almost guaranteed when Fisk decided he would not follow the Missouri upstream as in previous years, but would take a shortcut across country. Fisk was warned about hostile Lakotas, badlands, and poor grass and water, but he considered the warnings a trick to get him to go by river to Fort Berthold, where he would have to pay exorbitant prices for supplies.

General Sully had just fought the Sioux at Killdeer Mountain and in the Badlands, where he had to protect one train of what he called "draft dodging" miners, and he in no mood to protect another one. Nevertheless, Fisk pulled out of Fort Rice on 23 August, with 88 wagons and 200 emigrants. He even inveigled an escort of 47 soldiers under Lieutenant Smith of Company A, Dakota Cavalry. Sully wrote to Gen. John Pope, in command of the Department of the Northwest, that Fisk and his emigrants "can't go forward on their trail; there is no grass and very little water. Fisk was told of this before he started from here, but he, though he had never been over the country before, knew better."[1]

Fisk trailed up the Cannonball River and went about 130 miles west of Fort Rice when Sully's prediction came true. On 2 September, as they descended into one of the cutbanks of upper Deep Creek about ten miles east of the present-day town of Marmarth, North Dakota, one wagon overturned while struggling to cross the defile, and two more pulled over to assist. The train moved on while repairs were made, and nine soldiers stayed behind as guards. Fisk had only traveled one mile ahead when gunfire came from the direction of the creek behind him. He corralled the train while 50 soldiers and citizens hurried to the rescue.

Sitting Bull and 100 Hunkpapas attacked the unsuspecting wagons and grappled with the surprised whites in a hand-to-hand fight. One soldier put a bullet into Sitting Bull's left hip, which exited out of his back. White Bull and Jumping Bull pulled Sitting Bull to safety. Jumping Bull patched up Sitting Bull's wound, and he was spirited off to the Lakota village six miles distant to recover.

The Hunkpapas cut down most of the defenders in the first few minutes, using arrows, tomahawks, and knives, with only one escaping. The free man ran toward Fisk's Train, and was met by scout Jefferson Dilts, who was racing to the rescue ahead of the rest. Dilts recklessly charged the surprised Indians looting the wagons. Blasting away with his carbine and six-gun, he shot six Indians before reining his horse around and racing back. He was not fast enough; Dilts took three arrows in the back.

The men following Dilts now reached the scene and ran right into the Hunkpapas. They had to fort up and fight until sunset. After dark they headed back to the train. The rescue action cost the lives of ten soldiers and two civilians, including Dilts. Six Hunkpapas were killed, probably most of them by Dilts. One of the wagons captured by the Hunkpapas contained 4,000 bullets and many rifles, and another contained liquor and cigars. The Indians were perhaps too excited about their newfound jackpot to attack Fisk's wagons that night.

Fisk continued on a few miles the next morning but had to corral the wagons when the Indians renewed the attack. The defenders built sod walls six feet tall to protect themselves, and hollowed out gunslits for the mountain howitzer they carried. They named their fortification Fort Dilts in honor of the brave scout. More than 400 Lakotas probed the earthworks on 5 September, but the defenders took no casualties. Lieutenant Smith and 13 men crept out that night to ride to Fort Rice for help. The fortification proved secure; Fisk's trapped company had sufficient water from a nearby spring, and their wagons were loaded with plenty of supplies. Although Fisk was stuck at Fort Dilts for more than two weeks, the men did not suffer greatly. Smith and his men reached Fort Rice in 56 hours.

The Lakotas attacked several times during the siege, and one of the troopers spotted a white woman on a near-by bluff. It was Fanny Kelly. The Lakotas forced her to write a letter to negotiate for them. Under a truce flag, three warriors placed the note on a forked stick in plain sight of the circled wagons. Two other notes were exchanged. The Indians demanded supplies in exchange for Fanny and freedom for the wagon train to pass through the territory. Kelly carefully phrased the notes, warning of the Indians' treachery. Fisk responded, offering three horses, flour, sugar, and coffee for her, but the Lakotas wanted 40 head of cattle and four wagons. To Kelly's dismay, Fisk would not meet the demands; the Indians would not release her and rode away after a few more days.

Finally, on 18 September, an angry General Sully dispatched 900 men to rescue Fisk and escort the wagon train back to Fort Rice. The siege ended two days later. Fisk, however, was not pleased that the army demanded he return to Fort Rice. Fisk tried to talk them into escorting him west for two more days. When they refused, Fisk challenged the emigrants to either go forward with him to the Yellowstone or return with the soldiers to the Missouri. The officers would have none of it; they forced Fisk to return, and the result was the end of the Army Escort Service.[2]

As for Fanny Kelly, she remained captive nearly another two months. By October, the Lakotas had not driven the army out of their territory; and since it would be a dangerous winter with so many soldiers nearby, they suddenly became more conciliatory. On 23 October, about 200 Lakotas negotiated for peace with Capt. John H. Pell at Fort Sully. Pell pressed his advantage and said that the soldiers would not stop fighting until the white woman was released. Brings

## 19. The Fisk Wagon Train

Grave of Jefferson Dilts, buried within the corral of the Fisk Wagon Train, September 1864.

Plenty, Fanny's owner, would not negotiate until Sitting Bull intervened. Sitting Bull's honor was at stake more than his desire to help the white men, and the chief's implicit menace finally persuaded Brings Plenty. On 9 December a delegation of Blackfeet Sioux brought Fanny Kelly to Fort Sully. The gate opened, and once she crossed the threshold the gate slammed behind her. "Am I free, indeed free?" she asked.

Fanny remembered it differently. She said her captor sold her to the Blackfeet, who planned to use her as a decoy to get into the fort. She sent a note to the commander and warned him, and a number of soldiers of the 6th Iowa Cavalry stationed there confirmed her version. When the Blackfeet brought her in she was rushed through the gate, and the trailing Indians, decked out in paint and singing war songs, were shut out. She was poorly clad, her limbs were nearly frozen, and she had to be confined to the fort hospital for two months.[3]

Fanny finally was reunited with husband Josiah, and she became a minor celebrity. Josiah died in 1867, and Fanny was invited to Cheyenne, Wyoming, to share the home of Mr. and Mrs. Larimer. All was not well, however; for in October 1870 Fanny Kelly filed a lawsuit against Sarah Larimer. The women had agreed that they would prepare a joint memoir of their experiences, with both names appearing as co-authors; but in May 1869 Sarah took the manuscript to Philadelphia, where it was published in her name only and as her own work. Clearly, almost all of the Indian captivity experiences were Fanny's. At the first trial, Kelly recovered a judgment of $5,000. Two more appeals followed, and the women became bitter enemies. Fanny Kelly published her own version of the story in 1871. Neither woman, unlike Cresta in *Soldier Blue*, or Ellen Grange in *Duel at Diablo*, ever had intentions of returning to the Indians. Fanny died in 1904, and Sarah sometime after that.[4]

Although James Fisk captained a large train of 88 wagons and 200 men, it was the breakdown of one wagon that prompted the Indians to begin the attack. A similar breakdown of one

Sterling Holloway and Chill Wills stand by their lone wagon, figuring how to get their rifles through the pass guarded by Indians in *Kentucky Rifle* (Howco Productions Inc., 1956).

wagon gets the plot rolling in *Kentucky Rifle* (1956). Tobias Taylor (Chill Wills) and Jason Clay (Lance Fuller) are two men taking a wagonload of Kentucky Rifles west so that frontier settlers can defend themselves. When the wagon's axle snaps, the train has to move on, and several men and women remain behind until they can make repairs. When one man realizes the repairs will take longer than expected, he tries to get back to his wife in the main train that night, but Comanches kill him.

The next day the Indians come in to bargain, and when they discover the wagon contains rifles, they want to exchange the emigrants' lives for the guns. Clay refuses, but Dan Foster (Jess Barker) goes alone to the Comanche camp and tells them they will give the rifles for their lives. When Clay still refuses, the Indians say that they will not let Foster go, and will kill him unless they get the guns. Finally Clay agrees, but when Foster learns the Indians still plan to ambush the whites as they go through the mountain pass, he breaks free to try and warn them.

The Indians shoot Foster and attack the wagon, but are driven off by the few emigrants shooting their Kentucky Rifles, even while handicapped by the pacifist Preacher Bently (Henry Hull) and the inept Lon Setter (Sterling Holloway), with his Winnie the Pooh voice. After the whites nearly decimate the attacking Comanches, the Indians agree to let the emigrants go through the pass in peace ... almost. As the lone wagon traverses the pass, one renegade warrior shoots an arrow into Tobias's back, killing him. (In some respects, this is a relief, because Tobias spent half the movie singing "Sweet Betsy from Pike" and aggravatingly chirping praises of the amazing attributes of his beloved Kentucky Rifle.)

Overall, the movie is not very memorable, but it does illustrate that Indians did use captured whites in negotiations, and it shows the real threat faced by small parties of emigrants in the West, even with a large train just over the hill. What it does not show is that even a large train, such as Fisk's, was also at risk.

# 20

# The Ake-Wadsworth Wagon Train
(*The Outriders, How the West Was Won*)

## New Mexico, August 1861

The museum-historical facility in Abilene, called Frontier Texas, uses many innovative methods (including holograms) to tell the story of westward expansion. In the introductory video, a cowboy draws a line in the sand and says the line represents the frontier, one side known and the other side unknown. The nutshell explanation is not wholly accurate, for the frontier never was a solid line advancing west, and as we have seen with the Horn-Harris, Wilson, and McBride-Andrews trains, "go-backs" blurred any such line of demarcation.

Disgruntled emigrants were not the only ones heading back east. With the comparatively easy placer mining in California long played out, prospectors and traders from Shasta Valley, under John Richardson, were heading east to test their luck in the Idaho gold mines. On 24 June, 1864, they were on the Yreka-John Day Road near Silver Lake, Oregon, about 70 miles northeast of Fort Klamath, when Indians attacked. The Paiutes, under Howluck (Bigfoot), surprised the eight-wagon train, which included 23 men, two families, and about eight women, but the open country gave them time to circle their wagons into a defensive perimeter.

Even so, the war party severely wounded two men, stole seven cattle, cut out a few wagons, and destroyed 3,000 pounds of flour. Richardson retreated after the Paiutes pulled away, and came upon a second train under a Mr. Allen, heading out from Jacksonville, Oregon, with nine wagons and 21 men. Both trains fell back south to the ford on Sprague River about 30 miles east of Fort Klamath, where they found Lt. Col. Charles S. Drew, who was heading to the Owyhee Country with elements of the 1st Oregon Cavalry. Richardson and Allen decided against taking the Yreka-John Day Road and elected to accompany Drew as he broke new road heading east across southern Oregon.[1]

The Civil War years saw increased travel on the western trails and roads. A steady supply of gold was all-important to finance the Union war effort. Gold and silver shipments headed east, thousands of civilians fleeing the fighting in the east headed west, the southwest became a battleground between Union and Confederate forces, and Apaches began raiding with increased ferocity. Amid the turmoil and danger, many residents of New Mexico Territory decided to return east. Early in the war, in August 1861, a number of ranchers and farmers from the Tubac, Sonoita, and Tucson areas, many of them Confederate sympathizers, gathered together to follow the Union soldiers as they left for the eastern war zone. The largest group of wagons was under Felix Grundy Ake and William Wadsworth. In Tucson, Moses Carson, Kit Carson's half-brother, joined them. When they moved east in mid-month, the train consisted of six double wagons, two buggies, a single wagon, 24 men, 16 women, and seven children. They drove hundreds of cattle, sheep, goats, and horses.

While camped on the banks of the Mimbres River on the night of 26 August, they were visited by an excited man named Eugene Zimmer, who had been driving cattle east through Cooke's Canyon the day before. Indians attacked him, killed two of his Mexican herders and stealing the cattle. Zimmer, with his agitated manner and thick German accent, was not believed. The next morning the Ake-Wadsworth party moved east to enter Cooke's Canyon. Waiting for them were Cochise and Mangas Coloradas with nearly 200 warriors.

The livestock entered the pass first, followed by the mounted men, then the vehicles. At the narrowest point near the eastern end there was not enough room for two wagons to ride side by side. Just then, one man noticed the nude bodies of the Mexican herders killed the day before. When word was passed along the line, several riders at the rear of the column, including Sam Houston, nephew of the famous Texan, deserted and rode back to the Mimbres. This left only about 17 males to fight the Indians. When nothing else happened, the wagons continued cautiously forward. When the wagons were in the narrowest part of the canyon, however, the hillsides burst to life as more than 50 Apache rifles barked out. Leading the train, John St. Clair and James May were killed, and several horses went down, blocking the train's forward movement. William Redding and a few mounted settlers charged the Indians to divert their attention while Jack Pennington tried to turn the wagons around. A bullet broke Redding's leg, but he stayed in the saddle until several more shots killed him.

Robert and America Phillips grabbed their son, left their wagon, and made it back to a small triangle formed by Ake's wagons. From their little fort, Carson, Wadsworth, Ake, Nathaniel Sharp, and an Indian named Chickasaw Brown fought back with determination. While loading his musket, Jim Cotton accidentally discharged the weapon and sent the spear-like ramrod into his leg. Sharp caught an arrow in the neck and ear, but pulled the barb clean through and kept fighting. The Indians were more concerned with rounding up all the livestock, or they would surely have overrun them. As the attackers drove the animals away, Ake and Wadsworth left the fort and climbed a hill for a better shot. Chiricahua snipers pumped two bullets into Wadsworth, and Tom Farrell went out to aid the two men, shooting one Apache in the process but taking a bullet in the back for his efforts. Ake left his would-be rescuer lying on the ground and went back to the wagons, leaving Farrell for Sharp and Jack Pennington to retrieve.

The battle then evolved into a long-range sniping affair, with Cochise and Mangas seeing no need to rush the wagon corral. They had the stock that they wanted, and they had killed a few Americans. In the early afternoon, teamster Mariano Madrid killed one more Apache, and the Indians finally withdrew with perhaps 400 cattle and 900 sheep. The Apaches lost about five killed, while the returning emigrants had four killed and about eight wounded.[2]

The incident showed that Indians did ambush wagons at constricted points on the trails, as well as on the open prairie or desert. "Head 'em off at the pass" was in the Indians' tactical manual. It was also true that in many instances raiding Indians wanted to steal stock more than kill the owners. If American or Mexican freighters, teamsters, mule drivers, cowboys, or herders got in the way, they would probably be killed as a consequence; but many times, murder was not the main reason for the raid. Some Apaches realized that it would be folly to kill all the Anglos and Mexicans who trailed stock across their lands; if they were all dead, who would continue to bring them more?

In *The Outriders* (MGM, 1950), three Confederate soldiers, one of them Will Owens (Joel McCrae), escape from a Union prison camp and become unwillingly involved with guerrilla William Quantrill's raiders. They have to escort a wagon train leaving Santa Fe for Missouri, with the plan to lead the train, which is carrying gold, into Quantrill's hands. On the way, Will begins to have misgivings, especially when the beautiful Jen Gort (Arlene Dahl) distracts him from his task. There is the obligatory Indian menace; however, these Indians do not attack. Will Owens realizes that they are much more interested in the wagon train's horses than in killing the whites. When he turns the horses over to the Indians, they let the train proceed.

There is a scene in the epic *How the West Was Won* (MGM, 1962), filmed in Monument Valley, wherein Cheyennes attack a wagon train traveling through the desert. Being outnumbered, the wagon boss, Roger Morgan (Robert Preston), decides to run for it, but gambler Cleve Van Halen (Gregory Peck) questions his decision. Morgan says they'll run and then cut the lead horses loose for the Indians. "Chances are they want our stock more than they do us," he says.

The train races along, with a few wagons overturning and emigrants shooting at Indians from under the wagon covers. A number of men climb out onto the racing horses and mules and cut them loose. These animals, plus the cattle they round up are truly what the Indians wanted, and they break off the attack. Once again, movie plots echo history.

Cooke's Canyon, New Mexico, where the Ake-Wadsworth wagons were attacked in August 1861.

# 21

## The Blinn-Buttles Wagon Train (*Little Big Man, The Searchers*)

### Colorado, October 1868

Another party of would-be emigrants to the West found that conditions were not always as sanguine as pictured, and that maybe the old homestead back East wasn't so bad after all. Clara Isabel Harrington was born in Elmore, Ohio, in 1847. She married Civil War veteran Richard F. Blinn in 1865, and they settled in Perrysburg, Ohio. One year later they had a son, William. Clara was slightly built, with dimples and freckles. She was described as a practical joker, beautiful, exuberant, and vibrant. Her parents moved in 1868 to take up a new life in Ottawa, Kansas. The Blinns also pulled up stakes, but Richard thought they would go beyond Kansas. They left Ohio on 15 March, 1868, bound for, as Richard wrote in his diary, "Sand Creek Colorado Territory."

They took a train to Kansas City, where they bought mules and wagons and traveled west with a few others, including Richard Blinn's brother-in-law and sister, John F. Buttles and Sarah. The emigrants went to Fort Dodge and continued up the Arkansas River along the Santa Fe Trail, reaching Sand Creek on 20 April. "Here we are at last," Blinn recorded. "Everything looks nice. I like the place first rate."[1]

Richard ran a rest station near the mouth of the Big Sandy (Sand Creek) and the Arkansas River, but the job did not go well. Work was hard, and Richard's arm, wounded in the Civil War, never fully healed. Clara was homesick and fearful of Indians, so they decided to go back to Kansas and build a cabin near her parents. Richard formed a partnership with his brother-in-law, Jack Buttles, to furnish supplies to government posts as they headed east. They organized an eight-wagon train with 100 head of cattle and eight men, and left Boggsville, Colorado Territory, on 5 October. Clara carried all of the outfit's money, belonging to Richard, his brother Hubbell, and Jack Buttles—nearly $800 in greenbacks and gold coin.

By 9 October they had traveled about 50 miles along the Santa Fe Trail and stopped "this side of Sand Creek at three mile point" for an early dinner. After eating, they decided to put on a few more miles before nightfall. The largest wagon, with Clara and Willie aboard, pulled out ahead of the others. At that moment a band of about 75 Cheyennes attacked, split the train, and ran the lead wagon across the Arkansas River. The warriors cut off the men with the rear wagons, circled around, and shot flaming arrows, setting several wagons on fire. The defenders dug a breastwork around the wagons and were trapped there for five days, with the number of attacking Indians growing to nearly 200. Hubbell Blinn said no one was killed, but two suffered wounds, one in the nose and another in the knee. Finally, one or more of the men broke out and made it back to Fort Lyon, reaching there at three in the morning of 14 October. At daybreak, Lt. Henry H. Abell, 7th Cavalry, and ten soldiers rode to the rescue, but it was too late. They found the burned remains of the supply wagon, but Clara and Willie, who had been hiding under a feather bed, were long gone.[2]

After being captured, Clara, like Fanny Kelly, had the presence of mind to scribble a note on a card and drop it on a bush about four miles downstream from the attack site. It read: "Dear Dick, Willie and I are prisoners. They are going to keep us. If you live, save us if you can. We are with them. Clara Blinn." The other side read: "Dick, if you love us, save us." The card was found and given to the distraught Richard Blinn.[3]

The attacking Cheyennes were from bands that had been recently raiding in Kansas. The Arapahos, Cheyennes, Comanches, and Kiowas had promised, in treaties signed in 1865 and 1867, that they would stop depredating and taking white hostages; but the promises meant little.

Many of the raiders belonged to the band of Black Kettle, the ostensible "peace" chief of the Southern Cheyennes. Black Kettle's warriors were not new to the business of raiding, killing, and taking hostages. Back in 1864 they used Nancy Morton, Lucinda Eubank, and Laura Roper, along with four children, as hostage pawns in an attempt to buy peace — a move that backfired on them and resulted in the Battle of Sand Creek in November 1864. Black Kettle never could, or never bothered to, make his village off-limits to marauders.[4]

After the latest round of raids in Kansas, warriors vacated the state and headed for Indian Territory. Some of the bands swung into Colorado Territory first, where they destroyed the Blinn-Buttles Train and captured Clara and Willie. The Indians believed they had good bargaining chips with which to deal for peace, much as they had believed in the late summer of 1864. That idea had miscarried, as would this one.

In late October 1868, a trader operating out of Fort Cobb, William Griffenstein, learned that there was a white woman and child in Black Kettle's camp. Clara wrote a letter, dated 7 November, in which she pleaded for someone to buy her and her child. She said she would work for her rescuer and "do all that I could for you." She also told Kansas Governor Samuel Crawford that if peace was made she would be freed. "For our sakes," she penned, "do all you can and god will bless you."[5]

The Cheyennes had raped and abused other white captives, but Clara Blinn may not have been treated as badly, although Willie was apparently beaten and starved. The Cheyennes probably realized that if they were to use Blinn to get their demands, she must not be returned as "damaged goods." Griffenstein showed Clara's letter to Col. William B. Hazen, 38th Infantry, at Fort Cobb, Indian Territory. Hazen forwarded the letter to Gen.

Clara Blinn, taken from a wagon train in Colorado in October 1868 (courtesy Kansas State Historical Society).

William T. Sherman on 25 November, along with his own letter stating that he told Griffenstein to negotiate for the Blinns' release and "to spare no expense in his effort to reclaim these parties." The letter did not reach Sherman in St. Louis until 18 December.

On 20 November, Black Kettle, Big Mouth and other chiefs came to Fort Cobb to discuss peace and talk about ransoming white captives. Hazen knew the army was actively campaigning against them, and he could not make a separate treaty. Although Black Kettle was ostensibly at Fort Cobb to discuss peace, he did say, as Hazen recorded it, "that many of his men were then on the war path, and that their people did not want peace with the people above the Arkansas." Hazen directed them to go back to their villages and deal directly with General Sheridan. Clara and Willie Blinn were disposable pawns.[6]

On the same day Hazen forwarded Blinn's letter to Sherman, Lt. Col. George A. Custer and the 7th Cavalry were already in Indian Territory hunting the Cheyennes. Combating the cold, wind, and snow, Custer followed a fresh trail that led directly to Black Kettle's camp on the Washita River. Custer did not know about the white captives in the village, nor did he know whose village his cavalry struck on the frigid dawn of 27 November, 1868. As the troopers splashed across the Washita, chaos erupted and gunfire reverberated in the frosty air. Some Indians fought, but most of them scattered. Black Kettle and Little Rock were killed. Custer captured the camp, burned the teepees, and shot 875 Indian ponies. He reported killing 103 Indians and capturing 53. The battle was not one-sided, for 21 soldiers were killed and 16 were wounded. Among the casualties were Clara and Willie Blinn.

Custer pulled his troops out that evening, went back to Camp Supply, Indian Territory, obtained provisions and reinforcements (including the 19th Kansas Cavalry), and returned to the scene of the fight on 10 December. The Blinn bodies were discovered just east of the village site, in the direction most of the Indians fled. Doctor Bailey described a small white woman and an undernourished child with a bruised cheek. Doctor Henry Lippincott said Clara had one bullet hole above the left eyebrow, and that her head was scalped, her skull extensively fractured. Willie's body showed evidence of violence about the head and face. There was a report that one or both of Clara's breasts were hacked off, and that Willie's head was smashed against a tree. On Clara's stomach was a piece of cornbread, leading Bailey to speculate that she was trying to hide some food for an escape attempt. Nearby was a wrapped package of paper money and gold coins. Men of the 19th Kansas filed past the bodies until someone finally recognized them.[7]

Clara and Willie's bodies, along with that of Maj. Joel Elliott, who was killed in the battle, were wrapped in blankets and taken by ambulance for burial at Fort Arbuckle, IT. They were buried with military honors on Christmas Day, 1868. Richard Blinn still did not know of their fate, and spent the next four months searching for them. At Fort Cobb on 16 January, 1869, Blinn was given a piece of Clara's dress, her shoes, and Willie's hair. He went to Fort Arbuckle in February, where he finally reached the graves of his wife and child; but with little money, he gave up on the idea of taking their remains back to Kansas. Richard moved back to Perrysburg, Ohio, where he died of tuberculosis in 1873.

Some time after Fort Arbuckle was abandoned in June 1870, the bodies in the cemetery were reinterred at Fort Gibson, IT. By then, the identification of Clara and Willie Blinn's remains were lost. They rest today at the Fort Gibson Cemetery simply as "Unknown Woman" and "Unknown."[8]

A major episode in *Little Big Man* (1970) depicts Custer's attack on the Washita in a nascent example of what would become the standard treatment of the frontier military: Custer and his men are no better than savage murderers, killing men, women, and children without compunction or discrimination. There is absolutely no mention of white captives being held in the village.[9] Instead, one of the inhabitants is a white man, Jack Crabb (Dustin Hoffman), who has

Richard Mulligan as the insane George Custer just before his death at the Little Bighorn in ***Little Big Man*** (Stockbridge/Hiller, 1970). The film was a centerpiece for the transformation of Indians from villains to innocent victims, and white men from the good guys to the bad.

lived voluntarily with the Indians for many years ever since he and his sister were "rescued" from a wagon train destroyed by other Indians.

The scenario is outrageous. When Jack and his teenage sister Caroline (Carole Androsky) are taken by the Indians, it soon becomes apparent that Caroline *wants* to be raped, and is disappointed that she isn't. Her rather husky, masculine appearance apparently fools the Indians into thinking she is a boy. The Indians are embarrassed that they smoked a pipe with her in their teepee, and Caroline is embarrassed that they thought she was a male and didn't molest her. Caroline lights out for civilization, but Jack stays on with the tribe, becoming Little Big Man.

When Custer (Richard Mulligan), who is portrayed as a self-righteous, pompous glory-hunter, attacks the village of Old Lodge Skins (Chief Dan George), he lets his men run amok. Old Lodge Skins and Little Big Man escape, but Little Big Man's wife, Sunshine (Aimee Eccles), and her baby are mercilessly gunned down, along with most of the remaining villagers.

"Do you hate them now, grandfather?" Little Big Man asks Old Lodge Skins.

Perhaps surprisingly, the old man still tries to see good in mankind, even in the whites. The audience, however, has most likely come to hate the white soldiers (the movie was, in fact, an anti–Vietnam War polemic trying to draw parallels between the My Lai massacre and the Washita by showing American soldiers as savages and Indians as helpless victims).[10] The trend continued along the same avenue through *Dances with Wolves* (1990).

*Little Big Man* portrays Custer as a savage because he killed Indians, and the savagery extends to his order to destroy the Indians' ponies. The soldiers kill hundreds of snorting, squealing horses. Indeed, the white men must be barbarians to do such a thing to harmless horses. Yet, there was a military necessity to capture the horses needed for your own force and destroy the rest to prevent their use by the enemy. It was not a new or unique tactic. Other commanders, such as Col. Ranald Mackenzie, did the same.

A scene in *The Searchers*, wherein Ethan (John Wayne) and Martin (Jeffrey Hunter) reach the winter camp of Lieutenant Colonel Custer, is suggestive of Custer's camp after the Washita battle. In the film, the two searchers find several rescued white women and children, all much the worse for wear. In reality, Custer rescued no captives at the Washita, for Clara and Willie were killed before he could get to them. Learning of their deaths later, however, Custer changed his tactics when he next went after Indians who held white captives, and successfully recovered Sarah White and Anna Morgan without attacking the Indian villages.

# 22

## The Templeton, Kirkendall, and Floyd Wagon Trains (*Red River*)

### Wyoming, July 1866

Thus far, we have only examined one attack on the Bozeman Trail, that of the Townsend Wagon Train in 1864. Danger increased in 1866 after the army built a series of forts to "protect" travelers. Fort Reno on Powder River, Fort Phil Kearny on the Little Piney, and Fort C. F. Smith on the Bighorn were in operation in the summer of 1866, but their presence only seemed to anger the Indians and may have created more problems for travelers than they solved.

Peter Cazeau and Henry Arrison were traders from Fort Collins, Colorado Territory, using the Bozeman Trail. With them in their two wagons were three employees, Cazeau's Oglala wife Mary, and their four children. On 16 July, 1866, they were camped on Peno Creek, six miles north of Fort Phil Kearny, when a band of Northern Cheyennes joined them. The Cheyennes had just been in council with soldiers at the fort, and were peacefully inclined. Later, however, some angry Oglala Lakotas appeared, demanding that the Cheyennes join them in a war against the soldiers. "French Pete" Cazeau tried to remain neutral, while hoping that the Cheyennes would convince the Lakotas not to go to war — at least until he got away. The Cheyennes refused to fight, and the Lakotas, about 300 of them, called them cowards, whipped them, and drove them from the camp.

The Oglalas left at nightfall, and Cazeau may have thought he had dodged a bullet, but early the next morning the Oglalas returned and attacked the train that was trying to get out of the area. They killed Arrison, Cazeau, and the three hired men. Mary Cazeau and the children escaped into the brush; soldiers later found them and took them to the fort. Mary warned the military that there were thousands of hostile warriors in the area, and that they planned to steal all the stock from the fort, kill all Americans, and completely stop travel on the road.[1]

Mary Cazeau's warning proved prophetic. On 20 July, 1866, a small 18th Infantry detachment, under Lt. George Templeton, headed north to Fort Phil Kearny with 29 soldiers as an escort for the wife of Lt. Alexander Wands, the wife of Sgt. F. M. Fessenden, a servant, and several children. They passed Fort Reno and went down Dry Creek to its junction with Crazy Woman Creek. Scouting ahead, Templeton and Lt. Napoleon H. Daniels were jumped by more than 50 warriors. They killed Daniels, and Templeton barely made it back to the train with an arrow in his back and a wound to his face.

Still, he ordered the train corralled and organized the defense while the attacking Indians wounded several men and killed a few mules. In the afternoon, several soldiers slipped out to try and get water. At sunset, two soldiers volunteered to ride back to Fort Reno for help. Just then, another train of 34 wagons and 47 men, under Capt. Thomas B. Burrowes, was approaching from the northwest. Burrowes was unaware that anything was wrong until he sighted Templeton's corralled train and came across the body of Pvt. Terrence Callery, who had left the train earlier to hunt.

The two trains forted up together, and on 21 July scouts found the body of Lieutenant Daniels, stripped, scalped, and pierced with 22 arrows. Responding to the call for help, Lt. Thaddeus S. Kirtland and 13 men rode in, and Captain Burrowes took the lot of them back to Fort Reno on 22 July. Two men were killed and six wounded.[2]

After burying Lieutenant Daniels at Fort Reno, Captain Burrowes turned back to Fort Phil Kearny with the Templeton party and a large supply train of 100 wagons. On the 23rd he caught up with the civilian wagon train of Hugh Kirkendall, with 43 wagons; the Tootle and Leach Train of 24 wagons; and the John Walker Train of five wagons, which had left Fort Reno the day before. The combined trains consisted of nearly 200 wagons and stretched six miles across the plains.

The first wagons reached Clear Creek, near present-day Buffalo, Wyoming, on the afternoon of the 24th, and corralled. Kirkendall's Train lagged behind about six miles south and was unable to get in that evening. They circled their wagons for the night when 25 Indians unsuccessfully tried to stampede their mules. In the meantime, William Dillon, with the Tootle and Leach Train, left camp with five men to see what was holding up Kirkendall. When Indians found them, Dillon's small party dismounted, shot their horses, and used their bodies and the saddles as barricades. After four hours of fighting they tried to make a run for Kirkendall's corral. Dillon was critically wounded, and while two men carried him, the remaining three walked backwards, shooting at their pursuers. Finally, Kirkendall realized what was happening and sent a party out to their rescue. The sight of approaching rescuers convinced the Indians to break off their pursuit.

Burrowes learned of the attack and sent couriers to Fort Phil Kearny for help, while dispatching 16 men to assist Kirkendall and Dillon. They broke through the Indians' ring and rode into the encircled corrals, to the great relief of the defenders. Kirkendall finally moved his wagons north to Clear Creek. Dillon died that night and was later buried at Phil Kearny's post cemetery. On the morning of 25 July, 60 men and a howitzer, commanded by Lt. Nathaniel C. Kinney, arrived from the fort, and they all proceeded to that post.[3]

Incidents of these Indian attacks bore similarities to a scene in *Red River* (Monterey, 1948). Although centering on an 1865 cattle drive from Texas to Kansas, the film includes a few instances of Indians attacking wagons, including an attack on Thomas Dunson (John Wayne) and Nadine Groot's (Walter Brennan) lone wagon while camped at a river crossing. There is also an unseen attack on a large train, in which Dunson's old flame, Fen (Coleen Gray), is killed. A lone white boy, Matt Garth (Mickey Kuhn), survives, grows to be a man (Montgomery Clift), and becomes Dunson's partner. The attacks cause Groot to ask, "Why do Injuns always wanna be burnin' up good wagons?"

On the cattle drive north, Indians attack a half-dozen wagons carrying gamblers and prostitutes west. The cowboys come across the Indians circling the wagons and shooting. Matt Garth, Buster McGee (Noah Beery Jr.) and two others race their horses through the circling Indians and into the wagon corral. The cowboys are enough to tip the scales in favor of the defenders, and the Indians are repulsed, but not before one of the prostitutes, Tess Millay (Joanne Dru), gets an arrow in the shoulder. Garth, suggesting that it may be poisoned, has to suck on her shoulder, removing the poison and thereby apparently endearing himself to her.

There were no recorded poison arrow incidents in the attacks on the Bozeman Trail in July 1866, but there were similar rescues. The combined trains of Burrowes, Kirkendall, Dillon and

*Red River* (Monterey, 1948) is considered a seminal Western for Howard Hawks's direction, Montgomery Clift's excellent screen debut, and John Wayne's performance. "I didn't know the sonofabitch could act!" said John Ford.

others contained nearly 200 wagons and were some of the largest groups ever attacked by Indians in the West — although they were never assaulted while all together in one circle, but rather while separated (much as in the attacks on the Smart, Adams, and Kennedy trains in Idaho). There were plenty of Indians raiding along the entire trail, for on the same day Kirkendall and Dillon were attacked, warriors also hit the Floyd Wagon Train, about 100 miles to the southeast, with devastating results.

Nathan Floyd, an Irishman who had arrived in Montana Territory in 1863 from the Colorado mines, went back to Leavenworth in 1866 to purchase merchandise to bring back to Virginia City. On 24 July, the train he captained was trailing along the Bozeman route between Brown Springs and the Dry Fork of the Cheyenne when the Indians struck.

As the captain, Floyd was riding ahead of the wagons looking for the next water source when he was surprised and killed. Hearing the firing, 13 men, some armed with Spencer Rifles, rushed ahead to help, but they ran into a hornet's nest. Indians surrounded them, and in a few minutes eight men were dead or dying, and the remaining five, two of them wounded, managed to escape back to the main party. The 36-wagon train circled up and was besieged for two days before the Indians rode away.

The survivors cautiously crawled forward. They found Floyd with his head cut off. Charles Barton, who the travelers nicknamed "Blowhard" for his braggadocio, had 20 arrows in him, a knife protruding from his side, and his whiskers scalped from his chin. Like Barton, 18-year-old Zach Husted's body was similarly mangled. Most of the bodies were in such bad shape that they were all buried where they lay. Also killed were William H. Dearborn, Hiram H. Campbell,

John Little, Stephen Carson, and William Bothwell. Another man, John Sloss, had been wounded two days before the battle and died at Fort Reno. Emigrants coming along the trail later saw the graves and the dried blood and became frightened. Said George W. Fox, who passed by on 29 July, "this begins to make things look 'skaly.'"[4]

Contrary to what some New Western historians like to spin about non-violence in the Old West, and the comparative safety of a wagon trip west, the situation often did get very "skaly."

# 23

## The Hayden, Crow, Blanchard, Snyder, and Baca Wagon Trains (*Two Mules for Sister Sara*)

### Kansas, 1847, 1864

The Bozeman Trail was dangerous during the few years of its existence. The Santa Fe Trail was dangerous for six decades. Because the Santa Fe Trail was less a route for emigrants and more a commercial path, historians tend to ignore it when talking about trail dangers. Nevertheless, attacks occurred, and one of the peak periods of danger was during the Mexican War of 1846–48.

In the spring of 1847 a wagon train of Bent, St. Vrain and Co., commanded by Frank De Lise, was heading east to Missouri. On 28 May, De Lise selected a campsite at Walnut Creek, a wooded and watered site near the creek's junction with the Arkansas River near present-day Great Bend, Kansas. De Lise and another trader, William Tharp, went on a buffalo hunt the next morning. The livestock were let out of the corral to graze. Suddenly, mounted Indians attacked the circled wagons, the livestock, and the hunters all at once. Sixty of Tharp's mules, 40 of Bent and St. Vrain's mules and oxen, seven of John S. Smith's horses and mules, and two of Lewis Garrard's mules were run off.

Although caught by surprise, De Lise and Tharp held their ground and put up a staunch defense, shooting down five Indians; but despite a valiant effort, Tharp was killed and scalped before men from the train could rescue them. Tharp was buried at the Walnut Creek Crossing.[1]

The following month, Lt. John Love and Company B, 1st Dragoons were ordered to escort the paymaster, Maj. Charles Bodine, and his 12-wagon train containing $350,000 in specie from Fort Leavenworth, Kansas, to Santa Fe. On 23 June, at Pawnee Fork, two other wagon trains came in for protection. Trader Henry C. Miller joined government wagonmaster Hayden's 30-wagon train, and trader James S. Wethered hooked up with wagonmaster Fagan's 30-wagon train. Indians attacked Hayden and Fagan on the morning of 23 June, before Love's arrival, and three or four of Fagan's men were wounded. A Mr. Smith from Van Buren County, Missouri, was lanced seven times but managed to shoot and kill his attacker as he lay wounded. The same Indians attacked another train led by Mr. Bell and Colonel William H. Russell, and protected by a 15-man guard. The Indians drove off and slaughtered 160 oxen. Love assured Bell and Russell that he would seek revenge.[2]

On 24 June, Love's Dragoons, and Hayden and Fagan's trains, spent the day crossing the Pawnee River. The next day, Lieutenant Love ordered the two trains to stay close together so he could provide protection. Fagan was fine with that directive, but Hayden was stubborn and was

## 23. The Hayden, Crow, Blanchard, Snyder, and Baca Wagon Trains

Plain Encampment, Kansas, site of the attack on the Hayden and Fagan wagon trains.

determined to outdistance the others, causing the rest to travel until nightfall to reach him. Lieutenant Love camped next to the river, which provided grass and water and seemed fairly safe from any unexpected attack. This campground became known as Plain Encampment or Grand Prairie, and was located four miles southwest of the Big Coon Creek Crossing, and five miles southwest of present-day Garfield, Kansas. Fagan's train pulled in about 400 yards to the rear.

Saturday morning, 26 June, was a clear day with a gentle southerly breeze. Hayden, believing there was no danger, let his oxen out of the corral to graze under the watchful eyes of the herdsmen. Fagan also released his livestock. Lieutenant Love was on a high point overlooking the camps with his telescope when he heard some war whoops and screams from the direction of Hayden's camp. Mounted Comanches rose out of the tall grass, while others charged from the ravine near Big Coon Creek. The noise of rattles, and the sight of waving buffalo robes and charging horsemen, frightened the livestock and caused them to stampede. About 250 Comanches rode among the animals and lanced several. The herders could not stop the stampede. They placed themselves between the warriors and the livestock, but the Indians charged right through, wounding three.[3]

Love ordered his dragoons to pursue the Indians, when 200 more Comanches appeared south of the river directly across from the dragoon camp. The lieutenant realized his duty was to protect the paymaster and his train, so he ordered 25 dragoons to deploy around the camp to ward off an attack, while Sgt. Ben Bishop took 25 mounted dragoons in pursuit of the oxen and the other Indians. Bishop charged, expecting Hayden's teamsters and herders would join him; but when they saw ten times more Indians than soldiers, they fled for the safety of their camp. Bishop's dragoons fought bravely in hand-to-hand combat, but after five soldiers were killed and six wounded, Bishop ordered a retreat. The Comanches scalped three of the dragoons, cut the throat of one, and sliced off the ears of the last. The fight lasted 20 minutes. Soldiers saw a dozen or more Comanches fall, but their comrades removed the bodies. About 160 oxen were driven off.[4]

Lieutenant Love moved Hayden and Fagan together for safety, and then sent a messenger to Fort Leavenworth to inform them of their plight, while requesting new teams of oxen to take the train to Santa Fe. They waited until 2 July, when they considered the wounded were stable enough to be moved, and then traveled to Fort Mann, an abandoned post that still provided a degree of protection. By borrowing oxen from other trains, and leaving behind some equipment and wagons, Hayden managed to follow along as far as Fort Mann, where he waited for the additional stock from Leavenworth. Love, his dragoons, the paymaster and his entourage, and Fagan's train left Fort Mann on 8 July, and reached Santa Fe on 6 August. Lt. Col. Alton R. Easton and four companies of Missouri Volunteers reached Mann on 23 July with 360 head of oxen. They yoked them to Hayden's wagons, and he finally headed for Santa Fe.[5]

The bold Indian attack on a large train escorted by U.S. Dragoons gave ample warning that anyone traveling on the Santa Fe Trail was putting his life in jeopardy. Little had changed 17 years later, when Comanches and Kiowas were still running free and attacking wagon trains small and large.

On 18 July, 1864, warriors attacked the trains of Jerome (Jesse) E. Crow (21 wagons) and Richard F. Barret (nine wagons), with John Hiles as wagonmaster, on Walnut Creek, not far from present-day Great Bend. The two freighters rode together as they traveled from Fort Leavenworth, Kansas, to Fort Union, New Mexico Territory. They had safely corralled the evening before, but by ten in the morning they were strung out on the road when about 120 Indians struck.

The warriors divided and charged down each side of the train, shouting and shooting. In such a vulnerable position, the freighters had little chance. The Indians killed ten of them, scalped several, and wounded five more. The survivors got out and took up a defensive stand but could do little but watch as the warriors took all the wagon sheets, destroyed 132 sacks of flour, damaged nine wagons, and ran off 23 oxen. The losses totaled $4,526.

The night before, only about three miles away at a spot that would become Fort Zarah, Capt. O. F. Dunlop, Company H, 15th Kansas Cavalry, camped with his men. That evening Dunlop entertained a number of Kiowas and Arapahos who had come professing friendship. Dunlop warily treated with them, and by early morning they were gone, only to sweep down on Crow and Barret within sight of the army camp. Dunlop mounted up his men as fast as possible and rode out, even though he estimated the attacking Indians at more than 800; but when he arrived, the Indians had already scattered. Soldiers and teamsters thought that the Kiowas Kicking Bird and Little Heart participated in the attack.[6]

A week later, Kiowas under Satanta and Satank were back in the area. They killed a sentry at Fort Larned, stole horses from the post herd and moved west, striking at any convenient targets. At Cimarron Crossing of the Arkansas River they attacked a stage and killed two men. On 1 August, 1864, about 70 Comanches and Kiowas approached a small train owned by a Mr. Allison, camped at Lower Cimarron Springs (Wagon Bed Spring) about ten miles south of present-day Ulysses, Kansas (the same place that saw mountain man Jedediah Smith killed by Comanches in 1831). The Indians approached in a friendly manner and asked for food, when suddenly they attacked, killing Allison and the other four Americans in the party.

They spared the lives of the Mexican teamsters, telling them that they had no quarrel with them. The warriors gave them one wagon and a yoke of oxen and told them to leave the area. The Mexicans hurried west on the Santa Fe Trail, thankful for their lives. Capt. Nicholas S. Davis of the 1st California Infantry met the teamsters near the Canadian River. He said that the Kiowas told the Mexicans "to go back to New Mexico, as they did not wish to kill them; but that they would kill every white man that came on the road." Davis continued on to Wagon Bed Spring and buried the bodies of the five Americans.[7]

## 23. The Hayden, Crow, Blanchard, Snyder, and Baca Wagon Trains

**Wagon Bed Springs, Kansas, site of the 1864 attack on the Allison Wagon Train.**

Kiowas and Comanches were not the only tribes raiding the Santa Fe Trail in 1864. From their camps in western Kansas, Cheyennes sent out war parties to the Arkansas River. A Mexican train; a train of 14 wagons under Andrew Blanchard; the Stuart Train; and the Slemmons & Company Train under Charles P. McRae and John Sage were allowed to move beyond Fort Larned because they had 95 wagons and more than 100 armed men with them. At Middle Cimarron Crossing they found out that it still wasn't enough.

On 21 August, 1864, the combined trains approached the Arkansas River near the head of the Dry Route from Fort Larned, with McRae in front, followed by Sage, the Mexican train, and Blanchard. The first three trains formed up in a circle, leaving a portion open for Blanchard, but inexplicably he moved on and corralled one-half mile beyond McRae.

They were in camp early, resting for the long, dry journey ahead, and most of the men were asleep at one in the afternoon. Three men from McRae's Train were outside the wagons shooting prairie dogs when one of them shouted out, "Indians!" About 40 Cheyenne warriors under Little Robe charged from the north, trying to cut off the three hunters from the wagons. While most of the teamsters were sleeping, six black mess cooks grabbed rifles and advanced outside the wagon circle, firing and giving the three hunters time to escape into the corral. Five Indians led by Bear Man, riding a yellow pony, cut between McRae's and Blanchard's trains.

Andrew Blanchard, in a foolhardy move, drew his pistol and rode out after them, evidently not noticing the other Indians circling around his wagons or the greater number of mounted Indians still waiting on the bluffs. He was 200 yards from the camp when he realized his mistake. Most of the Cheyennes drove off his cattle, but several rode up to Blanchard and knocked him off his horse. About 15 of Blanchard's teamsters got their weapons and ran out after him, firing as they advanced. Blanchard was captured, but the warriors had to drop him when the teamsters closed in. Blanchard had been shot several times, with one arrow coming straight through his back and protruding out his stomach, and one lance wound through his shoulder.

The teamsters carried him back to the corral where he died within the hour. They buried him beside the road. Ten teamsters or hired hands also died in the attack.

Indians cut through McRae's herds, driving off 130 mules, about one-third of the total. All of Blanchard's stock was taken, except two oxen. The stock was driven south of the river where the Indians leisurely rested before moving away. That evening a messenger mounted Blanchard's horse and rode 65 miles back to Fort Larned for help. He met another train coming from Larned, escorted by Captain Hardy and a detachment of Colorado Cavalry, and rode in with them. The second morning after his departure they rumbled up to the stalled wagons at Cimarron Crossing.[8]

August of 1864 was a deadly month for Indian attacks all across the Central Plains. Just arrived in Denver, Colorado Territory, was Anna Snyder, who had come west at the bidding of her husband, a blacksmith at Fort Lyon. John Snyder, Company E, 1st Colorado Cavalry, talked the quartermaster into letting him have an ambulance (and accompanying him) to pick up his wife. A teamster named Bennett, and possibly a soldier (Joel H. Dyer of Company F), also went along. They fetched her in Denver, drove south to Pueblo and then east along the Arkansas River—the Mountain or "Wet" route of the Santa Fe Trail. When they stopped at Booneville, Eliza, an old woman who had lived with Colonel Albert G. Boone's family for years, told Mrs. Snyder, "You all got a mighty fine head of hair for the Injuns to git, honey."

The frightened woman answered, "Oh, don't say that, for I have heard such terrible stories of how they abuse the prisoners."

The next day the little group headed for Bent's Old Fort, but they never arrived. On 14 August they were attacked by a band of more than 40 Arapahos led by Little Raven's son, who the day before had led a raid at Point of Rocks Agency and stole 28 head of stock. The Indians overwhelmed them. The westbound stage came upon the wreckage shortly after, and Thomas Pollock reported finding the bodies of three men. John Snyder was scalped, and his testicles were cut off and stuffed into his mouth. One of his legs was cut off, and he was hung on the ambulance by the other leg. The two other men were also killed and mutilated. The woman was missing.

Capt. Isaac Gray, Company E, 1st Colorado Cavalry, took a detachment to the murder site. He sent scouts out in all directions, but they could not pick up a trail. All Gray found were the bodies, an ambulance, and a wagon containing the remnants of the Snyders' household furniture. He reported that "The inhabitants in this settlement are much excited, and a great many think of abandoning their farms." The captive Mrs. Snyder was taken to Black Kettle's Cheyenne camp where, disconsolate over her predicament, she hanged herself.[9]

Three years later, at the same spot where the Blanchard and McRae-Sage trains were attacked, Capt. Francisco Baca and his 80 wagons were camped at the Cimarron Crossing of the Arkansas. They were heading for Santa Fe with passengers, who included the first Catholic Bishop of Santa Fe, Jean Baptiste Lamy, ten priests, and six nuns.

Heading north from their camp on the Washita River were the Cheyenne Lame Bear and 75 of his warriors, including George Bent, mixed-blood son of trader and ex-agent William Bent. On 22 June, 1867, the Cheyennes swept in on the train and stole 50 mules, but were repelled by Baca's fast-shooting men before the attackers could do any more damage. Howling Wolf, who was trying to get the bell mare and lead all the animals away from the train, was wounded, and the Indians gave up the fight.

The priests tried to remain stoic, but the nuns were quite unsettled by what fate might be in store for them should they be captured. Eastern newspapers fueled the story, reporting that all the priests had been killed and the nuns abducted and raped. In fact, the passengers came through unscathed by Cheyenne bullets and arrows. Ten of the passengers died, nevertheless, including one nun. This time, however, the killer was an epidemic of cholera that was sweeping through Kansas in the summer of 1867.[10] Indian attack was not the only trail danger.

Even the remote possibility that nuns might be abducted on the western trails was explored briefly in *Two Mules for Sister Sara* (Universal, 1970). In the opening scene, Hogan (Clint Eastwood) happens upon three bandits in Mexico who have grabbed a "nun," Sister Sara (Shirley MacLaine), and are in the process of robbing, stripping, and attempting to rape her. Of course, Hogan kills the bandits and finds himself partnered with Sister Sara for the rest of the film. He helps her in return for information she knows about the defenses of a fort that Hogan and the rebel Juaristas want to capture. In the end we learn that Sara is not really a nun but a prostitute posing as a nun in her own undercover attempt to obtain information on the French Army. Thankfully, there were few instances of nuns being attacked on the trails, and even fewer films about them.

# 24

## The Cooke and Custard Wagon Trains (*The Massacre, Chuka*)

### Kansas, June 1867; Wyoming, July 1865

There were many wagon trains attacked during the Western migrations, most of which had surviving witnesses to tell the story. A few people may have survived the Bloody Point Massacre in 1852, and only the children were spared in the Fancher attack in 1857. No one survived the Gravelly Ford massacre in 1862. There may have been other Gravelly Ford–type attacks on lone wagons or small trains, but we will never know because there was no one left to report it.

So far we have dealt almost exclusively with Indian attacks on civilian wagon trains, but the army was not immune. They were involved with the Hayden and Fagan trains, the Fisk Train, and Sawyers Train to some degree; but the Cooke Train and the Custard Train were all military—and the latter was totally wiped out.

The Cooke Train is so named because it was nominally under the command of Lt. William W. Cooke, who was acting under orders from Lt. Col. George Custer. During Custer's 1867 summer campaign on the Central Plains, while camped in the neighborhood of present-day Benkleman, Nebraska, Custer sent about 12 wagons to Fort Wallace, Kansas, for supplies. The train, with Lt. Samuel M. Robbins and Company D, 7th Cavalry, as escort, consisted of about 50 men. Capt. Robert M. West, with Company K, traveled with them as far as Beaver Creek, where he went on a separate scout. Cooke's wagons safely made it to Fort Wallace, loaded up with supplies and headed north toward Custer.

While the train was gone, Custer skirmished with the Indians on 24 June. After that incident, he decided the wagon train might be in danger. He sent a squad of Company E, under Capt. Edward Meyers, south to find Captain West, with orders for both to find Cooke and escort the wagon train back.

On 26 June, half-way between Fort Wallace and Beaver Creek, more than 600 warriors appeared on the hills around the slow-moving train. Cooke and Robbins didn't circle up. Instead, they deployed the wagons into two parallel columns, wide enough to allow the horses to travel inside. The troopers dismounted and formed a circle around the perimeter while the entourage slowly advanced. The first attack came from the flank, but the troopers coolly knelt and used their seven-shot Spencers to good effect. Several Indians and ponies went down. The braves fell back while scout William Comstock taunted them in their own language.

In the next attack the warriors rode in circles around the train, constricting ever closer until the soldiers opened fire, again driving them back. The Indians kept up the pressure for three hours, as circling warriors swept in and out, drawing fire and using up the soldiers' last remaining ammunition. All the while the wagons kept moving.

## 24. The Cooke and Custard Wagon Trains

The standoff ended when Captains West and Meyers finally appeared on the northern horizon. The Indians contemplated going for the wagons in a last charge but decided that their mounts were too tired after hours of hard riding. They pulled away, and Cooke and his rescuers were able to reach Custer's main command. The Indians suffered five killed and a half-dozen wounded, while two troopers were wounded. The rolling wagon defense worked, mainly as a consequence of cool-headed troopers using repeating weapons.[1]

The episode could have had a tragic ending in more ways than one, and leads to a couple of "what ifs." Custer had previously sent a letter requesting his wife Libbie come to Fort Wallace. He figured she could accompany the supply train back to his command. Custer would get to see his wife. He would have no need to ride, as he later did, from Fort Wallace to Fort Riley to find her, and may have avoided the court martial that followed.

Then again, Libbie may not have survived the wagon train journey back to Custer's camp. By a twist of fate, and the good judgment of the post commander, Libbie was not allowed to join the train due to the hostile Indians. It was a good decision, because the wagon train was ambushed and Custer had already re-thought his plan to have Libbie join him. Would an officer really carry out his orders that Libbie was to be shot to prevent her from falling into the hands of the Indians (see Chapter 10)?

When Libbie next saw Lieutenant Cooke he told her, "The moment I found the Indians were on us, and we were in for a fight, I thought of you, and said to myself, 'If she were in the ambulance, before giving an order I would ride up and shoot her.'"

"Would you have given me no chance for life," she replied, "in case the battle had gone in your favor?"

"Not one," he said. "I should have been unnerved by the thought of the fate that awaited you, and I have promised the General not to take any chances, but to kill you before anything worse could happen."[2]

Both George and Libbie dodged the proverbial bullet in that instance.

Coincidentally, a wagon boss with a last name very similar to the lieutenant colonel who died on the Little Bighorn in 1876, Amos Jefferson Custard, also faced an Indian attack—with tragic consequences. Custard was born in Crawford County, Pennsylvania, in 1827. In 1853 Amos married and moved to Kansas, and in 1862 he enlisted in the 11th Kansas Cavalry. Instead of being sent east to fight in the Civil War, the 11th Kansas patrolled the trails west, and in the summer of 1865 it was embroiled in the great Indian raids that occurred along the roads in present-day Nebraska and Wyoming. Commissary Sergeant Custard, of Company H, took supply wagons and about 25 men from Companies H and D from Platte Bridge Station west to Sweetwater Station. With five wagons pulled by six-mule teams, they delivered their load and looked forward to returning to Platte Bridge, where they expected to be sent east to be mustered out after three years of service.

Custard followed the old Oregon Trail, "nooned" at Horse Creek, and camped for the night at Willow Springs, about 21 miles from Sweetwater and half-way to Platte Bridge. That evening Lt. Henry C. Bretney, 11th Ohio Cavalry, Capt. A. Smith Lybe, 6th Infantry, and a ten-man detachment rode through Custard's camp on the way to Platte Bridge. The men stopped to eat supper with Custard and tried to persuade the sergeant to accompany them to the station that night. Custard thought the mules were too tired and declined.

The next morning, 26 July, 1865, Custard left early and drove along a waterless stretch to where a branch of the trail split north to cross the divide at Emigrant Gap. Custard took the southern branch, where the telegraph was strung, closer to the North Platte River. Near the river bend east of Red Buttes, a 30-man patrol of the 11th Ohio was out trying to repair the cut telegraph line. They had been in the field several days; the telegraph lines were cut for about nine miles, and the patrol could not repair it. What was worse, they had been under constant attack by Indians and did not feel that they could safely reach Platte Bridge Station. They drew their wagons across the neck of a peninsula and dug rifle pits; they had been trapped there for three days already. The boom of the cannon at Platte Bridge could be heard from nine miles away. With Custard's arrival, the repair patrol figured they now had enough reinforcements to hold out until rescued.

When Custard was asked to join them, however, he replied, "No sir; we don't stop here. We are going to Platte Bridge in spite of all the redskins this side of Hell."

He was told that the station was surrounded by thousands of Indians, and the soldiers implored him to stay. Custard reportedly said, "You fellows are skeered. We will go on, and if you want to be safe, go on with us. We will cut our way through, or go to Hell a-trying. Forward, Men!"

Custard had been given two chances to save his train. He would not get a third.

About 11:30 A.M. soldiers at Platte Bridge saw the white tips of Custard's wagons on the far horizon to the west. The Indians saw them too. The fort's howitzer sent a couple of shots in that direction. Custard heard them and sent Cpl. James W. Shrader and four men ahead to see what the firing was about. When Indians appeared on three sides of them, Shrader dashed for the river about half a mile away. On the south bank, Indians approached from the direction of the fort. Pvt. Edwin Summers tried to ride off in the opposite direction, but was caught and killed. Pvt. James Ballau was killed on the riverbank. The three remaining men dashed for the fort. With some lucky shooting they killed Left Hand, the brother of the famous Cheyenne war leader Roman Nose. As the Indians gathered around their fallen leader, Shrader, and Pvts. Henry C. Smith and Byron Swain, all from Company D, 11th Kansas, crept close enough to the fort to be spotted by the soldiers, who rode out and brought them in. They were the only survivors.

By this time, Custard had decided that the only way to save themselves was to dash to the fort, so when the Indians swarmed upon them they were in no position to circle up for defense. Only the second and third wagons stopped next to each other, with the other three scattered as far as 140 yards away. The men of the rear wagon abandoned it and ran to the middle two. The soldiers cut the mules loose and hurriedly tried to make a defensive position. They were armed with Smith .50 caliber breech-loading carbines, a single-shot weapon that could be fired a dozen times a minute. Custard's men made good work of it at first, knocking a number of charging warriors off their ponies.

After the first charge, the Indians withdrew to reorganize, and the soldiers piled boxes, corn sacks, and bedding under the wagons. After another charge or two, the Cheyennes backed off in a wider circle, staying out of effective reach of the carbines. After a time, the warriors crawled closer — up depressions and ravines — pushing logs and rocks in front of them as moveable barriers, and lofting their arrows into the trapped men. After about four hours the fire from the doomed command slowed in intensity, as men were picked off one by one. Then, after one volley, the warriors rushed them; there was a short hand-to-hand struggle, and the Indians gave out a rousing whoop. The breeze carried the faint sound to the soldiers at Platte Bridge, and they knew that it was over.

The last few wounded soldiers were tortured, for the soldiers had inflicted substantial casualties on the Indians, and they exacted vengeance. The warriors scalped Custard and his men, but later threw them away, for too many Indians had been killed to celebrate the battle.[3]

There were not many films made in which the entire wagon train or central characters are wiped out, which would make for a short movie. One early exception was *The Massacre* (Biograph, 1912). In this 20-minute film by D. W. Griffith there were two massacres to suggest the title. Stephen (Wilfred Lucas) is an army scout who asks a woman (Blanche Sweet) to marry him but discovers she loves another man (Charles West). She marries West and has a child. Two years later they join a wagon train heading west. Stephen has participated in an army attack on

## 24. The Cooke and Custard Wagon Trains　　　　　　　129

Red Buttes, Wyoming, near the site of the July 1865 Custard Wagon Train Massacre.

an Indian village in which nearly all the inhabitants were killed. When he joins the wagon train as a guide for the military escort, the Indians seek revenge. The Indians attack the wagons, and the cavalry arrives too late; all are killed except the woman and her child—later found alive under a pile of dead soldiers.

Griffith, who was usually very effective in depicting the horrific effects of war, graphically shows that in battle even unarmed women and children can be killed and maimed, sometimes accidentally, sometimes purposely. The film explicitly depicted battle carnage in ways that were shunned by Hollywood for much of the next few decades.

Another film that killed off all the main protagonists was the like-titled *Massacre* (Fox, 1956). Ramon (Dane Clark) is a government agent trying to track down Comancheros and gunrunners who are supplying and inciting the Yaqui Indians of old Mexico. Ramon succeeds in destroying the gunrunners' arms cache. Unfortunately, he, along with the bad guys, meets his fate when the Indians wipe them all out.

*Chuka* (Rodlor, 1967) is another film where everyone (maybe) is massacred, although a fort is the target, not a wagon train. Fort Clendennon is the isolated outpost where all the army misfits have been sent. It contains a top-heavy assortment of officers, Col. Stuart Valois (John Mills), Major Benson (Louis Hayward), Captain Carrol (Hugh Reilly), and Lieutenant Daly (Gerald York). As for enlisted men, there is Sgt. Otto Hansbach (Ernest Borgnine) and only about 20 privates on the verge of mutiny. The only one who supports the disliked colonel is the sergeant, who served with him in Africa in the British Army. Valois saved his life in the Sudan, but the natives captured the colonel and cut him up, as the sergeant put it, so that he wasn't a full man anymore! Valois, now in the U. S. Army, has to prove to himself and everyone else that he indeed still is a man. The proof, unfortunately for those under him, is to be made by defending a doomed fort.

Into the mix rides a gunman, Chuka (Rod Taylor), and two beautiful women, Veronica Kleitz (Lucianna Paluzzi) and Helena Chavez (Victoria Vetri, billed as Angela Dorian). Chuka once had a fling with Veronica, but their lives were far too different for a marriage to succeed. Outside await the hungry and angry Arapahos, who want the supplies and ammunition in the fort. Chuka knows the Arapahos' needs—he once shared food with the leader, Hanu (Marco Lopez)—and he knows the Indians will not leave until they get the supplies.

Chuka tells Valois that he must give the Arapahos the supplies or they will massacre everyone in the fort. The colonel will not listen. After the last stage arrives, the Indians seal the place off, and the few civilian scouts, stage driver, and soldiers spend their time discussing options. Stage "shotgun" rider Baldwin (Joseph Sirola) makes the notable comment that he hates Indian war because so many horses get killed.

A soldier mutiny is quelled, and Valois sends out scout Lou Trent (James Whitmore) to get help. Trent is caught and tortured, and Chuka has to rescue him. When they return, Chuka again pleads with Valois that if any of them are to survive he must abandon the fort and give the guns and supplies to the Indians. Like Sergeant Custard, Valois again refuses his chance.

Finally, the Indians make an overwhelming attack on the small fort at night, shooting flaming arrows and climbing in on lances they have thrown into the outside walls. Valois is shot down before he can prove his manliness, and all in the fort are killed. Veronica dies from an arrow wound. Only Chuka and Helena are left, hiding under the stairs, when the rest of the Indians open the gates and stream in, loading wagons with the supplies and guns they wanted. Hanu, the last Indian out, sees the pair hiding. Chuka places his revolver to Helena's head, waiting to see what Hanu will do; but the chief just rides away.

In the final scenes, when an army rescue force arrives, they find only a grave on the parade ground. We are left to assume that Chuka buried his former love, Veronica, and that he and Helena escaped—perhaps. None are ever seen again.

Like Sergeant Custard, Colonel Valois had multiple chances to change his fate, but tragically lost his supplies, his life, and the lives of others, and all because of pride, honor, or just plain stubbornness.

Indian attacks on forts, although not as common as on wagon trains, were also a staple of decades of Western films. Attacking forts was also said to have been an invention of Hollywood. Not so. Indians attacked many forts and stockades east of the Mississippi during the Colonial and Revolutionary days, and even through the War of 1812. In the West, Indian attacks on forts were rare, but they did occur. The largest assault happened in Minnesota in 1862, an incident in a conflagration that may be the greatest single episode of settler killings and captures in American history. Death estimates ran as high as 2,000, according to the St. Peter *Tribune*; and six weeks after the uprising, burial parties were interring as many as 47 bodies a day. There were many bodies found lying in far off thickets and prairies, and thousands of settlers fled the state, never to return. Commissioner of Indian Affairs William Dole estimated Indians killed from 800 to 1,000 "inoffensive and unarmed settlers." Twenty-three counties were virtually depopulated. The official count was established at 644 dead, with about 300 captives taken.[4]

As the Dakotas swept through the countryside from their reservation along the Minnesota River, refugees fled their farms and congregated at Fort Ridgely. The soldiers were out trying to stem the Indians' advance or frantically looking for reinforcements. Lt. Thomas P. Gere, 5th Minnesota Infantry, was left in command at the fort. Survivors were pouring in, and he nervously wondered how he could defend the post. At noon on 19 August, Lt. Timothy J. Sheehan brought in reinforcements, and later another detachment came in after a 40-mile march. There were about 250 refugees in the fort and about 180 soldiers. Now they had a chance.

Thankfully there was no attack that day, but on the 20th a lone Indian, Chief Little Crow of the Mdewakanton band, rode up, ostensibly to demand a talk. It was only a diversion from the attack of perhaps 400 warriors that burst from the trees on the opposite side. Fort Ridgely did not have a walled perimeter; like most of the forts in the West, it was more or less a rough

The last stage rides into doomed Fort Clendennon, as Joseph Sirola, Luciana Paluzzi, Victoria Vetri, and Rod Taylor ponder their fate in *Chuka* (Rodlor, Inc., 1967).

square of buildings, with openings like a sieve. The warriors broke through the first defense line and reached the row of log houses forming the northern perimeter of the fort.

Sheehan rallied his men on the parade ground. The Indians prepared for another charge, and the Minnesota volunteers wavered. All the while, Sgt. John Jones was furiously giving some infantrymen a crash course in artillery firing. Six old howitzers were wheeled into place and loaded. Jones was ready just as Sheehan's line began to melt.

"Aim in the center and fire as rapidly as possible," Jones ordered.

The three old guns belched their haphazard loads of canister and solid shot. The Dakotas hesitated. Working like mad, the sergeant and his men rammed home another round, and another. At the third salvo, the Indians broke. They could face the musketry, but had a great fear of the "wagon guns." Jones had saved the day.

On the 22nd, Little Crow was back, this time with almost 800 warriors. The soldiers had repaired the damage, built up defenses, and placed their six trump howitzers in positions to cover all the approach angles. This time the Indians came from all sides, and Mankato's warriors got into the buildings on the southwest corner, setting fire to haystacks and woodpiles. Cannon fire blasted the buildings, and the Indians scattered back to the ravines and trees. More assaults were made, and all were repulsed by artillery blasts. In the timber, Little Crow was stunned by a shell burst. Realizing he could not take the fort, he called off the attack. For all the ferocity of the assault, the soldiers had lost only five killed and 22 wounded. About 100 Indian graves were found in the woods, and perhaps an equal number were wounded.[5]

Other forts were attacked. On 30 April, 1860, in present-day Arizona, Navajos attacked Fort Defiance. Since they had failed to clear the soldiers from their homeland in previous battles, the Navajos returned in force to the fort with several hundred men. As in *Chuka*, they attacked in the pre-dawn and charged the buildings with three columns of warriors. Defending the fort was Bvt. Major Oliver L. Shepherd and his Companies B, C, and E of the 3rd Infantry.

Defiance was another fort without an outside wall, and the Indians got into some of the outbuildings, but there was little to be done about it in the darkness. Muskets flashed in the gloom for two hours before the dawn illuminated the area enough for Shepherd to take control. He led his infantry in a series of charges that cleared out the buildings and drove the Navajos back into the foothills. Because much of the fighting was done at night, there were few casualties—only one soldier was killed and two wounded, while about 12 Navajos were killed or wounded.[6]

The Bozeman Trail forts Reno, Phil Kearny, and C. F. Smith were under a virtual siege at times in 1866 and 1867. Although the Indians did not attack these stockaded posts directly, they did make major assaults on detachments or fortified positions very close to the forts, such as the Hayfield Fight of 1 August, 1867, outside of C. F. Smith, and the Wagon Box fight on 2 August, 1867, near Phil Kearny. The battles had all the trappings of the best Hollywood could offer in the doomed-outpost-holds-out-until-rescued category. On 21 December, 1866, Indians also wiped out Capt. William J. Fetterman and 80 of his men, a reality that makes films like *Massacre* and *Chuka* pale by comparison.

# 25

# The Lyman Wagon Train and Beecher Island (*The Plainsman, The Oregon Trail*)

## Texas 1874; Colorado 1868

The Red River War in Texas and Indian Territory began largely as an Indian response to the white buffalo hunters encroaching on their lands. It was in full swing in September 1874 as several military expeditions crossed the area searching for Indians. In several instances it was the Indians who found the military first.

Capt. Wyllys Lyman and 104 men of Company I, 5th Infantry, and detachments of Companies H and I, 6th Cavalry, were on their way from Camp Supply in Indian Territory to meet Col. Nelson A. Miles and the main strike force to the south, near the Llano Estacado (Staked Plains). On 9 September, after the soldiers crossed the Canadian River, about 70 Kiowas discovered them and began following, harassing them and trying to steal the stock. Lyman kept Company I, 5th Infantry, out as skirmishers on either side of his double column of 36 wagons; and Lt. Frank West, with 13 troopers, rode in advance. The Kiowas rode in and fired, but the soldiers drove them back, allowing Lyman to move 12 miles south. By mid-afternoon they had reached the Washita River near the mouth of Gageby Creek.

Appearing suddenly were about 400 more Kiowas and Comanches under Lone Wolf, Mamanti, Satanta, Big Bow, and Big Tree. Lyman hastily corralled the wagons as the infantry wheeled to the right and left, forming two oblique lines like an arrowhead at the front of the train. Lt. Granville Lewis organized soldiers to defend the rear. They had practiced the maneuver, and it took less than a minute, yet the Indians were already upon them, charging with abandon and piercing the circle.

Sgt. William DeArmond fell dead, and Lieutenant Lewis took a severe wound in the knee. Within seconds the warriors slashed through and withdrew, taking positions all around the train. There were no more attacks during the afternoon, but near evening hundreds of warriors rode out and began slowly circling the besieged train in what was called "an awesome display of barbaric horsemanship." Some sat erect and stoic, others acrobatically rode hunched down on the far side of their ponies, firing from underneath their necks. Still others were seen standing on their ponies' backs, feathered ornamentations flowing in the wind, and defiantly gesturing and calling out curses to the soldiers. Hollywood could not have conjured up a finer display.

Come darkness, the soldiers dug breastworks in the sand with their hands and mess cups, and carried grain sacks and supply boxes to build up the perimeter. Teamster James McCoy was badly wounded carrying ammunition to the trenches. A sleepless night followed, with howling coyotes or warriors keeping the soldiers on edge. Four soldiers, each carrying six canteens, crept out to a buffalo wallow partially filled with water and returned successfully. With daylight, the soldiers could see that the buffalo wallow was now in range of the warriors' guns.

The Indians kept up sniper fire all day, as bullets kicked up puffs of sand and whisked through the grass, keeping the bluecoats pinned down. By the end of the second day the water in the kegs was nearly gone, and the men clamored for more. Lyman refused permission for any man to risk his life by crawling out to the water hole. Indians shot about 12 mules that day, and Sgt. Frederick Neilon was hit in the left leg.

At midnight a young scout of German descent, William Schmalsle, volunteered to ride to Camp Supply for help. With the activity of preparing for his escape focusing attention on one side of the corral, a small party of teamsters and soldiers took the opportunity to make a dash for water on the other side. With them was a boy of about 17 or 18, who may have been Thomas Huckobey. Huckobey was captured by the Indians in Texas in 1867, and lived with them for about seven years before being "rescued." He was camped with his band near the Canadian River and was out rounding up ponies when a detachment of 5th Infantrymen found him. The boy, known as "Tehan" to the Indians, could still speak English. He told his story to the soldiers, and said he would be happy to be returned to his white family. He was passed on to Captain Lyman as he came through with his supply train.

As the illicit party crawled out to get water, Indians discovered them and started firing. In the confusion, "Tehan" slipped away and went back to the Indians. The other whites scrambled pell mell back to the corral without obtaining any water.

On the third day of the siege, Botalye performed a feat of daring that became famous in the tribe. Several warriors talked about the boldness or foolishness of making a dash between two of the soldier trench lines. As they argued, the half–Kiowa, half–Mexican warrior ended the discussion by hopping on his pony and calling out, "I'm going to see how much power they have."

Botalye tied a white sheet around his waist and charged at the corral. With bullets kicking dust around him and whizzing by his head, he cut through the trenches, leapt over some startled soldiers, and exited the other side. When he returned unwounded, the other warriors were amazed; but Botalye was not done. He let his winded pony catch its breath and charged again. This time bullets cut off two feathers in his scalp lock. He slipped down over to one side of the pony and fired. A bullet clipped the saddle horn between his fingers and another slug cut the knot of the sheet at his back. He returned safely again. The Kiowas tried to grab him, but he wouldn't listen. He said he would make four charges, and he did. No warrior had ever seen anything like that before, and all thought he must have had great medicine with him that day.

Several chiefs congratulated him, including the famous Satanta, who said, "I could not have done it myself. No one ever came back from four charges." Botalye received a new name that day: Eadle-tau-hain, which meant He-Wouldn't-Listen-to-Them.

The display of showmanship, besides using up the soldiers' precious ammunition, probably chipped away at their morale. They sat, under siege, for another 36 hours, filled with the anxiety of not knowing if they would escape, if the scout got through, or if they would die from a bullet or thirst. Pvt. Daniel Buck was wounded in the head, and assistant wagonmaster James L. Stanford was hit as he carried ammunition to the forward gun pits. McCoy died and was buried next to DeArmond. The moans of the wounded made it worse for the rest. Desperate for liquids, soldiers broke into the supplies, hacked open cans of fruit, and drank the juice; the sweet syrups tasted heavenly. Unfortunately, some men broke into a store of vinegar and drank

*Opposite:* Although a rather slow-moving, contrived love story between Wild Bill Hickok and Calamity Jane, *The Plainsman* (Paramount, 1936) did offer a realistic scene in its depiction of a Beecher Island–type fight with the Indians.

**Site of the Battle of Beecher Island, Colorado Territory, 1868.**

it after mixing it with sugar. Some got sick, while one became violent and delirious, frothing at the mouth and appearing to have gone insane. It took him two days to recover.

On 12 September it began to rain, and the soldiers who had complained of the horrible heat, dryness, and thirst now contended with cold and water-logged conditions. The buffalo wallow filled up, and any ground depressions became mud-holes. The men sat shivering in puddles, wondering what their fate would be.

That night William Schmalsle reached a soldier hay camp 20 miles south of Camp Supply. When he rode out of the wagon circle, Indians chased him in the darkness for a time, but he escaped into a buffalo herd. Riding across the prairie, his horse stepped into a prairie dog hole, fell, and then ran away after Schmalsle was thrown off. The scout walked until daylight, hid, and walked again the next night. When he straggled into the hay camp, a mounted messenger rushed off to Camp Supply with the news.

About 10:30 P.M. on 13 September, Lyman's men heard Schmalsle's voice calling out in the darkness. He and five scouts had ridden back to deliver the news of help on its way. Lt. Henry P. Kingsbury, with 51 soldiers and scouts, and seven civilians, arrived at Lyman's corral about 2:30 in the morning of 14 September. With them came an ambulance and a doctor. They had covered 88 miles in about 38 hours. Despite the ordeal, by nine that morning, Lyman had his train prepared and resumed the drive toward Miles's command.[1]

Lyman's wagon train fight had all the ingredients for a great movie, and elements of the story were used time and again—whether Hollywood realized it or not. The story of besieged trains, desperate defenders, wounds, death, thirst, hunger, bravery, sacrifice, and rescue became standard fare for scores of plots. One of them, *The Plainsman* (Paramount, 1936), directed by Cecil B. De Mille, attempted to intermix the characters of William B. "Wild Bill" Hickok (Gary Cooper), William F. "Buffalo Bill" Cody (James Ellison), Martha Jean "Calamity Jane" Burke

(Jean Arthur), and George A. Custer (John Miljan). The result was a mediocre mix of fact and fiction — mostly fiction.

It is the job of the main characters to secure the frontier, which they go about while confronting the usual obstacles, such as bad Indians like Yellow Hand (Paul Harvey) and bad white men like John Lattimer (Charles Bickford), who sells guns to the Indians. George Custer meets his end at the Little Bighorn, and Wild Bill is shot and killed by Jack McCall (Porter Hall) in Deadwood. The film's final words: "It shall be as it was in the past.... Not with dreams, but with strength and with courage, Shall a nation be molded to last."

*The Plainsman* was a success at the box office, but DeMille's direction in his first epic western proved sub-par. The script was wordy and obvious, and the film suffered from too much studio shooting. With a big budget, DeMille strangely elected to mix genuine exteriors with phony studio sets, bouncing his actors on fake horse props and using back projection.

One part DeMille got right was a scene in which the Indians attack Buffalo Bill and an army detachment escorting wagons carrying ammunition and supplies. Certainly without realizing it, DeMille nearly encapsulated the Lyman Wagon Train episode. Calamity Jane and Wild Bill are captured by the Indians but are freed after Calamity spills the beans about what route the wagon train will take. They watch from a hill as the Indians, under Yellow Hand, take positions to surround and attack the wagons as they approach the river crossing.

"Caught like rats in a trap," Hickok says to Calamity. He climbs down a cliff, jumps the last Indian riding by and steals his horse. Hickok gives the horse to Calamity and tells her to ride to Custer for help. Then he somehow gets two more Indian ponies and rides, crouched between them, toward the wagon train, which has been attacked while crossing the river and is forted up on a small island.

With the soldiers' covering fire, Hickok makes it into the circle to add his carbine to the defense. Captain Wood (Purnell Pratt) is wounded in the arm, and Cody is wounded in the head, and the soldiers are being picked off one by one. Yet they hold out six or seven days — the enlisted men argue how long it has been — as the list of dead and wounded grows, and the men become exhausted, nervous wrecks. "Three days since the mule meat went bad," one soldier comments.

Finally the Indians mount what appears to be a final charge, splashing right down the river, but the concentrated army fire is too much, and the charge splits along both sides of the island. The bugler is killed, but the men think they hear a bugle blowing. They must be going crazy; but wait ... it is Custer and the 7th Cavalry coming to the rescue! Calamity Jane got through.

The wagon train fight in *The Plainsman* also has similarities to the Beecher Island fight of 17–21 September, 1868. If the writers of the film's storyline, Courtney R. Cooper and Frank J. Wilstach, based their tale on any historical model, it may well have been the Beecher Island episode, since it was showcased more often in history books than Lyman's fight.

In 1868 Gen. Philip Sheridan had the idea to help Kansas with its Indian problem. He directed Maj. George A. Forsyth to enlist a company of 50 frontiersmen to patrol the northwest frontier of the state. The 50 plainsmen moved out of Fort Hays on 29 August, traveling in a big loop to Fort Wallace, back to the railhead at Sheridan, then north toward the Republican River.

After two weeks in the saddle they picked up an Indian trail and followed the ever-increasing number of tracks up the Arikaree Fork into Colorado Territory. At dawn on 17 September, Indians drove off several of Forsyth's horses. He was saddling up for a chase when the few warriors turned into more than 500. The only hope was to get the command over to a small island in the Arikaree and try to hold them off. When they splashed across, the Indians quickly encircled them, and some men wanted to make a run for it.

"Stay where you are men," shouted Forsyth. "It's our only chance. I'll shoot down any man who attempts to leave the island."

And there they stayed, fighting off numerous mounted Cheyenne and Lakota charges down the river, and dodging the snipers along the north and south banks who were hidden in the tall grasses, picking them off one by one. Three times they held off massed frontal charges by Indians under Pawnee Killer, Tall Bull, Bull Bear, and White Bull, who bore down on the island only to split to both sides at the last second when it looked as if they might ride right over the top of the defenders. The frontiersmen's Spencer repeaters saved the day.

Forsyth was hit twice. As Dr. John Mooers crawled over to help him, the physician took a bullet in the forehead and slumped to the sand. Second in command Lt. Frederick Beecher was mortally wounded.

"My poor mother," he mumbled before he died.

Forsyth took a third hit from a bullet that grazed the top of his head. But the Indians had suffered casualties too. The prominent Cheyenne warrior Roman Nose entered the fray, even though he believed he would die because his spiritual medicine was not working. True to his premonition, Roman Nose led a charge and was cut down by a Spencer bullet. The battle faded out with the setting sun.

That night two scouts slipped out to try and reach Fort Wallace for help. At dawn on the 18th the fighting picked up with another half-hearted charge. Then the Indians settled down to a desultory sniping at the trapped defenders of what would come to be called Beecher Island. The second night two more scouts broke out to get help.

The fight continued for five days until, by the 21st, it appeared that almost all the Indians had disappeared. Now it was a fight against starvation. The horses were dead, and there were too many wounded to travel. The next meals were made of rancid horse meat. One of the scouts, Chauncey Whitney, scrawled in his diary, "My God! Have you deserted us?"

But the men who went for help did get through. Custer's 7th Cavalry did not rescue them as in *The Plainsman*, but on 25 September, Company H of the 10th Cavalry ("Buffalo Soldiers"), under Capt. Louis Carpenter, came riding in.[2]

As perhaps the most famous cavalry regiment in the west, the 7th Cavalry played a part in more than its fair share of movie rescues. *The Oregon Trail* (Universal, 1939), a 15-chapter serial, might set the record for the number of 7th Cavalry rescues in one film — with six!

In the first chapter, "Renegade's Revenge," Gen. Alfred Terry, while discussing the westward migrations and Indian attacks, tells Gen. William T. Sherman, "The disasters have occurred only to the biggest of the wagon trains, especially those headed to Oregon." He thinks white villains are behind it. Johnny Mack Brown, one of the top box-office draws of the time, plays Jeff Scott, the frontier scout hired to investigate, and who saves the day on many occasions—almost as often as Custer.

Scott and Deadwood Hawkins (Fuzzy Knight) join a wagon train to learn what they can, and soon suspect that bad guy Sam Morgan (James Blaine), in cahoots with an Eastern syndicate, controls the trade and does not want the area settled. With henchman Bull Bragg (Jack C. Smith), Morgan conspires with the Indians to stop the wagon train. One of the bad Indians is Yellow Snake, played by Jim Thorpe (who was of Sac and Fox ancestry, a gold medal Olympian, a professional baseball and football player, and named the greatest athlete in the first half of the 20th century).

The Indians attack the wagon train in chapter one, causing Scott to shout out his first "Form into a circle!" The segment ends with the Indians about to overwhelm the train, and heroine Margaret Mason (Louise Stanley) about to go over a cliff in a runaway wagon. The day is saved at the start of Chapter Two, "Flaming Forest," when Scott rescues Margaret, and the 7th Cavalry, led by none other than George Custer (Roy Barcroft), arrives just in time to save the wagons. The casting of Barcroft as hero Custer seems out of place today, given that Barcroft went on to become known as "King of the Bad Guys."

## 25. The Lyman Wagon Train and Beecher Island

Fuzzy Knight, Nell O'Day, and Johnny Mack Brown. The two men were partners in the 15-chapter serial *The Oregon Trail* (Universal, 1939).

The next chapters are chock full of typical serial perils and cliffhangers, such as prairie and forest fires, blind canyons, raging rivers, stampedes, powder kegs, landslides, Indian attacks, burning buildings, captures, and rescues. In Chapter Five, "Stampede," Indians trap Scott and Deadwood in a cabin, but Custer rides to the rescue, driving off the warriors and freeing the two heroes. In Chapter Eight, "Redskin's Revenge," the Indians, riding after Scott, are about to capture him when Custer and a handful of cavalrymen arrive to foil their plans.

"Avalanche of Doom," Chapter Nine, finds the Indians attacking the town, riding and whooping down the main street. Morgan shoots Scott off a wagon amid the chaos, and the Indians appear ready to capture the whole place when Custer and his troopers storm in from the other end, shooting down some Indians and scattering the rest. In the last chapter, "Trails End," Custer rescues heroes and heroines twice, once from the Indian camp and once during a final gunfight in town between the good guys and bad guys. Morgan is finally exposed and goes to jail, and Scott gets the girl.

Obviously, some western films went overboard in the depiction of the cavalry coming to the last-minute rescue. But it did happen. Hollywood was in tune with the concept.

# 26

## The Lyons, Shurly, Reel, and Hartz Wagon Trains (*Apache Rifles, Rio Grande, Broken Arrow, Hondo*)

### Texas 1849 and 1857; Wyoming 1867 and 1876

Indians attacked civilian emigrant trains, freight wagons, and military trains. All were fair game, from the Mexican to the Canadian border. With much historical and popular focus on the Oregon Trail, we forget the other routes that were fraught with danger. One of those was the Lower Military Road between San Antonio and El Paso. A train of five wagons, owned by Dr. Lyons and Nat Lewis of San Antonio, left El Paso in late June 1849 for the return trip home. Among the 13 men in the train were Ben Sanford, Emory Givens, John Crowder, Charley Hill, Jerry Priest, Charles Blawinsky, and men named Brown and McDonald. John L. Mann, who had been along the route several times, was the guide. Eight men on horseback rode along with them, but at Devil's River they left the slow wagons and went on ahead. Some of the remaining 13 men considered this to be an unlucky number and a bad omen.

At Deadman's Pass, north of present-day Comstock, Texas, a band of Comanches watched the riders go through, but waited for the slower wagons. Mann saw a lone man in the road far ahead. Thinking it was one of the riders who had recently left, Mann felt no cause for alarm. Walking in front of the train were Jerry Priest and an unnamed man they called the blacksmith. The latter had apparently lost his mind during the trip, and the others thought he was "perfectly crazy, but harmless." When the wagons climbed to the pass the Indians attacked from both sides of the road. Priest ran back and warned Mann, but the blacksmith just stood in the road and was killed in his tracks.

Brown, an old Indian fighter, calmly stood by his wagon and fired, knocking a warrior from his horse only 30 yards away. Bullets and arrows splintered the wagon's dubious protection. A fatal bullet struck Brown. Blawinsky, who the men called "Polander," was fighting near Brown and was mortally wounded. A few men from the next wagon ran out and pulled Blawinsky back with them. Nick Andres climbed into the wagon bed and was about to shoot over the rim when a bullet hit him in the throat and killed him. An unnamed old man who was in the wagon with Andres picked up the dead man's gun and ran to the next wagon, but went down with a bullet in the knee. Crowder and Givens were both wounded in the arm. The Indians captured the wagon in which Andres lay, pulled it out of range, and scalped him. Mann's wagon was ransacked and his best rifle stolen. He took a gun from a dead man and commenced firing. One bullet tore through his hat and creased his scalp.

## 26. The Lyons, Shurly, Reel, and Hartz Wagon Trains

The Indians besieged the desperate white survivors until about two in the morning. Blawinsky died. The defenders heard fewer shots, and Mann encouraged them by saying the Indians were out of ammunition and they would survive. True enough, the Indians pulled off about 400 yards, built a fire, and roasted the beef that was in Mann's wagon. At daylight they were gone. Charley Hill walked up a hill to look for Indian sign and was chased back to the wagons by four mounted warriors, but no further damage was done. About nine A.M. a small wagon train arrived with seven mounted Mexicans in advance. Mann explained the situation, and the Mexicans hurried up their train to form a secure corral with Mann's remaining wagons. They readied for another attack, but none came.

The Mexicans sent a rider north to a detachment of soldiers up Devil's River at Beaver Lake. They arrived the next day and took up the Indians' trail but never caught up with them. Two wagons were lost, a few oxen killed, and several stolen. The four dead men were buried in what came to be called Deadman's Pass.[1]

In Wyoming, two years after the destruction of Sergeant Custard and his wagons, Lt. Edmund R. P. Shurly, 27th Infantry, barely escaped the same fate. On 28 October, 1867, Lieutenant Shurly, with 40 27th Infantrymen, left Fort C. F. Smith with 25 empty wagons heading south to Fort Phil Kearny. Shurly reached a point six miles north of Phil Kearny when he met up with a Wells Fargo supply train escorted by Lt. Florence McCarthy, 27th Infantry. The two lieutenants agreed to "swap" trains, with McCarthy taking the empty wagons south and Shurly taking the Wells Fargo train on to Fort C. F. Smith. On 3 November, Shurly had his men store their knapsacks on the lead wagon of the 16-wagon train, which contained the ammunition stores. They headed north, but a snowstorm blew in and little progress was made.

The next morning Shurly got the train moving to a point east of present-day Sheridan, and then crossed over a divide to descend into the valley of Goose Creek. About 11 A.M. the train was strung out, with the lead wagons in the valley, the middle section negotiating a slippery hill, and the rear nearly out of sight a half mile from the hill. The ammunition was in front, the howitzers were in the rear, and the Wells Fargo teamsters were in the middle with rifles but no ammunition. From his position on the hill, Shurly saw Indians approaching, but there was little he could do.

About 300 Lakotas and Cheyennes attacked the front and rear simultaneously. The frightened mules bolted, and the first wagon ran into the arms of the warriors, who leapt aboard and drove it out of sight. While the other forward wagons corralled in the valley, the howitzer fired from the rear, and Shurly made his way toward the firing. He and seven men were cut off from the rest, but Cpl. Peter Donnelly, Company H, worked the howitzer fast enough to keep the Indians at bay. Finally, in order to save the gun, Shurly had it limbered up and drove it, disregarding all hazards, toward the corral. On the way, the lieutenant took an arrow through his foot but turned with revolver in hand and shot the Indian who just shot him. Pvt. Harold Partenheimer, Company D, was killed when two arrows pierced his lungs, and Cpl. Donnelly and Pvt. James McGeever were badly wounded. Cpl. Gordon Fitzgerald, Pvt. Michael Kerr, and civilian William Freeland were less seriously injured.

They finally reached the corral, but it was hastily set up in a narrow depression within rifle range of surrounding hills and thickets near the creek. With the ammunition wagon gone, Shurly made a quick count and found that they only had six shots for the howitzer and 40 rounds each for the remaining soldiers. The Indians, meanwhile, had gone to three wagons abandoned on the hill and ransacked their contents, carrying off or destroying some of the 700 sacks of corn, and making off with stores of red blankets. They were apparently satisfied enough with their plunder, for the firing became desultory and ended with the onset of darkness. Two men volunteered to ride to Fort Phil Kearny, reaching there at midnight with the news. At one A.M. Capt. John Green led two companies of 2nd Cavalry out of the fort, filming the besieged

Near Deadman's Pass, Texas, site of the July 1849 attack on the Lyons Wagons.

train at daylight. The trapped men groaned when they saw what appeared to be more Indians coming over the hill, but the groans turned to cheers when they recognized the horsemen as U.S. Cavalry.

While the wagons went on to Fort C. F. Smith, the dead and wounded were taken back to Phil Kearny. Shurly was incapacitated for almost eight months; Fitzgerald's hand was amputated; and Donnelly and McGeever later died of their wounds. They were buried in the post cemetery, along with Private Partenheimer. It was thought that about ten warriors were killed or wounded.[2]

A decade later the situation had not changed much on Wyoming's high plains. The summer of 1876 was a time of fear for emigrants, freighters, and settlers. The Battle of the Little Big Horn was still in the news, and Indians attacks increased along the North Platte River. Freighters hauling supplies up to Fort Laramie and Fort Fetterman had to be on guard. A. H. "Heck" Reel operated a freight outfit out of Cheyenne under army contract. In late July he organized a train of nine wagons in units of three, each drawn by 12 to 14 yoke of oxen. Each unit carried more than 24,000 pounds of freight.

The train left Cheyenne in late July with wagon boss George Throstle, second in command Sylvester Sherman, and a crew of 16 men. The supplies were destined for Gen. George Crook, then in camp on Little Goose Creek in Wyoming Territory, preparing to chase after the Indians who had defeated Lt. Col. George A. Custer. Reel told Throstle to furnish every man with a .45 revolver and a .44 Winchester rifle. The caravan rode north to the Chugwater, northwest to Cottonwood Creek, and on to the Overland Trail. On the night of 31 July they camped on Elkhorn Creek, about eight miles west of present-day Glendo, Wyoming.

Early on the first, the wagons started uphill north of the creek, trekked down into the valley of Coffee Creek, then traveled up another set of hills. The bluffs were steep and progress slow. It was four in the afternoon before they reached level ground on the divide south of the North Elkhorn. Throstle and Sherman rode ahead, talking of the ten miles they still had to go before reaching the next campsite on La Bonte Creek. Suddenly, about 30 Lakotas rode out from a deep draw north of the road. Three bullets hit Throstle, who yelled, "Oh, My God!" and fell from his horse. One bullet hit Sherman's saddle and creased his leg, but he spun his horse around and raced back to the wagons.

The Indians were upon the train before they could begin to corral. Teamster Irish Pete caught a bullet in his leg before the Indians broke away. The driver of the second unit deserted his post and jumped into the rear wagon of the first unit. The man in charge of the rear unit knew there was no chance to get his wagons into the corral, so he left it and drove in the abandoned second group. It looked like the Indians would get him, but he lashed the team with one hand while shooting his pistol with the other. In the corral, Sherman looked for the rifles; they were buried in a box under five thousand pounds of flour. The warriors circled the wagons, shooting from underneath their ponies' necks. They did not hit any more freighters, but wounded several oxen and saddle horses. When the freighters finally got the Winchesters working, the Indians fell back. In the deepening dusk, Irish Pete saw something move beyond the wagons and fired, killing a teamster's dog.

The Indians raided the rear wagon unit about 300 yards away, plundering and burning. They rolled away the beer kegs and set 10,000 pounds of bacon on fire; the flames rose 200 feet in the air. The wheel oxen of the rear unit burned to death, while the next animals pulled the front wheels off the wagon in their panic to escape the fire. By the light of the fires, the freighters kept close watch, but the Indians made no more charges. The next morning they were gone.

Sherman got the remainder of the train moving, and they soon found Throstle's body—stripped, scalped, and with his heart cut out. He was rolled in a tarpaulin and thrown on top of the supplies. In addition to Throstle's death and the wounding of Pete and Sherman, Reel lost three wagons, ten oxen, four horses, and thousands of dollars worth of goods.[3]

It was not only the Lakotas and Cheyenne of the northern plains who made it so dangerous for wagon trains. The Apaches had made southern Texas dangerous for Spanish, Mexicans, and Americans for 200 years. It was extremely hazardous for civilians, and not much safer for the U.S. Army. Regularly scheduled mail and passenger service between San Antonio, Texas, and San Diego, California, began in March 1857. First, George H. Giddings, and then James E. Birch, received contracts to carry the mail. Both used the Lower Military Road between Fort Lancaster and Fort Davis. The monthly express in the summer of 1857 consisted of an ambulance and a wagon escorted by Sgt. Ernest Schroeder, with six men of the 8th Infantry from Fort Davis, and Sergeant Libby with a wood detail of six men of the 1st Infantry from Fort Lancaster.

On the evening of 24 July, 1857, the party was about 25 miles west of Lancaster near Pecos Station when about 60 Mescalero Apaches attacked it. When the Indians approached, the two sergeants ordered the teams unhitched and the men to take cover. Some Indians approached with a white flag and shouted out in Spanish, but more warriors crept up in a nearby arroyo. Libby stepped forward, but Schroeder warned him: "Look out sergeant for the sons of bitches they will get the advantage of you if they can and don't put yourself in danger."

At that moment a bullet tore into Schroeder's chest and killed him. Libby ordered the party to retreat to Fort Lancaster. They fired as they fell back, keeping the Indians at bay, but the progress was slow and dangerous. Libby ordered them to abandon Schroeder's body and hurry on. At nightfall the Indians gave up the attack, and the tired men stumbled into the post at three o'clock the following morning.

Lt. Alexander M. Haskell, 1st Infantry, quickly organized a punitive expedition, but Lt. Edward Hartz, who was currently at Fort Lancaster with 46 men of the 8th Infantry, took command by seniority. Hartz had a plan. He had 80 men from Companies H and K, 1st Infantry, and Companies C, D, F, and H, 8th Infantry, climb aboard several wagons and hide. The canvas covers were drawn closed, and the force was disguised as a provision train. They set out immediately. Hartz hoped to lure the Indians close enough to throw back the covers and open fire on them. The stratagem was thought necessary because there were few other ways that foot soldiers could get close enough to the mobile Indians. A penny-pinching U.S. Congress had deemed cavalry too expensive—there were only five mounted regiments in the entire country at this time—and the slow-moving frontier infantry had to make the best of a bad situation.

The idea was sound, but the Apaches were not fooled. About 45 miles west of Fort Lancaster, about 40 warriors took the bait and began the attack. But upon seeing the commotion inside the wagons and the covers being pulled off, the warriors realized a surprise had been set for them and quickly pulled back out of range. Hartz ordered half of the soldiers out of the wagons to advance as skirmishers—in effect, placing his infantry in the same position they usually found themselves in: on foot and too slow to chase or counter the mounted warriors' moves. The Apaches set the prairie on fire, hoping to burn the wagons. Hartz recalled the soldiers and pulled his vehicles back to a bare, sandy depression; the crackling grass fire split in two and moved around them. When the fire passed and burned out, Hartz ordered his men forward, but by this time the Apaches were gone.

No soldiers were killed, and Hartz reported killing two Indians. He was critical in his report about the lack of mounted troops, claiming that infantry was powerless, and "the Indians are in virtual possession of the road."[4]

Hartz's stratagem was reproduced in many movies. It was used by Buck Jones in *Dawn on the Great Divide*. In *Apache Rifles* (Fox, 1964), Capt. Jeff Stanton (Audie Murphy), while on patrol looking for the Indians who massacred a party of miners, places some of his cavalrymen under cover in a wagon to lure the Indians. The tactic works and they capture Victorio's son, Red Hawk (Michael Dante), and force him to talk peace.

In *Rio Grande* (Republic, 1950), Col. Kirby York (John Wayne) charges his troopers into

Jeff Chandler and Jimmy Stewart discuss war and peace in *Broken Arrow* (Fox, 1950).

**John Wayne, as Hondo Lane, with his dog Sam in *Hondo* (Wayne-Fellows, 1953).**

an Apache–controlled adobe village, with some soldiers under cover in bouncing wagons, hellbent for battle. In Chapter Six, "Indian Vengeance," of the 15-part serial *The Oregon Trail* (Universal, 1939), Jeff Scott (Johnny Mack Brown) trades himself to the Indians in place of a captive white boy. A wagon train charges through the Indian village to aid in his rescue.

A wagon charge against Indians may seem far-fetched, even in a serial, but it did occur during the Indian wars in the West on at least one occasion. During the Red River War of 1874,

Lt. Frank D. Baldwin, with men of Company D, 6th Cavalry, and Company D, 5th Infantry, were escorting 23 wagons to Camp Supply in Indian Territory. On 8 November, 1874, Baldwin discovered Chief Grey Beard's Cheyenne village on McClellean Creek in the Texas Panhandle. With little time to formulate a plan, Baldwin formed his wagons in double column, placed the infantry in between, and surrounded the wagons with cavalry. The bugler sounded the charge, and the unorthodox procession galloped into the village.

Grey Beard held off the soldiers long enough to allow most of their women and children to escape, but lost about 20 warriors in the process. Baldwin took no casualties, rescued two white captives, and received a Medal of Honor for his efforts.[5]

For *Broken Arrow* (Fox, 1950), Delmer Daves directed the story of Tom Jeffords (James Stewart) making peace with Chiricahua Apache Cochise (Jeff Chandler). The plot is loosely based on fact but much over-romanticized, with a contrived love story between Jeffords and an (obviously white) Indian girl, Sonseeahray (Debra Paget). The film was hailed as one of the first to depict the Indians fairly and as human beings—which illustrates American audiences' and film critics' short memories, for such films were made many times during the silent era, with scores of them depicting white and Indian sweethearts and lovers.[6]

Jeffords's effort to bring peace to the Southwest resulted in a tentative trial run when Cochise promised not to molest any Butterfield stages. He did not, however, promise to refrain from attacking any military trains. As Colonel Burnall (Raymond Bramley) leads an army wagon train escorting Gen. Oliver O. Howard (Basil Ruysdael), Burnall comments that he hopes the Indians do attack, telling Howard he has 75 men, with 50 riflemen hidden under blankets in the wagons, ready to fight. Alas, Cochise is too smart for them and won't fall for the planned surprise. He attacks in three waves and draws the mounted escort away to kill them in an ambush. The wagons don't have a chance to circle; the soldiers jump out to fight, but are gunned down before they can form up. Nearly all the soldiers except Howard are killed, and the Indians steal the wagons with the guns and supplies that Burnall was supposed to protect.

One author praised *Broken Arrow* for a "burgeoning cultural awareness in Hollywood" and for portraying Indians as "multidimensional human beings." She apparently enjoyed director Daves showing the audience Cochise's military skill when he outfoxes the soldiers.[7] She may believe this was an accurate representation because it most likely fits her conceptions of the way things ought to have been, but the attack never happened. Cochise didn't wipe out an army wagon train.

Greater success at fighting Apaches from wagons was shown in the movie *Hondo* (Wayne-Fellows, 1953). The film's finale depicted a series of wagon train attacks, with soldiers riding under the canvas covers. The title character, Hondo Lane (John Wayne), gets involved with a frontier settler, Angie Lowe (Geraldine Page), married to no-good Ed Lowe (Leo Gordon). Ed leaves her and her son Johnny (Lee Aaker, who played Rusty in *Rin Tin Tin*) alone in dangerous Apache country, while he engages in nefarious activities. Lane becomes Angie's protector of sorts, in a role similar to Alan Ladd in *Shane* (Paramount, 1953).

Angie assumes she is safe because she has always been on friendly terms with Chief Vittorio (Michael Pate). Hondo has a fight with Ed Lowe, and has to kill him, not knowing he is Angie's husband until later, and not knowing when or how to tell her. When the Apaches capture Hondo, in order to save him and prevent a warrior taking her for his wife, Angie tells Vittorio that Hondo is her husband. Lane goes along with the story in order to get out of the predicament.

Eventually Hondo has to tell Angie that he killed her husband in a fight, but she already has divined that fact and accepts it. Vittorio and his warriors attack a wagon train of soldiers, but the chief is killed. The weary train of soldiers comes by Angie's cabin, where Hondo and Angie learn of Vittorio's death.

"It can't be," Angie says.

"Everybody gets dead," Hondo replies. "It was his turn."

## 26. The Lyons, Shurly, Reel, and Hartz Wagon Trains

In the end, cavalry scout Hondo leads the train of soldiers and settlers out of the embattled territory. He hides the troopers in the wagons, and they head out. When the Apaches attack, Hondo cries, "Circle the wagons!" Of course, the soldiers begin blasting the Apaches from beneath the wagon covers, one of which Hondo refers to as the "heavy artillery." The Indians fall back to begin the siege, but Hondo plans to keep moving. He starts the wagons racing forward, and the Apaches chase them again, only to have Hondo yell, "Circle the wagons!" The soldiers blast the Apaches once more. The warriors pull back. Hondo starts the wagon train dashing again, and the Indians follow. This time Hondo kills the Apache leader, and the dispirited warriors finally give up the chase.

"Wagons forward, Yo!" Hondo calls out as the train rolls on safely to the fort.

# 27

## The Sawyers Wagon Train (*Wagon Tracks*)

### Wyoming, August and September 1865

In March 1865, Congress appropriated $50,000 to build a wagon road from the junction of the Niobrara and Missouri Rivers to Virginia City, Montana Territory. Because of his political connections, James Sawyers was appointed to lead the expedition, which had the dual purpose of building a new road westward and publicizing a shorter route to the goldfields. Sawyers left the mouth of the Niobrara on 13 June, 1865, with 53 men and 15 wagons pulled by 45 yoke of oxen. His men included engineer Lewis H. Smith, expedition clerk and occasional scout Charles W. Sears, chief guide Ben F. Estes, assistant guide Baptiste Defonde, scout John F. Godfrey, physician Dr. Daniel W. Tingley, and James's younger brother, wagonmaster Newell M. Sawyers.

Escorting the expedition was the rather unwilling Capt. George Williford and 143 "Galvanized Yankees" of the 5th U.S. Volunteers (ex–Confederates who had taken the oath of allegiance and signed up to fight Indians), plus a detachment of 1st Dakota Cavalry under Lt. John R. Wood. The army escort had 25 wagons drawn by six mules each, and two 12-pound mountain howitzers. Joining them was an emigrant train of five wagons: one family of three men, two women, and three children; and two single males, Samuel H. Cassady and Edward H. Edwards. The largest section of the train was a freight outfit of 36 wagons, linked together to form 18 double wagons pulled by six yoke of oxen each, owned by Charles E. Hedges and Daniel T. Hedges of Sioux City, Iowa. John Hardin was wagonmaster, and Nathaniel D. Hedges, 19 years old, was in charge of the freight.

They traveled single file, with a squad of infantry and one howitzer in advance, followed by the escort wagons, then a squad of infantry, the expedition wagons, a squad of infantry, the emigrant and freight wagons, and a squad of infantry with a howitzer bringing up the rear. The guides and road laborers were kept in front of the train. The scouts and cavalry rode on the flanks to assure safety.[1]

Sawyers slowly traveled up the Niobrara, struggling through sand hills with the temperatures at times climbing over 100 degrees. By the time they reached the badlands of the upper White River, Williford's soldiers' clothing was in tatters, and he was short of supplies. By 9 August they had reached the upper Belle Fourche River and decided to strike northwest to the Powder River. A nearly waterless 32-mile trek over the next two days convinced Sawyers that it was not a place for a wagon road, and he retraced his steps.

They camped on Bone Pile Creek on 13 August, about ten miles southwest of the present town of Gillette, Wyoming. There, Cheyennes jumped Nate Hedges, who was out scouting only a mile and a half from the wagon corral. They killed him and ran off eight horses. Sawyers said that Hedges was "a genial and pleasant companion, and of very correct habits; his loss cast a gloom over the camp not soon dispelled."[2]

Sawyers moved the wagons a few miles down Bone Pile Creek to what appeared to be a better defensive position, corralled, and placed a strict guard. The men dug 20 or more rifle pits in a circle around the top of a knoll. Hedges was buried in the center of the corral and his grave concealed. On the 14th, the Indians appeared in force and made a dash at the herd, but the soldiers and civilians drove them off. The next day more than 500 Cheyennes and Lakotas appeared on the bluffs. They swept onto the plain, circling and shooting in a classic scene that would be recreated in many a Hollywood film, but were rebuffed again. At noon the Indians asked for a parley. Sawyers gave them a wagonload of sugar, bacon, coffee, flour, and tobacco in an attempt to buy his way out. George and Charles Bent, the mixed-blood sons of trader William Bent, rode with the Indians and acted as interpreters for the Oglala Red Cloud, the Northern Cheyenne Dull Knife, and the Southern Cheyenne Bull Bear.[3]

Captain Williford objected to giving gifts, certain that the Indians still meant to attack them, and he was proven correct. No sooner did Sawyers try to move when fighting broke out again. Dull Knife's Cheyennes had agreed to the bargain, but not some Lakotas who rode in after the gifts were distributed. The Lakotas shot and killed two Dakota Cavalrymen of Company B, John Rawze and Anthony Nelson, then pulled back to harass the train with long-range fire. By day's end, the warriors tired of the sport and rode away. Only Nelson's body could be recovered, and it was buried in the corral, much as Hedges had been. Five Lakotas were wounded, two of them mortally.[4]

On the morning of the 16th, Sawyers backtracked east to Caballo Creek, camping for two days while scouts brought in word that Gen. Patrick E. Connor was on Powder River on the west side of Pumpkin Buttes. Sawyers headed the train south to Fort Connor (later renamed Fort Reno), where he picked up an escort of 30 6th Michigan Cavalrymen and three officers, led by Capt. Don G. Lovell. They headed north along the eastern base of the Bighorn Mountains, now following the Bozeman Trail.

On 31 August, while approaching the Tongue River, Capt. Osmer F. Cole, 6th Michigan, rode ahead of the train and was caught and killed by about ten Arapahos. A short distance behind, Captain Lovell galloped up, fired on the Indians, and then retreated to the train for help. He returned with 12 cavalry troopers, but the Indians were gone, as was Cole's horse, equipment, and revolver. Cole was not scalped; the soldiers believed it was because he had only one arm, the other having been amputated in the Civil War.[5]

The next morning, 1 September, as the wagons forded Tongue River, a dozen Arapahos attacked the cattle herd at the rear of the train. The Indians captured several cattle and shot up the long train as it was strung out in the valley. Sawyers corralled the train while the soldiers ran out a howitzer to shell the Indians, killing war leader Heavy Horn and dispersing the rest. Sawyers's cook, Jack Marshall, was struck in the neck with a spent ball, but it did not break the skin. One horse was shot. A couple of hours later, with the warriors seemingly gone, the train moved north to the bluffs, only to find 75 more Arapahos firing from the shelter of the hills. Sawyers headed the wagons back toward the river, turned east, and moved downstream. This time, more Indians fired at them from hidden positions along the riverbank. Sawyers turned again and headed the train upriver.

The wagons corralled a second time, but they were still too near the river. Concealed Indians fired into the circle, mortally wounding teamster James Dilleland and emigrant E. G. Merrill. A bullet struck Dilleland on the left side of his back and exited near his naval. Another hit Merrill in the left breast and lodged under his left arm. Once again, Sawyers moved the wagons north, this time about 200 yards from the river. Late in the afternoon the Indians came in under a flag of truce to talk. Both sides seemed to be buying time. The Indians said they thought they were firing at General Connor's men, who had attacked their camp a few days earlier. As they parleyed, Sawyers hoped that messengers sent to Connor would soon return with reinforcements.

With nothing resolved, Sawyers readied the train for another attack and waited. Merrill died about ten o'clock that night, and Dilleland died 3 September. Cole, Dilleland, and Merrill were buried within the corral. Sawyers waited, trapped for nearly two weeks. The Indians made no more attacks, but their continued presence made Sawyers reluctant to proceed. A near-mutiny by his disgruntled employees forced him to turn back on 13 September. That evening, reinforcements of 2nd California Cavalry, under Capt. Albert E. Brown, arrived, and the weary men of the train, many of them disgusted with Sawyers's handling of the expedition, did another about-face and continued their long-delayed trek to Montana.[6]

The combined Sawyers Wagon Train comprised a substantial 81 wagons and about 250 people. Indians attacked trains with larger numbers of wagons and people, but they may not have attacked any other trains protected by a greater number of soldiers. When Captain Williford and Lieutenant Wood accompanied Sawyers on the first half of his journey, there were more than 160 soldiers defending the train. On many occasions during the Western Indian Wars the army tried to make it mandatory that wagon trains link up so that at least 100 armed men were with each train to make it "safe." The Indians apparently hadn't read the rules.

Sawyers's train, like Fisk's, was stopped by Indians who wanted to bargain before letting it proceed. They demanded payment of livestock or supplies to let the whites pass through their country. A twist on that scenario is seen in *Wagon Tracks* (Artcraft, 1919), produced by the well-known William S. Hart and Thomas H. Ince. The story takes place on the Santa Fe Trail, "where marched the pioneers, building a new empire in the sand-rimmed wilderness" (as the caption reads). Frontiersman Buckskin Hamilton (William S. Hart) travels from Santa Fe to Independence, Missouri, to meet his young brother Billy (Leo Pierson), freshly graduated from an Eastern medical school. Unbeknownst to Buckskin, Billy has been killed by David Washburn (Robert McKim) on a riverboat during a card game argument. Washburn's sister, Jane (Jane Novak), tries to stop the men as they wrestle with a gun. The weapon goes off, killing Billy. Jane faints, and David, with the help of his partner Guy Merton (Lloyd Bacon), tries to convince her that she is the one who killed the young man.

Buckskin arrives and learns the circumstances, but he is not convinced that the girl pulled the trigger. The entire party heads for Santa Fe, and Buckskin is elected captain of the wagon train. On the way, the grieving Buckskin and Jane fall in love, and Jane can no longer hold the secret; she believes it was her brother who pulled the trigger. Buckskin wants revenge, but he cannot take it without knowing for sure. He takes Washburn and Merton on a long trek through the desert, refusing to let them return for water until they confess. Finally, the two thirst-crazed men fight, and Merton reveals it was Washburn who did the killing. All of them make it back barely alive.

In the meantime, the wagons have corralled. The caption reads, "The Circle — a vital precaution for defense." While camped, many Kiowas ride in to parley and trade. One warrior tries to take a shawl from a woman's shoulders, and her husband shoots him dead. The angry Indians don't immediately retaliate; the chief informs the emigrants that if they want to proceed through their country, they must pay — not with supplies, but with a life. If they do not deliver up a prisoner for torture and death, the Indians will attack at dawn.

When Buckskin returns, the emigrants tell him of their dilemma. They are too few to resist an Indian attack, and they must select a man to sacrifice himself. (One wonders why they do not send the man who shot the warrior to his doom.) They decide to draw straws, but when Buckskin explains that Washburn murdered his brother, the emigrants decide that Washburn must be the victim. Washburn cringes and pleads, and Jane, who cannot let her brother be tortured and killed, implores Buckskin to find another solution. Buckskin, romantic and tragic hero that he is, decides that he will sacrifice himself instead, but Washburn will not be off the hook. Buckskin gives Washburn his gun, ordering that he must first shoot himself to pay for his crime. Instead, Washburn flees, but runs right into the Indians, who kill him anyway. Frontier justice, of sorts, is served, and the wagon train is allowed to proceed.

The storyline of *Wagon Tracks* may appear rather banal and juvenile to today's movie audiences, who have a century of film plots behind them. The success of the movie at the box office, however, inspired the production of *The Covered Wagon* four years later, which is said to be the first epic Western, and led to a long line of more sophisticated productions. For all its seeming implausibility, *Wagon Tracks* did have historical antecedents.

# 28

# The Burrell-Foster Wagon Train (*The Red Raiders, Westward Ho the Wagons*)

## Iowa 1854

Indians did not attack every wagon train. Many times, the emigrants' fears of what might happen were worse than what actually transpired. A significant number of pioneers never saw an Indian; others experienced more benign interactions, such as when Indians came in to trade or ask for something to eat. Indians did, however, successfully use hunger or the desire to barter as ruses to get in close to the wagons without arousing suspicion, and the emigrants always had to be on guard. Still, a number of emigrants learned to accept the appearance of Indians as a routine matter. A small sampling will illustrate the usual custom.

Jane Gould and her family headed west from Iowa in late April 1862, joining and leaving several larger trains as they traveled. On 30 May they were camped north of the Platte River in eastern Nebraska near Fremont. Jane wrote in her diary that day:

> While we were breakfasting this morning there was an Indian came in. He asked for something to eat. We gave him some doughnuts [and] offered him some milk which he declined. He peered around some time and finally said "coffee is good, sugar too." So I gave him some coffee with sugar in it. He took it and stirred it well and drank it leisurely with his biscuits. [When] we asked him if he was a Pawnee he said yes. Albert asked him if the Sioux were good [and] he [retorted], "Sioux no good, Cheyennes no good, Omaha good, Ottoes very good."[1]

The incident was not extraordinary. Jane got used to the Indians—at least until August, when she caught up with the Smart and Adams Train in present-day Idaho and just missed being involved in the attacks on those trains. Then, as we have seen, she changed her tune.

One train that had less trouble with Indians than with internal conflict and the weather was the famous Donner Party. Before they met their fate in the snows of the Sierras they were moving along as usual. On 16 June, 1846, at the junction of the North and South Platte Rivers in present-day Nebraska, Tamsen Donner wrote a letter. In it she said, "The Indians frequently come to see us and the chiefs of a tribe breakfasted at our tent this morning. All are so friendly that I cannot help feeling sympathy and friendship for them."[2]

Amelia Knight left Iowa for Oregon in 1853. Their wagons had not even gotten to the Missouri River when, about ten miles from Council Bluffs, they stopped for several days to "rest and recruit our cattle, wash, cook, etc." They saw their first Indians on 29 April. Amelia wrote, "Lucy and almira afraid and run into the wagon to hide."

By 2 May, the day before they were to start traveling again, they had been visited several times. "Indians came to our camp every day," Amelia wrote, "begging money and something to eat children are getting used to them."[3]

In 1854 Sarah Sutton traveled from Illinois to Oregon. On 17 July, nooning near Rock Creek in dangerous territory along the Snake River in Idaho, Sarah wrote, "this country for a few days travel has formerly been famous for Indians robbing and killing people, but good luck to us we have not seen one for several days."

Sarah didn't know how accurate, or lucky, she was, for a little farther down the road, and one month later, the Yantis, Perry, Ward, and Masterson families were all but destroyed by Indians. For Sarah, however, it was peaceful. On 21 July she wrote, "several more Indians came to see us before breakfast this morn. We could not feed them all much. We started early and left them all on the ground."[4]

Virgil K. Pringle left Missouri for Oregon in 1846. By 22 June, his wagon train came in sight of a party of Sioux packing up camp and moving toward Fort Laramie. They arrived near the fort about four that afternoon, where Pringle saw what he estimated were 200 lodges of Sioux. The next day he wrote:

> Camped last night with about 70 wagons. This morning all united in giving our Sioux brethren a feast with which they appeared highly pleased. It was conducted with considerable order and regularity on their part, smoking the pipe of peace and a friendly address from their chief and a present of powder, lead and tobacco on our part.[5]

Elizabeth Dixon Smith left Indiana for Oregon in 1847. By 13 July, the wagons were camped five miles past Fort Laramie. They had lost some cattle, and the men of the train paid some Indians to hunt for them. Elizabeth wrote in her diary, "The Indians came as before and set down in a circle and spread a blanket in their midst and beged [sic] presents we gave them provision and they dispersed." The next day Elizabeth wrote, "Layed by found the lost cattle payed the Indians for hunting 15 dollars although our men found them."[6]

Patty Sessions was in a Mormon wagon train heading from eastern Nebraska to Salt Lake City. On 5 August, 1847, she was also just beyond Fort Laramie when she recorded, "Go 7 miles pass fort larrimee [sic] see many Indians feed them but little feed yesterday and today I have fixed my wagon cover the girls baked currant pies."[7]

Although emigrants might see and interact with Indians anywhere along the route, it was often near Fort Laramie that many encounters occurred. It was there that a number of friendly bands, mostly Lakotas, congregated. They were sometimes deprecatingly termed the "Laramie loafers." The Burrell-Foster Wagon Train also met the Sioux at Fort Laramie—but it was not their first encounter.

Several families left the Plainfield, Illinois, area in the spring of 1854, headed for California. Among them were widowed Mary Burrell, her 18-year-old daughter Mary, and her son Edward, who was married to Louisa Hannibal Burrell. Wesley Tonner, young Mary's fiancé, was accompanying them. Isaac Foster was one of the leaders, and with him came his wife Grace and their two children. William and Mary Hannibal added a wagon. Putnam Robson, nephew of Mrs. Burrell, accompanied the train, as did Isaac Harter, brothers Silas and Oscar Wrightman, a Mr. and Mrs. Holmes, and four other young men, for a total of 21.

The train had barely reached Council Bluffs, Iowa, when an unfortunate encounter occurred. Young Mary Burrell wrote in her diary on 29 April, "had a fracas with the Indians. The emigrants killed 2. Wes got stabbed in the leg a little but not very seriously. got well frightened and left our old camp at dark & moved up to town."

Wesley Tonner described the incident in more detail. They were camped a few miles south of town when 11 Indians attacked a small train camped less than a mile from the Burrell-Foster

Train. Still being in Iowa, the warriors were certainly not Lakotas. They may have been Pawnees, but more likely Omahas, Iowas, or Otoes. When the emigrants ran to the Burrell-Foster train for help, Wes Tonner and several of "the boys" retrieved their weapons and rode over. They found the Indians in possession of the wagons, and it appeared that one warrior had been wounded in the scuffle. Tonner's boys only had pistols and couldn't compete with the Indians' rifles. They sent scattered shots into the wagons while one man rode to town for more help.

The implausible scene, with Indians defending the wagons and the emigrants firing at them from outside, didn't last long. The Indians soon disdained the wagon circle that emigrant and military defenders so cherished; fighting from a confined space was not their brand of warfare. Said Tonner, "They soon began to run each one his own way." Tonner and a companion rode after one warrior, who soon turned and, with a couple of other warriors, began to chase the emigrants. "We thought it our safest plan to wheel," Wes said, "which we did, and made for camp. Indians after us."

Back near the train, reinforcements from town arrived, and now it was the Indians' turn to wheel and run. Tonner and others went after two warriors riding one horse, when the duo stopped and began firing. When the Indians' rifles were empty, Tonner's party chased them about two miles along the Missouri River bottoms, firing all the time. They killed one, who dragged the other off the horse when he fell. The last warrior ran into the brush, and Tonner rode in after him, a near fatal move. "While trying to drop the villain with my revolver," Tonner said, "he ran up and gave me a dig in the leg with his knife before I could wheel the horse. We killed these two, and the one that was wounded, afterwards died."

Strangely enough, Tonner added, "There was talk of having us arrested," but apparently the authorities thought better of it. Tonner said he dared them. "I do not think there was any wrong about it. I fought for my rights, and tried to kill them lest they might attack our camp we knew not when." With a possible arrest pending, the train pulled out anyway, crossed the Missouri, and headed west. Tonner later learned that they had fought a renegade band that was molesting emigrants, that there might even have been a reward for them, and orders were sent to stop them at Fort Laramie. Nothing more came of it. "If any body had tried to take us after we were on the Plains," said Tonner, "they would have got reward with our Pistols for here we had the law in our own hands."[8]

The Burrell-Foster journey had barely begun when Indians attacked a nearby train, captured the wagons, and defended them from an emigrant counter-attack. The scenario appears so improbable that one might think only a screenwriter with a perverse sense of humor could have concocted it. And one did.

Screenwriter Marion Jackson may or may not have known that such an incident really happened, but it was a part of the action in *The Red Raiders* (First National, 1927). The movie is prefaced by the caption "The conquest of the West — led by a little band of fighting men whose deeds stand brilliant on the pages of our history." Similar introductions were common to early films but shunned by Hollywood in the latter half of the 20th century. The fighting men of this film are led by Lt. John Scott (Ken Maynard, in one of his better silent film performances), while the plot involves a band of Indians split into peace and war factions.

A number of real Indians played roles, which was not uncommon in the silent film era. The Sioux peace chief is played by White Man Runs Him, a Crow scout who actually accompanied Custer at the Battle of the Little Bighorn. Chief Yowlache is Lone Wolf, leader of the war faction.

Lone Wolf's continued raiding forces the white settlers to seek protection at the fort. The fort's commander, Captain Ortwell (J. P. McGowan), can't do anything because the president has given orders that the army must support the peace.

When the Indians continue to attack, the settlers are instructed to get into wagons and race for the fort as the Indians chase them. The film has plenty of spots for Maynard to show off his riding skills on his favorite stunt horse, Tarzan. He rides to recall two companies of cavalry that have been sent off on a wild goose chase.

The hard-pressed settlers reach the fort, and, in an odd scene, they ride their wagons in a circle around the fort, which they cannot get into while the gates are shut during the Indian attack. The wagons circle the fort, and the Indians circle around both. Warriors shoot flaming arrows into the covered wagons, and when some settlers abandon the vehicles, the Indians, in a reverse of the usual sequence, crawl under cover of the wagons to fight the settlers. Finally, Lieutenant Scott rides to the rescue with the cavalry, the Indians abandon the wagons, and Scott shoots down Lone Wolf. Even the most unlikely incidents in Western films often had historical counterparts.

Filming of *The Red Raiders*, which was partially shot on the actual Little Bighorn battlefield, had to be halted for a time when a chief was actually shot and killed. While the crew waited to see if there was going to be any retaliation by the Indians, it was learned that the dead Indian's son-in-law committed the murder, and filming resumed.

After the Burrell-Foster party had their run-in with Indians in Iowa, they continued their journey. They soon learned that an overland wagon trip west had its own way of quickly breaking in the travelers. This party had "seen the elephant" early, and was operating under its own rules in a short time. Future encounters with Indians were nowhere near as exciting. Several days later they met some Pawnees, and a few weeks after that were trading with Indians near Chimney Rock. They arrived at Fort Laramie on 29 May, two days before Mary Burrell's 19th birthday. She jotted in her diary:

> Two-story house made of Adobe. Wigwams in abundance. 5 Indian squaws came & begged for meat & bread, two men also, and in the afternoon 5 men came. I played on the melodeon for them. They were pleased & wanted Hannibal to dance. Got some cows shoed. Made fruit cakes, washed &c.

By this time in the journey, emigrants were generally used to the routine and ready to tackle the second half of the trip, which was where the most severe deserts and mountains would be encountered. The Burrell-Foster Train met a large, moving encampment of 400 Sioux farther up the Platte. They met and traded with some Indians, but warily avoided other bands west of Fort Bridger, near Pilot Peak, on the headwaters of the Humboldt and near Gravelly Ford. They reached California in late August.[9]

The experience of the Burrell-Foster Train, not having fought any major battle with the Indians, was actually more typical of western journeys. This, however, was not because battles and massacres never occurred, but because of the immense number of emigrants who made the trip. Historian Merrill Mattes estimated that 350,000 emigrants used the Oregon and California Trails from 1841 to 1866.[10] Of course, when we extend the time frame and include other trails, where fewer statistics were kept, the number of people going overland in the westward migrations from the 1830s to the 1870s easily reached half a million.

In 1956, Walt Disney Pictures produced *Westward Ho the Wagons*, one of the last wagon train movies that followed in the footsteps of *The Covered Wagon* and *The Big Trail*. Because many children would see the picture, Walt Disney wanted to emphasize an adventure where cooperation with the Indians was more typical than conflict.

As with the Burrell-Foster Train, Disney's movie emigrants heading west face the typical trials, beginning early in the opening scenes when Pawnees attack a train of 12 wagons and steal a number of horses. John "Doc" Grayson (Fess Parker) and Hank Breckinridge (Jeff York) are leading the train loaded with other Disney regulars, including a passel of "Mouseketeers," such as Karen Pendleton, Cubby O'Brien, Tommy Cole, and Doreen Tracey.

As "Doc" Grayson, Parker sings songs, one about the famous run of John Colter when he escaped from the Blackfeet. Shortly after, Dan Thompson (David Stollery, who appeared in other Disney productions, such as *Spin & Marty*) is captured. He escapes, running like John Colter, outdistancing his pursuers and making it back to the wagon train.

Pawnees chase the train. Grayson has placed the best shots in the two rear wagons, hidden under the covers. When the Indians catch them at the bluffs, Grayson orders that their horses be released, because that's what the Pawnees really want. It works.

At Fort Laramie, Hank yells, "Circle your wagons," and the train stops to prepare for the second half of the trip. There, as did so many emigrants from historical wagon trains, they meet the Sioux, albeit with some skepticism as to whether they will be friendly or not. Disney has his cast engage in some non-politically correct discourse. When "Doc" Grayson asks, "If an Indian wants something a white man has, what does he do?"

"Scalps him," says young Jerry Stephen (Cubby O'Brien).

Potential trouble arises when the Sioux chief decides he wants to trade for the pretty blond girl, Myra Thompson (Karen Pendleton), and is rebuffed. When the chief's son is badly injured falling from a horse, the medicine man, Many Stars (Iron Eyes Cody), cannot cure him. "Doc" Grayson decides to put his life on the line and give it a try. As Grayson, Fess Parker, fresh from his role as Davy Crockett, this time is less important as an Indian fighter than as a healer, for he cures the boy and secures the good graces of the Sioux, who then agree to guide the emigrants on their journey. The wagon train leaves Fort Laramie, accompanied by theme song "Westward Ho, the Wagons," and they travel safely and happily on to Oregon.

The idea of whites doctoring sick Indians is not a Disney invention. At many trading posts, missions, and later on the reservations, Indians tried the white man's medicine. Government initiatives additionally saw to the vaccinations of many. In 1836, nearly two decades before the Burrell-Foster Train, the missionary families of the Whitmans and Spaldings were among the first to take wagons west. The Whitmans settled in what is now southeast Washington, near Walla Walla, and began administering, treating, and teaching the local Indians. The Sager children, as discussed above, were taken to the Whitmans for care. Although Marcus and Narcissa Whitman tried their best, an epidemic of measles that swept through the area in 1847 killed many people, white and Indian alike.

The Cayuse tribe was divided between trusting Marcus and his medicine, or their own *tewats*, or medicine men. Both failed to stop the disease that claimed so many lives. Distrust, jealousies, and cultural challenges led the Indians to rise up and strike on 29 November, 1847, killing Marcus, Narcissa, and about eight others, and capturing 49 whites and mixed-bloods living at the mission. The failure of a white doctor to cure his Indian patients was a major factor in the catastrophe that followed.[11] The challenge of "Doc" Grayson in *Westward Ho* reflected this historical peril.

Producer Walt Disney at first did not want Indians shown killing anyone while attacking a wagon train. Second-unit director Yakima Canutt protested, saying that people died during attacks on wagon trains, and that it would not be realistic to leave that out. But, since children would be watching the movie, Disney insisted there should be no killing shown. After screening the film, however, Disney realized the attack looked too phony and told Canutt to re-film the attack scenes. Canutt told him it would take another week and several hundred thousand dollars, but Disney gave the okay. He realized he needed to get it right.

Even Disney, the force behind scores of family-oriented productions, knew he should not attempt to change some basic facts of American history: although many emigrants passed through unscathed, Indians attacked wagon trains and people were killed.

Just how horrible an experience awaited the unlucky ones is graphically illustrated by the fate of the German family.

# 29

# The German Wagon Train
## (*Rio Grande, Lonesome Dove, Last Train from Gun Hill*)

### Kansas, September 1874

The era of western exodus by wagon train was over by the 1870s. The days of the six-month journey across half the continent at a walking pace received its death knell in 1869. On 10 May, at Promontory Point in the northwest corner of present-day Utah, and just south of the Hudspeth Cut-Off of the old Oregon Trail, the "wedding" of the Central Pacific and Union Pacific Railroads was consummated with the driving of the final golden spike. Finally, the Missouri River was connected with the Pacific Ocean.[1]

Although the years of the great wagon migrations were over, not everyone could afford to travel west by railroad. One family searching for its dreams in the West left Georgia for Colorado in 1870. It was a long, slow journey for John and Lydia German; four years after starting out, they still had not arrived. They spent time in Missouri and southeastern Kansas, finally leaving Elgin on 15 August, 1874. Several railroads were in operation by then, and there were few emigrants using the old wagon roads; but John and Lydia, now both 44 years old, could not afford the fare. With one wagon and several oxen they walked west, following the old Smoky Hill Trail across central Kansas. Their seven children, Rebecca Jane (age 20), Stephen (19), Catherine (17), Joanna (15), Sophia (12), Julia (7), and Nancy "Addie" Adelaide (5), helped in whatever ways they could. On the night of 10 September they camped on the banks of the Smoky Hill about a dozen miles east of Fort Wallace.

By sunrise they were awake and driving the wagon up the bluffs. Rebecca and Lydia were on the driver's seat, John walked ahead carrying his musket, and Stephen and Catherine walked herd on their cattle. Stephen thought he saw an antelope and pointed toward the bluffs. But he and Catherine were both startled to see Indians charging down. They ran. From the wagon, Sophia counted 19 Indians.

They were Cheyennes, and they included Medicine Water, his wife Mochi, and his brother Cometsevah. They had all survived the 1864 battle at Sand Creek. One warrior shot John in the back, and Mochi plunged a hatchet into his skull. Lydia jumped off the wagon and ran to him, crying, "Oh let me get to father!" She was murdered next to her husband. Lydia was pregnant, and the Cheyennes sliced open her belly and tore her unborn child from her. Rebecca grabbed an ax and tried to defend herself, but she was knocked senseless and several Indians raped her. When they were done, and while Rebecca lay unconscious, they covered her with bedclothes from the wagon, set her on fire, and burned her to death.

Site of the September 1874 German Family massacre along the Smoky Hill River, Kansas.

Indians killed Stephen and shot Catherine in the leg with an arrow. Medicine Water pulled out the shaft and threw her onto his bay horse. The Indian pulled the four youngest sisters out of the wagon and tore their bonnets off their heads to see who had the longest locks. Joanna's long blonde hair made her the choice. She was shot in the head and scalped. Addie began to cry, but Julia was so shocked that, as she later said, "I could not cry. There wasn't enough tears in my eyes."[2]

It had been 45 years, 75 miles, and hundreds of attacks since the 1829 raid on Bent's Wagon Train. Little had changed.

The Cheyenne marauders took whatever loot they could carry, rounded up four cows and two calves, hoisted the four surviving sisters on horses, and rode south to the Texas Panhandle. Nearly three weeks after the massacre a hunter discovered the charred wagons, and the news was reported to Fort Wallace. As a result, Lt. Christian C. Hewitt, 19th Infantry, led a patrol to the scene. In the dirt was a family bible with nine names inscribed. The numbers didn't match the bodies, and the soldiers knew that there were four missing girls. For the next few months the girls' rescue was a primary goal for most of the army on the southern Plains. Nine miles from the massacre site the Cheyennes camped and divided up the spoils, including the girls. The warriors raped Catherine and Sophia.

Over the next weeks the girls were treated very cruelly, suffering from exposure, beatings, and starvation. Sophia's ankles were tied to a horse so tightly with rawhide straps that they ripped through her skin, leaving her scarred 60 years later. The two elder sisters were forced into concubinage, made to do backbreaking labor, and abused by the Cheyenne women. Mochi, said Catherine, "seemed delighted to see us tortured or frightened." For one of her ordeals, Catherine said, "I was stripped naked, and painted by the old squaws, and made the wife of the chief who could catch me when fastened upon the back of a horse and set loose on the prairie. I don't know what Indian caught me." Later she declared that "nearly all in the tribe" had raped her.[3]

## 29. The German Wagon Train

On 24 September, near North McClellan Creek, southeast of present-day Pampa, Texas, the Cheyennes spotted a herd of bison. In the warriors' excitement, the two who usually had charge of the two youngest sisters set them down and rode away. Catherine tried to rein up and see what was happening, but other warriors lashed her forward. Catherine assumed that the girls were such a burden that the Indians had killed them. She told Sophia what she saw, and Sophia sadly replied, "They are better off than we are!"[4]

Julia and Addie wandered around until they saw some wagon tracks, followed them to an abandoned army camp, and found hardtack, horse corn, wild berries, and onions to eat. Wolves threatened them, but they drove them away. Incredibly, the little girls survived for about six weeks on their own. During that time, soldiers had been combing the plains searching for the captured girls, while fighting with the Indians in numerous actions that became known as the Red River War. Stone Calf and his Cheyenne band, with which Catherine and Sophia were now living, was aware that the army knew of the four captive girls. He realized

Sophia German and Catherine German (courtesy of Arlene Feldmann Jauken).

that if he was caught and confronted with that fact, he needed to have four girls, not just two. He sent out scouts, who found the two missing captives and returned them to the village. The girls were given raw meat to eat, but being near death, neither could even chew.[5]

On Sunday, 8 November, it was still uncertain whether Julia and Addie's luck in being "rescued" was good or bad, for that morning, Lt. Frank D. Baldwin, with Company D, 6th Cavalry, and Company D, 5th Infantry, made a wagon train charge into Grey Beard's village on North Fork McClellan Creek. Grey Beard's warriors held the soldiers off for a time while the women and children scattered. Among those gathered up and taken away were Catherine and Sophia German. Sophia had learned a few words of Cheyenne and heard the Indians say it would be best to kill her little sisters; one rode back to do so. Julia crawled under some buffalo robes near a fallen lodge. A warrior fired at the robes, but a soldier immediately shot and killed him. As the soldiers rummaged through the wreckage, George James, 5th Infantry, lifted the robes and saw a starved white child.

"What is your name, dear little girl?" he asked.

"My name is Julia German," she answered, "and Addie and Sophia were here a while ago."[6]

The soldiers searched the other lodges and finally found Addie. She could hardly walk. A Sergeant Mahoney arrived and picked Addie up. He held her close and wept. One hardened teamster remarked, "I have driven my mules over these plains for three months, but I will stay forever or until we get them other girls." Said George James, "I give you my word, the condition those girls were in almost set us hard boiled soldiers to blubbering." Fifty years later, Addie remembered, "How good the soldiers were to sister and myself."[7]

Julia German and Adelaide German (courtesy of Arlene Feldmann Jauken).

The soldiers tried to force the Indians onto the reservation and obtain the last two captives. In late December 1874, Cheyennes surrendering at Darlington, IT, informed the agent that one sister (Catherine) was in Stone Calf's village, the property of Long Back, who made money gambling with her and farming her out as a prostitute; while the other (Sophia) belonged to Wolf Robe, who was in Grey Beard's Band. In January 1875, Col. Nelson A. Miles sent a friendly

## 29. The German Wagon Train

German Family gravesite, Fort Wallace Cemetery, Kansas.

Indian to take a message to the "Misses Germaine" that their little sisters were safe, and that every effort was being made to rescue them.

Constant pressure from the troops, starvation, and despair finally had their effect, and on 6 March, 1875, Stone Calf, Grey Beard, and 820 Indians surrendered at Darlington. Catherine, nearly 18 years old, weighed 80 pounds, and Sophia, nearly 13, weighed 65 pounds. The soldiers and employees took up a collection for them.

Julia and Addie went to Fort Leavenworth in December, and Catherine and Sophia went there in April 1875. With no parents or nearby relatives, Colonel Miles became their guardian. In 1879 Congress finally appropriated money for the care of the German Sisters. Catherine died in 1932, Addie died in 1942, and Sophia died in 1949. In 1957 Julia was a guest of the Fort Wallace Memorial Association when the old prairie graves of the German family were located and a new stone dedicated at the Fort Wallace Cemetery. Julia died on 1 June, 1959, at age 92, the last white captive taken from a wagon train.[8]

Hollywood of the first half of the 20th century could offer some realism when depicting scenes of Indian outrage upon white victims—but not much. In *Rio Grande* (Republic, 1950), Apaches attack an army-escorted wagon train leaving a wilderness post and heading to Fort Bliss. The wagons race from the attackers, with the attendant chaos of spilled horses and riders, and stuntmen falling under rolling wagons. The train finally, sensibly, circles up, and the soldiers tip the wagons over to use as firing barricades. One trooper, Jefferson York (Claude Jarman Jr.), rides for help.

The Apaches break off the attack, for they have cut out a couple of wagons with white women and children. They take them south of the Rio Grande into Mexico, to a small village that they have taken from the Mexicans. Col. Kirby York (John Wayne), following Gen. Phil Sheridan's (J. Carrol Naish) verbal "suggestion," crosses the river into Mexico to punish the Apaches and rescue the women and children.[9] On the way they find a wrecked wagon. Nearby

The last film in John Ford's cavalry trilogy, *Rio Grande* (Republic, 1950) had historical antecedents in depicting the capture and rescue of white children, with soldiers chasing Indians across the border into Mexico.

is the body of Mrs. Bell, wife of Corporal Bell, who is in the rescue party. He wants to see the body, but Colonel York refuses his request in order to spare him the sight. Director John Ford only allows the audience to see Mrs. Bell's bonnet lying in the mud amid the charred wreckage.

When the soldiers approach the village, Troopers Travis Tyree (Ben Johnson), Daniel "Sandy" Boone (Harry Carey Jr.), and Jeff York volunteer to sneak inside and find the children. They locate the captives in an old adobe church—clean, clothed, unharmed, and apparently as happy as on a picnic. The boys still wear army kepis, and one girl, Margaret Mary (Karolyn Grimes—Zuzu Baily in *It's a Wonderful Life*), is so cheerful and talkative that she has to be hushed three times so she won't reveal the soldiers' presence. She is allowed to go into the steeple to ring the church bell as a signal to Colonel York to begin the attack.

York charges in with some mounted troopers, and with others riding in the backs of bouncing wagons, much as in the actual fight on McClellan Creek in 1874 when Lieutenant Baldwin charged his wagons into the Indian camp to rescue Julia and Addie German. The three troopers in the church at the other end of the village begin firing, and the Apaches attack them, only to be shot down by the soldiers shooting through a cross-shaped opening in the wooden door. Colonel York is wounded by an arrow, but the Apaches are vanquished and all the children saved—without injury and with hardly a hair out of place. The smiling boys and girls will probably look back on their encounter as a fun, trauma-free adventure. Details of their captivity are not addressed, and their happy faces reflect an experience far removed from the ordeal of the German Sisters—and that of scores of other captive children.[10]

More realism in depicting the fate often in store for captives, and far removed from the fairy tale lived by Cresta (Candace Bergen) in *Soldier Blue*, was seen in the TV mini-series *Lonesome Dove* (1989). When Lorena Wood (Diane Lane) is captured by the renegade Indian Blue Duck (Frederic Forrest), her experience is much akin to that of Catherine German. Lorena is raped by a band of Kiowas, serves as high stakes in a dice game, and is starved and beaten until near death. It takes her much time to physically recover, and psychologically she never heals.

The same year that Julia German died, *The Last Train from Gun Hill* (Paramount, 1959) appeared. The entire plot stems from opening scenes in which the white bad guy, Rick Belden (Earl Holliman), rapes and kills an Indian woman (Ziva Rodann). By that time, a major shift in Western movie themes was already in the making. Few people would have cared to tell the German Sisters' story, for old villains were becoming heroes, and old heroes were becoming villains. It is unfortunate that, before Julia died, she could not have talked with some of the young filmmakers and historians who would leave their politically correct marks on the latter half of the 20th century.

# 30

## Trail Deaths
## (*The Covered Wagon, The Big Trail, Westward the Women, How the West Was Won*)

That the road west was fraught with danger is illustrated by the hundreds of emigrants killed, wounded, or captured by Indians.[1] Death, however, was ever present in many other forms. Accidental fatalities, listed by historian Merrill Mattes in descending order of deadliness, were caused by shootings, drownings, crushing by wagon wheels and domestic animals, falling objects, sharp instruments, rattlesnakes, buffalo hunts, hail, and lightning. The emigrants, called "walking arsenals" by Mattes, killed or wounded themselves more than they did Indians.[2]

One example, detailed earlier, was when little Catherine Sager jumped off a moving wagon and fell beneath a wheel, which crushed her leg. More tragic was the experience of the Martin and Mary Ringo Family. As they traveled west in 1864, in the vicinity of present-day Glenrock, Wyoming, Martin Ringo stepped atop his wagon to pull out his shotgun. A witness named Davenport wrote of what happened. The gun went off, "the load entering his right eye and coming out the top of his head. At the report of the gun I saw his hat blown up twenty feet in the air, and his brains were scattered in all directions."

Mary Ringo later recorded in her diary: "And now Oh God comes the saddest record of my life for this day (July 30) my husband accidentally shot himself and was buried by the wayside and oh, my heart is breaking, if I had no children how gladly I would lay me down with my dead."[3]

The remaining Ringos were not yet done with hardship and heartache. At another fort beyond, possibly at Fort Bridger or Camp Douglas near Salt Lake City, the army offered an escort of soldiers to see the Ringos back to Missouri; but Mrs. Ringo, according to one of the children, Mattie Bell, said she was as much afraid of soldiers as she was of Indians, and besides, Missouri "wouldn't seem like home without father."

In late September in eastern Nevada, camped near the Ringos was the wagon of a Mrs. Richardson, who gave birth to a baby son. The incident certainly reminded the pregnant Mary Ringo that her time of confinement was also near. They reached Austin, Nevada, in early October, with tragedy right behind. Mary gave birth to a stillborn son. According to Mattie Bell, this may have been for the best, since the baby "was terribly disfigured from mother seeing father after he was shot."

The Ringos had five children. The eldest at the time was 14-year-old John, who commented that, disfigured or not, the baby "looked just like father did." After selling some oxen and a wagon, the family finally made it to California. The fatherless boy eventually went "bad," drifting to Texas and Arizona, and becoming the notorious gunfighter Johnny Ringo.[4]

Most families traveling west did not experience the great tragedies of the Ringos, but thousands dealt with disease, accidents, birth, and death. A small sampling will suffice as illustration.

In 1851 Jean Rio Baker sailed with a group of English Mormons across the Atlantic, up the Mississippi River, and to Iowa, where they joined a wagon train to Salt Lake City. In Baker's lengthy diary we see one of the party succumbing near present-day Grand Island, Nebraska, about 20 July. "We remained in camp repairing damages," Baker wrote, "this day at half past two o'clock, Sister Kempton died, she came with us from London, and was in her usual health till two days ago, Aunt Bateman and I laid her out, and sewed her body up in a sheet, she was buried by the Brethern at sunset, on the summit of a small hill, where there are 5 more graves."

From the rapidity of Kempton's demise we can speculate that she was carried away by a quick-acting, deadly disease, although Baker mentions no epidemic among the emigrants. One month later, on the North Platte beyond Fort Laramie, the wheel of life came full circle. On 19 August, Baker wrote, "Remained in camp all day, repairing damages, Sister Sharkey gave birth to a daughter, doing well."

Six days later Baker recorded, "I was sent for Sister Henderson, who had been sick for two days. In one hour, I was enabled to assist her in giving birth to a daughter, but the Mother is so much exhausted that I fear she will not rally again." Two days later he wrote, "Sister Henderson died to-day at noon, we buried her at 9 P.M., she left seven children."[5]

Sarah M. Mousley traveled in another Mormon wagon train to Salt Lake City in 1857. On 12 July, near Prairie Creek, not far from where Sister Kempton died, Sarah recorded in her diary: "Encamped for dinner and here visited or went to see the corps of an aged Sister who had been subject to disease of the heart and died from fright by her husband being kicked by one of his oxen."

Two days later Sarah wrote: "Just after our encampment for the night we were called to receive a little stranger in our midst," the offspring of a Mrs. Forman. "Mother and daughter doing well," Sarah said, "retired early to rest after service."[6]

In 1848 Keturah Belknap and her family headed to Oregon. Tragedy visited the train early in the journey while still near St. Joseph, Missouri. They debated whether to move on a Sunday and "break the Sabbath," but the more eager among them prevailed. Keturah recorded: "So we all started but had only gone about 5 miles when a little boy was run over by the wagon and instantly killed. We then stopped and buried the child. We were near a settlement so it was not left there alone."

Far along the trail near Fort Hall, in present-day Idaho, Keturah's three-year-old boy Jesse "was very sick with Mountain Fever," and the parents despaired that he might die. After sitting up with him all night, the fever broke, and they were able to travel again. Keturah delivered another baby son, Lorenzo, on 10 August, 1848, in eastern Oregon. Far too busy now, Keturah recorded no further entries in her diary.[7]

Francis Sawyer left Kentucky in 1852, heading for California. On 16 July, in Hot Springs Valley in eastern Nevada, Francis reported that the "Digger Indians" killed a white man, who was buried alongside the trail. In early August along the Carson River, Francis and her family nooned with another family. The woman had just delivered a son. "The arrival of the little stranger," Francis wrote, "made it necessary for his friends to go into camp for a week or more.... I have heard of several children being born on the plains, though it is not a very pleasant place for the little fellows to first see the light of day."[8]

Hannah Tapfield King emigrated from England to Utah in 1853. In her journal she recorded that on 22 August, while in the vicinity of Devil's Gate, Wyoming, she "first saw a splendid bearded Comet." Since it was quite common at the time to associate comets with upcoming misfortune, perhaps it was with some resignation that Hannah also recorded the death of a man she knew only as "Vincent." "This death makes me feel gloomy," she wrote.

Nearing Green River on 2 September, the wheel turned again. "Yesterday Sister Jones was confined with a daughter amid Thunder & Lightening," Hannah wrote. Still concerned with omens, she added, "I should think something of it were it my case."[9]

In these peripatetic communities on wheels, disease was even more deadly than accidents. The two most dreaded by travelers and Indians alike were cholera and smallpox, which seemed to sweep the plains in cycles. John Unruh estimated that there might have been 10,000 emigrant deaths during the westward migrations, with nine out of ten attributable to diseases. One traveler along the Oregon Trail in 1852 recorded 401 fresh graves along the way, and another believed that within ten years "the road will be a complete graveyard."[10]

Although wagon train movies have scarcely touched upon the danger of disease on the trail, they have conventionally depicted deaths and births. The movie journeys are almost always for the purposes of settlement, with a community of families having to overcome great hazards to follow their dreams. Although many of the hazards stem from Indian attacks, the more mundane cycle of death and birth is evident in these communities on wheels.

Considered an influential and milestone film, *The Covered Wagon* (Paramount, 1923) introduced the epic tradition to the Western movie and gave it a grand scale. Shot in Utah and Nevada, the film offered some striking sequences, showing 400 wagons crossing rivers, buffalo hunts, campfire-singing, snow and mud, prairie fires, and an Indian attack on the wagon train in a box canyon, complete with a dramatic cavalry rescue.

"Not a false whisker in the film," claimed director James Cruze, who used genuine Conestoga wagons and a cast of 3,000, including 1,000 Indians. *The Covered Wagon* was steeped in romantic myths of nation-building. As a grand gathering of emigrants head west along the Oregon Trail in 1848, narrative cards inform the audience: "The blood of America is the blood of pioneers—the blood of lion-hearted men and women who carved a splendid civilization out of an uncharted wilderness." Other cards tell us that the journey was one of "crushing hardship, discontent and homesickness ... grinding toil" and "staggering loss of wagons and stock."[11]

For the first two weeks of the journey the emigrants evidently feel safe, and the wagons aren't circled up at night. A fortnight into the trek the first emigrants begin turning around after finding the journey to be harder than they imagined. Those who continue begin to abandon treasured possessions when many heretofore essential keepsakes become unnecessary weight. Soon, old Mrs. Wattles sickens and dies, although of what malady we aren't told. The funeral is held, and she is buried by the trail in an unmarked grave. The travelers throw ashes and sticks over the area, and the rolling wagons blot out every trace of her existence. At the same time, a new baby is born to another woman in the train, and the life and death cycle continues, with the pioneers' journey a microcosm of a larger scheme.

Within the larger train are the Wingate and Woodhull groups, but philosophical, temperamental, and romantic differences cause them to split up. In one scene, gruff Sam Woodhull (Alan Hale) shoots an Indian who demands money to ferry their wagons across the Platte. The Pawnees attack and kill many of Woodhull's train, but he escapes. Later, along the Snake River, Woodhull fights Will Banion (J. Warren Kerrigan) over, among other things, the affections of pretty Molly Wingate (Lois Wilson). One group, with the Woodhulls, splits off to California, while another, under old Jesse Wingate (Charles Ogle), stays on track for Oregon.

*Opposite:* **Considered the first epic Western, *The Covered Wagon* (Paramount, 1923) was grand in scope and had a documentary quality, almost as if James Cruz had filmed an actual wagon train in the 1840s.**

The separation is shown by the abandoned plows on the roadside. Wingate warns about the lure of gold: "The pick and the shovel never built a country—you've got to have a plow." Will Banion, however, is no farmer. He and his companions, Jim Bridger (Tully Marshall) and William Jackson (Ernest Torrence), in the same roles they later played in *Fighting Caravans* (1931), head for the gold fields. Banion's trip is only temporary, however. After he makes his fortune, he returns to Oregon to marry his sweetheart, Molly. The journey is over, the families have been re-settled, and, presumably, the birth and death cycle will continue.[12]

In a similar vein, *The Big Trail* (1930) presented scenes of people and animals dying throughout the long journey. After the wagons are lowered down their version of "Windlass Hill," the emigrants cross a desert. Oxen and mules succumb in the waterless stretches, as do several people, who are buried by the trail while the wagons roll over the nameless graves. After the climactic Indian attack the emigrants are left to bury about a dozen victims of the fighting, from old to young. This time, mounds of dirt and stones marked with crosses memorialize their passing. "Old Wendy has gone on another trail," Breck Coleman (John Wayne) tells Zeke (Tully Marshall), trying to console him. In a poignant scene, one emigrant leaves a ragdoll on a little girl's grave.

Touching scenes of death on the trail were the staple of many wagon train Westerns. In *Westward the Women* (MGM, 1952), directed by William Wellman, there is a severe lack of marriageable women on Roy Whitman's (John McIntyre) California farm. Whitman goes to Chicago to recruit about 150 potential brides. Buck Wyatt (Robert Taylor) reluctantly leads the wagon train, believing that women will not be able to handle the demands of 2,000 miles of trail.

To the contrary, the women, including Patience Hawley (Hope Emerson) and fiery Fifi Danon (Denise Darcel), prove every bit as capable of handling the wagons as any men, braving weather, fire, flood, drought, runaway wagons, rape, murder, and Indians attacks. Emotive scenes include a military-like roll call of fatalities after an Indian attack, and the tragic death of a little Italian boy, followed by the birth of a baby under a blistering desert sun. The survivors do reach California, receiving the respect they won and deserve by their rite of passage.

In *How the West Was Won* (MGM, 1962), buffalo are the cause of many trail deaths. The Indians, angered by the railroad building its iron tracks through their country, stampede a herd of bison through the railroad camp. The thundering animals destroy buildings and equipment, and trample people. After the dust settles, we see one little boy crying over his mother's crushed body.

Scout Zeb Rawlings (George Peppard) argues with railroad boss Mike King (Richard Widmark) about the efficacy of his plan to build through Indian country. As the child wails, Rawlings queries King, asking if he can live with the sound of suffering in his ears. King brushes off the question. "That ain't crying," he says, "that's first new life goin' on."

In regards to deaths on the trail, Hollywood got the concept right, and even did a pretty good job with the details.

# 31

# Stagecoach Attacks
# (*Stagecoach*)

Corollary to attacks on wagon trains were attacks on stagecoaches, but the subject of Indians versus stagecoaches would merit another book, so a few examples will have to suffice here. It would be difficult to name even a handful of Westerns that did not have stagecoaches in them, and those films where white bandits or Indians chased a stage were nearly as numerous. The attacks were not something that Hollywood made up. They occurred across the entire West.

One author has written that the first time white bandits attacked a moving stagecoach occurred in California in August 1856.[1] Indians attacked coaches before that. One incident happened on the Lower Military Road in southern Texas in 1854, when Henry Skillman and George H. Giddings operated the San Antonio to El Paso mail. The first coach under their new partnership left for El Paso on 1 November, led by George's brother Frank and James Hunter. Skillman and merchant A. C. Rand followed behind them one day later. Two Mexican guards rode along, and the driver was a rough, notorious character named Jack Gordon. Heavy rain slowed both parties, but on the night of the 14th Skillman caught up with Giddings in west Texas at El Muerto Springs, near present-day Valentine. They breakfasted together the next morning.

Skillman got started earlier, promising to wait for Giddings at Eagle Springs. Several miles west of El Muerto, Skillman met an eastbound coach, and the two parties exchanged news. Skillman continued for another dozen miles before stopping to shoe a mule. In the meantime, Giddings began rolling; but before he could catch up to Skillman, about 50 Mescalero Apaches caught up with him.

The Indians reined up about 200 yards away and called out, "Amigos!" When the Apache leader came forward, guard Louis Dixon warned them to stay back if they wanted to stay alive. The warriors pulled back and began circling. One of them waved a bloody soldier's jacket that belonged to a dispatch rider who they killed a week earlier west of Fort Clark. Instead of charging Giddings, however, they sped off after Skillman. Reaching his coach, they tried their ruse of friendship again, also to no avail. Skillman waved them away, and the Indians opened fire. Things got even hotter when Gidding's coach galloped up, broke through the circling warriors, and joined Skillman.

"The prettiest part of the fight was now coming on, and the fun was not stopped 'till sundown," a coach passenger said. Fifteen hard-fighting and straight-shooting Texans coolly met the circling Indians and held off their repeated charges. Some Mescaleros climbed a rise a few hundred yards away and began lobbing shots into the Texans' position. Two passengers were wounded, and several mules were hit, including Skillman's favorite animal. Giddings hitched up the teams to pull out of range while Skillman covered him. Eyewitnesses said that Skillman was an excellent rifle shot, and he killed three Indians at 300 yards. Rand fired one dozen times with his Sharps, and the sure, steady fire drove the Indians out of range. They continued the siege from a respectful distance, and finally left the determined Texans at nightfall. When the expressmen reached El Paso and their story was told, they were treated as heroes.[2]

In the summer of 1861 the Civil War was heating up. In Virginia on 21 July the first bloody clash of the war was being fought near a little stream called Bull Run. The same day, 2,000 miles west, a small group of Unionists decided to abandon Franklin (El Paso), Texas, upon seeing the approach of Confederate forces. Some of them were former Butterfield employees, and they agreed to take the San Antonio and San Diego Mail Company's coach to California. Leaders of the party were Freeman Thomas and Emmitt Mills, brother of Anson Mills, who would become a brigadier general in the Union Army. Other members were Joe Roescher, Mat Champion, Robert Aveline, John Portell, and John Wilson.

The party was experienced and well armed, but not for what they would find in Cooke's Range to the west. They camped at the abandoned stage station near Cooke's Springs on the 20th, and continued the next morning. Only one mile into the canyon about 150 Apache warriors, under Mangas Coloradas and Cochise, attacked. The coachmen ran for a side canyon, hoping to reach higher ground. There they stripped the coach of its guns, ammunition, and water, and sent the team downhill, hoping it would satisfy the Indians. It did not. The Americans built two-foot stone breastworks from which to fire behind, and the Apaches surrounded them and fired into their position throughout the day and into the next.

Four of the party were killed within the breastworks; two apparently made it about 50 yards before they were killed; while John Wilson got 150 yards away before he was finished off. A few days after the fight, freighters Alejandro Daguerre and J. J. Thibault found their bodies. Wilson had 12 arrows in him. The bodies were stripped, with all of their arms broken and their heads riddled with bullets—probably a testimony to the hard fight they exhibited. The freighters found battered bullets strewn all over the ground, and one tree about 150 yards from the breastwork had 11 balls in it. A penciled note was found that said the fight lasted two days, and at that time five of the Americans were dead. It was said that Cochise and his eldest son Taza were wounded. Mangas was supposed to have said that 25 Apaches were killed, and concluded that if the Apaches were as brave "as these few white men, he could whip the world."[3]

Apache attacks on stagecoaches are a staple of many western films. They happened quite often, but unlike in the famous scene from *Broken Arrow* (Fox, 1950), Cochise (Jeff Chandler) did not make a pact with Tom Jeffords (James Stewart) to stop attacking coaches and mail riders of the Butterfield Overland. Throughout the Civil War Years, and until Cochise finally made peace with Gen. Oliver O. Howard in late 1872, no stages or riders were safe. Author Edwin Sweeney, who has researched the episode thoroughly, concluded that "no such pact existed" between Jeffords and Cochise.[4] For Hollywood in this instance, the Jeffords-Cochise legend, and the wish to portray Indians in a better light, outweighed the facts.

In central Kansas, on 11 June, 1865, Lt. Richard W. Jenkins, Company I, 2nd Colorado Cavalry, left Cow Creek Station with the mail coach heading to Fort Zarah. With him as escort were three men of his company and three men of Company G, 7th Iowa Cavalry. Three miles from the station they passed a slow-moving wagon train. One mile beyond that 100 Indians, probably Kiowas, stormed the coach. The driver spun the stage around, but the warriors soon caught up and stabbed their lances through the windows while the passengers blasted away at them. One Indian was killed and four ponies were shot. Two soldiers, Privates Cutting and Platt, Company G, took lance wounds to the head.

Capt. Elisha Hammer, Company G, 7th Iowa Cavalry, in command of Cow Creek Station, was on the roof of one of the buildings and watched the action. He quickly readied 26 men of Company I, 2nd Colorado, and 29 men of Company G, 7th Iowa, and rushed to Jenkins's relief. The Indians pulled back at Hammer's approach. Jenkins took command of the Company I

The author sits on the remnants of the breastworks built by Freeman Thomas's men during the July 1861 fight in Cooke's Canyon, New Mexico.

contingent as they chased the Indians. They trotted and galloped about six miles southwest to the banks of the Arkansas River, where they caught the Indians trying to cross to the south bank.

The soldiers were, Hammer said, "close enough to empty eight saddles, a portion of the Indians floating down the river, killing and wounding at least fifteen Indians. We killed or wounded three Indians on the south bank with carbines from the north side."

With the Indians driven from the riverbanks, Jenkins crossed over and covered the approaches as Hammer crossed. They continued the chase three miles south of the Arkansas, but the warriors were too far ahead by this time, and Hammer rode back to the post.[5]

Raiding warriors cared little if they attacked civilians or soldiers. On 8 November, 1866, a stage pulled out of Silver City, Idaho Territory, on its way to Virginia City, Nevada. At ten A.M. Paiutes attacked the coach about four miles east of Owyhee Ferry in eastern Oregon. The warriors fired a volley while concealed behind a rock wall they had built near the road. One bullet tore into passenger W. Wilcox's chest.

"Oh my God, I'm killed!" he cried out, and his head slumped onto George Harrington's knee. Seconds later, Harrington caught a bullet in the left hip. One bullet tore through the carriage and clipped driver Wash Waltermire in the side, causing a minor wound. Waltermire whipped the horses into a run but galloped right into a mounted party of Indians who were waiting down the road. He tried to go around them, but the band that had first fired on the stage soon caught up with the coach.

Now two groups of warriors rode on both sides, trying to catch the stage in between. As Wash whipped the horses, guard James McRae fired his carbine, keeping the Indians at bay for about two miles. A bullet hit one of the wheel horses and it fell, dragging the stage to a halt. Two other horses were wounded. While Wash unhitched the horses, McRae kept firing, and Harrington got out of the coach, assisted by the last two passengers, J. M. Holland and P. Casey.

They tried to get on the horses, but the spooked animals bolted; one ran off and the other two were unmanageable. The men stumbled and ran the last two miles to the ferry. As they approached, the employees and soldiers stationed there heard the firing and prepared for action. When the breathless survivors came in, a Sergeant Brown, 11 soldiers, and four station men hurried back to the stage. The Indians were already gone, but not before they had cut out Wilcox's heart, scalped him, and stripped his clothes. They cut up the mail sacks and tossed the mail to the wind, but did not have enough time to destroy the coach. The soldiers buried Wilcox, pulled the stage to the station, and repaired it. Harrington was cared for, and by that evening, with a fresh team of horses, the stage continued on its journey.[6]

In Colorado, stages and stations on the eastern plains were inviting targets for raiders. At Fort Wallace in western Kansas, Lt. James M. Bell, Company I, 7th Cavalry, spent much of the year of 1867 constantly juggling his few troopers among the stage stations, trying to protect the passengers that traveled to Denver and back east. On one return trip from Denver the Indian scare was so bad that Bell could find no passengers to ride east with him on the stage. With only one driver and one mail guard, he started the journey.

In eastern Colorado he picked up three men of his company, and at the next station he took aboard a sick private from Company E, 3rd Infantry. They reached Cheyenne Wells, where the wife of the station keeper begged Bell to let her go east with them. On 11 June the stage continued on until it crossed a dry fork of the Smoky Hill River, four miles from Big Timber Station, which was located about one mile east of the Kansas-Colorado border.

While the tired animals dragged the coach through the sand of the creek bed, about 25 Cheyennes opened fire on them, riddling the coach with bullets. Bell and his three troopers grabbed their Spencer carbines and returned fire. Once across the creek bed the stage halted, and they got out to shoot. Bell told the woman to lie flat on the floor. The sick infantryman tried to crawl down from the top of the stage where he had been riding, but he was hit while hanging in front of the open doorway.

"I am killed," he said, as he slumped to the sand. He tried to give Bell his dying message to his mother, but the hot fire kept Bell too busy. The rapid-firing Spencers kept the Indians at bay. Bell saw them place the bodies of two warriors on horseback and ride off. The stage got rolling once more, but the warriors came on for another try. One was shot from his horse, and after two hours the rest of them gave up. Bell's stage, with badly wounded horses, finally pulled into Big Timber Station.[7]

These stage attacks are only a tiny sampling. Indian attacks on stages were a staple of Hollywood Westerns, and the instances may have occurred as often in reality as they did onscreen. One of the most well-known and analyzed films of the genre is *Stagecoach* (Walter Wanger Productions, 1939). John Ford's first Western in 13 years has been called the most significant sound Western ever made, the first film made in Monument Valley, the film that rescued John Wayne from the "B" Western doldrums, the first of the genre of modern Westerns, and the film that bridged the gap between the "A" and "B" Western.[8]

The clichéd main plot centers on the Ringo Kid (John Wayne) searching for the murderers of his father and brother. The Kid breaks out of prison and heads for Lordsburg, but when his horse dies in the desert, he is picked up by a stagecoach, and Marshal Curly Wilcox (George Bancroft) takes him into custody.

The coach is a microcosm of stereotypes: drunken Doc Boone (Thomas Mitchell), Southern gambler Hatfield (John Carradine); crooked banker Gatewood (Henry Churchill); pregnant army wife Lucy Mallory (Louise Platt); effeminate whiskey peddler Peacock (Donald Meek); fat, comical stage driver Buck (Andy Devine); and kindly whore Dallas (Claire Trevor). All of the characters, social outcasts in one way or another, reveal their true nature during the course of the journey from Tonto to Lordsburg; but with the desert and the raiding Apaches to

*Stagecoach* (Walter Wanger Productions, 1939) was the first of John Ford's movies to be filmed in Monument Valley, Arizona. It has been called the first modern Western and the most significant sound Western ever made.

contend with, they realize they must work together, and thus reveal an innate nobility in each of them.

When the Apaches attack, the Kid has to choose between escape and helping the passengers survive. He chooses the latter, gives his word, and Marshal Curly gives him back his gun to help fight. Thus, the Kid, with his professional violence, again becomes an accepted member of society. The scene is attendant with all the spills and thrills of the stagecoach chase, made all the more spectacular by stuntmen Yakima Canutt and Iron Eyes Cody managing and participating in the falling, diving, jumping, and dragging. The classic scene of a man leaping among the galloping horses pulling the stage was copied many times, even as late as 1970, when Jack Crabb (Dustin Hoffman) spoofed the action in *Little Big Man*.

Of course, the 7th Cavalry comes to the rescue, and the stage eventually reaches Lordsburg. The Kid has his confrontation with the Plummer Gang, and kills Luke Plummer (Tom Tyler), who murdered his father. Because the Kid has redeemed himself, Marshal Curly lets him go. The Kid and Dallas, however, cannot find a real place in society; they declare their love for each other and escape to a little ranch the Kid has in old Mexico. America, it appeared, was still not tolerant enough to welcome all would-be members of its community. The dream for some was ever onward, beyond the next horizon.

*Stagecoach* possesses elements of both the "A" Western, which focused on the epic journey and its process of moving and becoming, and the "B" Western, which more often focused on the problems of a single agricultural community. The film was free of specific historical connections, and thus could be seen as a fable or folk story, while illustrating some of the very real trials and tribulations of the Western experience.

While *Stagecoach* has garnered great praise, some critics seemed to have missed the point. One reviewer wondered how the stage could have been surprised, because the Apaches would have had to travel for miles across open country, and would have been seen and heard. She also questioned how an Apache with a bow and arrow could have gotten close enough to the coach to fire an arrow into it; and why the Apaches can't seem to hit anyone, while the whites in the coach can't seem to miss. Of course, she also dismisses such inconsistencies, saying that the mistakes were "irrelevant to audiences" because speed and action were important, "not reality."[9]

Unfortunately, some critics don't know history. The stage chase in *Stagecoach* was played out in reality many times. Indians did surprise coaches in all types of terrain. One instance occurred along the Virginia City to Silver City road in southeast Oregon, on 3 July, 1865, when a wagon train with outriders were traveling across an open sage plain.

Suddenly, 50 Paiutes appeared as if they had sprung from the ground. No one expected to be attacked in a seemingly safe, open space. The warriors had been cleverly hidden behind large sagebrush along the trail. They had tied down their horses with a rope looped around the horses' necks and pulled up tight under one of their forefeet. The animals were hunched down and helpless until the rope was pulled with a jerk, and the horses sprang up. At the same time about 20 rifles barked out, and four of the white men were hit.[10]

Indians could, and did, surprise wagon trains and stages. And they did get close enough not only to shoot arrows into the vehicles, but, as illustrated earlier via the 1865 raid near Cow Creek Station in Kansas, they even rode up close enough during the chase to lance two soldiers in the head!

Another critic who should have known better, given his claims of being an old-time cowboy, was William S. Hart. Hart, who had acted in or directed nearly 100 films, was an aging ex-star in his 70s when he commented on *Stagecoach*. The movie was magnificent but unrealistic. Why? Hart believed that the Indians, being intelligent warriors, would have just shot down the horses and ended the chase before it began. John Ford commented on the seeming inconsistency, stating that he couldn't have had the Indians shoot the horses because "it would have been the end of the picture."[11]

Besides the cinematic necessity to keep the horses alive, the pursuing Indians generally had the same end in mind. A contemporary observer in 1840s New Mexico Territory wrote that the Utes, Navajos, and Apaches would never kill all the Mexicans, nor steal all their horses and sheep, because they performed a service by raising stock; and the Indians knew that they should leave enough alive for a new flock the next year. The pure murder raid was far less frequent than the raid looking for horses and plunder. Horses and mules were wealth for almost every western Indian tribe, and if at all possible they would try to capture the animals, not kill them. That fact is represented in a number of Westerns, including *The Outriders* (1950), *How the West Was Won* (1962), and *Westward Ho the Wagons* (1956).

If it seems unreal to some folks that the Indians hit fewer targets than the whites, it is nevertheless true. Unless they orchestrate a complete tactical surprise, attackers almost always take more casualties than defenders. "Classic" Hollywood film coverage of the Indian Wars centers on the years from 1850 to 1890. During that time span there were about 21,400 casualties, both Indian and white. Of that number, about 6,500 were army and civilian losses, while Indian losses totaled about 14,900.[12]

Some critics may have thought *Stagecoach* was not realistic enough, but many of its scenarios had historical antecedents. Once again, Hollywood, through hard research or serendipity, understood some basic facts of the West better than some of its detractors.

# 32

## The Elm Creek Raid
## (*The Searchers*)

### Texas, October 1864

One of the most famous of all Western movies was *The Searchers* (Warner Brothers, 1956). Based on the Alan Le May novel, the story, although not about a wagon train attack, did have historical connections. The incident that piqued Le May's interest was the infamous Elm Creek Raid. Nearly 500 Comanche and Kiowa raiders struck Young County, Texas, in the fall of 1864, along Elm Creek, a tributary of the Brazos River northwest of Fort Belknap. Sweeping south out of Indian Territory, the warriors wreaked chaos across the countryside. Some settlers hid, some fled, and others played "Paul Revere," riding to outlying ranches to give warning. A number of settlers "forted up" at George Bragg's Ranch. The defenders of "Fort Bragg," and another strongpoint, "Fort Murrah," held off the Indians. The Comanche Little Buffalo, who organized the raid, was killed while fighting at Bragg's.

Lt. N. Carson, Company D, of Colonel James Bourland's Border Regiment, pursued about 300 raiders who drove off hundreds of horses. Carson's men rode into an ambush and were forced to retreat. As they fell back, the soldiers rescued two women from the McCoy house. During the raid the Indians lost about 20 warriors, mostly in the fight at Bragg's Ranch and with Carson's soldiers. Carson lost five killed and about five wounded, while seven civilians were killed and two wounded.

The most memorable incident of the raid occurred during late morning on Thursday, 13 October, only a few miles northwest of Fort Belknap, when the Indians swept down on the Fitzpatrick Ranch, a two-story house once called the Carter trading post. The 21-year-old Milly Susanna Carter Durkin futilely tried to defend the others with a shotgun, but she was tomahawked, gang-raped, scalped, and killed. There were no men home that day. Inside the house were Milly's mother, Elizabeth Ann Carter Sprague Fitzpatrick (age 38); her brother Elijah Carter (13); Milly's daughter Charlotte Elizabeth "Lottie" Durkin (5); Milly's daughter Milly Jane (2); and Milly's newborn, unnamed son. A black family also lived there, with Britt Johnson the head of their household, but Britt was away working at the mill. Britt's pregnant wife, Mary Johnson (24), was home with her daughter (4) and two sons (5 and 7).[1]

While Milly Susanna was being raped, the elder Johnson boy, Jim, ran from the house, but Indians killed him. These murders caused the others to realize that resistance was useless. Even so, when the Indians found the Durkin baby hidden in a box under the bed, they pulled him out and smashed him against a wall. The rest of them were tied on ponies, and when the Kiowa Satanta blew a bugle, the raiders took them away.

They rode northwest for almost two days and nights before stopping on Saturday morning near the Pease River. Elijah Carter was sick and too ill to travel. The Indians built a fire in a brush heap and threw the boy in it. They forced Elizabeth Fitzpatrick to watch her grandson burn to death. From there the Indians headed into the north Texas Panhandle. It is uncertain if all the captives were kept together, but at least some of them were in the Indian village on the Canadian River near Bent's old adobe fort when soldiers attacked on 25 November.

Col. Christopher "Kit" Carson left Fort Bascom on 12 November with about 335 cavalrymen and infantrymen, searching for Kiowas and Comanches who had been raiding along the Santa Fe Trail. Carson first hit the 150-lodge village of Little Mountain's Kiowas. They fled downstream, and Carson followed, coming upon more Indians as he went. When he approached Stumbling Bear's 350 lodges, about 1,000 warriors confronted him. Satanta was present, again blowing his bugle, and now it was Carson's turn to fall back. Only the howitzers kept the charging warriors at bay. Carson wisely vacated the area, but he torched the lodges and supplies before he left — a severe blow to the Indians at the onset of winter. Three soldiers and a scout were killed, and 29 soldiers and scouts were wounded; while the Indians lost about 60 killed and wounded. Some of the captive whites were indirect casualties of the attack.

Little Milly Jane Durkin had been hidden in the bushes when Carson approached Stumbling Bear's village, and she was whisked away when the Indians counterattacked. When the soldiers were gone, the angry Indians rode off for help from their kinsmen on the Cimarron River. The months of December 1864 and January 1865 were cold and harsh, and the Indians and their captives suffered greatly. Many perished due to starvation and exposure. Milly Jane was one of them, dying during what the Kiowas called the "Muddy Traveling Winter." The Indians blamed the "Great Father" for all of their deaths.[2]

The five remaining captives spent the winter and spring in various Indian camps. Few inquiries were made concerning their fate, possibly because they were illiterate and had few relatives in Texas, while Young County had a very small population and an inefficient government, one barely able to manage its own affairs, let alone organize a rescue attempt. Apparently the only male relative able and willing to try to rescue the captives was Mary's husband, Britt Johnson. Johnson was strong, honest, respected, and a brave Indian fighter, and he made several trips into Indian Territory looking for his wife, children, and the Fitzpatricks and Durkins.[3]

Johnson went to the Indian Territory with David White, who was looking for his own captured son, with the assistance of Brig. Gen. James W. Throckmorton, commander of the First Frontier District in Texas. In late May 1865 a grand council with many of the Plains tribes was held at Camp Napoleon at Cottonwood Grove, now Verden, Oklahoma. There Throckmorton arranged for the release of nine white captives, including members of the Fitzpatrick-Durkin clan, the Johnsons, and White's son Elonzo.[4]

The Comanche Asa Havey, who knew Britt Johnson when the Comanches lived on the Clear Fork Reservation in Texas in 1858–59, was instrumental in gaining their release. For a number of horses, blankets, supplies, and a $20 gold piece, Asa Havey retrieved the captives from Tosawi's Comanches and turned them over to Texas agents at Cottonwood Grove. The first to be released were Mary Johnson, her five-year-old son, seven-year-old daughter, an infant born to Mrs. Johnson during her captivity, and Lottie Durkin. Britt Johnson gave seven ponies for the return of his family.

Lottie was separated from her grandmother and her sister after Carson's attack in November 1864. The Indians had tattooed her arms, and tattooed a dime-sized blue moon on her forehead, marking her for life. The freed captives were sent to Decatur, Texas, where Britt Johnson may have picked them up. By mid-summer of 1865 they all went to Veal's Station in Parker County, where Britt had relocated after the Elm Creek attack.[5]

Elizabeth Fitzpatrick was still with the Indians. She had not been sold with her granddaughter or the Johnsons, but was held by different bands, and at one time was with Satanta's

## 32. The Elm Creek Raid

Kiowas. The Indians met the whites again for a peace conference, this time on the Little Arkansas in Kansas in October 1865. Again Britt Johnson was there, trying to recover Texas captives. Before the commissioners would distribute the treaty goods, they demanded that the Indians turn over their prisoners. The Kiowas admitted to having four, and the Comanches had three, but all of them, they claimed, were not with the bands on the Little Arkansas. Five Texas captives were eventually brought in, but Elizabeth Fitzpatrick was not among them.[6]

Jesse H. Leavenworth, at times colonel, commissioner, and agent, was busy rounding up any other captives he could locate. With the help of mixed-blood Jesse Chisholm, Leavenworth rode to Fort Zarah on the Arkansas River. On 2 November, 1865, north of the post on Walnut Creek, Leavenworth found a white woman and a small white girl, Alice Taylor, working like slaves in a Kiowa camp. The woman was Elizabeth Ann Fitzpatrick, and she knew right away what the soldiers were doing there, although she "thought they must be beings from another world" because "their white faces and blue uniforms looked so beautiful."[7]

Elizabeth had been captive just over one year. She had been starved, beaten, and raped, and her obviously pregnant belly was a constant reminder of her treatment. Leavenworth took both of them to another Comanche camp where he recovered James Benson (age 9), who was taken from his home near Burnet, Texas, in 1865. A Mr. W. Dunlap, of Kansas, bought Benson with a number of steers. Leavenworth took the three freed captives to the Kaw Agency at Council Grove. On the trip, Elizabeth questioned Leavenworth and learned that her granddaughter, Lottie, had been returned to Texas four months ago. She also learned that Milly Jane died the previous winter, but she refused to believe it.[8]

Born in Alabama in 1825, Elizabeth Ann Fitzpatrick had married a free black man, Alexander J. Carter, who ran a trading post on the frontier near Fort Belknap. Carter was murdered in September 1857. Elizabeth's daughter, Milly Susanna, had married Pvt. Owen Durkin the same year, and Elizabeth married Lt. Owen A. Sprague in 1858. Apparently the lieutenant did not relish his situation, for he soon disappeared. Milly lost her husband in 1859 when soldiers at Belknap murdered him. Milly had another child out of wedlock in 1862, and the same year Elizabeth Ann married Thomas Fitzpatrick. This marriage lasted 18 months, until Fitzpatrick was murdered in 1864. Once again Elizabeth Ann was a widow. The next disaster occurred seven months later during the Elm Creek Raid when Indians massacred some of her family and captured the rest.[9]

At the Kaw Agency, Elizabeth Ann met the other Texas women and children who had been rescued: Caroline McDonald, Rebecca McDonald, James Taylor, Dorcas Taylor, and James Ball. Along with Alice Taylor and James Benson, "Grandma" Elizabeth, only 39 years old, took on the duties of supervising and caring for seven women and children. In addition, Agent Hiram W. Farnsworth hired Elizabeth Ann at three dollars per week to cook, clean, sew, and nurse the growing number of people and employees at the agency. In December, Elizabeth was expected to deliver her child, but apparently the baby was stillborn.

In early 1866 the arrangements were nearly complete to send the freed captives back home. Commissioner D. N. Cooley appointed Leavenworth to take them back to Texas, but the agent demurred, arguing that Mrs. McDonald "might be confined any day," and that the trip south would be too hazardous. He figured it would be easier for the captives to travel to St. Louis, down the Mississippi, and up the Red River to Shreveport, Louisiana; and the trip should be done in the spring. The postponement might also allow him to recover the Fitzpatrick and McDonald girls.

Additionally, the women did not want to travel 1,000 miles by wagon, as they were in fear of being captured again. Mrs. McDonald gave birth to a boy in March 1866 and was finally ready to go home, if only she could get her last daughter, Mahala, back from the Indians. Elizabeth, too, was sure that Milly Jane was alive and did not want to leave without her. In June, Leavenworth and Elizabeth rode out, and in two weeks they returned with Caroline's five-year-old child Mahala. It seemed that everyone was together except for Milly Jane. Finally, on 27 August, 1866, after more problems regarding financing the trip, the women and children began their trek back to Texas—by wagon.[10]

The trip was long and dangerous. The same month that the freed captives set out, Kiowas, under Satanta, raided Montague County—the very area the recovered captives would pass through—attacking the James Box family, killing the husband and a baby, and carrying off five females. After the Kiowa raid, the returning ex-captives came through and went south to Decatur, where the passengers were split up into several parties to continue on to their various homes. Elizabeth finally reached Parker County in October, where she finally met the Johnsons and her granddaughter, Lottie Durkin.

In 1869, Elizabeth married Isaiah Clifton. They moved to Shackleford County, near the booming area around Fort Griffin. Lottie moved with them. In May 1871, Gen. William T. Sherman was at Fort Griffin, and Elizabeth Ann Clifton and Lottie Durkin called on him. They described their ordeal during the 1864 Elm Creek Raid and their subsequent captivity. Elizabeth made it clear that she was not convinced that her granddaughter Milly Jane was killed in the winter of 1865. She pleaded with Sherman to re-institute the search, and the general promised that he would.[11]

In November 1880, Isaiah Clifton had a stroke and died; Elizabeth Ann had been abandoned by one husband and buried three others. She became more depressed and morose than anyone had seen. Her spirit was gone. Seeming older than her 57 years, she steadily deteriorated in health until she died on 18 June, 1882. Elizabeth Ann Carter Sprague Fitzpatrick Clifton was buried next to Isaiah in a mesquite-covered graveyard near the Clear Fork of the Brazos, somewhere below Fort Griffin. The graves were unmarked.[12]

Of the captives of 1864, only Lottie Durkin remained. In 1874, at age 15, she married David H. Barker, the marshal of the town of Fort Griffin. They had two daughters, Ada and Ida. When the buffalo played out, Fort Griffin began a quick decline, and Barker took his family west to the Panhandle, stopping near the Sweetwater, a few miles from Fort Elliott, at a place that would eventually become Mobeetie. Barker became a deputy, but Mobeetie was doomed also—from drought, prairie fire, cattle fever, and lack of a railroad. In 1886 they moved on to Tascosa, Texas. Lottie's health was never good since her captivity, and she declined more after the birth of a son in July 1887. On 10 August cholera took the life of her little baby, and on the same day "childbirth fever" claimed Lottie. The lady with the blue moon on her forehead was only 27 years old.

The last of the Elm Creek Raid captives was gone. The story persisted that Milly Jane Durkin was still alive and living with the Kiowas. Britt Johnson was said to have made several trips looking for her. Elizabeth Ann insisted she had seen her with Chief Sun Boy's Kiowas near the Little Arkansas in 1865. Vincent Colyer, Secretary of the Board of Indian Commissioners, while riding near Fort Bascom, met a band of Kiowas who claimed to have a girl named "Molly" in captivity, but Colyer's questions assured him that the captive was too old to be Milly Jane. Agents Lawrie Tatum and James Haworth initiated searches for the girl, but could not locate her. The Indians always insisted that Milly Jane died during the first harsh winter after her capture. The woman who married the Kiowa Chief Goombi, and died in 1934 at Mountain View, Oklahoma, likely was not Milly Jane Durkin.[13]

The long and involved odyssey of the Elm Creek captives was the inspiration for *The Searchers*.[14] Many diverse analyses about the nature of this movie have focused on whether John Ford used it as a commentary on racism, on civil rights, as an ideological play of counterinsurgency against Communism, or to explore any number of psychological, sociological, or cultural issues.[15] All of the sometimes nonsensical analyses aside, Alan Le May had a simpler and sounder objective: write a good story based on real frontier incidents.

## 32. The Elm Creek Raid

Calm before the storm: The Edwards Family is reunited — shortly before the Comanches all but destroy them. Prodigal son John Wayne sits in the rocker as Dorothy Jordan, Pippa Scott, Lana Wood, and Walter Coy question him in *The Searchers* (Warner Brothers, 1956).

The movie opens with long-lost former Confederate Ethan Edwards (John Wayne) returning home from the Civil War, Texas Rangers, and fighting in Mexico. His brother Aaron (Walter Coy), and sister-in-law Martha (Dorothy Jordan) and their children, welcome him back. It appears as if the prodigal may finally begin to settle down, but things go drastically wrong. Comanches, led by Scar (Henry Brandon, who played Quanah Parker in *Two Rode Together*), attack the cabin. Aaron is killed, while Martha is raped, mutilated, and killed. Aaron's son is killed. Daughter Lucy (Pippa Scott) is carried away, only to be raped and killed along the trail. Little Debbie (Lana Wood) is taken to be raised in the tribe as an Indian.

The scene of destruction is thankfully shielded from the audiences' eyes, but it is evident in the rage it engenders in Ethan. He demands vengeance, and he desperately wants to rescue his two nieces. As the searchers cross the countryside looking for the Indians' trail, Ethan goes alone into a canyon and finds Lucy's raped and mutilated body. He tries to keep it a secret from the rest, particularly Brad Jorgensen (Harry Carey Jr.), who was Lucy's sweetheart. Brad later thinks he sees Lucy in the Indian camp they have crept up on. He wants to rescue her, but Ethan shatters Brad's hopes.

"What you saw wasn't Lucy," he says. "What you saw was a buck wearin' Lucy's dress. I found Lucy back in the canyon. I wrapped her in my coat. Buried her with my own hands. Thought it best to keep it from ya."

"Did they," Brad mutters, "was she...."

**On the trail of the Indians who captured little Debbie Edwards are *The Searchers*: Harry Carey Jr., Jeffrey Hunter, and John Wayne.**

"What do you want me to do, draw you a picture?!" Ethan explodes. "Spell it out? Don't ever ask me. Long as you live, don't ever ask me more."

The distraught Brad, half-crazy with anger, charges alone into the Indian camp, where he is killed.

There are only two searchers left, Ethan and Martin Pawley (Jeffrey Hunter). The two men hunt for years, once coming upon Lieutenant Colonel Custer's winter camp and finding a number of women and children, ex-captives recently freed from the Indians. Most are in bad shape, some also appearing demented. By this time Ethan knows that little Debbie, if she is still alive, is a young woman and certainly has been "defiled" by the Comanche warriors. Ethan realizes that he will have to kill Debbie in order to release her from her "fate worse than death." Martin, a quarter-blood Cherokee, is appalled that Ethan would want to destroy her.

In the end, soldiers and Rangers attack Scar's village. Martin ends up killing Scar, and Ethan has a last-second change of heart. He lifts the older Debbie (Natalie Wood) up in his arms. The audience is still not sure if he will kill her.

"Let's go home, Debbie," he says.

John Ford offered a different ending than novelist Alan Le May. In the book, the "Ethan" character (Amos Edwards) is shot and killed by an Indian woman who Ethan fails to shoot because he thinks she might be Debbie. While Ford chose a happier ending, Le May more accurately depicted his model, Britt Johnson's, actual demise. On 24 January, 1871, Britt and two companions, Dennis Cureton and Paint Crawford, were hauling supplies along the Fort Richardson–Fort Griffin road in north Texas. About 25 Kiowas and Comanches spotted them and attacked. The three men rode into a small depression called Turtle Hole, killed their horses to form a barricade, and fought for their lives. The three made a good showing; it was reported that more than 170 empty cartridges were found by their bodies. The stand was hopeless, however, for the warriors overran, scalped, and mutilated them.[16]

Thus ended the life of the real searcher. Once again, novelists and Hollywood drew their inspiration from history.

# 33

## Charles Goodnight and Oliver Loving (*Lonesome Dove*)

### New Mexico, August 1867

Larry McMurtry's novel *Lonesome Dove*, a Pulitzer Prize winner, was published in 1985 and became a six-hour television mini-series in 1989. It has been called one of the best stories and movies ever written or filmed, and has been read and seen by millions. The epic story focuses on Augustus McCrae (Robert Duvall) and Woodrow Call (Tommy Lee Jones), aging ex–Texas Rangers seeking to finally make their fortune by driving a herd of cattle from Texas to Montana. In the book and movie version of *Lonesome Dove*, the drive gets underway about the spring of 1878.

Although a work of historical fiction, the story has temporal and geographical connections to the Old West that it depicts, and one would expect that those connections be viable. Nevertheless, there are several problems with this 1878 cattle drive of Call and McCrae's and their Hat Creek Cattle Company. The drive originates along the Rio Grande south of the Nueces River. The country from there to San Antonio is described as tree-covered and rough, while north of San Antonio they say it opens up, levels out, and becomes less wooded. On the contrary, this is the area of the Edwards Plateau, the Texas hill country, with canyon, creeks, trees and hills, which gets quite rough in many places as the streams cut through the limestone escarpment and drain to the sea.

Gus McCrea goes to what he calls Clara's Orchard, where he and his old sweetheart used to court in the peaceful days 15 years before. But by the book's time frame, 15 years ago was in the middle of the Civil War, and Gus was supposed to be fighting Indians in the Frontier Battalion. The orchard, too, is said to be on the Guadalupe River, 20 miles west of Austin, but the Guadalupe's nearest point to Austin is about 50 miles southwest. McMurtry probably should have placed McCrea's courting spot on the Pedernales.

Call and McCrae trail up to Fort Worth, where Lorie (Diane Lane), the "soiled dove" that McCrae has become very fond of, is captured by the renegade Blue Duck (Frederic Forrest). Gus trails them northwest and has a big shoot-out just west of Adobe Walls near the Canadian River. In the book, Gus takes Lorie to Adobe Walls and tells her of the big fight between Indians and buffalo hunters that took place there two years earlier; the actual fight occurred in 1874, *four* years before. In fact, if McCrea trailed Blue Duck through this area in 1878, as the novel and movie imply, he would be crossing the vast ranch of cattleman Charles Goodnight, who took over the Palo Duro area for his herds in 1876. In 1877, Goodnight and partner John Adair ran a ranch with 100,000 head on a million acres. By 1878 there were several large spreads in the area. The region was not a wilderness.

## 33. Charles Goodnight and Oliver Loving

The book and movie, however, have Call back in Fort Worth, about to lead the first trail drive through the area. Gus and Lorie figure they can wait in the Adobe Walls area for Call to catch up with the herd. If they did, they'd have a long wait, for the actual trail passed about 200 miles east of them. Before Call heads north he cautions his cowboys that it will be a hard drive — there would not be another town until they reached Ogallala, Nebraska, on the South Platte. Of course, by 1878 there were many settlements between Fort Worth and Ogallala. They could pass through a number of towns, plus cross about three or more railroads on the way. Tracing their track via clues in the book, we find that Call and McCrae, instead of blazing a new trail, are really following the already established Western Cattle Trail.

Eventually Gus and Lorie meet up with the herd. They move north, cross the Arkansas, then the Republican (after which they would have been trampling across many ranches and homesteads), and reach the Platte east

Robert Duvall, as Gus McCrae, and Tommy Lee Jones, as Woodrow Call, in *Lonesome Dove* (Alianza Films International, 1989). Novelist Larry McMurtry modeled the main characters on real-life cattlemen Oliver Loving and Charles Goodnight.

of Ogallala. Here they learn that no one can travel east because they are in the middle of Red Cloud's War, and no one in central Nebraska is safe. In reality, by 1878, Red Cloud had been peacefully on the reservation for a decade, and the last Indian raid along the Platte in central Nebraska took place near Spring Creek in 1870.

Call and McCrea leave Ogallala for Montana. Somehow, geography has again gone awry, for they trail west from Ogallala "several days" to where the river turns south; so they then take the north fork. Ogallala is on the South Platte. If they trailed several days in that direction they would be around the site of present-day Sterling, Colorado, before they decided they had better take the North Platte — way too late. At any rate, they reach central Wyoming in the Casper area and then begin an 80-mile waterless stretch trying to reach Powder River. In reality, this famous waterless stretch was between the Concho and Pecos in Texas.

On the Powder they come across an Indian camp, and their faithful guide and partner, Josh Deets (Danny Glover), is killed by a starving Indian boy who runs a lance through him. Call carves out a marker for Deets: "Served with me 30 years. Fought in 21 engagements with the Comanche and Kiowa. Cherful in all weathers, never sherked a task. Splendid behavior."

When they finally reach Montana they are delighted. An old Ranger partner, Jake Spoon (Robert Urich), who they reluctantly hanged along the way for stealing horses, had told them how nice it would be. And, here, in 1878, Call declares they are the only cattlemen in Montana; in actuality, Nelson Story had brought Longhorns to Montana from Texas as early as 1866. It is here that we reach a climax of the story when Gus and a character named Pea Eye Parker (Tim

Scott) go ahead across the Yellowstone to scout out a route to the Milk River. Someone should have told them that about 100 miles ahead they would have had to cross the Missouri River first. At any rate, at "over 100 miles" past the Yellowstone, they get into trouble with some Indians. In the movie they are Sioux, which is probably more accurate than in the book, where their opponents are Bloods (by this time, that tribe was on a reserve 400 miles to the northwest and up in Canada).

Gus goes chasing after buffalo, only to come riding back with 20 Indians chasing him. He and Pea Eye run for a creek to the east, which we later learn from the book is the Musselshell River. They jump the bluffs (in the book they dig out a cave in the sandy banks, in the movie the cave is already there) and settle in for a siege. Two arrows hit Gus in the leg, and Pea Eye takes a bullet clear through his shoulder. Gus complains that the warrior who shot him full force with the arrow was only 20 yards away, and that's why it went half way into the calf of his leg! We have heard the stories of an Indian shooting an arrow with such force that it could go clear through a buffalo. Remember, the young Indian boy drove a lance all the way through Deets, but a warrior at 20 yards couldn't put an arrow all the way through McCrea's calf. Old Gus must have been made of tougher hide than we could have imagined.

While besieged, Pea Eye is concerned, lest the Indians shoot them from far off, but Gus is not worried. He tells Pea Eye that the Indians don't have good eyesight because they spend too much time sitting in smoky teepees! (At least we didn't have to hear that one in the movie.)

Gus kills seven warriors throughout the day, and when night falls the rain falls too. Gus tells Pea Eye he must head off downstream for help, for Gus can't walk and is worried about losing his leg. Pea Eye heads out, and in the book he manages to lose his gun, food, and all his clothes in the river. In the movie we are spared that sight, and see Pea Eye tromping across the plains in his long underwear.

Pea Eye is eventually found and rescued. Meanwhile, the Indians leave, and Gus tries to walk back on his own. He figures he is 30 or 40 miles northwest of Miles City on the Yellowstone, but when first attacked they were said to be 100 miles north. He will follow the creek he is on, all the way down. The nearest point of the Musselshell to Miles City, however, is about 90 miles, and it flow north to the Missouri, not south to the Yellowstone. While Call is looking for Gus, an old prospector eventually finds the wounded man and helps him get to Miles City. In the book, a doctor amputates his left leg; in the movie, it's his right leg, and the doc warns that Gus will die unless the other leg is also cut off. Call finds McCrea, but Woodrow's pleas will not change Gus's mind. He will die before he loses both legs. And so he does. But before he goes he makes Call promise that he will carry his remains back to Texas.

With winter approaching, Call has the body packed in charcoal and salt, boxed, and set in a shed. (In the book, he returns in the spring to find that an animal has knocked over the box and stolen the amputated leg.) The coffin is repacked, reinforced, and placed in a buggy, and Call begins the trip south. He journeys through Wyoming and back to Ogallala, Nebraska, where he delivers letters to McCrea's women friends, Clara Allen (Anjelica Huston) and Lorie. He is then halfway through Kansas when he finds that his fame has preceded him, and he has to explain to scores of homesteaders, cowboys, and even Indians the purpose of his hauling a coffin to Texas. The Indians, who are riding free through central Kansas in 1879, are said to be Sioux, Arapaho, and even Pawnee! Only one year prior, Call told his cowboys that this area contained nary a town or a human.

Call is tired of meeting people and explaining his story, so from central Kansas he turns west and rides to Denver, as if he would find less people in Denver. From there he heads south to Pueblo, then to Raton Pass. He spends one night on the Purgatoire River when a lone rider, Charles Goodnight, happens to come upon his camp. Woodrow Call has just met the historical character he is modeled after! It appears that Call had ridden with Goodnight back in the 1850s in the Frontier Regiment; but he never liked him much, he said, because Goodnight was "indifferent to authority, or at least unlikely to put any above his own." Goodnight has business in Pueblo and must continue riding. He points to the coffin and says, "I reckon that's McCrea." It truly appears that Call's odyssey was known country-wide.

Call continues south and witnesses the attempted hanging of Blue Duck in Santa Rosa, New Mexico Territory. It is here where a reporter catches up to him and asks him why he's carried Captain McCrae 3,000 miles (it actually would have been about 1,000 at this point), and about how it was to start the "first ranch in Montana."

"They say you're a man of vision," the reporter says.

"Yes, a hell of a vision," Call responds as his movie-ending reply.

But Call still has to make it all the way down the Pecos, through New Mexico, and to Horsehead Crossing in Texas, where Indians attack him and he temporarily loses McCrea's body in the river. He eludes them, recovers the body, crosses the 80-mile waterless stretch, and finally makes it to Clara's Orchard. There he buries Gus by the banks of the Guadalupe. Once again back in Lonesome Dove, Call notices the burnt down saloon where McCrea spent so much time with Lorie, cutting cards for a "poke." An old man tells him that the owner burned it down with himself inside. Call asks why. The old man answers that when she left, he couldn't stand it. He sat in her room a month and then he burned it. "Who?" Call asks him. "The woman," the man answers. "The woman. They say he missed that whore."

These were the final words in the book version. It was a fine dual explanation that also echoed the end of Gus McCrea, but it wasn't the type of ending for an epic Western movie. The "vision" statement was a better closer for a film, which shows the connection — tenuous, but a connection nevertheless — that Hollywood still has with the propagation of the Western myth.

Larry McMurtry was credited with writing some fine historical fiction, but just how much he modeled his story on actual people and events may be surprising. His character Gus McCrae was really Oliver Loving, who drove some of his cattle as far as Illinois in the late 1850s, and took his first herd to Colorado in 1860, avoiding the angry farmers in eastern Kansas who were afraid of Texas Fever. He left in the fall from the upper Brazos with about 3,000 head, trailed through Indian Territory, up to the Arkansas, and west and north. He sold the cattle in Denver in the spring of 1861. After that, the Civil War effectively cut off any large trail drives to northern markets.

In 1866, Loving teamed up with Charles Goodnight, the character Woodrow Call is based on, to drive north again. This time they avoided all the troubles in Indian Territory and Kansas, and cashed in on the new market in the mining country of Colorado. They set out from the Fort Belknap area on 6 June, 1866, with 2,000 cattle and 18 armed men, headed west on the old Butterfield Stage route to the North Concho, and across an 80-mile waterless stretch to the Horsehead Crossing of the Pecos. From there they trailed up the Pecos to Fort Sumner, where they sold more than half the herd to the army. Loving took the remaining 800 head up to Denver, where he sold them to J.W. Iliff; while Goodnight rode back to Texas to gather up another herd.

They successfully made a couple of drives before the dramatic events of 1867. In west Texas, during the second season of drives, Loving became impatient with the slow progress of the cattle moving up the Pecos River. As it was late July, and contracts were to be given in August for next year's drive, he decided to leave the main herd and move ahead on his own. Goodnight cautioned against it, but Loving's mind was made up.

Loving would take a companion. In the book and movie, this was Pea Eye. In reality, the man who joined him was a man named Bill Wilson. He had been in trouble most of his life and never seemed to have much luck. He farmed, worked cattle, and ran a saloon. In Jacksboro after the Civil War he was robbed, and what were called the Yankee Carpetbag courts would do nothing for him. Wilson and another fellow found the thief one night and shot him dead. Wilson was caught and taken to Fort Richardson. Goodnight found out, and arranged for some friends to get the guards drunk the night before they were to take him to trial. Wilson spurred his horse while he and the drunk guards crossed the Trinity bottoms, and he broke free. The guards shot up the woods but could not catch him. Wilson quickly joined up with Goodnight and Loving, who were just heading their herd west. Wilson had to get out of the country, for he was easily recognizable. Why? He only had one arm. Not too concerned with political correctness back in those days, folks had a practical name for him that didn't seem to bother anyone. They called him "One Arm" Wilson. Today he'd have to be called "Digitally Challenged Wilson" or some such moniker.

Now, in July of 1867, when Loving saddled up to head north, "One Arm" Wilson rode with him. They rode during the nights, passing Pope's Crossing near the Texas-New Mexico state line, taking the high trail above the Delaware River and over to Black River. Loving detested night riding, and since they had seen no sign of Indians, he talked Wilson into riding by day. Moving across the open plain north of Black River, they spotted a large band of Indians riding fast toward them from the Guadalupe Mountains to the west, from the neighborhood of today's Carlsbad Caverns.

The two cowmen broke into a four-mile run for the breaks of the Pecos River to the east. They rode over the bluff and over a sand dune that snaked between the bluff and the river, about 100 yards farther on. They gathered their weapons, set loose the horses and took shelter behind the protection of the dune. Wilson had Goodnight's revolving six-shooter rifle, as well as his own pistol, and Loving had sidearms and a repeating Henry Rifle. The Indians poured over the bluffs, crossed the river (at that point about 30 yards wide), and surrounded them. Wilson thought there were several hundred of them. The only opening in the circle of dunes was toward the river, but Loving shot the first Indian who tried to get a bead on them from that angle.

Late in the evening someone called to them from the bluffs in Spanish, proposing surrender terms. The cowmen suspected treachery, but Wilson wanted to try to talk if Loving would cover him. He stepped up on the dune, with Loving carrying the Henry behind him. Indians already moved in behind them, and as they climbed the dune a bullet ripped through Loving's wrist and into his side. They dove back into the ditch and fired at the charging Indians, who broke and fell back. They wrapped up Loving's wounds and settled in for the siege.

The warriors showered their position with rocks and high-angled arrows, but none of the missiles hit. Wilson watched the brush nearby and detected movement. He shifted and readied his gun to fire when the Comanche would appear, but instead the warrior disturbed a rattlesnake and backed off much faster than he had crept in. That evening Loving was feverish, and Wilson slipped to the river to get a boot full of water for him. Loving felt sure he would die, and urged Wilson to get away that night. He said he would keep a six-gun and take as many Indians as he could before putting his last bullet into his own head. If the Indians left, Loving said he would get into the water and move one mile downriver to hide and wait for help. Wilson should be able to move downriver and run into Goodnight and the rest of the cowboys who were slowly moving upstream a few days behind them.

Wilson agreed to go, and took the Henry, for the metallic cartridges would be unaffected by the water. He removed all of his clothing but his hat, drawers, and undershirt, and moved into the stream. Wilson saw an Indian sitting on his horse in the middle of the stream, lazily splashing his feet in the water. The river at that point was only three or four feet deep, but the night was moonless. Wilson paddled by along the bank, and then struck deep water. With one arm he could not swim with the rifle. He jammed the barrel deep into the sand below the surface so the Indians could not find it, and swam off weaponless. Downstream, Wilson climbed out, and by daybreak he was well on his way. Unfortunately, Goodnight had not pushed the herd hard, but had stopped to give them a rest and let the men wash their clothes. Instead of 40 miles away, he was probably 80 miles south. Wilson kept on, walking shoeless across the cactus and rocks. He walked for three days.

Ahead of the herd, Charles Goodnight thought he saw someone come out of a cave near the riverbank. The person looked red, but Goodnight spurred his horse ahead to take a look. Said Goodnight, "The river water was red with sediment, and his underclothes were as red as the river itself. But when he beckoned to me, I knew positively that it was Wilson." Wilson could barely talk, his eyes were bloodshot, his feet were swollen, and he left bloody steps in the sand. Goodnight put him on his horse and hurried him back to the outfit, where they wrapped his feet in damp blankets, cleaned him, and fed him. When he related the story, Goodnight took six men and raced ahead to find Loving.

The rescuers rode the rest of the evening and all night, following Wilson's description of their trail. On the way, they found a torn page from Loving's journal, showing they were on the right path. They reached the edge of the bluffs and, believing the Indians were still there surrounding Loving, charged over the bank, fully intending to fight their way in to rescue him. The Indians were gone, along with Loving.

They found the dune where the cowmen had fought. It was half-filled with stones, and, said Goodnight, "its banks perforated with probably a hundred arrow shafts.... I knew they had not got him, as there was ample evidence that they had been hunting for him everywhere." They searched downriver but could find no trace. Where had Loving gone?

When Wilson left, Loving fought off his attackers for two more days and nights. They tunneled through the sand within feet of him but did not have the courage to break in on him. Loving figured that Wilson might have been killed — maybe Goodnight too. On the third night he slipped into the river, but instead of going downstream like he told Wilson, he went upstream, hoping to reach the trail that neared the river about six miles north of there, and perhaps be found by some passer-by. Eventually he gained the trail and lay down in the brush under a small tree near the river. Without food, and only able to suck on a water-moistened handkerchief, Loving finally passed out.

Several Mexicans traveling to Texas with a wagon and oxen found him. They fixed him some *atole*, similar to corn-meal mush, and he regained his senses. Loving offered them $250 to take him to Fort Sumner, about 150 miles away, and they swung the wagon around and headed north. They met up with other cowmen on the trail, under Jim Burleson, who rode hard and took word to Sumner. An ambulance was sent out and took Loving to the fort. Burleson then hurried downriver to find out about the cattle. When he met up with Goodnight he related his recent encounter.

"Loving was killed by Indians, way below on the Pecos," Goodnight said.

"Loving is at Fort Sumner," Burleson replied. Whereupon Goodnight saddled up his best mule, Jenny, who could canter all day long, and rode the 110 miles to Sumner in one day and night. Loving's side had healed up, but the shattered wrist was infected and gangrenous. He did not want the amputation, and the doctor seemed reluctant to perform it because he thought that Loving would not be able to survive the shock. Goodnight told the doctor in no uncertain terms that he would operate or fight him instead. The amputation was performed, but the artery could not successfully be tied off; it kept breaking open and bleeding. Loving was given chloroform and the artery re-tied, but his system could not take the strain. He weakened.

"I regret to have to be laid away in a foreign country," Loving told Goodnight before he died.

He should have no fear, Goodnight replied, and promised to take his remains to his home cemetery back in Texas. Loving died 25 September, 1867. He was buried temporarily at Sumner. When Goodnight finished transacting their business, he set about fulfilling his promise the next winter. His cowboys fashioned a tin casket for the body. They placed the wooden casket inside it, packed it with powdered charcoal, sealed it, and placed it in a wagon. They left Sumner on 8 February, 1868, six big mules pulling the funeral wagon, with Texas cowmen riding front and rear. The cavalcade took the Goodnight-Loving Trail, and the trip was absolutely peaceful and uneventful the whole way. They got back to Loving's spread at Weatherford, Texas. The Masonic Lodge buried him with fraternal honors.[1] This incident became the central episode in Larry McMurtry's novel (and the subsequent television Western) *Lonesome Dove*. The climactic scenes from the book and movie were very close to reality.

McMurtry's character Josh Deets (played by Danny Glover) also had an historical counterpart. A former slave from Mississippi whose owner moved to the Cross Timbers country of Texas, Bose Ikard hooked up with Loving and became a wonderful rider, a great night-herder, a good cook, a jack-of-all trades, and a man Loving thought had more endurance and stamina than any of them. Ikard, however, was not killed up on Powder River as in the book and movie. He came back to Texas with Goodnight in 1869 and bought himself a farm. Bose Ikard lived until January 1929. When he died and was buried in Weatherford, Texas, Charles Goodnight, who died later that same year, inscribed on the marker: "Bose Ikard. Served with me four years on the Goodnight-Loving Trail, never shirked a duty or disobeyed an order, rode with me in many stampedes, participated in three engagements with the Comanches, splendid behavior." We see from this exactly where McMurtry drew his inspiration for the Josh Deets character.

We can learn some history from *Lonesome Dove*. The book and film are well done, at least in the sense of telling a good tale. There are historical errors in both, and geographical ones also, which are particularly noticeable in the book. Nevertheless, the book and movie were historical fiction, and as such they can be cut some slack. What is apparent, again, is that novelists and filmmakers can successfully use real incidents from the American West to tell epic stories of the country's formative years. What is also apparent, at least in this instance, is that art attempts to imitate life, and although it may come close, it is not as good as the real thing. We can probably find errors in any historical fiction, and also in the movies that profess to be accurate depictions of history. But is it really that important that a movie Indian doesn't wear the proper feather ornamentation in his hair? Sometimes we pick at the minutia and miss the big picture.

# 34

## *How the West Was Won* and *Into the West*

Baby boomers born in the 1940s and 1950s grew up learning a very different brand of American history than the generations coming of age during the past four decades. It was a time when radio, movies, and the comparatively new phenomenon of television reinforced a positive message: America was a good place to live, its people were outstanding nation-builders, and its ancestors were men and women of vision who spread liberty and democracy across the land. We learned the same story in school, and we could end each day feeling good about our country and ourselves.

Not anymore.

Admittedly, nostalgia is painted in golden hues, but the post–World War II years possessed a distinctly different tone than what is in evidence today. Some of us may remember the cowboy stars of the Fifties, who were pictured as genuine frontier heroes, models that children wanted to emulate. In the late Fifties, TV westerns, with lawmen as heroes, were in vogue, and represented more than one-quarter of all network prime-time shows. To a later generation, those shows may have been seen as an unrealistic depiction of our past. Yet they showed America as a land of idealism and optimism where right would always triumph.

"Manifest Destiny," described in pejorative terms today as nothing more than a smokescreen for greed and conquest, was viewed as a beneficial process whereby Americans could pass the gifts of liberty and democracy to the less privileged, all the while fulfilling their own dreams. The 1962 movie *How the West Was Won* was the supreme paean to Manifest Destiny. Filmed in Cinerama by three directors using an all-star cast, and backed by a beautiful mix of traditional folk music and original composition, the film told the story of four generations of the Prescott and Rawlings families as they pursued their destiny across the American continent. Segments titled "The Rivers," "The Plains," "The Civil War," "The Railroads," and "The Outlaws" encapsulated the western movement. There was tribulation and tragedy, but there was triumph in the end. Progress was seen as inevitable and good. It was an epic tribute to our past and gave hope for the future.

*How the West Was Won*, however, did not tell the full story. Watching it today one will immediately notice it is told from the white European standpoint. There are few, if any, scenes from Indian, Hispanic, or any minorities' point of view. We see white families boating down the Ohio River and fighting river pirates. We see white families emigrating across the plains. There are wagon trains, Indian fights, and buffalo stampedes. The Civil War is encapsulated in the Battle of Shiloh, with a fictional encounter between a Rebel (Russ Tamblyn) and a Yankee (George Peppard), as the former tries to assassinate Gen. Ulysses S. Grant (Henry Morgan). There is a great railroad chase, and the outlaws are duly dispatched. Law and order reigns supreme.

The Indian problem has just turned more serious, as discussed by Richard Widmark (left) and Henry Fonda in *How the West Was Won* (MGM, 1962).

Most of the characters eventually reach California, build homes, start families, or otherwise fulfill their destinies. The 19th century is shown as a seminal time of constructing the foundation of a pyramid that others will build upon.

*How the West Was Won* was accurate in its broad overview: emigrants floated down the Ohio River; they crossed the plains and deserts; there was a great Civil War; Indians and outlaws had to be overcome in "taming" the West. There were no portrayals, however, of any specific historical events. There were no Parker's Fort, Sutter's Mill, Whitman Mission, Van Ornum Wagon Train, Grattan Massacre, Sand Creek, Washita, or Little Bighorn battles. The specifics were fictional while the overall picture was true. The final scene shows a wagon trail evolve into a road and then into a concrete highway, and a small village change into a great city. America is seen as a dynamic land with even better things in store for the future.

The optimism expressed in *How the West Was Won* soon came to a grinding halt. Only a few years later the movie could never have been made. President John Kennedy was killed the following year, and the Civil Rights movement and the escalating war in Viet Nam all contributed to distorting the way we looked at ourselves. A darker mood descended. Soldiers, cowboys, and frontiersmen were no longer heroes. An anti-military/industrial complex attitude was in the saddle. The standard westerns of the 1920s to the 1950s were replaced by what were termed the "Spaghetti Westerns," generally filmed overseas, where the good guy was nearly indistinguishable from the bad—and all of them were ugly. Movies emphasized violence on a scale never before seen, and in many instances the violence was perpetrated by white Americans against

## 34. How the West Was Won *and* Into the West

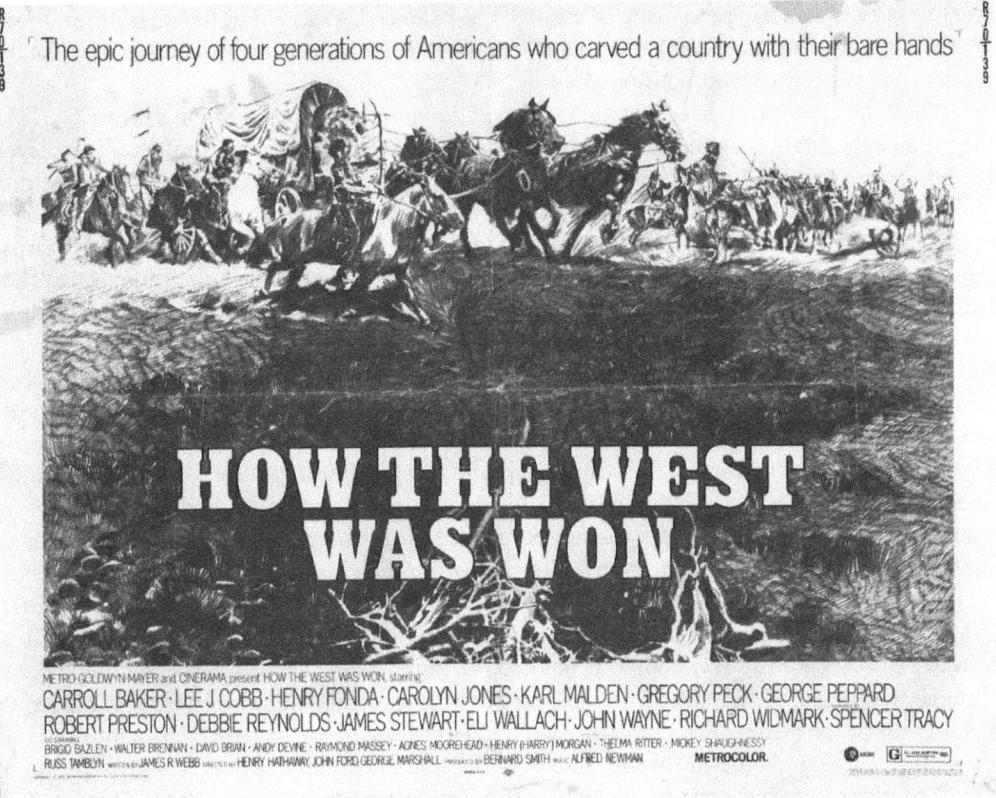

The first feature film to use Cinerama, *How the West Was Won* (MGM, 1962) was a sprawling paean to Manifest Destiny and a tribute to the pioneers who shaped America.

Indians and minorities. In 1970, *Little Big Man* showed a glory-hunting, insane George A. Custer slaughtering Indians at the Washita and soliloquizing like Hamlet at his death scene at the Little Bighorn. *Soldier Blue* gave us a similarly crazed John Chivington-type character butchering Indians at Sand Creek.

Books such as *Bury My Heart at Wounded Knee* served to fan the flames. The times were ripe for the book, and it trampled the one-time soldier/cowboy heroes into the dirt. The Indian was raised to the status of patriot hero, and perhaps, unwittingly, into the perpetual victim. It was a good story, but poor history, and by then people didn't seem to care — or know the difference.

America had been "dissed," and the disparagement only got worse. Films such as *Dances with Wolves* followed the trend. By now, almost all whites, save a precious few, were depicted as murderers or crazy. Even the new victims, the Lakotas, were being picked on by the Pawnees!

Just how far the situation has deteriorated is evidenced in the 2005 TNT production *Into the West*. The concept for *Into the West* is similar to *How the West Was Won*. *Into the West* is divided into six parts: "Wheel to the Stars," "Manifest Destiny," "Dreams & Schemes," "Hell on Wheels," "Casualties of War," and "Ghost Dance." It traces the conquest of the West through the eyes of the white Wheeler Family and a family of Lakotas. The concept is good. Telling the story of the western movement needs the balance of various viewpoints. Beyond this, the gulf between the two films is enormous.

In *Into the West*, minorities, Hispanics, Indians, and women are all victims of debauched, murderous, power-hungry, racist white men. As in so many of the films that preceded it, nearly every soldier is depicted as egoistic or mentally unbalanced. Facts about major confrontations at Sand Creek, Washita, Little Big Horn and Wounded Knee are seriously distorted to make the soldiers appear in the worst light possible.

There are enough incorrect details to drive a student of western history to distraction. Take the Sand Creek affair, for example. The bodies of the murdered Hungate Family were displayed in Denver in June 1864, not in September. Colorado Territorial Governor John Evans didn't authorize formation of the 3rd Colorado Cavalry. Col. John Chivington was not in command of the 3rd — George Shoup was. The words spoken at the Camp Weld Council were badly misrepresented. Evans all but promised the Indians that winter was his time for fighting — that they would be attacked. The Indians came away from the council knowing that no peace was made — they told trader John Prowers exactly that.

While the Indian chiefs were in Denver talking peace, their villages and warriors were in Kansas raiding and battling the soldiers. Chivington was under direct orders to attack the Indians. Even so, he did not attack peaceful bands. Chief Friday's Arapahos, for instance, were camped much closer to Denver, but Chivington did not go after them. He went after the guilty ones. The Indians had never been living on the Sand Creek Reservation, and they were not on it on the day of the battle. They were not peaceful, but had been raiding, raping, killing, and capturing all summer. They had seven white captives in the village until shortly before the battle. Three women were beaten and raped, but *Into the West* makes no mention of any of this.

Fort Lyon did not have a wooden stockade. Maj. Edward Wynkoop did not give an American flag to Black Kettle. Wynkoop was not even at Sand Creek. There was no mounted charge through the village. Chief White Antelope was not killed stoically standing in front of his teepee holding his peace medal. The first two people killed in the battle were soldiers shot down by the Indians. The Indians fled the village before the soldiers entered. There was no mention of the 76 soldier casualties—one of the highest casualty counts in the Indian Wars. There was no mention of the white scalps found in the village. Black Kettle did not walk out of the village carrying his wounded wife; he abandoned her and fled. The soldiers did not kill all; they captured and saved about ten Indians and mixed-bloods, plus a few whites who were in the village trading. In summary, the Indians were not peaceful, they were not under protection, and they were not killed in the village.

This type of distortion runs rampant throughout *Into the West*. Custer's words about waiting for reinforcements before the Battle of the Little Bighorn are purposely altered to show him in a poorer light. The Indians did fire first at Wounded Knee, contrary to the film's depiction. One might read Robert Utley's *Last Days of the Sioux Nation* for an understanding of the true sequence of events. Even the Indian school at Carlisle, Pennsylvania, conceived by a good man like Richard H. Pratt, is shown to be no better than a concentration camp run by Gestapo-like guards. One could even complain that Quantrill's Raiders are shown sacking and burning Lawrence, Kansas, in mid-winter snow instead of in mid-summer, as in reality; or that clean-shaven mountain man Jedediah Smith is always incorrectly shown as bearded and dirty.

Misrepresentation and playing loose with the facts are the bread and butter of *Into the West*. It gets nearly as much wrong as right, and its sole purpose appears to be to pile another guilt-trip on Americans. Where *How the West Was Won* was idealistic, optimistic, and bright, *Into the West* is nihilistic, pessimistic, and bleak. Even the score is melancholy, bordering on a funeral dirge, and the screen is painted in somber colors. In the final scene the heads of the main white and Lakota families tell their children the "tale" of how the west was won, which would smother one family with shame and guilt, and paint the other as perpetual victims. It is not a happy denouement for either side.

Neither *How the West Was Won* nor *Into the West* gives a true picture of the westward movement. The former was guilty of omission rather than distortion, while the latter was guilty of distortion *and* omission. There seems little doubt as to which view is healthier. Where did TNT and one-time Crockett fan Steven Spielberg (here serving as co-executive producer) get their jaundiced views of history? A companion volume to the film *Into the West* was written by Max McCoy, and although it does give warning that it is "a work of fiction," the folks watching the film don't receive that red flag. Viewers are likely to believe that what they are seeing is true, particularly given the constant bombardment of politically correct history the post-baby boomer generations have been force-fed during the past four decades.

*Into the West* sprang from suspect origins, and, like Harriet Beecher Stowe's Topsy, it just "grow'd." It seems to belong to what may be termed the "Everybody Knows" school of history. The "facts" are suspect, but somehow everybody knows they must be true. The propaganda has had its effect. It is history by repetition. If you hear it or see it enough, it becomes true by volume alone.

"Everybody Knows" history is closely related to history by popular vote. Americans have a penchant for putting truth to the vote test. It is said that about two-thirds of Americans believe that John F. Kennedy was a victim of a conspiracy. That doesn't make it true. A significant percentage of Americans are also said to believe that space aliens have visited the Earth. The proposition that we can vote on truth is ludicrous, and we should not allow our history to be written or taught with such shoddy methodologies.

Have we progressed in understanding during the four decades between *How the West Was Won* to *Into the West*? Very doubtful. The history portrayed in the latter is arguably worse than in the old versions. The disparagement of America is self-destructive, but the dark view of our past that *Into the West* presents is only a manifestation of our times. The generational cycle will inevitably shift again, and many of us hope that the currently politically correct press and publishers will soon come to their senses. Maybe Hollywood will follow along. Maybe Hollywood can lead the way.

# 35

# Riding into the Sunset

"Guns Don't Kill, Movies Kill" was the title of a talk given by Michael Bellesiles at the 1999 Western History Association Conference (discussed briefly in this book's introduction). The conference featured a number of scholars in a roundtable discussion, all of whom shared beliefs that the West was not shaped by violence. It was the media, Bellesiles said, that played the decisive role in convincing most Americans that the frontier was a violent place. Movies are the culprits that have made us into a gun-toting, confrontational nation.

According to Stuart Udall, there are teachers who declare that "perhaps 90 percent of Americans acquire their beliefs about our past from watching movies or television." Udall believes that filmmakers only concentrate on isolated violent occurrences, and by doing so, "History is wrenched out of shape and a great myth is born that frontier violence forged the essential American character."

Robert Dykstra said frontier violence was not as American as apple pie. "It's a hoax, folks," he affirmed. Paula Mitchell Marks concurred, stating that "the real frontier West had little relation to the Wild West, that violent murderous place of popular imagination, and this distortion is a creation primarily of the media."[1]

The authors and historians at that conference were united in their belief that Hollywood was, and is, shaping how Americans view their past, and paving the way to a possibly disastrous future. These scholars definitely had agendas, with gun control high on the list. In their push for a kinder, gentler world, however, they may be distorting history more than Hollywood ever did.

A case in point is that of Bellesiles, then a professor at Emory University. His book *Arming America* won the Bancroft Prize for the best work of American history published in 2000. Bellesiles' thesis states that guns were scarce in early America, Americans were never well-armed, and most were uninterested in owning guns. Gun ownership was just an "invented tradition" concocted by historians and the media. It was a powerful declaration.

The major problem was that it wasn't true. When scholars and reporters from across the nation began investigating Bellesiles' claims and checking his footnotes, the entire façade came crashing down. "Virtually every aspect" of his conclusions were based "on faulty, at times nonexistent, evidence and biased research."[2]

Bellesiles wanted so badly to "prove" his point that he misused the historical documents, distorted them, or even concocted them. He is not alone in this type of deception. Ward Churchill, recently fired from a professorship at the University of Colorado, was under investigation for similar actions, including plagiarism. Whereas Bellesiles' agenda is gun control, Churchill's is genocide. He so desires everyone to believe that Native Americans were victims of genocide that his "scholarly" publications are rife with the type of falsifications that led to Bellesiles' downfall.

Churchill's works have made their way into discussions about the meaning and direction of Western films, possibly leading authors to conclusions that tend to support Churchill's advocacy of violence, and his world view of a monstrous conspiracy of white men out to destroy all other non-white cultures. One professor of Film Studies at the University of California apparently has bought into Churchill's arguments and believes he, among others, has "eloquently exposed" America's creation myth that conquering the Indians was a necessary by-product of westward expansion. Scholarly dishonesty in using selective evidence, distorting the facts, or making up statistics can seduce the uninitiated, and it is more insidious than plagiarism.[3] There are no people as potentially dangerous as those who possess the "truth," yet will use any means to justify their personal agendas.

The Western History Association's panel denied frontier violence in an attempt to downplay contemporary violence. It is part of a trend by historians trying to cure what they don't like in the present by re-writing the past. Judging from what Hollywood has shown us in the last four or five decades, some of those historians must be pleased.

Westerns have drastically changed from what they were in the first half of the 20th century. The number of Western movies has dropped drastically, although violence is still part of the stories. There are still shootings, lynchings, cattle drives, stagecoach attacks, wagon trains, Indians, cowboys, rustlers, and battles between the army and the Indians. The current trend in Hollywood, however, is role reversals: whereas traditionally the army, emigrants, cowboys, and settlers were the "good guys," and the Indians were usually the "bad guys," there has been a 180-degree turnaround. For the last several decades the white man has been given the "black" hat, while the Indian wears the "white" hat. The earlier depiction was not accurate, but neither is the latter. All parties could more accurately be painted in shades of gray.

Unknown to all but the hardcore Western film mavens, the earliest Western movies were filmed on the East Coast, and plots concerning Indian-white friendships and interracial romances were more common. In 1911 the film industry made its own westward migration, settling down in the Los Angeles area. Newspapers and magazines reported that the Western movie was dead, but in reality there was a rejuvenation and metamorphosis. The silent Westerns of the Teens and Twenties recast the Indian as a villain, a role he was relegated to for another four decades.[4]

The changing scene, labeled by author Richard Slotkin as the "Cult of the Indian," was evident as early as the 1949 films *Apache Chief, Daughter of the West*, and *The Cowboy and the Indians*, and in the 1950 films *Broken Arrow* and *Devil's Doorway*. Others followed, such as the 1952 films *Hiawatha, Navaho*, and *Rose of Cimarron*. *Apache* (1954), *Apache Woman* (1955), and *White Feather* (1956) continued the trend.[5]

A more sympathetic view of Indians was necessary to counter the negative image they had been given in many films from the Teens to the Forties. The trend accelerated in the Sixties, with *Cheyenne Autumn* (1964), as an example, portraying the Indians "as a metaphor for the oppressed."[6] But like the proverbial snowball rolling down the hill, the trend picked up speed and mass until it grew into a monster that could not be controlled.

Perhaps it was a combination of the Civil Rights movement, the Feminist movement, the backlash against the war in Vietnam, and the general distrust of the military-industrial complex, but it was during the radicalized decade of the Sixties that the role reversal went beyond its fail-safe point. The white and black hats were switched, and the new black-hatters were being vilified more than the Indians ever were.

The year 1970 saw the release of a book and two movies that epitomized the change in attitude. Dee Brown's *Bury My Heart at Wounded Knee*, subtitled *An Indian History of the American West*, struck a resonant chord. Never mind the fact that Brown's historical methodologies were very suspect—the book is rife with distortions, omissions, and selective evidence use. It didn't seem to matter. Americans were apparently tired of the old myths and legends. A reviewer for *Newsweek* summed up the new conscience. White Americans were now the villains, and Brown had presented "a damning case against our national roots in greed, perfidy, ignorance and malice." The reviewer claimed to have read hundreds of books, but none of them, he said, "has saddened me and shamed me as much as this book has."[7] Brown's flawed history was taken as 100 percent truth, and part of its legacy has served to curtail rational dialogue throughout the subsequent decades.

Appearing the same year was the film *Little Big Man* (Stockbridge/Hiller), which Slotkin called "a vehicle for overtly anti-war polemics." Nevertheless, or perhaps because it was so outrageous, the movie was a big hit. The movie's hero, Jack Crabb (Dustin Hoffman), and his sister Caroline (Carole Androsky), are the only two survivors of a Pawnee attack on a wagon train. Cheyennes find them and take them to their village. When the Indians don't molest Caroline, she heads back to the white world.

Crabb then experiences a series of highly improbable, but comic, misadventures trying to live in two worlds. Director Arthur Penn satirizes both cultures, but hits harder when targeting the whites. At one juncture Crabb takes up with traveling snake oil salesman Alardyce T. Merriweather (Martin Balsam). Merriweather passes on many words of wisdom, but one pearl in particular stands out. He tells Crabb that, "two legged creatures will believe anything, and the more preposterous the better."

The line epitomizes the entire film, for by the end, an unsophisticated audience would come to believe that almost every Indian travels the moral and spiritual high ground, while almost every white man is a thief, a killer, a buffoon, or completely insane. The portrayal of George Custer (Richard Mulligan) as a raving lunatic earned laughs, but, unfortunately, it also was taken for reality by many Americans who get their "history" solely from movies. It was said that the popular film did more to humanize American Indians than any newspapers, books, or documentaries could have done. It was not said that the movie also played a large part in the eventual demonizing of the military and the pioneers.[8]

Merriweather's line in *Little Big Man* that people will believe anything was not the first or last time that sentiment was expressed in Western movies. In *Fort Apache* (RKO, 1948), Lt. Col. Owen Thursday (Henry Fonda) is the Custer-like character who leads his troops to destruction. At the film's end, Lt. Col. Kirby York (John Wayne) talks to a group of reporters about the disaster. When one praises Thursday, York, although he despised Thursday, responds, "No man died more gallantly, nor won more honor for his regiment."

They discuss the new painting of "Thursday's Last Charge," and another reporter declares it to be a magnificent work, with massed Apaches attacking and Thursday leading his men in a final charge.

"Correct in every detail," York responds, although he knows, and the audience knows, that the painting was nothing like the final battle it purports to depict. The important message that director John Ford wanted to send was that it was good for the nation to have heroes; it was vital for a people to have heroic myths and legends in which to believe.[9]

John Ford took that idea one step farther, and in a more ominous way, at the end of his film *The Man Who Shot Liberty Valence* (John Ford/Paramount, 1962). Ransom Stoddard (James Stewart) has made his fame and fortune as the man who shot the outlaw Liberty Valence (Lee Marvin), but only he and his wife Hallie (Vera Miles) know the truth — that Tom Doniphon (John Wayne) killed Valence. Stoddard's successful career was built on a deception.

Years later Doniphon dies, and Stoddard attends the funeral. Newspapermen converge to get the story of how Stoddard killed Valence so many years ago. Stoddard, however, decides to tell the truth. When he explains what really happened and asks that they print it, the newsmen decline, stating, "When legend becomes a fact, print the legend."

Grant Withers, Victor McLaglen, John Wayne, Henry Fonda, and George O'Brien face Cochise in *Fort Apache* (RKO, 1948). Fonda, as Lt. Col. Owen Thursday, plays a disciplinarian who is about to begin the fatal battle.

In an interview, John Ford was asked if he really believed that. "Yes—" Ford said, "because I think it's good for the country." Ford said that plenty of men in America's past have been made out to be great heroes when they weren't. "But," he reiterated, "it's good for the country to have heroes to look up to."[10]

Unknown to Ford, the result of his films, along with others being produced by Hollywood in increasing numbers in the Sixties and Seventies, was to knock nearly every frontier hero off his pedestal. Ford, who died in 1973, never witnessed what Hollywood later did to the heroes he sought to protect. By the end of the 20th century, all the Custers, Sheridans, Carsons, Earps, Codys, Hickoks, Crocketts and the like were portrayed not as heroes but as villains, agents of an evil white America despoiling the land and the indigenous people.

The idea that American history was concocted to fool the people appeared full blown in *Buffalo Bill and the Indians, or Sitting Bull's History Lesson* (De Laurentis, 1976). The opening scenes show a family of settlers near a little cabin. Suddenly, Indian raiders attack, shooting the men and abducting a young white woman. It is a scene that truly occurred many times in the nation's history, but this time a voice calls out "Cease the action," and music plays and credits roll. It is only an act.

The implication is that such scenes were only created by novelists or moviemakers, or in this case by the showman William F. "Buffalo Bill" Cody. Cody's Wild West Show was said to have created many American icons and legends. Director and screenwriter Robert Altman uses Cody's show, which ran on and off from 1883 until Cody died in 1917, as a vehicle to debunk

American history. Appearing during the year of America's bicentennial celebration, the film also marked what one author believes was the year that the Western genre died.

Buffalo Bill, who actually was a genuine frontier hero who participated in significant historical events, is portrayed (by Paul Newman) "as a vainglorious, hypocritical, impotent, drunken racist."[11] In Altman's vision, American history is nothing more than fiction, a phony collection of fantasies made up by the likes of Bill Cody and his popularizer, Ned Buntline (Burt Lancaster).

In one scene Cody argues with Annie Oakley (Geraldine Chapman) about getting Sitting Bull (Frank Kaquitts) to join the show. The problem is that Sitting Bull has his own conception of the "truth," while showman Cody has another, and Annie thinks Sitting Bull's is the more correct.

Angry because Annie has threatened to quit the show, Cody asks her, "What did Bull ever do for you?"

"He wanted to show the truth to the people," Annie answers. "Why can't you accept that just once?"

"Because I got a better sense of history than that!" Cody replies.

In another scene, Ned Buntline talks about Cody, the man he helped create. "No ordinary man would have had the foresight to take credit for acts of bravery and heroism that he couldn't have done. And no ordinary man would have realized what tremendous profit could be made by telling a pack of lies in front of witnesses like it was the truth."

Thus, a man who was an authentic frontier hero is portrayed as a liar—a snake oil salesman like Merriweather in *Little Big Man*—and one who can get "two legged creatures" to believe anything.

And what is Sitting Bull's vision of times past? "History," Bull says through his interpreter Halsey (Will Sampson), "is nothing more than disrespect for the dead." The description, sadly, in early 21st century terms, has become more literal than metaphorical, and our dead American forefathers are the ones being held in contempt.[12]

By 1978 it was standard operating procedure to treat all Western history as bunk. The film *China 9, Liberty 37* (CEA/ASPA Productions)[13] included the same sentiment that was expressed at the end of *Liberty Valence* and throughout *Buffalo Bill and the Indians*. The main conflict involves a love/hate triangle among the gunslinger Clayton Drumm (Fabio Testi), Matthew Sebanek (Warren Oates), and Catherine Sebanek (Jenny Agutter). At one point Drumm meets Wilbur Olsen (Sam Peckinpah), a dime novelist who wants to write Drumm's story and, like Ned Buntline did for Buffalo Bill Cody, "create" a legendary hero.

"I bring the West to the East," Olsen explains to Drumm. "People say I write lies, but the truth is ... it's dead in a year or less."

"What do you want?" Drumm asks.

"A touch of pulchritude for the people back east," Olsen explains, "a piece of the American West they can believe in."

"You mean lie to them?" Drumm asks.

"Of course. The lies, they need, we all need."

"My life is not for sale," Drumm says.

"Nonsense!" Olsen insists. "It's only a question of who pays, and when."

By the 1980s, Westerns were certainly out of fashion. The depths to which the genre had sunk could be seen in a remake of *Stagecoach*. Actually, the first remake was done in 1966, with Alex Cord playing the role of the Ringo Kid. It was bad, but the 1986 re-remake was even worse. Starring Kris Kristofferson as the Ringo Kid, Willie Nelson as Doc Holliday, Johnny Cash as Marshal Curly, and Waylon Jennings as Hatfield the gambler, the movie simply appeared to be a vehicle to cash in on the celebrity of several popular country singers.

In the original version, John Ford used the Indians as a viable menace to knit the little band of passengers together into a social community. In the 1986 film, the Indians are no danger at all; they have become victims of the white man and are now an oppressed minority. When Doc (Willie Nelson) makes speeches about how the Indians have been mistreated and misunderstood, it becomes propaganda. One author said that the movie failed because the Indians ceased being a danger and became objects of condescension. "The film is interesting," she wrote, "only in its ladling out of white guilt and its patronizing understanding of the 'misunderstood' Geronimo."[14]

In 1990's *Dances with Wolves* (TIG Productions), Kevin Costner, as director, producer, and star, presented his version of America's past. The vision was bleak. To his credit, Costner used talented Indian actors to depict the Native Americans as real people and not the clichéd stereotypes of the past. There was a price, however. For the most part, Costner could only elevate the Indians by degrading the whites.

Whereas at the end of *Little Big Man* the audience comes to believe that most white men are ignorant fools, by the end of *Dances with Wolves*, white men are objects of disgust and hatred. The Lakotas are the rational, just, peaceful people (unlike their enemies, the Pawnees), and the whites are filthy, ignorant liars and violent killers — or, as in *Little Big Man*, blithering idiots.

In an early scene in *Dances with Wolves* we catch a glimpse of how the military will be portrayed. "Sir Knight," the half-crazy Major Fambrough (Maury Chaykin) says to Lieutenant Dunbar (Costner), "I've just pissed in my pants, and nobody can do anything about it." (In the director's cut, the officer is also masturbating!) The stereotype of the mentally unstable army officer appears to be one of the latest clichés for the frontier military.

Dunbar leaves the craziness of "civilization" behind so he can see the frontier "before it's gone." But he can't really escape the degenerate whites. They find him, and for no apparent reason the soldiers kill Dunbar's horse, Cisco, and his wolf, Two Socks, animals that the audience has come to love. They try to take Dunbar back to receive military justice as a deserter and renegade, but when the Lakotas attack their small caravan, the audience is cheering for the Indians to massacre every one of the despicable white soldiers.

It is quite a turnaround. The Western of the first half of the 20th century generally depicted Indians as villains; by the century's end the white man was the villain. Not only was he the villain, he had become more loathsome than any movie Indian had ever been. The shaming and disgracing of the frontier military, the emigrants, and the pioneers is a very disturbing trend.

Today, movies with attitudes like this have colored the mindset of many. One author explains, "How and what we write and interpret about history matters to people who will never go to college or read a book." Another says, "For many, Hollywood History is the only history," and still another speculates that moviegoers "basically think whatever they see is true."[15] The lesson is clear for the importance of historical accuracy.

Many years ago historian Bernard De Voto said that the folk mind was often wiser than the intellectuals because it knew its heroes and embraced them stubbornly, even when heroes were out of fashion.[16] The observation may have been true during the mid–20th century, but today, sadly, most people have come to believe that there were no white heroes, that they were all spoilers, hypocrites, and liars. The very real accomplishments and deeds of our ancestors are now shown only as false myths and legends created for our own gratification. It is untrue, and it is destructive to our sense of pride in being American.

Post-baby boomer generations watching movies made between the 1920s and the 1960s see Indians attacking and killing, while the army and settlers are portrayed in a positive light. Many of these younger viewers probably conclude that all those old movies must be inaccurate and racist because they don't jibe with portrayals in newer Westerns (those made during the past four decades). Obviously, the old ones must be wrong, if for no other reason than they just aren't being made like that anymore. Like the commercials tell us, new goes with improved, and repetition is equated with truth.

Times change, obviously, and writers and filmmakers' attitudes change with them. As has been shown here, however, Hollywood in its first half-century did a remarkably good job depicting America's westward migration. The vision of the old emigrant wagon trains trekking to the promised land under the threat of attacking Indians was not a fabrication of film. It has been said that the Western fell into disfavor because it did not provide all of the correct details. To the contrary, the Western film began declining when too much fuss was made about the details while all the heroic myths and legends were being demolished. Today, cynicism is viewed as accuracy.

The "New Western" historian version of our West emerged between *The Outlaw Josey Wales* (1976) and *Dances with Wolves* (1990). The old, optimistic, Turnerian version of America's growth was replaced by themes of dislocation, environmental calamity, economic exploitation, merciless conquest of indigenous peoples, and individual failure.[17] The current picture is neither pretty nor accurate.

In depicting the western migration, early Hollywood is the winner. During the first half-century, Hollywood nailed the concept but was remiss in portraying the details; in the second half-century, Hollywood did better with the details but lost sight of the concept. Getting the costume, the model of the gun, or the color of the war paint correct is not that important — if, as a consequence, heroes are demolished and an entire group of people is vilified.

So, for all you doubting, cynical historians and moviemakers out there, there are several things you should know for future projects: Indians attacked wagon trains of any size; they killed people, sometimes mercilessly; wagon trains circled up for defense; Indians circled around wagon trains; and the army did come to the rescue. Deal with it.

Tim McCoy, an actor in many "B" westerns of the 1920s and 1930s, said shortly before his death in 1978 that he was disturbed at the recent trend in Hollywood movies. In nearly every movie he saw, the heroes were out and the bad guys were in. He said:

> Why this is I do not know. I cannot condemn the trend, for it is like everything else I have observed, part of ongoing change. But I do mourn the passing of the hero, for we gave the young people someone to look up to, a figure to emulate, and, more often than is generally supposed, imposed upon ourselves an obligation to be true to that image. If people must live their lives cast in various parts, why should the prevailing roles not be dedicated to the highest standards and principles?[18]

Why not, indeed?

Are we in danger of becoming what the books and movies of late tell us we are: gun-toting, guilt-ridden self-haters living on false legends? We still have a chance to save the situation if we circle the wagons and give it our best shot. We can still fight for accuracy in books and movies.

Historians, please tell us the truth.

Hollywood, give us back our history.

# Appendix A: The Wagon Train Movies

The following are brief summaries of a number of films in which wagon trains play at least a minor part in the storyline. The list is not all-inclusive. Filmography abbreviations: *d* director; *p* producer; *s* screenwriter; *st* story; *c* cinematographer; *lp* leading players.

***Abilene Town*** (United Artists, 1946). *d* Edwin L. Marin, *p* Jules Levey; *s* Harold Schumate; *c* Archie Stout; *lp* Randolph Scott, Ann Dvorak, Lloyd Bridges, Rhonda Fleming, Edgar Buchanan, Howard Freeman.

It's cattlemen versus settlers in the frontier town of Abilene. Dan Mitchell (Randolph Scott) tries to calm the situation in which Sheriff Bravo Trimble (Edgar Buchanan) would rather drink than fight; and the cattlemen's henchman, Jet Younger (Jack Lambert), and the settlers' leader, Henry Dreiser (Lloyd Bridges), are on a collision course.

This is not strictly a wagon train movie, but the cattlemen do make a night raid on a circle of emigrant wagons. The settlers win in the end, and Mitchell forsakes the nice girl (Rhonda Fleming) for the dancehall floozie (Ann Dvorak).

***Across the Plains*** (1939). *d* Spencer G. Bennett; *p* Robert E, Tansey; *s* Robert E. Tansey; *c* Bert Longenecker; *lp* Addison (Jack) Randall, Frank Yaconelli, Joyce Bryant, Hal Price, Dennis Moore, Glenn Strange, Bud Osborne.

Young brothers Jack Winters (Jack Randall) and Jimmy Winters (Dennis Moore) are separated when Indians attack their wagon train and kill their parents. One is raised by Indians and the other by an outlaw gang leader. Years later, Jimmy and his outlaw band attack a train led by Indian-raised brother Jack.

***After the Massacre*** (Reliance, 1913). This action-drama film focuses on Indian attacks on wagon trains and pioneer settlements.

***The Angel of Dawson's Claim*** (Lubin, 1910). *lp* Harry Myers.

A five-year-old child is the sole survivor of a wagon train massacre. A miner, Harry Myers, finds her and tries to raise her, but is unable to. He gives the girl to a woman he loves, but the girl wants to stay with the man who rescued her. The woman ends up marrying the miner so all three can be together.

***The Apache Kid*** (1941). *d* George Sherman; *s* Eliot Gibbons; *st* Richard Murphy; *c* Harry Neumann; *lp* Don "Red" Berry, Lynn Merrick, LeRoy Mason, Robert Fiske, John Elliott, Forbes Murray, Monte Montague, Al St. John.

Pete Dawson (Don "Red" Barry) leads a group of emigrants from Missouri to Oregon Territory. The villain, Joe Walker (Robert Fiske), has his henchmen dress as Indians to attack the train. They drive off the stock and destroy the supplies, making the emigrants dependent on Walker for help.

***Apache Rifles*** (Fox, 1964). *d* William Witney; *p* Grant Whytock; *s* Charles B. Smith; *c* Archie L. Dalzell; *lp* Audie Murphy, Michael Dante, Linda Lawson, L. Q. Jones, Ken Lynch, Joseph Vitale, Robert Brubaker, Eugene Iglesias, Pat O'Malley.

Wagon train attacks play only a minor role in this film, but Capt. Jeff Stanton (Audie Murphy) does place soldiers under cover in wagons to draw the Apaches into an attack. Also, Apaches under Red Hawk (Michael Dante) trap an army wagon train in a canyon, and the soldiers have to overturn the wagons to use as barricades.

The love interest springs from Stanton, depicted as an Indian-hating racist in the beginning, falling in love with Dawn Gillis (Linda Lawson), a half–Comanche "squaw." Red Hawk lances Stanton, but he recovers, resigns his commission, and gets the girl.

**The Aryan** (Triangle, 1916). *d* William S. Hart; *s* C. Gardner Sullivan; *lp* William S. Hart, Bessie Love, Louise Glaum, Gertrude Claire, Charles French, Herschel Mayall, Swallow.

Steve Denton (William S. Hart) is an outlaw with scruples. He and his gang find a wagon train stranded in the desert, with the travelers dying of thirst. The gang members want to exploit the situation and take the women captive, but Hart, falling for pretty Mary Jane Garth (Bessie Love), bargains with them for their freedom and leads the train out of the desert.

**Attack on an Emigrant Train** (Biograph, 1907). A blend of stage and film, this was one of the earliest depiction of Indians attacking wagon trains.

**The Bad Lands** (PDC, 1925). *d* Dell Henderson; *s* Harvey Gates; *lp* Harry Carey, Wilfred Lucas, Lee Shumway, Gaston Glass, Joe Rickson, Trilby Clark.

Patrick O'Toole (Harry Carey) is a frontiersman who heads to an isolated army fort to investigate liquor and gun smugglers. Indians attack the wagon train he's riding. They narrowly escape with their lives when a young officer, Hal Owen (Gaston Glass), abandons them rather than fight the Indians. Owen is the son of Colonel Owen (Wilfred Lucas), who is in charge of the fort. Hal, who owes gambling debts, tries to hold up the Pony Express, but it is O'Toole who is falsely accused. When the colonel marches out with his troops to look for the raiding Indians, young Owen is placed in charge of the fort. The Indians attack the undermanned post, and O'Toole finds Owen hiding in a corner. He forces the young officer to fight, and Owen finally makes up for his past cowardice but is fatally wounded. Colonel Owen returns to rescue the fort just in time, and Hal clears O'Toole before he dies.

**Bend of the River** (Universal, 1952). *d* Anthony Mann; *p* Aaron Rosenberg; *s* Borden Chase; *c* Irving Glassberg; *lp* James Stewart, Arthur Kennedy, Rock Hudson, Jay C. Flippen, Julie Adams, Stepin Fetchit.

A wagon train of emigrants heads toward Oregon, led by Glyn McLyntock (James Stewart). Indians attack, but an even bigger problem arises when Glyn's partner, Emerson Cole (Arthur Kennedy), plots to take the emigrants' much-needed food supply and sell it to some miners for gold.

**The Big Trail** (Fox, 1930). *d* Raoul Walsh; *s* Jack Peabody, Marie Boyle, Florence Postal, Fred Sersen; *c* Lucien Androit, Arthur Edeson; *lp* John Wayne, Marguerite Churchill, Ward Bond, Tyrone Power Sr., Charles Stevens, Ian Keith, Tully Marshall.

Discussed in text.

**Blazing the Trail** (Bison, 1912). *d* Thomas H. Ince; *lp* Francis Ford, Ethel Grandin, J. Barney Sherry, Ann Little.

Francis Ford, John Ford's older brother, starred in this film, directed by Thomas H. Ince, about Indians battling pioneers. Indians claim friendship with emigrants but attack their wagon train. Some emigrants are killed, and an adult brother and sister are captured but later rescued from the Indian camp. In the end, the "orphans" leave crosses on their parents' graves and continue the journey west.

**Brigham Young** (Fox, 1940). *d* Henry Hathaway; *p* Kenneth MacGowan; *s* Lamar Trotti; *c* Arthur Miller; *lp* Tyrone Power, Linda Darnell, Dean Jagger, Brian Donlevy, Jane Darwell, Vincent Price, Mary Astor.

The story involves the trials of Mormon leader Brigham Young (Dean Jagger) in bringing his followers overland to settle in the Salt Lake area. Lead characters Jonathan Kent (Tyrone Power) and Zina Webb (Linda Darnell) face renegade Indians and white villains bent on disrupting their journey to the promised land.

**Buffalo Bill on the U. P. Trail** (Sunset, 1926). *d* Frank S. Mattison; *lp* Roy Stewart, Cullen Landis, Kathryn McGuire, Sheldon Lewis, Milburn Morante, Earl Metcalfe.

Mainly about the railroads, this film also includes scenes in which the frontier scout Gordon Kent (Cullen Landis) guides a wagon train of emigrants across the plains.

**California** (Paramount, 1946). *d* John Farrow; *p* Seton I. Miller; *s* Frank Butler, Theodore Strauss; *c* Ray Rennahan; *lp* Ray Milland, Barbara Stanwyck, Barry Fitzgerald, George Coulouris, Anthony Quinn.

Called an "unofficial remake of *The Covered Wagon*," this star-laden drama is rather slow-moving and dull. The early sequences show a wagon train heading to California, which soon scatters when news arrives of gold strikes in California.

***The Call of the Blood*** (Kinemacolor, 1913). A pioneer family tries to cross the plains to reach the closest settlement when Indians attack their covered wagon. The warriors kill the father and take the pregnant mother captive, while the boy escapes to the fort. Before the mother dies, she gives birth to a girl, who grows up with the Indians, never knowing her heritage. The boy later becomes an army officer and meets his long-lost sister when he discovers she wears a family locket.

***Cherokee Uprising*** (Monogram, 1950). *d* Lewis D. Collins; *p* Vincent M. Fennelly; *c* Gilbert Warrenton; *s* Daniel B. Ullman; *lp* Whip Wilson, Andy Clyde, Lois Hall, Sam Flint, Forrest Taylor, Marshall Reed, Iron Eyes Cody, Chief Yowlache, Lee Roberts, Stanley Price, Lyle Talbot.

Though set in a time, according to the narrator, "Long after the Indian and white man were at peace," renegade Indians and white men are still attacking wagon trains. Marshal Bob Foster (Whip Wilson) has to deal with the white villains and Indian warriors who continue to attack emigrant wagons, killing the pioneers and stealing their supplies and stock so they can buy whiskey.

***The Covered Wagon*** (Paramount, 1923). *d* James Cruze; *p* Jesse L. Lasky; *s* Jack Cunningham; *st* Emerson Hough; *c* Karl Brown; *lp* J. Warren Kerrigan, Lois Wilson, Ernest Torrence, Alan Hale, Tully Marshall, Charles Ogle, Ethel Wales, Guy Oliver, Johnny Fox.

Discussed in text.

***The Cowboy's Baby*** (Selig, 1908). *d* Francis Boggs; *p* William Nicholas Selig; *lp* Fred Church.

The central portion of this short drama focuses on Indians attacking a wagon train. The star, Fred Church, appeared in nearly 250 movies from 1908 to 1935.

***Custer's Last Stand*** (Weiss Productions, 1936). *d* Elmer Clifton; *p* Louis Weiss; *s* George Arthur Durlam, Eddie Granemann, William Lively; *c* Bert Longenecker; *lp* Rex Lease, Lona Andre, William Farnum, Ruth Mix, Jack Mulhall, Nancy Caswell, George Chesebro, Dorothy Gulliver, Frank McGlynn Jr., Helen Gibson, Josef Swickard, Chief Thundercloud, Reed Howes, Bobby Nelson, Robert Walker.

This 15-chapter serial is chock-full of characters, quests, perils and plot twists. The main story revolves around an Indian medicine arrow with encoded directions to a secret cave of gold, with white villains, led by Tom "Keen" Blade (Reed Howes), as well as Indians, trying to get it. Kit Cardigan (Rex Lease) is the hero, and Barbara Trent (Nancy Caswell) the sweetheart. Frank McGlynn Jr. plays General Custer, and Ruth Mix is his wife Elizabeth.

In the first chapter, "Perils of the Plains," Indians attack wagon trains twice. The first time they wipe out all but four emigrants. Henry Trent (Josef Swickard) finds the medicine arrow on a dead Indian and gets the ball rolling. The second train has time to circle before the Indians hit, and the emigrants stuff mattresses and supplies between the wagons to plug the gaps. Kit Cardigan rides into the circle in time to help save them by getting young Bobby Trent (Bobby Nelson) to blow the bugle and fool the Indians into believing the army is coming to the rescue.

In Chapter Three, "Red Vengeance," the Indians attack the town of Blackpool, much as they did in the serial *The Oregon Trail* (1936). In Chapter Ten, "Flaming Arrows," the Indians attack Fort Henry, riding around and shooting at the wooden stockade, and sneak into the fort through a secret trap door. The bad Indian, Young Wolf (Chief Thundercloud), tries to kill Libbie Custer but is foiled. In the end, Custer dies at the Little Bighorn, but Young Wolf also dies when he falls on the medicine arrow. No one finds the gold.

***Cyclone of the Saddle*** (Argosy Productions Corporation, 1935). *d* Elmer Clifton; *p* George M. Merrick, Louis Weiss; *s* Elmer Clifton, George M. Merrick; *c* Edward Linden; *lp* Rex Lease, Janet Chandler, Bobby Nelson, Yakima Canutt, Helen Gibson, Milburn Morante, George Chesebro.

The army sends Andy Thomas (Rex Lease), posing as a renegade, to join a wagon train to learn who has been attacking the emigrants and freighters. The gunrunner villains are Cherokee Charlie (George Chesebro) and whip-wielding Snake (Yakima Canutt), who kill two Indians and blame it on the pioneers to start an uprising. The Indians retaliate by attacking the wagons, but Andy saves the day and gets the girl, Sue Carter (Janet Chandler).

***Davy Crockett, Indian Scout*** (Edward Small Productions/Reliance Pictures, 1950). *d* Lew Landers; *p* Edward Small; *st* Ford Beebe; *c* George E. Diskant; *lp* George Montgomery, Ellen Drew, Phillip Reed, Noah Beery Jr., Paul Guilfoyle, Addison Richards, Chief Thundercloud.

It's not the "real" Davy Crockett, but his nephew (George Montgomery), who leads a wagon train of emigrants and an army escort across dangerous Indian country in 1848. Because of a spy among them, they contend with several attacks by Indians who always know just what trail and pass they will follow. The cast also includes Ellen Drew as Francis Oatman, and Noah Beery Jr. as Tex McGee.

**The Dawn of Understanding** (Vitagraph, 1918). *d* David Smith; *s* Edward J. Montagne; *lp* Bessie Love, George A. Williams, John Gilbert, George Kunkel, Frank Glendon.

A romantic drama set in 1849, the film tells the story of Sue Prescott (Bessie Love) and her trying experiences traveling in a wagon train on the way to California. Her mother dies during the trek, and Sue decides not to continue west, but goes to work for, and falls in love with, frontiersman Ira Beasley (John Gilbert).

**Dawn on the Great Divide** (Monogram, 1942). *d* Howard Bretherton; *p* Scott R. Dunlap; *s* Adele S. Buffington; *st* James Oliver Curwood; *c* Harry Neumann; *lp* Buck Jones, Mona Barrie, Raymond Hatton, Rex Bell, Robert Lowery, Maude Eburne, Christine McIntyre, Roy Barcroft, Robert Frazer, Harry Woods, Tristram Coffin.

Discussed in text.

**Days of Daring** (Aywon, 1920). *d* Tom Mix.

Tom Mix is a Pony Express rider in 1849, more than a decade before the Pony Express actually began. He quits his job to take his sweetheart and her brother to California. Indians attack their wagon on the way west, but they are rescued at the last minute.

**The Deserter** (Triangle, 1916). *d* Scott Sidney; *p* Thomas H. Ince; *s* Thomas H. Ince, Richard V. Spencer; *lp* Charles Ray, Rita Stanwood, Wedgwood Nowell, Hazel Belford, Joseph J. Dowling.

In a plot similar to the 1912 Bison film of the same name, Lieutenant Parker (Charles Ray) is the officer who strikes his captain while drunk. He is put in the guardhouse but escapes, and is branded a deserter. Parker finds a wagon train attacked by Indians and rides to the fort for help. The emigrants are rescued, but Parker is mortally wounded. He is finally buried with military honors.

**The Devil Horse** (Pathé, 1926). *d* Fred Jackman; *p* Hal Roach; *st* Hal Roach; *lp* Yakima Canutt, Gladys McConnell, Robert Kortman, Roy Clements, Fred Jackman Jr.

Young Dave Garson (Fred Jackman Jr.) cares for his favorite horse as a boy, but he is separated from it after Indians attack the wagon train, killing his parents. The boy grows into a man (Yakima Canutt) who dislikes Indians—as does the horse because the Indians have mistreated it.

When Indians capture Garson years later, they force him to fight the "devil horse" (Rex the Wonder Horse); but it is his old pal, and they are reunited and escape. The bad Indian Chief Prowling Wolf (Robert Kortman) desires the daughter of an army officer and foments an uprising so he can capture her, but Garson, riding the "devil horse," comes to the rescue.

It may be surprising to learn that this generally anti–Indian film was produced by Hal Roach, a king of comedy-film productions, while the story was co-written by Roach and Stan Laurel, of Laurel and Hardy fame.

**Duel at Diablo** (United Artists, 1966). *d/co-p* Ralph Nelson; *co-p* Fred Engel; *s* Marvin H. Albert, Michael M. Grilikhes; *c* Charles F. Wheeler; *lp* James Garner, Sidney Poitier, Bibi Andersson, Bill Travers, John Hoyt, Dennis Weaver.

Discussed in text.

**Early Days in the West** (Bison, 1912). *lp* Wallace Reid, Dolly Larkin, George Field, Ray Francis, W. G. Rice, Paul Machette.

A wagon train guide and scout, Mahomena (George Field), who is a full-blood Indian, loves Eunice (Dolly Larkin), a white woman, but she rejects him. To exact revenge he leads the wagon train into a Sioux ambush.

**Fighting Caravans** (Paramount, 1931). *d* Otto Brower, David Burton; *s* Edward E. Paramore Jr., Keene Thompson, Agnes Brand Leahy; *c* Lee Garmes, Henry Gerrard; *lp* Gary Cooper, Lily Damita, Ernest Torrence, Fred Kohler, Tully Marshall, Syd Saylor.

Discussed in text.

**Fighting Pioneers** (Resolute Pictures Corp., 1935) *d* Harry L. Fraser; *p* Alfred T. Mannon; *s* Harry L. Fraser, Charles E. Roberts; *c* Robert E. Cline; *lp* Rex Bell, Ruth Mix, Buzz Barton, Stanley Blystone, Earl Dwire, Chief Thundercloud, Chief Standing Bear, Chuck Morrison, John Elliott, Roger Williams.

The cavalry is having problems with the Indians, especially since they are being supplied with arms from the fort's armory. Lieutenant Bentley (Rex Bell) saves the day by rescuing a wagon train and capturing the white gunrunners.

***For the Service*** (Buck Jones Productions/Universal, 1936). *d* Buck Jones; *p* Buck Jones; *s* Isadore Bernstein; *c* Herbert Kirkpatrick, Allen Q. Thompson; *lp* Buck Jones, Phillip Trent, Edward Keane, Fred Kohler, Beth Marion, Frank McGlynn Sr., Ben Corbett, Chief Thunderbird, Robert McKenzie, Silver.

Buck Jones produced, directed and starred in this story about army scout Buck O'Bryan contending with white villains, Indian raiders, settlers, and a coward, George Murphy (Philip Trent). The main problem is that Murphy is the son of an officer who wants him included in the scouting details. Murphy, however, is terrified of Indians since he saw his mother and sister massacred by Indians when he was a child.

When they ride into an Indian attack on a wagon train, Murphy wants to flee, and O'Bryan forces him to ride for help by threatening to shoot him. On another patrol they run into the white and Indian renegades led by Bruce Howard (Fred Kohler). Murphy cries out in terror. Howard kills Murphy, but O'Bryan kills Howard and the gang is wiped out. The young man is carried back to the post as a hero, with only O'Bryan knowing the truth.

***The Forty-Niners*** (Monarch, 1932). *d* John P. McCarthy; *p* Burton L. King; *c* Edward A. Kull; *s* F. McGrew; *lp* Tom Tyler, Betty Mack, Al Bridge, Fern Emmett, Gordon DeMain, Mildred Rodgers, Fred Ritter, Frank Ball, Florence Wells.

"Tennessee" Matthews (Tom Tyler) is a trader near Fort Laramie, in conflict with "Squaw" O'Hara (Al Bridge), the villain who makes a living by leading wagon trains into traps where white renegades and Indians can attack and plunder them. Both men fall in love with Virginia Hawkins (Betty Mack), who, with her father, is waiting for an escort for their wagons.

Virginia's preference for Matthews only makes O'Hara more ornery, and he leads the wagon train to the place of its intended destruction. Matthews, nevertheless, saves the train and wins the girl.

***Frontier Uprising*** (Zenith Pictures, 1961). *d* Edward L. Cahn; *p* Robert E. Kent; *s* Orville H. Hampton; *st* George Bruce; *c* Maury Gertsman; *lp* Jim Davis, Nancy Hadley, Ken Mayer, Nestor Paiva, Don Kelly, Stuart Randall, Eugene Iglesias, John Marshall, David Renard, Tudor Owen, Renata Vanni, Addison Richards, Herman Rudin, Jan Arvan.

Scout Jim Stockton (Jim Davis) leads a wagon train to California, unaware that the U.S. and Mexico have just gone to war. Mexican General Torena (John Marshall) has formed an alliance with Indian Chief Taztay (Herman Rudin) to stop all foreign incursions into Mexican Territory.

Taztay attacks but is repulsed. The wagons arrive at Monterey in time for Torena's attack on the American garrison. Stockton helps the commander dynamite the fort rather than let it fall into Torena's hands. The explosions demoralize the Mexican Army, which runs away, and Stockton celebrates by marrying wagon train passenger Consuela Montalvo (Nancy Hadley).

***The Glory Trail*** (Crescent Pictures Corporation, 1936). *d* Lynn Shores; *p* E. B. Derr; *s* John T. Neville; *c* Arthur Martinelli; *lp* Tom Keene, Joan Barclay, Walter Long, James Bush, E. H. Calvert, Frank Melton.

This film uses the familiar plot wherein white villains team up with Indians to attack wagon trains on the Bozeman Trail. This time, ex–Confederate soldiers, led by Capt. John Morgan (Tom Keene), team up with Union soldiers to fight a gang of renegades led by Riley (Walter Long), whose line of work is to sell guns to the Sioux and lead wagon trains into traps.

***Hondo*** (Wayne-Fellows, 1953). *d* John Farrow; *p* Robert Fellows; *s* James Edward Grant; *st* Louis L'Amour; *c* Robert Burks, Archie Stout; *lp* John Wayne, Geraldine Page, Ward Bond, James Arness, Michael Pate, Leo Gordon, Paul Fix, Rodolfo Acosta, Lee Aaker, Tom Irish.

Discussed in text.

***How the West Was Won*** (MGM, 1962). *d* Henry Hathaway ("The Rivers," "The Plains," "The Outlaws"), John Ford ("The Civil War"), George Marshall ("The Railroad"); *p* Bernard Smith; *s* James R. Webb; *c* William H. Daniels, Milton Krasner, Charles Lang Jr., Joseph La Shelle; *lp* Spencer Tracy (Narrator), Carroll Baker, Lee J. Cobb, Henry Fonda, Gregory Peck, George Peppard, James Stewart, John Wayne, Richard Widmark, Henry Morgan, Karl Malden.

Discussed in text.

***In the Days of the Thundering Herd*** (Selig, 1914). *d* Colin Campbell; *s* Gilson Willets; *lp* Tom Mix, Bessie Eyton, Wheeler Oakman, Red Wing.

Tom Mingle (Tom Mix) is a Pony Express rider who leaves to join his sweetheart Sally Madison (Bessie Eyton) as she journeys west in a wagon train to meet her father, who has struck a rich mining claim. Indians, under Chief Swift Wing (Wheeler Oakman), attack the wagons, and Tom and Sally are the only survivors. A friendly Indian girl, Starlight (Red Wing), helps them escape. They join a party of hunters but are attacked again by the same Indians. This time Sally escapes to bring another party of hunters to rescue them.

***The Indian Scout's Vengeance*** (Kalem, 1910). *d* Sidney Olcott; *s* Sidney Olcott; *lp* Ruth Roland, Jack Conway.

A family of pioneers heading west in a wagon train befriends a Mexican drifter. The drifter makes amorous advances towards the daughter (Ruth Roland), but she rejects him because she loves the scout (Jack Conway) who is guiding the train. The Mexican seeks revenge by inciting a band of Indians to attack. They wipe out the train, except for the young woman and the scout. The Mexican captures the woman and takes her to the Indian village. The scout vows vengeance, kills the Indians, kills the Mexican in a knife fight, and rides off with his sweetheart.

***The Indians Are Coming*** (Universal, 1930). *d* Henry MacRae; *s* George Plympton, Ford Beebe; *lp* Allene Ray, Tim McCoy, Edmund Cobb, Francis Ford, Bud Osborne, Wilbur McGaugh.

This 12-part serial was released in both silent and sound versions, and opened on Broadway. Produced for $160,000 and grossing one million dollars, it proved that sound Westerns were profitable. It also reportedly brought back millions of children to the movie houses. The hero, Jack Manning (Tim McCoy), and heroine, Mary Woods (Allene Ray), are beset by numerous trials, involving villain Rance Carter (Wilbur McGaugh), prairie fires, and Indians, as they journey west. In the chapters "Red Terror" and "Circle of Death," Indians attack the wagon train. Dynamite the Dog plays the canine character Pal.

***The Invaders*** (Syndicate, 1929). *d* J. P. McGowan; *s* Walter Sterret; *lp* Bob Steele, Edna Aslin, Thomas Lingham, J. P. McGowan, Bud Osborne, Chief Yowlache.

A brother and sister are the only survivors of an Indian massacre of a wagon train. The girl is raised by the Indians, while the boy is raised by an army officer and later joins the cavalry. When they are adults, an Indian maiden tells the brother of the identity of his lost sister.

***Kentucky Rifle*** (Howco Productions Inc., 1956). *d-p* Carl K. Hittleman; *s* Francis Chase Jr., Lee Hewitt, Carl K. Hittleman; *c* Paul Ivano; *lp* Chill Wills, Lance Fuller, Cathy Downs, Sterling Holloway, Henry Hull, Jeanne Cagney, I. Stanford Jolley, Jess Barker, Rory Mallinson.

Discussed in text.

***Kit Carson*** (United Artists, 1940). *d* George B. Seitz; *p* Edward Small; *s* George Bruce; *c* John Mescall, Robert Pittack; *lp* Jon Hall, Lynn Bari, Dana Andrews, Ward Bond, Clayton Moore, Raymond Hatton.

Kit Carson (Jon Hall) leads a wagon train to California, along with a company of explorers under Capt. John C. Fremont (Dana Andrews). The Mexican Government is stirring up the Indians to keep the Americans out. The caravan is ambushed in a canyon, circles up, and uses stratagems to fool the Indians, such as making their numbers appear larger and sending a dead man riding on a horse to draw the Indians off.

***The Last Drop of Water*** (Biograph, 1911). *d* D. W. Grifith; *s* S. E. V. Taylor; *lp* Blanche Sweet, Joseph Graybill, Charles H. West, Mack Sennett, Alfred Paget, Robert Harron.

Some consider this short film by director D. W. Griffith one of the best depictions of an Indian attack on a wagon train and the survivors' subsequent battle for survival. It was an extensive production for its time, with a cast of hundreds, and numerous horses and wagons, to give it a grand scope.

***The Last Frontier*** (PDC, 1926). *d* George B. Seitz; *s* Will M. Ritchey; *lp* William Boyd, Marguerite De La Motte, Jack Hoxie, J. Farrell MacDonald, Junior Coghlan.

Because of the success of *The Covered Wagon*, Thomas H. Ince conceived another epic film dealing with the Westward movement. He began shooting but died before he could complete it. Finished by director George B. Seitz, *The Last Frontier* lacked the spark of its precursor. Beth (Marguerite De la Motte) and Tom Kirby (William Boyd, who later played Hopalong Cassidy) are the young sweethearts traveling west in a wagon train. Indians attack and kill Beth's parents; she blames Tom for the disaster. She later takes up with an unscrupulous trader, Lige (Mitchell Lewis), but Beth does not realize he is a villain until nearly too late during a buffalo stampede. Tom saves Beth, and they live happily ever after.

***The Last Wagon*** (Fox, 1956). *d/co-s* Delmer Daves; *p* William B. Hawks; *co-s* James Edward Grant, Gwen Bagni Gielgud; *c* Wilfrid Cline; *lp* Richard Widmark, Felicia Farr, Susan Kohner, Stephanie Griffin, Nick Adams, Ray Stricklyn, George Mathews, Douglas Kennedy, Timothy Carey, Tommy Rettig, James Drury.

Discussed in text.

***Lawless Plainsmen*** (Columbia, 1942). *d* William Berke; *p* Jack Fier; *s* Luci Ward; *c* Benjamin Kline; *lp* Charles Starrlett, Russell Hayden, Cliff Edwards, Luana Walters, Frank LaRue, Ray Bennett.

In this series Western, Steve Rideen (Charles Starrett) and Lucky Bannon (Russell Hayden) trail a herd of cattle to market, get in trouble, join a wagon train, and are attacked by Indians. The 7th Cavalry comes to the rescue.

***The Life of Buffalo Bill*** (Buffalo Bill and Pawnee Bill Film Company, 1912). *d* Paul Panzer; *p* Harry Davis, John P. Harris; *lp* William F. Cody, William J. Craft, Irving Cummings, Paul Panzer, Pearl White, William V. Ranous.

William F. Cody plays himself here, while a younger actor plays him in his dream sequences. Bill saves a stagecoach, captures an outlaw gang, fights Chief Yellow Hair, and saves a wagon train from Indian attack.

***The Lone Wagon*** (Sanford, 1923). *d* Frank Mattison; *p* F. M. Sanford; *s* Frank Mattison; *c* Elmer Dyer; *lp* Matty Mattison, Vivian Rich, Lafayette McKee, Earl Metcalfe, Gene Crosby.

A family travels across the plains. Matty Mattison plays a Mexican who accompanies the family so he can be near the pretty daughter, played by Vivian Rich. Indians plague them all the way, and at the end all are wiped out except for the daughter, who marries the Mexican scout.

***The Massacre*** (Biograph, 1912). *d* D. W. Griffith; *s* D. W. Griffith; *lp* Charles H. West, Wilfred Lucas, Blanche Sweet, Eddie Dillon, Claire McDowell, Robert Herron, Jack Pickford, Lionel Barrymore.

Discussed in the text.

***Old Overland Trail*** (Republic, 1953). *d* William Witney; *p* Edward J. White; *s* Milton Raison; *c* John MacBurnie; *lp* Rex Allen, Koko, Slim Pickens, Virginia Hall, Roy Barcroft, Leonard Nimoy, Gil Herman, Zon Murray.

The bad white guys, led by John Anchor (Roy Barcroft), are again stirring up Indian trouble, this time getting Black Hawk's (Leonard Nimoy) Apaches to attack a wagon train of pioneers. Rex Allen (Rex Allen) and his sidekick Slim Pickens (Slim Pickens) are on hand to save the emigrants, but not before the Indians circle, shoot up, and burn the train.

***The Oregon Trail*** (Universal, 1923). *d* Ed Laemmle; *s* Anthony Coldeway, Douglas Bronston, Jefferson Moffitt; *lp* Art Acord, Louise Lorraine, Jim Corey, Duke R. Lee, Sidney De Gray.

This 18-chapter serial borrowed from several historical events in the Westward movement, loosely focusing on Marcus Whitman (Duke R. Lee) and Narcissa Whitman (Ruth Royce), missionaries to the Indians of the Pacific Northwest. (Narcissa Whitman and Eliza Spaulding were said to be the first white women to take wagons west across the Rocky Mountains.)

***The Oregon Trail*** (Republic, 1936). *d* Scott Pembroke; *p* Paul Malvern; *s* Jack Natteford, Lindsley Parsons, Robert Emmett; *c* Gus Peterson; *lp* John Wayne, Ann Rutherford, Yakima Canutt, Frank Rice, Fern Emmett, Jack Rutherford.

In what was essentially a remake of *The Big Trail* (1930), John Wayne, as Capt. John Delmont, takes a leave of absence to find out who murdered his father. He leads a wagon train west, contending with the terrain, villains, Indians, and women, before winning the day.

***The Oregon Trail*** (Universal, 1939). *d* Ford Beebe, Saul A. Goodkind; *p* Henry MacRae; *s* George Plympton, Basil Dickey, Edmund Kelso, W.W. Watson; *c* Jerry Ash; *lp* Johnny Mack Brown, Louise Stanley, Fuzzy Knight, Roy Barcroft, Lane Chandler, Charles King.

Discussed in text.

***The Oregon Trail*** (Fox, 1959). *d/co-s* Gene Fowler Jr.; *p* Richard Einfeld; *co-s* Louise Vittes; *c* Kay Norton; *lp* Fred MacMurray, William Bishop, Nina Shipman, Gloria Talbot, John Caradine, Henry Hull.

Neil Harris (Fred MacMurray), a reporter for the *New York Herald*, goes west in 1846 to learn if the army is really sending soldiers disguised as settlers to strengthen American claims to the Northwest. Harris joins a wagon train in Missouri and travels across the country, experiencing the usual hard trail, rough crossings, droughts, storms, and Indian troubles.

Plenty of stock shots and indoor studio sets make a poor contrast to the original outdoor footage. In the end the Indians do attack the wagons, and Harris is captured and staked out to die, but is saved. The attack causes an Indian girl to renounce her people.

***The Overland Stage*** (First National, 1927). *d* Albert Rogell; *s* Marion Jackson; *lp* Ken Maynard, Katlneen Collins, Sheldon Lewis, Tom Santschi, Dot Farley, Florence Turner.

Jack Jessup (Ken Maynard) is a scout for the stage company who faces a corrupt trader, outlaws, and Indians. Hawk Lespard (Tom Santschi), the trader, has fomented the Indians to attack. Maynard tries to defuse the situation, but Lespard convinces the renegade Indians to attack a wagon train. Maynard warns the pioneers in time to prevent a massacre.

***The Painted Stallion*** (Republic, 1937). *d* William Witney, Ray Taylor, Alan James; *p* J. Laurence Wickland; *s* Barry Shipman, Winston Miller; *c* William Nobles, Edgar Lyons; *lp* Ray Corrigan, Hoot Gibson, Sammy McKim, Jack Perrin, Hal Taliaferro (Wally Wales), Julia Thayer, Duncan Renaldo, LeRoy Mason.

Discussed in text.

***Pawnee*** (Republic, 1957). *d/co-s* George Waggner; *p* Jack J. Gross, Philip N. Krasne; *co-s* Louis Vittes, Endre Bohem; *c* Hal McAlpin; *lp* George Montgomery, Bill Williams, Lola Albright, Charles Horvath, Charlotte Austin, Raymond Hatton.

George Montgomery plays a white man captured as a boy and raised by the Pawnees. When emigrants begin crossing Pawnee lands, the chief sends his "son," Pale Arrow, a.k.a. Paul Fletcher, to go with the wagons and "learn the ways of the white man." Fletcher joins a wagon train on the Oregon Trail, but when the chief dies, Crazy Fox (Paul Horvath) takes to the warpath.

Fletcher tries to stop the attack. When his background is discovered he is banished as a renegade. In the end he has to summon the 7th Cavalry for help, leave his Pawnee sweetheart, Dancing Fawn (Charlotte Austin), and hook up with his white love, Meg Alden (Lola Albright).

***The Pioneer Scout*** (Paramount, 1928). *d* Lloyd Ingraham, Alfred L. Werker; *s* Frank Clifton; *lp* Fred Thomson, Nora Lane, Tom Wilson, William Courtwright.

A gang of outlaws posing as raiding Indians goes after a small wagon train. Fred (Fred Thomson) is the scout who battles the bad guys.

***Pioneers Crossing the Plains in '49*** (Pathé, 1908). Hostile Indians attack a small wagon train, kill the pioneers and capture a young white woman and her sweetheart. The duo later manage to escape.

***Pioneers of the West*** (Republic, 1940). *d* Lester Orlebeck; *p* Harry Grey; *s* Karen DeWolf, Gerald Geraghty, Jack Natteford; *c* Jack Marta; *lp* Robert Livingston, Raymond Hatton, Duncan Renaldo, Noah Beery, Beatrice Roberts, George Cleveland, Lane Chandler, Wally Wales, Yakima Canutt, Joe McGuinn.

The Three Mesquiteers, Stony Brooke (Robert Livingston), Rusty Joslin (Raymond Hatton), and Rico (Duncan Renaldo), ride again. Indians attack a wagon train traveling to California in 1876 and kill the wagonmaster. The Mesquiteers volunteer to take the emigrants to the promised land, only to have white villains swindle them with poor land and high taxes.

***The Plainsman*** (Paramount, 1936). *d/p* Cecil B. De Mille; *s* Waldemar Young, Harold Lamb, Lynn Riggs; *st* Courtney R. Cooper, Frank J. Wilstach; *c* Victor Milner, George Robinson; *lp* Gary Cooper, Jean Arthur, James Ellison, Charles Bickford, Helen Burgess, Fred Kohler, Paul Harvey, Porter Hall, John Miljan, Granville Bates.

Discussed in text.

***The Prairie*** (Zenith, 1947). *d* Frank Wisbar; *p* George Moskov; *s* Arthur St. Claire; *c* James S. Brown Jr.; *lp* Lenore Aubert, Alan Baxter, Charles Evans, Jay Silverheels, Russ Vincent, Jack Mitchum.

This rather dull version of James F. Cooper's novel dwells more on the natural hazards faced by a wagon train of emigrants than on Indian attacks. Ellen Wade (Lenore Aubert), however, is a sole survivor of an Indian massacre. Chief Thundercloud, Chief Yowlache, and Jay Silverheels (Tonto from *The Lone Ranger* series) make appearances.

***Prairie Emigrant Train Crossing the Plains*** (Lubin, 1903). Indians attack a wagon train, but the emigrants are saved by "Buffalo Bill" and a number of scouts and cowboys.

***Prairie Schooners*** (Columbia, 1940). *d* Sam Nelson; *p* Leon Barsha; *s* Robert Lee Johnson, Fred Myton; *st* George Cory Franklin; *c* George Meehan; *lp* Bill Elliott, Evelyn Young, Dub Taylor, Kenneth Harlan, Ray Teal, Bob Burns, Netta Packer, Jim Thorpe, Richard Fiske.

Wild Bill Hickok (Bill Elliott) and his partner Cannonball (Dub Taylor) lead a wagon train of dispossessed Kansas farmers to Colorado. Dalton Stull (Kenneth Harlan) is the white land baron who forecloses on and drives out most of the settlers, and who incites the Pawnees under Chief Sanche (Jim Thorpe) to attack the wagon train so the emigrants won't interfere with his fur business in Colorado. Bill's sweetheart, Virginia Benton (Evelyn Young), is captured, and Bill and Cannonball have to rescue her, save the wagon train from the Indians, and bring the bad guys to justice.

***Ranger Courage*** (Columbia, 1937). *d* Spencer G. Bennet; *p* Larry Darmour; *s* Nate Gatzert; *c* Arthur Reed; *lp* Bob Allen, Martha Tibbetts, Walter Miller, Bob Kortman, Buzz Henry, Bud Osborne.

Bob Allen (Robert Allen) is the ranger who saves the Harper Wagon Train, carrying a strongbox full of money, from white villains and renegade Indians.

***The Ranger's Romance*** (Selig, 1914). *d* Tom Mix; *st* Tom Mix; *lp* Tom Mix, Goldie Colwell, Roy Watson, Inez Walker.

The Ranger (Tom Mix) cannot guide a wagon train across Indian lands because he is assigned to track down a bootlegger. When the Ranger captures his man, he learns that Indians attacked him. Worried that they may also go after the wagons, the Ranger rides to the rescue.

Meanwhile, Indians have already struck. One of the settlers (Roy Watson) is knocked out, and his daughter Sally (Goldie Colwell), after holding off the Indians with a rifle, is captured. The Ranger tracks the Indians back to their camp and rescues Sally.

***The Red Raiders*** (First National, 1927). *d* Albert Rogell; *s* Marion Jackson; *lp* Ken Maynard, Ann Drew, J. P. McGowan, Paul Hurst, Chief Yowlache, Ben Corbett.

Discussed in text.

***Red River*** (Monterey, 1948). *d/p* Howard Hawks; *s* Borden Chase, Charles Schnee; *c* Russell Harlan; *lp* John Wayne, Montgomery Clift, Joanne Dru, Walter Brennan, Coleen Gray, John Ireland, Harry Carey, Harry Carey Jr., Noah Beery Jr., Paul Fix, Wally Wales, Hank Worden, Wally Wales, Paul Fierro, Ray Hyke, Chief Yowlache.

Discussed in text.

***Ride, Ranger, Ride*** (Republic, 1936). *d* Joseph Kane; *p* Nat Levine; *st* Bernard McConville, Karen DeWolf; *s* Dorrell McGowan, Stuart E. McGowan; *c* William Nobles; *lp* Gene Autry, Smiley Burnette, Kay Hughes, Monte Blue, George J. Lewis, Max Terhune, Robert Homans, Lloyd Whitlock, Chief Thundercloud, the Tennessee Ramblers.

Texas Ranger Gene Autry and pal Frog Millhouse (Smiley Burnette) are riding with an army supply train as an escort. The military doesn't believe there is any danger until the Comanches arrive. As usual, they had been stirred up by the bad white guys.

***Roll, Wagons, Roll*** (Monogram, 1940). *d* Albert Herman; *p* Scott R. Dunlap, Edward Finney; *s/st* Victor Adamson, Edmond Kelso, Roger Merton; *c* Marcel Le Picard; *lp* Tex Ritter, Nelson McDowell, Muriel Evans, Nolan Willis, Steve Clark, Tom London, Reed Howes, Frank Ellis, Kenne Duncan, Frank La Rue, Chick Hannon, White Flash.

Tex Masters (Tex Ritter) goes undercover for the army to discover who is supplying guns to the Indians. He and his saddlemate Rawhide (Nelson McDowell) join a wagon train. When bad guy Matt Grimes (Tom London) tries to make sure the train suffers "accidents," Tex insists that the wagons take a different route than what Grimes had planned.

Grimes leaves the train and sets the Indians against the wagons. Tex saves them, but some members of the train come to believe Tex is in cahoots with the Indians. In town, Tex discovers fur trader Steve Coleman (Reed Howes) has a store full of rifles about to be sold to the Indians. Tex hears of the plot but is accidentally locked in the storeroom while Colemen sends his gang to join up with the Indians and attack the wagon train. Tex escapes, sends Rawhide for the army, and reaches the train just in time.

***Rollin' Plains*** (Grand National, 1938). *d* Albert Herman; *p* Edward Finney; *s* Lindsley Parsons, Edmond Kelso; *st* Jacques Jaccard, Celia Jaccard; *c* Gus Peterson; *lp* Tex Ritter, Horace "Snub" Pollard, Harriet Bennet, Hobart Bosworth, Ed Cassidy, Karl Hackett, Charles King, Ernie Adams, Lynton Brent, White Flash.

Tex Lawrence (Tex Ritter) tries to make peace between cowmen and sheepmen. Trigger Gargan (Charles King), a sheepman, frames a man for murder to try to run off the cowmen. Tex battles the bad guys, and there is a shoot-out between the two factions, with an unfortunate wagon train caught in between as the bullets fly.

***A Romance of the Rio Grande*** (Selig, 1911). *d* O. B. Thayer; *st* O. B. Thayer; *lp* Tom Mix, William Duncan, Myrtle Stedman.

Tom Mix portrays Tom Wilson, a Texas Ranger who battles Mexican whiskey smugglers and drunken Indians. When his sweetheart, Nellie Smith (Myrtle Stedman), and her father journey overland, they are attacked by Indians. Wilson gathers a posse of cowboys and arrives in time to find old man Smith tied to a burning wagon; but Nellie has been captured. Wilson and his posse catch the warriors, kill them, and rescue Nellie.

***Santa Fe Passage*** (Republic, 1955). *d* William Witney; *p* Sidney Picker; *s* Lillie Hayward; *c* Bud Thackery; *lp* John Payne, Faith Domergue, Rod Cameron, Slim Pickens, Anthony Caruso, Irene Tedrow, George Keymas.

Kirby Randolph (John Payne) is a scout who has been disgraced because it is believed he was to blame for the massacre of an entire wagon train by Kiowas under Satank (George Keymas). After a struggle, he and his saddlemate, Sam Beekman (Slim Pickins), are hired to take a wagon train full of ammunition to Santa Fe.

Part-owner of the train Aurelie St. Clair (Faith Domergue) doesn't like Randolph at first, but changes her mind when he saves them from a wild horse stampede initiated by Satank. She has her eye on Randolph, but since she is half–Indian she does not believe that Randolph will love her. When he does, her partner, Jess Griswold (Rod Cameron), becomes jealous and makes a deal with Satank, intending to turn Randolph over to the Indian in trade for safe passage of the wagons.

Satank agrees, but plans instead to get Randolph and the wagons and guns. Double-crossed, Griswold redeems himself by staying behind to allow Randolph and Aurelie to escape.

***The Santa Fe Trail*** (Arrow, 1923). *d* Ashton Dearholt, Robert Dillon; *st* Robert Dillon; *lp* Jack Perrin, Neva Gerber.

This 15-chapter serial depicted the (fictitious) adventures of Kit Carson (Jack Perrin), with plenty of wagon trains and Indian attacks.

***Santa Fe Trail*** (Warner Brothers, 1940). *d* Michael Curtiz; *p* Robert Fellows; *s* Robert Buckner; *c* Sol Polito; *lp* Errol Flynn, Olivia De Havilland, Raymond Massey, Ronald Reagan, Alan Hale, Van Heflin, Guinn Williams, William Lundigan.

This is not a wagon train movie, but the story of John Brown and "Bleeding Kansas." It does, however, feature a scene in which a young George Custer (Ronald Reagan) and a young J. E. B. Stuart (Errol Flynn) lead a freight wagon train on the Santa Fe Trail. John Brown (Raymond Massey) attacks to steal the rifles that are hidden in boxes marked "bibles."

***Senor Daredevil*** (First National, 1926). *d* Al Rogell; *s* Marion Jackson; *lp* Ken Maynard, Dorothy Devore, George Nicholls, Sheldon Lewis, Josef Swickard, Buck Black.

Don Luis O'Flaherty (Ken Maynard) guides a freight wagon train to a mining camp, encountering the usual pitfalls of terrain, weather, and outlaws. This was Maynard's debut in a lead role.

***Seven Alone*** (Doty-Dayton Releasing, 1974). *d* Earl Bellamy; *p* Lyman Dayton; *s* Douglas C. Stewart, Eleanor Lamb; *st* Honore Morrow; *c* Robert W. Stum; *lp* Dewey Martin, Aldo Ray, Anne Collings, Dean Smith, James Griffith, Stewart Petersen, Scott Petersen, Diane Petersen, Suzanne Petersen, Julie Petersen, Debbie van Orden, Christy Clark, Bea Morris, Dehl Berti.

Discussed in text.

***Sitting Bull—the Hostile Sioux Indian Chief*** (American Rotograph, 1914). The Randall Family has had much bad luck with the Indians. Early on, Chief Crazy Horse attacks the family while they travel in a covered wagon, but a scout helps them escape. Years later, Indians attack them again, and they are saved this time by the cavalry. A third Indian attack results in the death of the whole family except for Ruth Randall and a younger sister, both of whom are again saved by the army.

***Tumbleweed*** (Universal International, 1953). *d* Nathan Juran; *p* Ross Hunter; *s* John M. Lucas; *st* Kenneth Perkins; *c* Russell Metty; *lp* Audie Murphy, Lori Nelson, Chill Wills, Roy Roberts, Russell Johnson, Ralph Moody, Madge Meredith, Lee Van Cleef, I. Stanford Jolley, Eugene Iglesias.

Jim Harvey (Audie Murphy) is hired to guide a wagon train going west. Indians attack. Harvey tries to negotiate safe passage, and is able to talk to chief Aguila (Ralph Moody) because he once saved the chief's son's life. Harvey is captured, however, and the Indians wipe out the emigrants, except for two sisters.

An old Indian woman frees Harvey, and he makes it to town. Sheriff Murchoree (Chill Wills), however, wants to hang him as a deserter and coward. Harvey flees, and the sheriff and posse catch up, but the Indians attack them. They defeat the Indians, and Aguila is mortally wounded; but before dying he reveals that white villains instigated the wagon train massacre.

***Two Rode Together*** (Ford-Shpetner Productions/Columbia, 1961). *d* John Ford; *p* Stan Shpetner; *s* Frank Nugent; *st* Will Cook; *c* Charles Lawton Jr.; *lp* James Stewart, Richard Widmark, Shirley Jones, Andy Devine, John McIntyre, Linda Cristal, Paul Birch, Willis Bouchey, Henry Brandon, David Kent, Harry Carey Jr., Ken Curtis, Mae Marsh, Regina Carrol, Ford Rainey, Woody Strode, Jeanette Nolan, Cliff Lyons.

Discussed in text.

***Under the Star Spangled Banner*** (Kalem, 1908). This was one of the first films to depict an Indian attack on a family of white emigrants traveling west in a covered wagon.

***The Vanishing Pioneer*** (Paramount, 1928). *d* John Waters; *s* John F. Goodrich; *st* Zane Grey; *c* Charles E. Schoenbaum; *lp* Jack Holt, Sally Blane, William Powell, Fred Kohler, Guy Oliver, Roscoe Karns, Tim Holt, Marcia Manon.

John Ballard (Jack Holt) is the leader of a pioneer settlement beset by outlaws and crooked town politicians. After trying to solve the community problems, most of the settlers sell their property and head out in a long wagon train, once again seeking a new, more peaceful land.

***The Wagon Master*** (Universal, 1929). *d* Harry J. Brown; *s* Marion Jackson; *lp* Ken Maynard, Edith Roberts, Frederick Dana, Tom Santschi, Al Ferguson.

This film, released in silent and sound versions, was Ken Maynard's first talking role. The Rambler (Maynard) becomes wagon master when outlaws murder the first guide while trying to prevent the train from reaching its destination. Jake Lynch (Tom Santschi) is the boss of a gang trying to destroy competition and keep other wagons away from the mining camp of Gold Hill, which he alone hopes to supply. The Rambler defeats the villains at every turn.

***Wagon Tracks*** (Artcraft, 1919). *d* Lambert Hillyer; *s* C. Gardner Sullivan; *lp* William S. Hart, Jane Novak, Robert McKim, Lloyd Bacon, Leo Pierson, Ben Sprotte, Charles Arling.

Discussed in text.

***Wagon Train***. This television series was shown on NBC from 1957 to 1962, and on ABC from 1962 to 1965. With 284 60-minute episodes and 32 90-minutes episodes, *Wagon Train* encompassed just about every overland wagon train scenario one could imagine. The earlier episodes starred Ward Bond as wagonmaster Major Seth Adams, and Robert Horton as scout Flint McCullough. Later shows starred John McIntyre as wagonmaster Christopher Hale, aided by scouts Duke Shannon (Denny Miller) and Cooper Smith (Robert Fuller).

***Wagon Wheels*** (Paramount, 1934). *d* Charles Barton; *p* Harold Hurley; *s* Jack Cunningham, Charles Logan, Carl A. Buss; *c* William Mellor; *lp* Randolph Scott, Gail Patrick, Billie Lee, Raymond Hatton, Monte Blue, Leila Bennett.

In this remake of *Fighting Caravans* (1931), with Randolph Scott in the lead role, Indians attack a wagon train of emigrants on the way to Oregon in 1844.

***Wagonmaster*** (Argosy/RKO, 1950). *d/co-p* John Ford; *co-p* Merian C. Cooper; *s* Frank S. Nugent, Patrick Ford; *c* Bert Glennon; *lp* Ben Johnson, Harry Carey Jr., Ward Bond, Charles Kemper, Joanne Dru, Alan Mowbray, Ruth Clifford.

Horse traders Travis (Ben Johnson) and Sandy (Harry Carey Jr.) join a Mormon wagon train to guide it through hostile territory. The emigrants, nominally led by the worldly Elder Wiggs (Ward Bond), are joined by a broken down traveling medicine show, along with "scarlet woman" Denver (Joanne Dru). They are plagued less by Indians than by crazy outlaws under Shiloh Clegg (Charles Kemper).

***Wagons East*** (Tri Star, 1994). *d* Peter Markle; *p* Gary Goodman; *s* Matthew Carlson; *st* Jerry Abrahamson; *c* Frank Tidy; *lp* John Candy, Richard Lewis, John C. McGinley, Ellen Greene, Robert Picardo, Ed Lauter, William Sanderson, Rodney A. Grant.

This comedy film came with the tagline "They came, they saw, they changed their minds." Many of the folks from the town of Prosperity figure they cannot live in the West and decide to head east. Before they go, they argue about it, saying they can't go because it's "against the code." What code? "The code of the West." Ahh, the code that also says, "The only good Indian is a dead Indian," and "They died with their boots on."

After such banter they decide to form up a wagon train, to be led by James Harlow (John Candy in his last film), who also led the ill-fated Donner Party. The wagons go east, escorted by Indians who want the whites out of their country. The railroad bosses, however, don't want the whites to leave because they will lose money. They get the 7th Cavalry to attack the wagon train to keep them in the West. One escorting Indian even yells out for the whites to "Square the wagons" because it will make it harder for the army to ride around!

The writers and director poked fun at many Wild West clichés, but probably never realized that their main premise, taking wagons east, was not extraordinary at all. For instance, a great portion of the Rockies and inter-mountain West was initially settled by folks leaving the Pacific Coast and heading east.

**Wagons West** (Monogram, 1952). *d* Ford Beebe; *p* Vincent M. Fennelly; *s* Daniel B. Ullman; *c* Harry Neumann; *lp* Rod Cameron, Noah Beery Jr., Frank Ferguson, Michael Chapin, Peggie Castle, Henry Brandon, Sara Haden, Anne Kimball, Wheaton Chambers, I. Stanford Jolley.

Jeff Curtis (Rod Cameron) is the wagonmaster taking a wagon train to Oregon and trying to protect it from raiding Indians being supplied by white gunrunners, who are members of the same train.

**War on the Plains** (Bison, 1912). *d* Thomas H. Ince; *s* Thomas H. Ince, William Eagleshirt, Ray Meyers; *lp* Francis Ford, William Eagleshirt, Ray Meyers.

*War on the Plains* is considered to be one of the earliest "epic" films. Thomas H. Ince directed this, the first of his movies done in "Inceville" near Santa Monica, California, instead of in the "wilds" of New Jersey. The storyline involves two prospectors dying in the desert. One of them, the villainous Drake (Francis Ford), steals all the water and makes it to a wagon train. He regales the emigrants with tales of his daring, and nearly steals the heart of young Ethel (Ethel Grandin), the daughter of the wagon master, to the chagrin of her sweetheart (Ray Myers).

When Indians attack the wagons, Drake shows his true colors by running away, and Ethel has to grab a rifle to help defend the emigrants. Myers rides off to the fort to get the cavalry, who come to the rescue just in time. Drake dies in the desert just as miserably as the partner he first abandoned.

**The Way of a Man** (Pathé, 1924). *d* George B. Seitz; *st* George B. Seitz; *lp* Allene Ray, Harold Miller, Florence Lee, Bud Osborne, Carl Silvera, Lillian Adrian.

This film was simultaneously released as a feature movie and a 10-chapter serial. It includes the journey of a young man (Harold Miller) heading west in a wagon train to find a property deed stolen from his murdered father. The train experiences an Indian attack, with a white renegade as the chief villain.

**The Way West** (Harold Hecht Productions, 1967). *d* Andrew V. McLaglen; *p* Harold Hecht; *s* Ben Maddow, Mitch Lindemann; *c* William Clothier; *lp* Kirk Douglas, Robert Mitchum, Richard Widmark, Sally Field, Lola Albright, Stubby Kaye, Jack Elam, Harry Carey Jr.

In 1843, ex–Senator William J. Tadlock (Kirk Douglas), dreaming of a New Jerusalem in Oregon, organizes a wagon train, which includes scout Dick Summers (Robert Mitchum) and farmer Lije Evans (Richard Widmark). Tadlock drives his train mercilessly until Evans takes over, and they confront the usual hardships of weather, terrain, internal strife, and hostile Indians. The subplots were said to be enough to run a full season of soap operas.

**Western Frontier** (Columbia, 1935). *d* Albert Herman; *p* Larry Darmour; *st* Ken Maynard; *s* Nate Gatzert; *c* James S. Brown Jr., Herbert Kirkpatrick; *lp* Ken Maynard, Lucile Browne, Nora Lane, Robert "Buzz" Henry, Frank Yaconelli, Otis Harlan, Harold Goodwin, Frank Hagney, Gordon Griffith, James A. Marcus.

This is essentially a story about the white good guys battling the white bad guys, led by a white woman, Goldie (Nora Lane). The storyline, however, begins when Indians massacre settlers in a wagon train, and a white brother and sister are separated. One, Ken Masters (Ken Maynard), grows up to uphold the law, while his sister, Nora Masters, is brought up by the Indians and becomes the rustler known as Goldie. Goldie makes amends, however, by stepping in the line of fire and taking a bullet meant for her brother.

**Westward Ho the Wagons** (Walt Disney Pictures, 1956). *d* William Beaudine; *p* Bill Walsh; *s* Tom Blackburn; *c* Charles Boyle; *lp* Fess Parker, Jeff York, Kathleen Crowly, Sebastian Cabot, George Reeves, Karen Pendelton.

Discussed in text.

**Westward the Women** (MGM, 1952). *d* William A. Wellman; *p.* Dore Schary; *s.* Charles Schnee; *c* William Mellor; *lp* Robert Taylor, Denise Darcel, John McIntire, Hope Emerson, Marilyn Erskine, Lenore Lonergan.

Discussed in text.

***White Oak*** (Paramount, 1921). *d* Lambert Hillyer; *s* Bennett Musson; *lp* William S. Hart, Vola Vale, Robert Walker, Bert Sprotte, Chief Standing Bear.

Oak Miller (William S. Hart) is an honest gambler who tries to track down Mark Granger (Alexander Gaden), the man who seduced his sister. While on Granger's trail, Oak is arrested for a murder he didn't commit. Granger is free to plot an attack on a wagon train in collusion with Indians under Long Knife (Chief Standing Bear).

When the Indians attack, the pioneers are in desperate trouble, but a woman who knows Oak sends him a message by way of her faithful dog. The dog reaches Oak, and he gets out of jail in time to rush into the battle, capture Long Knife, and hold him hostage until the other Indians disperse.

***Wyoming*** (MGM, 1928). *d* W. S. Van Dyke; *s* Madeleine Ruthven, Ross B. Wills; *lp* Tim McCoy, Dorothy Sebastien, Charles Bell, William Fairbanks, Chief Big Tree.

Lt. Jack Colton (Tim McCoy) is a cavalry officer with a life-long pledge of friendship to Big Cloud (Charles Bell). The friendship is put to the test when Big Cloud breaks the treaty with the U.S. Government because of white encroachment on Indian lands. Colton has to fight when Big Cloud attacks a wagon train that Colton is escorting. The cavalry fends off the attack, but peace is not made until Chief Big Tree (John Big Tree) kills Big Cloud, his rebellious son.

***The Yellow Bullet*** (General Film Company, 1917). *d* Harry Harvey; *s* William H. Lippert; *lp* Robyn Adair, Lucy Payton, Bruce Smith, Neil Hardin.

This drama about treachery, greed, and gold lust begins with an Indian attack on a wagon train, leaving three survivors and a secret map to a gold mine.

# Appendix B: Wagon Trains Referenced in This Study

|  | Wagons | People | Casualties |
|---|---|---|---|
| 1829 KS, Bent | 38 | 79 | 1 killed |
| 1836 TX, Horn-Harris | 3 | 16 | 16 killed or captured |
| 1839 TX, Webster | 2 | 22 | 19 killed, 3 captured |
| 1844 WY, Sager | 1 | 9 | 2 died |
| 1847 KS, De Lise | ? | ? | 1 killed |
| 1847 KS, Hayden-Fagan | 64 | ? | 5 killed, 10 wounded |
| 1848 CO, Towne-Tevis | ? | 21 | 5 killed, 13 wounded, 2 captured |
| 1849 TX, Lyons | 5 | 13 | 4 killed, 2 wounded |
| 1851 AZ, Oatman | 1 | 9 | 9 killed or captured |
| 1852 CA, Bloody Point | ? | 65 | 62 killed, 1 wounded, 2 captured |
| 1853 TX, Wilson | 22 | 68 | 2 killed |
| 1853 TX | 2 | 9 | 8 killed or captured |
| 1854 IO, Burrell-Foster | 5 | 21 | 1 wounded |
| 1854 ID, Ward-Masterson | 12 | 65 | 18 killed |
| 1856 NE, Babbitt | 4 | ? | 4 killed, 1 wounded |
| 1856 NE | 1 | 3 | 3 killed |
| 1856 NE, Schevekendeck | ? | ? | 1 killed, 1 captured |
| 1856 NE, Mormon | ? | ? | 4 killed, 1 captured |
| 1857 NV, Holloway | 2 | 10 | 4 killed, 2 wounded |
| 1857 TX, Hartz | 7 | 80 | — |
| 1857 UT, Fancher-Baker | 40 | 140 | 123 killed, 17 captured |
| 1858 AZ, Rose-Baley | ? | 92 | 7 killed, 12 wounded |
| 1859 ID, Shepherd | 3 | 20 | 5 killed, 2 wounded |
| 1859 ID, Miltimore | 4 | 19 | 7 killed |
| 1859 ID, Carpenter | 5 | 20 | 1 killed, 3 wounded |
| 1860 ID, Utter–Van Ornum | 8 | 44 | 30 killed or captured |
| 1861 NM, Ake-Wadsworth | 15 | 47 | 2 killed, 5 wounded |
| 1862 NV, Gravelly Ford | ? | ? | about 17 killed |

## Wagon Trains Referenced in This Study

| | Wagons | People | Casualties |
|---|---|---|---|
| 1862 ID, Smith | 11 | ? | 5 killed |
| 1862 ID, Smart | 11 | 28 | 2 killed, 2 wounded |
| 1862 ID, Adams | ? | 13 | 4 killed |
| 1862 ID, Walker | 111 | 200 | — |
| 1862 ID, McBride-Andrews | ? | 15 | 6 killed, 2 wounded |
| 1864 KS, Allison | ? | ? | 4 killed |
| 1864 NE, Bowler | 26 | ? | — |
| 1864 NE, Morton-Marble | 12 | 18 | 13 killed, 2 captured |
| 1864 KS, Crow-Barret | 30 | ? | 10 killed, 5 wounded |
| 1864 KS, Blanchard-McRae-Sage | 95 | ? | 11 killed |
| 1864 CO, Snyder | 1 | 4 | 3 killed, 1 captured and died |
| 1864 OR, Richardson | 8 | 31 | 2 wounded |
| 1864 WY, Townsend | 150 | 467 | 4 killed, 1 wounded |
| 1864 WY, Kelly-Larimer | 3 | 11 | 4 killed, 2 wounded, 4 captured |
| 1864 ND, Fisk | 88 | 200 | 12 killed |
| 1865 WY, Fletcher | 2 | 6 | 1 killed, 1 wounded, 2 captured |
| 1865 WY, Custard | 5 | 25 | 22 killed |
| 1865 WY, Sawyer | 81 | 253 | 6 killed |
| 1866 TX, Box | 1 | 6 | 2 killed, 4 captured |
| 1866 WY, Cazeau | 2 | 10 | 5 killed |
| 1866 WY, Templeton-Kirkendall | 200 | ? | 3 killed, 6 wounded |
| 1866 WY, Floyd | 36 | ? | 8 killed, 2 wounded |
| 1867 KS, Baca | 80 | ? | — |
| 1867 KS, Cooke | 12 | 50 | 2 wounded |
| 1867 WY, Shurly | 16 | 41 | 3 killed, 4 wounded |
| 1868 CO, Blinn | 8 | 10 | 2 wounded, 2 captured and killed |
| 1871 TX, Warren | 10 | 12 | 7 killed, 5 wounded |
| 1872 TX, Gonzales | ? | ? | about 10 killed, 2 captured |
| 1874 TX, Baldwin | 23 | ? | — |
| 1874 TX, Lyman | 36 | 105 | 2 killed, 5 wounded |
| 1874 OK, Hennessey | 3 | 4 | 4 killed |
| 1874 KS, German | 1 | 9 | 5 killed, 4 captured |
| 1876 WY, Reel | 27 | 18 | 1 killed, 2 wounded |

# Chapter Notes

## Introduction

1. Jones, *Great Expectations*, 396.
2. Jones, *Great Expectations*, 2, 23, 42, 50–52; Light, *Baby Boomers*, 126–29; Lusted, *The Western*, 12, 119–20.
3. Strauss and Howe, *Generations*, 32–35. The authors place the boomers in a block of years slightly earlier than their peak birth years, stating the boomer generation encompassed the years 1943 to 1960.
4. Everson, *The Western Film*, 212, 214.
5. Michno, *Encyclopedia of Indian Wars*, 367.
6. Udall, "The 'Wild' Old West," 65, 68–69.
7. Udall, Dykstra, Bellesiles, Marks, Nobles, "How the West Got Wild," 277, 284.
8. Udall, "The 'Wild' Old West," 67; Mattes, *Platte River Road*, 23; Unruh, *Plains Across*, 185; Root and Hickman, "Pike's Peak Express," 507.
9. Mattes, *Platte River Road*, 56, 65, 232, 516.
10. Faragher, *Women and Men on the Overland*, 31–32.
11. Stewart, *The California Trail*, 322–23.
12. Unruh, *Plains Across*, 19, 156, 408.
13. Riley, *Women and Indians*, 98, 105, 155, 247; Schlissel, *Women's Diaries*, passim. Riley states that of 150 diaries she surveyed, only 15 reported major difficulties with Indians. This is ten percent. The enormity of the ratio is illustrated by a 20th Century comparison. The United States lost about one-quarter of a million men and women in the armed forces during WWII, out of about 15 million who served — less than two percent.
14. Myres, *Westering Women*, xviii, 55–57.
15. Munkres, "Plains Indian Threat," 242–43, 250, 263, 273.
16. White, *It's Your Misfortune*, 199, 204, 210, 211; Hine and Faragher, *The American West*, 571–72. Bellesiles and Brown are discussed in the last chapter.
17. Tate, *Indians and Emigrants*, 182, 233.

## Chapter 1

1. The best summary of the Utter–Van Ornum disaster is in Smith, "The Oregon Trail's Utter Tragedy." Other sources are Unruh, *Plains Across*; Madsen, *Shoshoni Frontier*; Schlicke, "Massacre on the Oregon Trail"; Shannon, *The Utter Disaster*; and Emeline Fuller (Trimble), *Left by the Indians*. For more about the captivity of the Van Ornum children, see Michno, *A Fate Worse Than Death*. The family names are sometimes written as Otter and Van Orman.

## Chapter 2

1. Hyslop, *Bound for Santa Fe*, 103, 113, 165–71; Lavender, *Bent's Fort*, 95–106.
2. Lecompte, "Manco Burro," 309–12; Smith, *Borderlander*, 196; Chalfant, *Dangerous Passage*, 257; Barry, *Beginnings of the West*, 756–57.
3. Lecompte, "Manco Burro," 312–14.

## Chapter 3

1. Rister, *Bondage*, 51–61, 78–79.
2. Rister, *Bondage*, 89–92, 123–24.
3. DeShields, *Border Wars*, 138; Rister, *Border Captives*, 63; Rister, *Bondage*, 124–31.
4. Rister, *Bondage*, 140–52.
5. Rister, *Bondage*, 153–55.
6. Rister, *Bondage*, 158–63; DeShields, *Border Wars*, 139–40.
7. Rister, *Bondage*, 165–66; DeShields, *Border Wars*, 140.
8. Exley, *Frontier Blood*, 84, 91; DeShields, *Border Wars*, 140; Rister, *Bondage*, 184n. In order to make some money, Mrs. Harris may have cooperated with publishers Perry and Cooke in 1838 to produce a semi-fictional account of her captivity under the name of Caroline Harris. See Hunter, "Southwestern Captivity Narratives," 141–44.
9. Rister, *Bondage*, 98, 184–87; "Sarah Ann Newton Horn," Handbook of Texas Online. Sarah's story first appeared in *A Narrative of the Captivity of Mrs. Horn, and Her Two Children, with Mrs. Harris, by the Comanche Indians*, written by E. House (St. Louis: C. Keemle, 1839).
10. Stewart, *California Trail*, 314–15; Madsen, *Bear River*, 78.

## Chapter 4

1. Dolbeare, *Dolly Webster*, 2–3.
2. Dolbeare, *Dolly Webster*, 3–7.
3. Dolbeare, *Dolly Webster*, 8–12.
4. Dolbeare, *Dolly Webster*, 13–19.
5. Dolbeare, *Dolly Webster*, 20–23.
6. Dolbeare, *Dolly Webster*, 27–33; Hunter, ed., "Memoirs of Mrs. Maverick," 6. Mary Maverick in Green, *Maverick*, 38, says that Webster walked into the town on 26 March.
7. Green, *Maverick*, 30–31, 38–42; Dolbeare, *Dolly Webster*, ix, 33–34.

8. A discussion of these authors' studies appears in Michno, *A Fate Worse Than Death*.

## Chapter 5

1. Wilson, *Sufferings*, 9–10.
2. Wilson, *Sufferings*, 10–14. The Comanches were probably Tehnahwahs, an offshoot of the Nokoni band. Winfrey and Day, *Texas Indian Papers*, 5, 171; Fehrenbach, *Comanches*, 144.
3. Wilson, *Sufferings*, 15–20.
4. Wilson, *Sufferings*, 21–25.
5. Wilson, *Sufferings*, 25–26; Hunter, ed., "Capture of Mrs. Wilson," 23; Hunter, "Southwestern Captivity Narratives," 178. Hunter indicates Wilson was cared for by Mexican women in the town of "Ysleta."
6. Wilson, *Sufferings*, 26–27; Thompson, *Sibley*, 99–100.
7. Winfrey and Day, *Texas Indian Papers*, 3, 182; 5, 169–70, 171–72. Hunter, "Southwestern Captivity Narratives," 177, cites a source that claims one of the Wilson boys was recovered a few months after Jane's escape, and spent some time at Fort Phantom Hill. Meredith's age has been given as seven, eight, and ten.
8. Wilson, *Sufferings*, 5–6, 28; Hunter, ed., "Capture of Mrs. Wilson," 23; Hunter, "Southwestern Captivity Narratives," 169–70.
9. Kenner, *Comanchero Frontier*, 140, 151, 155, 173.

## Chapter 6

1. Dunn, *Massacres*, 140–41; Stratton, *Oatman*, 26–38; Heard, *White Into Red*, 85; Thrapp, *Frontier Biography*, 1071; McGinty, *Oatman Massacre*, 41.
2. Stratton, *Oatman*, vii, 48–52; Dunn, *Massacres*, 141.
3. Stratton, *Oatman*, 63–64, 67–68, 72; Dunn, *Massacres*, 142–44.
4. Stratton, *Oatman*, 75.
5. Stratton, *Oatman*, 79.
6. Dunn, *Massacres*, 148–49; Stratton, *Oatman*, 85–86.
7. Dunn, *Massacres*, 148–51.
8. Stratton, *Oatman*, 116, 122, 134, 140; Dunn, *Massacres*, 152–53.
9. Stratton, *Oatman*, 181–83; Dunn, *Massacres*, 155–57.
10. Dunn, *Massacres*, 157–64.
11. McGinty, *Oatman Massacre*, 151, 156.
12. Thrapp, *Frontier Biography*, 1071; Stratton, *Oatman*, ix–x; Dunn, *Massacres*, 164; Hunter, "Southwestern Captivity Narratives," 184–85, 206, 220n26.
13. Michno, *A Fate Worse Than Death*, 38–39, 267–68, 304–05, 325.
14. Among the many films that addressed the situation were: *The Broken Trap* (1911); *Broncho Billy's Indian Romance* (1914); *The Call of the Wild* (1908); *Chief White Eagle* (1912); *The Crow's Nest* (1922); *The Curse of the Lake* (1912); *A Daughter of the Navajos* (1911); *The Flower of the Tribe* (1911); *The Heart of a Sioux* (1910); *The Huntress* (1923); *Indian Blood* (1914); *The Indian Flute* (1911); *The Indian Squaw's Sacrifice* (1910); *The Kentuckian* (1908); *Love in a Teepee* (1911); *The Mesquite's Gratitude* (1911); *The Outcast* (1912); *Red Clay* (1927); *A Red Man's Love* (1909); *The Red Red Heart* (1918); *The Red Rider* (1925); *A Romance of the Western Hills* (1910); *The Scarlet West* (1925); *The Squaw Man* (1914); *Strongheart* (1914), and *Where the Trail Divides* (1914).
15. Zesch, *Captured*, 120.

## Chapter 7

1. Shannon, *Boise Massacre on the Oregon Trail*, 5–8.
2. Shannon, *Boise Massacre on the Oregon Trail*, 66–67.
3. Shannon, *Boise Massacre on the Oregon Trail*, 68.
4. Shannon, *Boise Massacre on the Oregon Trail*, 78–79, 84.
5. Shannon, *Boise Massacre on the Oregon Trail*, 85–88, 95–98, 103; *Commissioner of Indian Affairs 1854*, 278–79. According to William Ward, "They found all but two children, my youngest brother and my aunt's son." Thomas may have died before the family began their journey, but he is also mentioned as having been captured at the time of the massacre, since no physical remains were discovered at the site.
6. Shannon, *Boise Massacre on the Oregon Trail*, 103–04.
7. Shannon, *Boise Massacre on the Oregon Trail*, 151–55
8. Kilpatrick, *Celluloid Indians*, 77–79, 90; Slotkin, *Gunfighter Nation*, 466; Walker, *Westerns Films Through History*, 223–24, 227.

## Chapter 8

1. Denton, *American Massacre*, 93, 96–100, 113–17, 126–42, 157; Dunn, *Massacres of the Mountains*, 253–64; Brooks, *Mountain Meadows*, 69–96.
2. Denton, *American Massacre*, 140–41.

## Chapter 9

1. Shannon, *Boise Massacre*, 177–87; Madsen, *Bear River*, 102–03; Unruh, *Plains Across*, 195–96.
2. Shannon, *Boise Massacre*, 197–211; Madsen, *Bear River*, 105–06; Unruh, *Plains Across*, 195.
3. Hardy, *The Western*, 73.

## Chapter 10

1. Nye, *Carbine & Lance*, 40; Robinson, *Satanta*, 48.
2. Lonnie J. White, "White Women Captives," 332; Gallaway, ed., *Texas: The Dark Corner of the Confederacy*, 110–11.
3. White, "White Women Captives," 332–33; Lee Herron, "Story of the Box Rescue," essay, Western History Department, Denver Public Library, Denver, CO; Winfrey and Day, *Indian Papers of Texas*, IV, 107, 114.
4. White, "White Women Captives," 333.
5. White, "White Women Captives," 333; G. A. Custer, *My Life on the Plains*, 60; Court of Claims, December Term, 1892, Indian Depredation, No. 5732. This band of Indians also stole 72 horses and 52 mules from brothers James and John Davenport in Cooke County. Charles M. Robinson III, in his book *Satanta*, 48, states that Box's ten-year-old son was also mortally wounded in the attack, and G. A. Custer, in *My Life*, 59, also states that one child was killed in the initial attack; however, the mother never mentioned a son in her story.
6. Mrs. W. R. Potter, *History of Montague County*, 24–26.
7. G. A. Custer, *My Life on the Plains*, 59, 60, 62.
8. White, "White Women Captives," 333.
9. Barnett, *Touched by Fire*, 170; G.A. Custer, *My Life on the Plains*, 60, 62.
10. White, "White Women Captives," 332; G. A. Custer, *My Life on the Plains*, 62.

11. *Commissioner of Indian Affairs 1866*, 280–81.
12. *Commissioner of Indian Affairs 1866*, 280–81; White, "White Women Captives," 330–332; Herron, "Box Rescue."
13. White, "White Women Captives," 332. Herron's statement is not likely accurate, given the short time span between Margaret's capture and rescue.
14. Herron, "Box Rescue." Herron states that for volunteering for the dangerous mission, he and McLaurie received "words of personal congratulation" from General Sherman.
15. Robinson, *Satanta*, 48; *Commissioner of Indian Affairs 1866*, 281.
16. E. B. Custer, *Following the Guidon*, 223–24.
17. G. A. Custer, *My Life on the Plains*, 60, 62; E. B. Custer, *Following the Guidon*, 222–223.
18. *Ibid.*, 223.
19. G. A. Custer, *My Life on the Plains*, 59–60.
20. *Ibid.*, 60, 62.
21. E. B. Custer, *Boots and Saddles*, 56–7.
22. E. B. Custer, *Boots and Saddles,* 133; Marquis, *Keep the Last Bullet for Yourself*, 176.
23. Biddle, *Reminiscences of a Soldier's Wife*, 160; Summerhayes, *Vanished Arizona*, 110–111; Barnett, *Touched by Fire*, 169–171.
24. White, "White Women Captives," 333; Herron, "Box Rescue."
25. Potter, *Montague County*, 26.
26. Marquis, *Keep the Last Bullet for Yourself*, 179. The theme of killing oneself to prevent capture was grossly overstated by Marquis when he contended that a large portion of Custer's men committed suicide at the Little Bighorn.
27. *Commissioner of Indian Affairs 1866*, 281.
28. Lillian Gish first played a mother defending a cabin against an Indian attack 46 years earlier, in the 1914 D. W. Griffith film *The Battle at Elderbush Gulch*.

## Chapter 11

1. Baley, *Disaster at the Colorado*, 1, 4, 15, 31, 35, 59–72, 97.
2. Rothel, *Ambush of Ghosts*, 133–37. Among the films shot in Monument Valley over the years were *Stagecoach* (1939), *Kit Carson* (1940), *Billy the Kid* (1941), *My Darling Clementine* (1946), *Fort Apache* (1948), *She Wore a Yellow Ribbon* (1949), *Rio Grande* and *Wagonmaster* (both 1950), *The Searchers* (1956), *Sergeant Rutledge* (1960), *How the West Was Won* (1962), *Cheyenne Autumn* (1964), *The Trial of Billy Jack* (1973), *The Legend of the Lone Ranger* (1981), and *Back to the Future III* (1990).

## Chapter 12

1. Sager, *Whitman Massacre*, 9–11, 152, 177–78 n9–10.
2. Sager, *Whitman Massacre*, 12–13, 156–57, 179n12, 179n14, 180n15, 16. Catherine recorded the birth date as May 22; however, Naomi stated it was the last day of May.
3. Sager, *Whitman Massacre*, 14–15, 159–61, 181 n21, 182n22, 23, 186n30.
4. Sager, *Whitman Massacre*, 15–17, 162–65, 187n33, 188n36, 188–90n37, 38, 190–91n39, 191n40, 41.
5. Sager, *Whitman Massacre*, 18, 21, 165–67, 170–71.
6. Sager, *Whitman Massacre*, 90; Michno, *A Fate Worse Than Death*, 92–99.
7. Sager, *Whitman Massacre*, 137–38, 145, 149–150; "Whitman Massacre—Whitman Massacre Roster," 1, http://www.oregonpioneers.com/whitman4.htm.

## Chapter 13

1. Czaplewski, *Captive of the Cheyenne*, sec. 2, 12.
2. Becher, *Massacre Along the Medicine Road*, 252, 255.
3. Czaplewski, *Captive of the Cheyenne*, sec. 2, 14; Becher, *Massacre Along the Medicine Road*, 252–56, 260.
4. Becher, *Massacre Along the Medicine Road*, 258; Czaplewski, *Captive of the Cheyenne*, sec. 1, 69. Hoig [*Peace Chiefs*, 109] incorrectly claims that Daniel Marble was captured on the Blue River in Kansas.
5. Czaplewski, *Captive of the Cheyenne*, sec. 1, 67, sec. 2, 15–17; Nancy Morton Depredation Claim, RG 75, #332.
6. Becher, *Massacre Along the Medicine Road*, 266.
7. Becher, *Massacre Along the Medicine Road*, 260, 262, 266, 314; Czaplewski, *Captive of the Cheyenne*, sec. 2, 17–18.
8. Becher, *Massacre Along the Medicine Road*, 326–27, 438.
9. Becher, *Massacre Along the Medicine Road*, 356, 358; Czaplewski, *Captive of the Cheyenne*, sec. 1, 72, sec. 2, 28–29.
10. Czaplewski, *Captive of the Cheyenne*, sec. 2, 45; Becher, *Massacre Along the Medicine Road*, 366–67, 429, 433n21.
11. Sanford, *Mollie*, 189–90; Becher, *Massacre Along the Medicine Road*, 328, 329n7.
12. Carroll, *Sand Creek Documents*, iii; Becher, *Massacre Along the Medicine Road*, 376, 430–31.
13. Langman, *Silent Westerns*, 158.
14. Langman, *Silent Westerns*, 190–91.
15. Marshall, *A Cry Unheard*, 13.
16. Halaas and Masich, *Halfbreed*, 378n53; Czaplewski, *Captive of the Cheyenne*, Sec. 1, 72; Nancy Morton Depredation Claim #332.
17. Michno, *A Fate Worse Than Death*, 475, shows only one girl out of 40 wanted to stay with the Indians, while only two boys out of 50 returned to them.

## Chapter 14

1. Thrapp, *Frontier Biography*, 1014; Stratton, *Pioneer Women*, 123; Spotts, *Campaigning with Custer*, 208; Broome, *Dog Soldier Justice*, 52, 207–08.
2. James S. Morgan Depredation Claim #3644; White, "White Women Captives," 337; Spotts, *Campaigning with Custer*, 208; Broome, *Dog Soldier Justice*, 53–54.
3. James S. Morgan Depredation Claim #3644; Spotts, *Campaigning with Custer*, 208–09; Stratton, *Pioneer Women*, 123–24; Broome, *Dog Soldier Justice*, 53–54.
4. Spotts, *Campaigning with Custer*, 209–10; Broome, *Dog Soldier Justice*, 55; Stratton, *Pioneer Women*, 124.
5. Stratton, *Pioneer Women*, 124; Broome, *Dog Soldier Justice*, 69; Crawford, *Kansas in the Sixties*, 332; Custer, *My Life on the Plains*, 280–81.
6. Custer, *My Life on the Plains*, 371–72; Dixon, "Sweetwater Hostages," 98; Crawford, *Kansas in the Sixties*, 334.
7. Custer, *My Life on the Plains*, 371–75; Dixon, "Sweetwater Hostages," 100; White, "White Women Captives," 342.
8. Spotts, *Campaigning with Custer*, 159.
9. White, "White Women Captives, 341–42; Broome, *Dog Soldier Justice*, 69; G. A. Custer, *My Life on the Plains*, 373, 374; E. B. Custer, *Following the Guidon*, 60; Spotts, *Campaigning with Custer*, 209.
10. Stratton, *Pioneer Women*, 125. Some of this story, printed 38 years after the fact, is wrong. For instance, Anna's brother did not walk into her tent in the Indian

camp. Authors have used this statement to "prove" that Indian captivity was not all bad.

11. Spotts, *Campaigning with Custer*, 210; Broome, *Dog Soldier Justice*, 144; E. B. Custer, *Following the Guidon*, 62.

12. Stratton, *Pioneer Women*, 125; Broome, *Dog Soldier Justice*, 144–45.

13. Stratton, *Pioneer Women*, 111, 121, 126; Powell, *Sacred Mountain*, 717.

## Chapter 15

1. Tate, *Indians and Emigrants*, xvi, 178–82.
2. Chalfant, *Cheyennes and Horse Soldiers*, 41–44.
3. Erb, Brown, and Hughes, *Overland Trail*, 45.
4. Fletcher-Cook Depredation Claim #5072.
5. Fletcher-Cook Depredation Claim #5072. The true story of Amanda Fletcher's captivity from her own, her father's, and her rescuer's testimony differs a great deal from the standard tale repeated by historians. For example, Berthrong, *Southern Cheyennes*, 258; Hyde, *George Bent*, 251; Halaas and Masich, *Halfbreed*, 192, 208; Hoig, *Peace Chiefs*, 113; Powell, *Sacred Mountain* I, 407; Kraft, "Between the Army and the Cheyennes," 52; Gerboth, *Tall Chief*, 26, 134n42; and McDermott, *Circle of Fire*, 81, contain variations of errors in Amanda's name (calling her Mary), age, place of capture, captor, treatment, and rescuer. Halaas and Masich misleadingly indicate that the Cheyennes gave Fletcher to Wynkoop out of respect. Powell claims that the Cheyenne Sand Hill owned her for a time, treated her kindly, and turned her over to interpreter John Smith. Amanda belies all of this.
6. Fletcher-Cook Depredation Claim #5072.
7. Custer, *Life on the Plains*, 62–63. Trenholm, *Arapahoes*, 262, without citing a source, says that Lizzie's sister Mary (*sic*) saw and identified her in Casper, Wyoming, but that Lizzie denied being white and wanted to remain living with the Arapahos. In fact, in 20 years of depredation claim records, Amanda never said she had seen Lizzie, and assumed she was dead. For Amanda Fletcher's full story, see Michno, *A Fate Worse Than Death*, 144–50.
8. Fletcher-Cook Depredation Claim #5072; Tate, *Indians and Emigrants*, 188. For whitewashed accounts of Amanda's experience, see Hyde, *George Bent*, 258; and Powell, *Sacred Mountain* I, 407.
9. Michno, *A Fate Worse Than Death*, 475.
10. Nye, *Carbine & Lance*, 151–52; Michno, *Encyclopedia of Indian Wars*, 251–52, 278.

## Chapter 16

1. Glassley, *Pacific Northwest*, 152; Murray, *Modocs*, 24. Sometimes the attack is said to have occurred in 1851. Murray believes this attack is a composite of several attacks on emigrants. Casualty estimates range from 33 to 70.
2. Angel, *History of Nevada*, 178; Rogers, *Soldiers of the Overland*, 29; *OR*: V.50, 123–25. Angel writes of this incident as occurring in 1861. McGarry's chastisement of the Indians appears in Michno, *Encyclopedia of Indian Wars*, 105.
3. Webber, *Oregon Trail Emigrant Massacre of 1862*, 11–12.
4. Webber, *Oregon Trail Emigrant Massacre of 1862*, 40–43.
5. These episodes belie historian George Stewart's belief that it would be preposterous for Indians to behave in this manner. Stewart, *The California Trail*, 322–23.
6. Webber, *Oregon Trail Emigrant Massacre of 1862*, 9, 33–34; Webber, *The Oregon & California Trail Diary of Jane Gould in 1862*, 58–59.
7. Webber, *Oregon Trail Emigrant Massacre of 1862*, 16–19, 23, 34.
8. Webber, *Oregon Trail Emigrant Massacre of 1862*, 8–10, 19, 33–36; Madsen, *Bear River*, 160.
9. Webber, *Diary of Jane Gould in 1862*, 61; Webber, *Emigrant Massacre of 1862*, 35.
10. Webber, *Diary of Jane Gould in 1862*, 61.
11. Rogers, *Soldiers of the Overland*, 29–31; Madsen, *Bear River*, 162.
12. Some of the dog hero movies are: *Clash of the Wolves*, 1925; *Fangs of Wolfheart*, 1925; *Shadows of the North*, 1923; *The Silent Call*, 1921; *Silent Pal*, 1925; *Teeth*, 1924; *The Wild Girl*, 1925; *Wings of the Storm*, 1926; *Wolf's Trail*, 1927; *Lightning Warrior*, 1931; *Law of the Wild*, 1934; *Trigger Trio*, 1937; *Call the Mesquiteers*, 1938; and *Phantom Gold*, 1938.
13. *Adjutant General's Office*, 20; McNitt, *Navajo Wars*, 380–81; Bailey, *Bosque Redondo*, 39–40.

## Chapter 17

1. Doyle, *Land of Gold*, 224; Johnson, *Bloody Bozeman*, 130–32.
2. Doyle, *Land of Gold*, 151–53.
3. Doyle, *Land of Gold*, 151–53, 208–210, 225, 240–41, 248, 252; Johnson, *Bloody Bozeman*, 134.

## Chapter 18

1. Kelly, *My Captivity*, 11–13, 20; Doyle, *Land of Gold*, 153; Farley, "An Indian Captivity," 249. Mary was said to be either five or eight years old.
2. Kelly, *My Captivity*, 21–27; Doyle, *Land of Gold*, 154; Andrew Sharp Depredation Claim #1520.
3. Farley, "An Indian Captivity," 249; Kelly, *My Captivity*, 27, 37–40.
4. Farley, "An Indian Captivity, 250; Unrau, *Talking Wire*, 154–55; Vaughn, *Indian Fights*, 6–9; Doyle, *Land of Gold*, 744; Kelly, *My Captivity*, 32–33.
5. Kelly, *My Captivity*, 54–55; Farley, "An Indian Captivity," 250. Sarah later wrote a book titled *The Capture and Escape; or, Life Among the Sioux*. Only a few pages deal with her capture, and the book was mainly a plagiarism of the book Fanny would write of her own experience.
6. Kelly, *My Captivity*, 64; Bradley, *March of the Montana Column*, 112–13.

## Chapter 19

1. Jackson, *Wagon Roads West*, 274–75; Clodfelter, *Dakota War*, 193–94.
2. Clodfelter, *Dakota War*, 193–96; Farley, "An Indian Captivity," 251–52; Jackson, *Wagon Roads West*, 276.
3. Clodfelter, *Dakota War*, 199–200; Kelly, *My Captivity*, 208–10; Utley, *Lance and Shield*, 63; Farley, "An Indian Captivity," 252–53.
4. Farley, "An Indian Captivity," 253–56; Drimmer, *Captured by the Indians*, 331.

## Chapter 20

1. Michno, *Deadliest Indian War*, 54–55.
2. Sweeney, *Mangas Coloradas*, 416–20; Roberts, *With*

*Their Own Blood*, 105–16. Zimmer is sometimes identified as Anton Brewer.

## Chapter 21

1. Justus, "Saga of Clara Blinn," 11; Richard Blinn Diary.
2. Justus, "Saga of Clara Blinn," 12; Blinn Diary; Hubbell Blinn letter to Bowling Green, OH, newspaper, 27 February, 1893.
3. Justus, "Saga of Clara Blinn," 12–13.
4. Broome, *Dog Soldier Justice*, 11; Berthrong, *Southern Cheyennes*, 306; Powell, *Sacred Mountain*, 568; Hyde, *George Bent*, 288–89.
5. Justus, "Saga of Clara Blinn," 13; Hyde, *George Bent*, 279.
6. Justus, "Saga of Clara Blinn," 13; Kroeker, *Great Plains Command*, 77–80.
7. Hoig, *Washita*, 211–13, gives a concise sample of the various accounts of their deaths.
8. Justus, "Saga of Clara Blinn," 19. A more complete story of the Blinn captivity is found in Michno, *A Fate Worse Than Death*, 151–56.
9. Black Kettle, always depicted as a lover of peace, held a number of white captives over the years, including Nancy Morton, Daniel Marble, Lucinda Eubank, Isabelle Eubank, Willie Eubank, Ambrose Asher, Laura Roper, Anna Snyder, Clara Blinn, and Willie Blinn.
10. Slotkin, *Gunfighter Nation*, 576, 590.

## Chapter 22

1. Doyle, *Land of Gold*, 430.
2. Doyle, *Land of Gold*, 431; Johnson, *Bloody Bozeman*, 207–08.
3. Doyle, *Land of Gold*, 432; Johnson, *Bloody Bozeman*, 208–09.
4. Doyle, *Land of Gold*, 433–34, 600, 637, 661; Hagen, *Exactly in the Right Place*, 39–40.

## Chapter 23

1. Chalfant, *Dangerous Passage*, 158; Garrard, *Wah-to-yah*, 295; Barry, *Beginning of the West*, 686.
2. Chalfant, *Dangerous Passage*, 87–93.
3. Chalfant, *Dangerous Passage*, 94–95.
4. Barry, *Beginning of the West*, 694; Chalfant, *Dangerous Passage*, 94–99. The casualties were: Pvts. Jonathan Arledge, Moses Short, John Dickhart, George Gaskill, and J.H. Blake killed; Sgt. Ben Bishop, and Pvts. Henry Vancaster, John Lovelace, Thomas Ward, James Bush (Burk), and Willis Wilson wounded.
5. Chalfant, *Dangerous Passage*, 100–01; Barry, *Beginning of West*, 700, 705–06.
6. Richard F. Barret Depredation Claim #1679; Jerome E. Crow Depredation Claim #998.
7. OR: V.41/1, 212–13; Oliva, *Fort Union and the Frontier Army*, 307; Simmons, *Santa Fe Trail*, 146.
8. OR: V.41/1, 212–13; OR: V.41/2, 827–29; Ryus, *Second William Penn*, 167–73.
9. Hoig, *Sand Creek Massacre*, 88–89; White, *Hostiles & Horse Soldiers*, 46n.30; OR: V.41/2, 766–67.
10. Powell, *Sacred Mountain*, 477; Burkey, *Come at Once*, 35; Hyde, *George Bent*, 270.

## Chapter 24

1. Michno, *Encyclopedia of Indian Wars*, 200.
2. Barnett, *Touched by Fire*, 168; E. B. Custer, *Tenting on the Plains*, 353–55; Michno, "The Box Family," 7.
3. Vaughn, *Platte Bridge*, 22–34, 77–86; Powell, *Sacred Mountain*, 342.
4. Oehler, *Great Sioux Uprising*, 234–36; *Commissioner of Indian Affairs 1862*, 171; Carley, *Dakota War of 1862*, 65; Michno, *Encyclopedia of Indian Wars*, 96.
5. Wellman, *Death on the Prairie*, 10–13; Schultz, *Over the Earth*, 117–20, 145–50.
6. Utley, *Frontiersmen*, 170; *Adjutant General's Office*, 21.

## Chapter 25

1. Nye, *Carbine & Lance*, 215–19; Michno, *A Fate Worse Than Death*, 373; Neal, *Valor Across the Lone Star*, 141–51. Twelve of Lyman's soldiers received the Medal of Honor for this action.
2. Michno, *Encyclopedia of Indian Wars*, 223–24.

## Chapter 26

1. Sowell, *Early Settlers*, 172–77.
2. Hagan, *Exactly in the Right Place*, 159–68.
3. Vaughn, *Indian Fights*, 167–75.
4. Francell, *Ft. Lancaster*, 51–53; Webb, *List of Engagements*, 17.
5. Michno, *Encyclopedia of Indian Wars*, 287–88. The story of the captives Julia and Addie German is discussed later.
6. See note 14, Chapter 6.
7. Kilpatrick, *Celluloid Indians*, 59.

## Chapter 27

1. Doyle, *Land of Gold*, 345, 346, 348.
2. Doyle, *Land of Gold*, 349, 358.
3. Doyle, *Land of Gold*, 349, 358, 359.
4. Hafen, *Powder River Campaigns*, 222, 227, 238, 245–58; Rosenberg, "Sawyers Wagon Road Expeditions and Related Rifle Pit Sites," 69–82; Powell, *Sacred Mountain*, 377–78.
5. Doyle, *Land of Gold*, 363, 400.
6. Doyle, *Land of Gold*, 346–51, 402–06; Hafen, *Powder River Campaigns*, 320–34.

## Chapter 28

1. Webber, *Diary of Jane Gould in 1862*, 13, 20.
2. Holmes, *Covered Wagon Women*, v. 1, 71.
3. Holmes, *Covered Wagon Women*, v. 6, 40–41.
4. Holmes, *Covered Wagon Women*, v. 7, 61, 63.
5. Webber, *Applegate Trail*, 51.
6. Holmes, *Covered Wagon Women*, v. 1, 125.
7. Holmes, *Covered Wagon Women*, v. 1, 176.
8. Holmes, *Covered Wagon Women*, v. 6, 228, 255, 259–61.
9. Holmes, *Covered Wagon Women*, v. 6, 226, 236, 237, 241, 244, 246, 248.
10. Mattes, *Platte River Road*, 23.
11. Jeffrey, *Converting the West*, 124, 126; Michno, *A Fate Worse Than Death*, 90–94.

## Chapter 29

1. Contrary to popular belief, a traveler could still not travel uninterrupted from coast to coast. There was no railroad bridge over the Missouri River between Council Bluffs and Omaha until 1872.
2. Jauken, *Moccasin Speaks*, 58–66, 231–32; Lee and Raynesford, *Trails of the Smoky Hill*, 214–16; Powell, *Sacred Mountain 2*, 868–69, sugarcoats the Cheyenne outrages, blaming what the Indians did on Chivington's attack at Sand Creek ten years earlier. Powell fails to mention slicing open the pregnant Mrs. German or burning Rebecca alive.
3. Jauken, *Moccasin Speaks*, 71, 73, 78–80; Haley, *Buffalo War*, 145; Powell, *Sacred Mountain 2*, 869. Incredibly, Powell states that the Cheyennes cooked for their captives, and claims that "mistreating of a captive woman was not usual among the People [Cheyennes]."
4. Jauken, *Moccasin Speaks*, 87–88.
5. Jauken, *Moccasin Speaks*, 88–90, 110; Lee and Raynesford, *Trails of the Smoky Hill*, 216–17; Powell, *Sacred Mountain*, 883–84.
6. Jauken, *Moccasin Speaks*, 112–15; Lee and Raynesford, *Trails of the Smoky Hill*, 217; Michno, *Encyclopedia of Indian Wars*, 287–88; Powell, *Sacred Mountain*, 884; Hyde, *George Bent*, 363.
7. Jauken, *Moccasin Speaks*, 115–17; Miles, *Personal Recollections 1*, 175.
8. Miles, *Personal Recollections 1*, 181; Jauken, *Moccasin Speaks*, 181, 191, 194, 201–09.
9. This scene is also reminiscent of an actual event: In May 1873, Col. Ranald S. Mackenzie led his 4th U.S. Cavalrymen into Coahuila, Mexico, to attack Kickapoos and Lipan Apaches who had been raiding in Texas.
10. See Michno, *A Fate Worse Than Death*, passim.

## Chapter 30

1. See Appendix B.
2. Mattes, *Platte River Road*, 90–99.
3. Holmes, *Covered Wagon Women*, v. 8, 200, 217–18.
4. Holmes, *Covered Wagon Women*, v. 8, 203, 227–29.
5. Holmes, *Covered Wagon Women*, v. 3, 205, 261, 265–66.
6. Holmes, *Covered Wagon Women*, v. 7, 173–74.
7. Holmes, *Covered Wagon Women*, v. 1, 190–91, 222, 229.
8. Holmes, *Covered Wagon Women*, v. 4, 105, 109–10.
9. Holmes, *Covered Wagon Women*, v. 6, 217–19.
10. Unruh, *Plains Across*, 408–09; Tate, *Indians and Emigrants*, 132–36. The nonsense that the army purposely spread smallpox to the tribes on the upper Missouri River in 1837 is amply exposed in R. G. Robertson's *Rotting Face: Smallpox and the American Indian* (Caxton Press, 2001).
11. Everson, *The Western Film*, 70; Lusted, *The Western*, 129–30.
12. Lusted, *The Western*, 130–34.

## Chapter 31

1. Wilson, *Stagecoach Robberies*, 16–17.
2. Austerman, *Sharps Rifles*, 58–62.
3. Williams, *Last Frontier*, 11; Tevis, *Arizona in the 50's*, 229; Sweeney, *Mangas*, 413–16.
4. Sweeney, *Cochise*, 294–95.
5. *OR*: V.48/1, 313–14.
6. *Owyhee Avalanche*, November 17, 1866; *Idaho World*, November 3, 1866, November 24, 1866.
7. Lee, *Trails of the Smoky Hill*, 108–09; Chandler, *Garryowen in Glory*, 7.
8. Hardy, *The Western*, 97; Simmon, *Invention of the Western*, 169.
9. Kilpatrick, *Celluloid Indians*, 53–54.
10. Michno, *Deadliest Indian War*, 96–97.
11. Everson, *The Western Film*, 173; Kilpatrick, *Celluloid Indian*, 54.
12. Hyslop, *Bound for Santa Fe*, 353; Michno, *Encyclopedia of Indian Wars*, 353.

## Chapter 32

1. Groneman, *Battlefields*, 151–52; *OR*: V.41/1, 886; Gallaway, *Dark Corner*, 228–30; Ledbetter, *Fort Belknap*, 117–18, 121, 135–36; Smith, *Frontier Defense in the Civil War*, 132–33.
2. Ledbetter, *Fort Belknap*, 6–7, 12n36, 118–19, 145–46; Michno, *Encyclopedia of Indian Wars*, 156–57; Nye, *Carbine & Lance*, 37. The standard story, first begun by historian W. S. Nye, is that Milly Jane married a Kiowa named Goombi and lived as an Indian until her death in 1934. Nye later admitted that his scenario was in error.
3. According to Ledbetter (*Fort Belknap*, 135), Britt did not rescue Fitzpatrick, Durkin, or his own family.
4. Michno, *A Fate Worse Than Death*, 261–63; Ledbetter, *Fort Belknap*, 135, 156n5; Smith, *Frontier Defense in Civil War*, 143; Richardson, *Comanche Barrier*, 233n17; Huckabay, *Jack County*, 511.
5. Ledbetter, *Fort Belknap*, 135–36, 157n11, 12; Kingman, "Diary of Samuel Kingman," 447; Phin W. Reynolds later went to school with Lottie Durkin and remembers she had "a red and blue circle on her forehead" [Gallaway, *Dark Corner*, 230].
6. *Commissioner of Indian Affairs 1865*, 531–32, 535; Ledbetter, *Fort Belknap*, 140, 200; Kingman, "Diary of Samuel Kingman," 447–49. The five captives were Cola Caroline McDonald, Rebecca J. McDonald, James Taylor, Dorcas Taylor, and James Ball. The latter is sometimes recorded as James Burrow. Ledbetter (*Fort Belknap*, 8, 68) discounts much of Britt Johnson's exploits, although it is clear that he made a few excursions into Indian Territory and Kansas to rescue captives. Sam Kingman specifically mentioned him being at the Little Arkansas Treaty on 15 October, 1865, where Kingman commented, "I hope no treaty will be made till all the prisoners are delivered up."
7. Ledbetter, *Fort Belknap*, 141, 143.
8. Ledbetter, *Fort Belknap*, 143, 145–46, 151; Winfrey and Day, *Texas Indian Papers 4*, 165.
9. Ledbetter, *Fort Belknap*, 33, 34, 42, 55, 64, 73, 75–76, 88, 104, 106.
10. Ledbetter, *Fort Belknap*, 147–49, 163–176; Foreman, "Jesse Leavenworth," 21.
11. Ledbetter, *Fort Belknap*, 177–79, 193–94, 196, 199–200.
12. Ledbetter, *Fort Belknap*, 213, 215, 217n18, 218–20.
13. Ledbetter, *Fort Belknap*, 5–8, 200–01, 209, 223–26, 231–33; *Commissioner of Indian Affairs 1869*, 86–87.
14. Le May's inspiration is sometimes thought to have been the 1836 raid on Parker's Fort, and the capture of Cynthia Ann Parker. Researcher Scott Zesch, who has spent much time studying the Britt Johnson story, extensively reviewed Le May's notes. He found many references to Johnson, but none to Cynthia Parker or her relatives James or Isaac Parker, who also looked long and hard for Cynthia.
15. Slotkin, *Gunfighter Nation*, 461–73.
16. Michno, *Encyclopedia of Indian Wars*, 247.

## Chapter 33

1. Haley, *Charles Goodnight*, 169–84.

## Chapter 35

1. Udall, Dykstra, Bellesisles, Marks, Nobles, "How the West Got Wild," 277–95.
2. Malcolm, "Disarming History," 1–2, 18–19.
3. Malcolm, "Disarming History," 5; Eddins, "Smallpox"; Lewy, "Genocide"; Walker, *Western Films Through History*, 10, 12, 220.
4. Lusted, *The Western*, 80–82; Simmon, *Invention of the Western*, 25–32, 37, 89.
5. Slotkin, *Gunfighter Nation*, 366–67; Simmon, *Invention of the Western*, 271; Buscombe and Pearson, *Back in the Saddle*, 8, 16.
6. Kilpatrick, *Celluloid Indians*, 67.
7. The comments are from Geoffrey Wolff, printed on the inside jacket cover of the Bantam paperback edition.
8. Kilpatrick, *Celluloid Indians*, 94. This author once discussed the film with a fellow who "knew" all about George Custer and the fact that he was "clinically insane." How did he know? He said he saw it all in *Little Big Man*!
9. Ironically, Dee Brown criticized *Fort Apache* for not being historically accurate, when historical inaccuracies are numerous in his most famous work, *Bury My Heart at Wounded Knee*. Mico, *Past Imperfect*, 150–53.
10. Hutton, "Correct in Every Detail," 29–30.
11. Coyne, *Crowded Prairie*, 168.
12. Simon and Spence, "Cowboy Wonderland," 90–92; Coyne, *Crowded Prairie*, 168.
13. The film was titled *Amore, Piombo e Furore* in Italy. The American version took its title from a roadside mileage post in the desert.
14. Kilpatrick, *Celluloid Indians*, 103–04.
15. Limerick, *Something in the Soil*, 239; Mico, *Past Imperfect*, 9, 23.
16. Stegner, *Marking the Sparrow's Fall*, 205.
17. Lusted, *The Western*, 33.
18. McCoy, *Tim McCoy Remembers*, 263–64.

# Bibliography

Adjutant General's Office. *Chronological List of Actions &c., with the Indians from January 15, 1837, to January, 1891.* Washington: GPO, 1891.

Ambrose, Stephen E. *Crazy Horse and Custer.* Garden City, NY: Doubleday, 1975.

Angel, Myron. *History of Nevada.* Oakland, CA: Thompson and West, 1881.

Aquila, Richard, ed. *Wanted Dead or Alive: The American West in Popular Culture.* Urbana, IL: University of Illinois Press, 1996.

Athearn, Robert G. *The Mythic West in Twentieth-Century America.* Foreword by Elliott West. Lawrence, KS: University Press of Kansas, 1986.

_____. *William Tecumseh Sherman and the Settlement of the West.* Foreword by William M. Ferraro and Thomas J. Murphy. Norman, OK: University of Oklahoma Press, 1995.

Austerman, Wayne R. *Sharps Rifles and Spanish Mules: The San Antonio-El Paso Mail, 1851–1881.* College Station, TX: Texas A&M University Press, 1985.

Babb, T. A. *In the Bosom of the Comanches.* Amarillo, TX: T. A. Babb, 1912. Reprint, Azle, TX: Bois d'Arc Press, 1990.

Bailey, Lynn R. *Bosque Redondo: The Navajo Internment at Fort Sumner New Mexico, 1863–1868.* Tucson, AZ: Westernlore Press, 1998.

Baley, Charles W. *Disaster at the Colorado: Beale's Wagon Road and the First Emigrant Party.* Logan, UT: Utah State University Press, 2002.

Barnett, Louise. *Touched by Fire: The Life, Death, and Mythic Afterlife of George Armstrong Custer.* New York: Henry Holt, 1996.

Barry, Louise. *The Beginning of the West: Annals of the Kansas Gateway to the American West 1540–1854.* Topeka, KS: Kansas State Historical Society, 1972.

Becher, Ronald. *Massacre Along the Medicine Road: A Social History of the Indian War of 1864 in Nebraska Territory.* Caldwell, ID: Caxton Press, 1999.

Bellesiles, Michael A. *Arming America: The Origins of a National Gun Culture.* New York: Vintage Books, 2001.

Berthrong, Donald J. *The Southern Cheyennes.* Norman, OK: University of Oklahoma Press, 1963.

Biddle, Ellen McGowan. *Reminiscences of a Soldier's Wife.* Mechanicsburg, PA: Stackpole, 2002.

Bradley, Lt. James H. *The March of the Montana Column: A Prelude to the Custer Disaster.* Edited by Edgar I. Stewart. Foreword by Paul L. Hedren. Norman, OK: University of Oklahoma Press, 1991.

Brooks, James F. *Captives & Cousins: Slavery, Kinship, and Community in the Southwest Borderlands.* Chapel Hill, NC: University of North Carolina Press, 2002.

Brooks, Juanita, *The Mountain Meadows Massacre.* Norman, OK: University of Oklahoma Press, 1950.

Broome, Jeff. *Dog Soldier Justice: The Ordeal of Susanna Alderdice in the Kansas Indian War.* Lincoln, KS: Lincoln County Historical Society, 2003.

Brown, Dee. *Bury My Heart at Wounded Knee.* New York: Holt, Rinehart & Winston, 1970.

Burkey, Blaine. *Custer, Come at Once!* Hays, KS: Thomas More Prep, 1976.

Buscombe, Edward, and Roberta E. Pierson, eds. *Back in the Saddle Again: New Essays on the Western.* London: British Film Institute, 1998.

Carley, Kenneth. *The Dakota War of 1862: Minnesota's Other Civil War.* St. Paul, MN: Minnesota Historical Society, 1976.

Chalfant, William Y. *Cheyennes and Horse Soldiers.* Foreword by Robert M. Utley. Norman, OK: University of Oklahoma Press, 1989.

_____. *Dangerous Passage: The Santa Fe Trail and the Mexican War.* Foreword by Marc Simmons. Norman, OK: University of Oklahoma Press, 1994.

Chandler, Melbourne C. *Of Garryowen in Glory: A History of the Seventh U.S. Cavalry Regiment.* Annandale, VA: Turnpike Press, 1960.

Clodfelter, Micheal. *The Dakota War: The United States Army Versus the Sioux, 1862–1865.* Jefferson, NC: McFarland, 1998.

Coyne, Michael. *The Crowded Prairie: American National Identity in the Hollywood Western.* London: I. B. Taurus Publishers, 1998.

Crawford, Samuel J. *Kansas in the Sixties.* Ottawa, KS: Kansas Heritage Press, 1994.

Custer, Elizabeth B. *"Boots and Saddles," or Life in Dakota with General Custer.* Reprint. Introduction by Jane R. Stewart. Norman, OK: University of Oklahoma Press, 1961.

_____. *Following the Guidon.* New York: Harper & Brothers, 1890. Reprint. Introduction by Shirley A.

Leckie. Lincoln, NE: University of Nebraska Press, 1994.

\_\_\_\_\_. *Tenting on the Plains, or General Custer in Kansas and Texas*. Norman, OK: University of Oklahoma Press, 1994.

Custer, George Armstrong. *My Life on the Plains*. Introduction by Edgar I. Stewart. Norman, OK: University of Oklahoma Press, 1962.

Czaplewski, Russ. *Captive of the Cheyenne: The Story of Nancy Jane Morton and the Plum Creek Massacre*. Lexington, NE: Dawson County Historical Society, 1993.

Denton, Sally. *American Massacre: The Tragedy at Mountain Meadows, September 1857*. New York: Vintage Books, 2004.

Derounian-Stodola, Kathryn Zabelle, and James Arthur Levernier. *The Indian Captivity Narrative, 1550–1900*. New York: Twayne Publishers, 1993.

DeShields, James T. *Border Wars of Texas*. 1912. Reprint. Austin, TX: State House Press, 1993.

Dippie, Brian W. *Custer's Last Stand: The Anatomy of an American Myth*. Lincoln, NE: University of Nebraska Press, 1976.

\_\_\_\_\_. *The Vanishing American: White Attitudes and U.S. Indian Policy*. Lawrence, KS: University Press of Kansas, 1982.

Dixon, David. "Custer and the Sweetwater Hostages." In *Custer and His Times, Book Three*, edited by Gregory J.W. Urwin and Roberta E. Fagan, 82–108. El Paso, TX, and Conway, AR: Little Big Horn Associates and University of Central Arkansas Press, 1987.

Dolbeare, Dr. Benjamin. *A Narrative of the Captivity and Suffering of Dolly Webster Among the Comanche Indians in Texas*. Clarksburg, VA: M'Granaghan & M'Carty, 1843. Reprint. New Haven, CT: Yale University Library, 1986.

Doyle, Susan Badger, ed. *Journeys to the Land of Gold: Emigrant Diaries from the Bozeman Trail, 1863–1866*. Helena, MT: Montana Historical Society Press, 2000.

Drimmer, Frederick, ed. *Captured by the Indians: 15 Firsthand Accounts, 1750–1870*. New York: Dover Publications, 1985.

Drinnon, Richard. *Facing West: The Metaphysics of Indian-Hating and Empire Building*. Norman, OK: University of Oklahoma Press, 1997.

Dunn, J.P., Jr. *Massacres of the Mountains: A History of the Indian Wars of the Far West 1815 – 1875*. New York: Archer House, nd.

Ellenbecker, John G. *Tragedy at the Little Blue*. Introduction by Lyn Ryder. Niwot, CO: Prairie Lark Publications, 1993.

Erb, Louise Bruning, Ann B. Brown, and Gilberta B. Hughes. *The Bridger Pass Overland Trail 1862–1869 Through Colorado and Wyoming*. Littleton, CO: Erbgem Publishing, 1989.

Etulain, Richard W. *Re-imagining the Modern American West: A Century of Fiction, History, and Art*. Tucson, AZ: University of Arizona Press, 1996.

Everson, William K. *A Pictorial History of the Western Film*. Secaucus, NJ: Citadel Press, 1969.

Exley, Jo Ella Powell. *Frontier Blood: The Saga of the Parker Family*. College Station, TX: Texas A&M University Press, 2001.

Faragher, John Mack. *Women and Men on the Overland Trail*. New Haven, CT: Yale University Press, 1979.

Farley, Alan W. "An Indian Captivity and Its Legal Aftermath." *Kansas Historical Quarterly* 2, no. 4 (Winter 1954), pp. 247–56.

Foreman, Carolyn Thomas. "Col. Jesse Henry Leavenworth." *Chronicles of Oklahoma* 13, no. 1 (March 1935), pp. 14–29.

Francell, Lawrence John. *Fort Lancaster Texas Frontier Sentinel*. Austin, TX: Texas State Historical Association, 1999.

Fuller, Emeline L. *Left by the Indians and Massacre on the Oregon Trail in the Year 1860*. Fairfield, WA: Ye Galleon Press, 1992.

Gallaway, B.P., ed. *Texas: The Dark Corner of the Confederacy*. Lincoln: University of Nebraska Press, 1994.

Garrard, Lewis H. *Wah-to-yah and the Taos Trail*. Introduction by A. B. Guthrie, Jr. Norman, OK: University of Oklahoma Press, 1955.

Gerboth, Christopher B., ed. *The Tall Chief: The Autobiography of Edward W. Wynkoop*. Denver, CO: Colorado Historical Society, 1994.

Glassley, Ray Hoard. *Indian Wars of the Pacific Northwest*. Portland, OR: Binfords & Mort, 1972.

Green, Rena Maverick, ed. *Memoirs of Mary A. Maverick*. San Antonio, TX: Alamo Printing, 1921. Reprint. Introduction by Sandra L. Myres. Lincoln, NE: University of Nebraska Press, 1989.

Grinnell, George B. *The Cheyenne Indians*. Lincoln, NE: University of Nebraska Press, 1972.

\_\_\_\_\_. *The Fighting Cheyennes*. Norman, OK: University of Oklahoma Press, 1966.

Groneman, Bill. *Battlefields of Texas*. Plano, TX: Republic of Texas Press, 1998.

Hafen, Leroy R. *Powder River Campaigns and Sawyers Expedition of 1865*. Glendale, CA: Arthur H. Clark, 1961.

Hagan, Barry J., C.S.C. *Exactly in the Right Place: A History of Fort C.F. Smith, Montana Territory, 1866–1868*. El Segundo, CA: Upton & Sons, 1999.

Halaas, David F., and Andrew E. Masich. *Halfbreed: The Remarkable True Story of George Bent*. Cambridge, MA: Da Capo Press, 2004.

Haley, J. Evetts. *Charles Goodnight, Cowman and Plainsman*. Norman, OK: University of Oklahoma Press, 1949.

Haley, James L. *The Buffalo War: The History of the Red River Indian Uprising of 1874*. Norman, OK: University of Oklahoma Press, 1985.

Hardy, Phil. *The Overlook Film Encyclopedia: The Western*. Woodstock, NY: Overlook Press, 1994.

Harris, Caroline. *History of the Captivity and Providential Release Therefrom of Mrs. Caroline Harris*. New York: Perry and Cooke, 1838.

Heard, J. Norman. *White into Red: A Study of the Assimilation of White Persons Captured by Indians*. Metuchen, NJ: Scarecrow Press, 1973.

Herron, Lee. *Story of the Box Rescue*. St. Paul, NE: n.d. Denver Public Library, M 349.

Hoig, Stan. *The Battle of the Washita: The Sheridan-Custer Campaign of 1867–69*. Lincoln, NE: University of Nebraska Press, 1979.

_____. *Kicking Bird and the Legend of the Kiowas*. Niwot, CO: University Press of Colorado, 2000.

_____. *The Peace Chiefs of the Cheyennes*. Foreword by Boyce D. Timmons. Norman, OK: University of Oklahoma Press, 1980.

_____. *The Sand Creek Massacre*. Norman: University of Oklahoma Press, 1961.

Holmes, Kenneth L., ed. *Covered Wagon Women Diaries & Letters from the Western Trails*. 9 vols. Lincoln, NE: University of Nebraska Press, 1995.

Huckabay, Ida Lasater. *Ninety-Four Years in Jack County 1854–1948*. Waco, TX: By the author, 1949.

Hunter, Carolyn Berry. *Ten Southwestern Captivity Narratives*. Ph.D. diss.: Northern Arizona University, 1992.

Hunter, Marvin J., ed. "The Capture of Mrs. Wilson." *Frontier Times* 1, no. 9 (June 1924), pp. 22–23.

_____. "Memoirs of Mrs. Maverick." *Frontier Times* 2, no. 5 (February 1925), pp. 1–7.

Hutton, Paul Andrew. "'Correct in Every Detail': General Custer in Hollywood." *Montana: The Magazine of Western History* 41, no. 1 (Winter 1991), pp. 28–57.

Hyde, George E. *Life of George Bent Written from His Letters*. Edited by Savoie Lottinville. Norman, OK: University of Oklahoma Press, 1968.

Hyslop, Stephen G. *Bound for Santa Fe: The Road to New Mexico and the American Conquest, 1806–1848*. Norman, OK: University of Oklahoma Press, 2002.

Jackson, W. Turrentine. *Wagon Roads West: A Study of Federal Road Surveys and Construction in the Trans-Mississippi West, 1846–1869*. New Haven, CT: Yale University Press, 1965.

Jauken, Arlene Feldmann. *The Moccasin Speaks: Living as Captives of the Dog Soldier Warriors*. Lincoln, NE: Dageford Publishing, 1998.

Jeffrey, Julie Roy. *Converting the West: A Biography of Narcissa Whitman*. Norman, OK: University of Oklahoma Press, 1991.

Johnson, Dorothy M. *The Bloody Bozeman: The Perilous Trail to Montana's Gold*. Missoula, MT: Mountain Press, 1983.

Jones, Landon Y. *Great Expectations: America and the Baby Boom Generation*. New York: Ballantine Books, 1981.

Justus, Judith P. "The Saga of Clara H. Blinn at the Battle of the Washita." *Research Review* 14, no. 1 (Winter 2000), pp. 11–20, 31.

Kelly, Fanny. *My Captivity Among the Sioux Indians*. New York: Carol Publishing Group, 1993.

Kenner, Charles L. *The Comanchero Frontier: A History of New Mexican-Plains Indian Relations*. Norman, OK: University of Oklahoma Press, 1994.

Kilpatrick, Jacquelyn. *Celluloid Indians: Native Americans and Film*. Lincoln, NE: University of Nebraska Press, 1999.

Kingman, Samuel A. "Diary of Samuel A. Kingman at Indian Treaty in 1865." *Kansas Historical Quarterly* 1, no. 5 (November 1932), pp. 442–450.

Kraft, Louis. "Between the Army and the Cheyennes." *MHQ* (Winter 2002), pp. 48–55.

Kroeker, Marvin E. *Great Plains Command William B. Hazen in the Frontier West*. Norman, OK: University of Oklahoma Press, 1976.

Langman, Larry. *A Guide to Silent Westerns*. Westport, CT: Greenwood Press, 1992.

Lavender, David. *Bent's Fort*. Lincoln, NE: University of Nebraska Press, 1972.

Leckie, Shirley A. *Elizabeth Bacon Custer and the Making of a Myth*. Norman, OK: University of Oklahoma Press, 1993.

Ledbetter, Barbara A. Neal. *Fort Belknap Frontier Saga: Indians, Negroes and Anglo-Americans on the Texas Frontier*. NL Ranch Headquarters, TX: Lavender Books, 1982.

Lee, Wayne C., and Howard C. Raynesford. *Trails of the Smoky Hill: From Coronado to the Cow Towns*. Caldwell, ID: Caxton Printers, 1980.

Light, Paul C. *Baby Boomers*. New York: W.W. Norton, 1990.

Limerick, Patricia Nelson. *The Legacy of Conquest: The Unbroken Past of the American West*. New York: W.W. Norton, 1987.

Lusted, David. *The Western*. Harlow, Essex, England: Pearson Education, 2003.

Madsen, Brigham D. *The Shoshoni Frontier and the Bear River Massacre*. Foreword by Charles S. Peterson. Salt Lake City, UT: University of Utah Press, 1985.

Malcolm, Joyce Lee. "Disarming History: How an Award-winning Scholar Twisted the Truth About America's Gun Culture — and Almost Got Away with It." *Reason Magazine* (March 2003).

Marquis, Thomas B. *Keep the Last Bullet for Yourself: The True Story of Custer's Last Stand*. Algonac, MI: Reference Publications, 1976.

Marshall, Doyle. *A Cry Unheard: The Story of Indian Attacks in and Around Parker County, Texas, 1858–1872*. Annetta Valley Farm Press, 1990.

Mattes, Merrill J. *The Great Platte River Road*. Lincoln, NE: Nebraska State Historical Society, 1969.

McConnell, Joseph Carroll. *The West Texas Frontier, or a Descriptive History of Early Times in Western Texas*. 2 Vols. Palo Pinto, TX: Texas Legal Bank and Book, 1939.

McCoy, Tim, with Ronald McCoy. *Tim McCoy Remembers the West*. Lincoln, NE: University of Nebraska Press, 1988.

McDermott, John D. *Circle of Fire: The Indian War of 1865*. Mechanicsburg, PA: Stackpole Books, 2003.

McGee, Patrick. *From Shane to Kill Bill: Rethinking the Western*. Malden. MA: Blackwell Publishing, 2007.

McNitt, Frank. *Navajo Wars: Military Campaigns, Slave Raids and Reprisals*. Albuquerque, NM: University of New Mexico Press, 1972.

Michno, Gregory F. *Battle at Sand Creek: The Military Perspective*. El Segundo, CA: Upton & Sons, 2004.

\_\_\_\_\_. *Deadliest Indian War in the West: The Snake Conflict, 1864–68.* Caldwell, ID: Caxton Press, 2007.

\_\_\_\_\_. *Encyclopedia of Indian Wars: Western Battles and Skirmishes, 1850–1890.* Missoula, MT: Mountain Press, 2003.

Michno, Gregory, and Susan Michno. *A Fate Worse Than Death: Indian Captivities in the West, 1830–1885.* Caldwell, ID: Caxton Press, 2007.

Michno, Susan J. "The Box Family, the Custers, and the Last Bullet." *Research Review* 20, no. 1 (Winter 2006), pp. 2–7, 31.

Mico, Ted, John Miller-Monzon, and David Rubel, eds. *Past Imperfect: History According to the Movies.* New York: Henry Holt, 1996.

Miles, General Nelson A. *Personal Recollections and Observations of General Nelson A. Miles.* Lincoln, NE: University of Nebraska Press, 1992.

Munkres, Robert L. *Saleratus and Sagebrush: People and Places on the Road West.* Zanesville, OH: New Concord Press, 2003.

Murray, Keith A. *The Modocs and Their War.* Norman, OK: University of Oklahoma Press, 1959.

Myres, Sandra L. *Westering Women and the Frontier Experience, 1800–1915.* Albuquerque, NM: University of New Mexico Press, 1982.

Nash, Gerald D. *Creating the West: Historical Interpretations, 1890–1990.* Albuquerque, NM: University of New Mexico Press, 1991.

Nash, Gerald D., and Richard W. Etulain, eds. *The Twentieth-Century West: Historical Interpretations.* Albuquerque, NM: University of New Mexico Press, 1991.

Neal, Charles M. Jr. *Valor Across the Lone Star: The Congressional Medal of Honor in Frontier Texas.* Austin, TX: Texas State Historical Association, 2002.

Nott, Robert. *Last of the Cowboy Heroes.* Foreword by Budd Boetticher. Jefferson, NC: McFarland, 2000.

Nye, Col. W. S. *Carbine and Lance: The Story of Old Fort Sill.* Norman, OK: University of Oklahoma Press, 1969.

Oehler, C. M. *The Great Sioux Uprising.* New York: Oxford University Press, 1959.

Oliva, Leo E. *Fort Union and the Frontier Army in the Southwest.* Southwest Cultural Resources Center Professional Papers No. 41. Santa Fe, NM: NPS, 1993.

Potter, Mrs. W. R. *History of Montague County, Texas.* Reprint. Salem, MS: Higginson Book, 1957.

Powell, Father Peter John. *People of the Sacred Mountain: A History of the Northern Cheyenne Chiefs and Warrior Societies, 1830–1879.* 2 Vols. San Francisco, CA: Harper & Row, 1981.

Prucha, Francis Paul, ed. *Documents of United States Indian Policy.* Lincoln, NE: University of Nebraska Press, 1990.

*Report of the Commissioner of Indian Affairs, 1862–1870.* Washington: GPO, 1863–1870.

Richardson, Rupert N. *The Comanche Barrier to South Plains Settlement.* Austin, TX: Eakin Press, 1996.

Riley, Glenda. *The Female Frontier: A Comparative View of Women on the Prairie and Plains.* Lawrence, KS: University Press of Kansas, 1988.

\_\_\_\_\_. *Women and Indians on the Frontier, 1825–1915.* Albuquerque, NM: University of New Mexico Press, 1984.

Rister, Carl Coke. *Border Captives: The Traffic in Prisoners by Southern Plains Indians, 1835–1875.* Norman, OK: University of Oklahoma Press, 1940.

\_\_\_\_\_. *Comanche Bondage: Beales's Settlement and Sarah Ann Horn's Narrative.* Glendale, CA: Arthur H. Clark Company, 1955. Reprint. Introduction by Don Worcester. Lincoln, NE: University of Nebraska Press, 1989.

Roberts, Virginia Culin. *With Their Own Blood: A Saga of Southwestern Pioneers.* Ft. Worth, TX: Texas Christian University Press, 1992.

Robertson, R. G. *Rotting Face: Smallpox and the American Indian.* Caldwell, ID: Caxton Press, 2001.

Robinson, Charles M. III. *Satanta: The Life and Death of a War Chief.* Austin, TX: State House Press, 1997.

Rogers, Fred B. *Soldiers of the Overland: Being Some Account of the Services of General Patrick Edward Connor and His Volunteers in the Old West.* San Francisco, CA: Grabhorn Press, 1938.

Root, George A., and Russell K. Hickman. "Pike's Peak Express Companies Part III — The Platte Route." *Kansas Historical Quarterly* 13, no. 8 (November 1945), pp. 485–526.

Rothel, David. *An Ambush of Ghosts: A Personal Guide to Favorite Western Film Locations.* Madison, NC: Empire Publishing, 1990.

Ryus, William H. *The Second William Penn: Treating with Indians on the Santa Fe Trail, 1860–66.* Kansas City, MO: Frank T. Riley Publishing, 1913.

Sager, Catherine. *The Whitman Massacre of 1847.* Fairfield, WA: Ye Galleon Press, 2004.

*Sand Creek Massacre, The: A Documentary History.* Introduction by John M. Carroll. New York: Sol Lewis, 1973.

Sandoz, Mari. *Cheyenne Autumn.* New York: Hastings House, 1953.

Sanford, Mollie D. *Mollie: The Journal of Mollie Dorsey Sanford in Nebraska and Colorado Territories, 1857–1866.* Introduction and notes by Donald F. Danker. Lincoln, NE: University of Nebraska Press, 1976.

Schlicke, Carl. *Left by the Indians and Massacre on the Oregon Trail in the Year 1860.* Fairfield, WA: Ye Galleon Press, 1992.

Schlissel, Lillian. *Women's Diaries of the Westward Journey.* New York: Schocken Books, 1982.

Schultz, Duane. *Over the Earth I Come: The Great Sioux Uprising of 1862.* New York: St. Martin's Press, 1992.

Shannon, Donald H. *The Utter Disaster on the Oregon Trail: The Utter and Van Ornum Massacres of 1860.* Caldwell, ID: Snake Country Publishing, 1993.

Simmon, Scott. *The Invention of the Western Film: A Cultural History of the Genre's First Half-Century.* Cambridge, UK: Cambridge University Press, 2003.

Simmons, Marc. *Following the Santa Fe Trail: A Guide for Modern Travelers.* Santa Fe, NM: Ancient City Press, 1984.

Simon, William G., and Louise Spence. "Cowboy

Wonderland: History and Myth: 'It Ain't All That Different Than Real Life.'" In *Western Films Through History*, ed. Janet Walker, pp. 89–108. New York: Routledge, 2001.

Skogen, Larry C. *Indian Depredation Claims, 1796–1920*. Norman, OK: University of Oklahoma Press, 1996.

Slotkin, Richard. *Fatal Environment: The Myth of the Frontier in the Age of Industrialization, 1800–1890*. New York: HarperCollins, 1994.

_____. *Gunfighter Nation: The Myth of the Frontier in 20th Century America*. New York: HarperCollins, 1992.

Smith, David Paul. *Frontier Defense in the Civil War: Texas' Rangers and Rebels*. College Station, TX: Texas A&M University Press, 1992.

Smith, Maurice E. "The Oregon Trail's Utter Tragedy." *Wild West* (April 2000), pp. 42–48, 80.

Smith, Sherry L. *The View from Officer's Row: Army Perceptions of Western Indians*. Tucson, AZ: University of Arizona Press, 1990.

Sowell, A. J. *Early Settlers and Indian Fighters of Southwest Texas*. Austin, TX: Benjamin C. Jones, 1900. Reprint. Austin, TX: State House Press, 1986.

Spotts, David L. *Campaigning with Custer, 1868–69*. Edited by D. A. Brininstool. Lincoln, NE: University of Nebraska Press, 1988.

Steckmesser, Kent Ladd. *The Western Hero in History and Legend*. Norman, OK: University of Oklahoma Press, 1997.

Stewart, George R. *The California Trail*. New York: McGraw-Hill, 1962.

Stratton, Joanna L. *Pioneer Women: Voices from the Kansas Frontier*. Introduction by Arthur M. Schlesinger, Jr. New York: Simon and Schuster, 1982.

Stratton, R.B. *Captivity of the Oatman Girls*. Foreword by Wilcomb E. Washburn. Lincoln, NE: University of Nebraska Press, 1983.

Strauss, William, and Neil Howe. *Generations: The History of America's Future, 1584 to 2069*. New York: William Morrow, 1991.

Summerhayes, Martha. *Vanished Arizona Recollections of the Army Life of a New England Woman*. Lincoln, NE: University of Nebraska Press, 1979.

Sweeney, Edwin R. *Cochise, Chiricahua Apache Chief*. Norman, OK: University of Oklahoma Press, 1991.

_____. *Mangas Coloradas, Chief of the Chiricahua Apaches*. Norman, OK: University of Oklahoma Press, 1998.

Tate, Michael L. *Indians and Emigrants: Encounters on the Overland Trails*. Norman, OK: University of Oklahoma Press, 2006.

Tevis, Captain James H. *Arizona in the '50s*. Albuquerque, NM: University of New Mexico Press, 1954.

Thrapp, Dan L. *Encyclopedia of Frontier Biography in Three Volumes*. Lincoln, NE: University of Nebraska Press, 199.

Thompson, Jerry. *Confederate General of the West: Henry Hopkins Sibley*. Foreword by Frank E. Vandiver. College Station, TX: Texas A&M University Press, 1996.

Trenholm, Virginia Cole. *The Arapahoes, Our People*. Norman, OK: University of Oklahoma Press, 1970.

Udall, Stewart L. "The 'Wild' Old West — A Different View." *Montana: The Magazine of Western History* 49, no. 4 (Winter 1999), pp. 64–71.

Udall, Stewart L., Robert Dykstra, Michael L. Bellesisles, Paula Mitchell Marks, and Gregory H. Nobles. "How the West Got Wild: American Media and Frontier Violence, A Roundtable." *Western Historical Quarterly* 31, no. 3 (Autumn 2000), pp. 277–295.

Unrau, William E., ed. *Tending the Talking Wire: A Buck Soldier's View of Indian Country, 1863–1866*. Salt Lake City, UT: University of Utah Press, 1990.

Unruh, John D., Jr. *The Plains Across: The Overland Emigrants and the Trans-Mississippi West, 1840–60*. Urbana, IL: University of Illinois Press, 1993.

U.S. War Department. *The War of the Rebellion: A Compilation of the Official Records of the Union and Confederate Armies*. Washington: GPO, 1880–1901.

Utley, Robert M. *Frontier Regulars: The U.S. Army and the Indian, 1866–1891*. New York: Macmillan, 1973.

_____. *The Lance and the Shield: The Life and Times of Sitting Bull*. New York: Henry Holt, 1993.

Vaughn, J. W. *The Battle of Platte Bridge*. Norman, OK: University of Oklahoma Press, 1963.

_____. *Indian Fights: New Facts on Seven Encounters*. Norman, OK: University of Oklahoma Press, 1966.

Walker, Janet, ed. *Westerns Films Through History*. New York: Routledge, 2001.

Webb, George W. *Chronological List of Engagements Between the Regular Army of the United States and Various Tribes of Hostile Indians*. St. Joseph, MO: Wing Print, 1939.

Webb, Walter Prescott, and H. Bailey Carroll, eds. *The Handbook of Texas*. Two Volumes. Austin, TX: Texas State Historical Association, 1952.

Webber, Bert. *Oregon Trail Emigrant Massacre of 1862 and Port-Neuf Muzzle-Loaders Rendezvous Massacre, Rocks, Idaho*. Medford, OR: Webb Research Group, 1987.

_____. *Over the Applegate Trail to Oregon in 1846*. Medford, OR: Webb Research Group, 1996.

Webber, Bert, ed. *The Oregon and California Trail Diary of Jane Gould in 1862*. Medford, OR: Webb Research Group, 1987.

Wellman, Paul I. *Death on the Prairie: The Thirty Years' Struggle for the Western Plains*. Lincoln, NE: University of Nebraska Press, 1987.

White, Lonnie J. *Hostiles and Horse Soldiers: Indian Battles and Campaigns in the West*. Foreword by Merrill J. Mattes. Boulder, CO: Pruett Publishing, 1972.

_____. "White Woman Captives of Southern Plains Indians, 1866–1875." *Journal of the West* VIII, no. 8 (July 1969), pp. 327–354.

Williams, Clayton W. *Texas' Last Frontier: Fort Stockton and the Trans-Pecos, 1861–1895*. College Station, TX: Texas A&M Press, 1982.

Wilson, Jane Adeline. *A Thrilling Narrative of the Sufferings of Mrs. Jane Adeline Wilson During Her Captivity Among the Comanche Indians. Rochester, NY: Dellon M. Dewey, 1854. Reprint. Fairfield, WA: Ye Galleon Press, 1971.

Wilson, R. Michael. *Great Stage Robberies of the Old West*. Guilford, CT: Globe Pequot Press, 2007.

Winfrey, Dornum H., and James M. Day, eds. *The Indian Papers of Texas and the Southwest, 1825–1916*. 5 Vols. Austin, TX: Pemberton Press, 1966. Reprint. Introduction by Michael L. Tate. Austin, TX: Texas State Historical Association, 1995.

Wynkoop, Edward W. *The Tall Chief: The Autobiography of Edward W. Wynkoop*. Edited and with an Introductory Biography by Christopher B. Gerboth. Denver, CO: Colorado Historical Society, 1994.

Zesch, Scott. *The Captured: A True Story of Abduction by Indians on the Texas Frontier*. New York: St. Martin's Press, 2004.

## Internet Sources

Eddins, O. Ned. "Plains Indian Smallpox." www.mountainofstone.com/indian_smallpox.htm.

Lewy, Guenter. "Were American Indians the Victims of Genocide?" History News Network. George Mason University. http://hnn.us/articles/7302.html.

Nowak. "Painted Post Crossroads," in forttours.com/pages/ewhite.

"Sarah Ann Newton Horn," *Handbook of Texas Online*. www,tsha.utexas.edu/handbook/online/articles.

"Whitman Massacre — Whitman Massacre Roster," 1, http://www.oregonpioneers.com/whit man4.htm.

## Unpublished

*Richard Blinn Diary*. Ford County, KS Historical Society.

Rosenberg, Robert G. "Historical Investigations of the Sawyers Wagon Road Expeditions of 1865 and 1866." Site study prepared for AMAX Coal Company.

## National Archives

National Archives and Records Administration, Washington, D.C. Records Group 75 and 123, U.S. Court of Claims, Indian Depredation Files:
   Barret, Richard F. RG 123 #1679
   Crow, Jerome E. RG 123 #998
   Davenport, James. RG 123 #5732
   Fletcher, Amanda. RG 123 #5072
   Morgan, James. RG 75 #3644
   Morton, Nancy. RG 75 #332
   Sharp, Andrew. RG 123 #1520

## Newspapers

*Idaho World* (Idaho City, Idaho)
*Nebraska City Daily Press* (Nebraska City, Nebraska)
*Owyhee Avalanche* (Silver City, Idaho)

# Index

Aaker, Lee 94, 146
Abell, Henry H. 112
Adair, John 182
Adams, Charles 38, 39, 40
Adams, Elizabeth 92, 93
Adams, George 92
Adams, George W. 92
Adams, Nick 46, 56
Adams, Thomas 38, 39, 40
Adams, Thomas J. 93
Adams Wagon Train 152
Aden, William 45
*The Adventures of Rin Tin Tin* 94, 146
Agar, John 87
Agutter, Jenny 198
Ake, Felix G. 108, 109
Ake-Wadsworth Wagon Train 108–110
Akey, Ed 64
Akins, Claude 31
Alamo 20
Allen, Clara 184
Allen, Mr. 108
Allen, Rex 6
Allison, Mr. 122, 123
Altman, Robert 197, 198
Ames (Amen), Mr. 40
Anderson, Bronco Billy 6
Anderson, John 42
Andersson, Bibi 86
Andres, Nick 140
Andrews, John 94
Androsky, Carole 114, 196
*Apache* (1954) 195
*Apache Chief* (1949) 195
*Apache Rifles* (1964) 144
*Apache Woman* (1955) 195
Applegate Trail 90
*Arming America* 194
Arrison, Henry 116
Arthur, Jean 135, 137
Asa Havey 176
Asher, Ambrose 72, 73
Autry, Gene 5, 6
Aveline, Robert 170
Avery, George 49

Babbitt, Almon W. 83
Babcock, William 38–40
Baby Boomers 5, 6, 189, 193, 199

Baca, Francisco 124
Baca Wagon Train 120
Bacon, Lloyd 150
Bailey, Dr. 113
Baily, Zuzu 163
Baker, Bob 6
Baker, Jean Rio 165
Baker, John T. 44–46
Baldwin 130
Baldwin, Frank D. 146, 159, 163
Baley, Gillum 64
Baley, William R. 64
Ball, James 177
Ballau, James 128
Balsam, Martin 196
Bancroft, George 172
Banion, Will 166, 168
Barcroft, Roy 138
Barker, Ada 178
Barker, David H. 178
Barker, Ida 178
Barker, Jess 106
Barret, Richard F. 122
*The Barrier of Blood* (1913) 36
Barton, Charles 118
*Bat Masterson* 6
Bateman, William 45
Baylor, Mr. 24
Beale, Edward F. 63
Beales, John C. 20
Beale's Wagon Road 63, 64
*Bear Hunt Romance* (1911) 36
Bear Man 123
Beck, Preston 17
Becknell, William 16
Beecher, Frederick 138
Beecher Island fight 137–138
Beery, Noah, Jr. 117
Beery, Wallace 6
Belden, Rick 163
Belknap, Jesse 165
Belknap, Keturah 165
Belknap, Lorenzo 165
Bell, Corporal 163
Bell, James M. 172
Bell, John C. 40
Bell, Mrs. 42, 163
Bell, Rex 48
Bellesisles, Michael 8, 194
Belmet, Clint 52
Bennett, Emerson 74

Bennett, Mr. 124
Benson, James 177
Benson, Major 129
Bent, Charles 16, 17, 149
Bent, George 74, 124, 149
Bent, William 16, 17, 84, 120, 124, 149
Bent Wagon Train 1, 16–17, 158
Bentner family 64
Bent's Fort 17, 18, 44, 66, 124, 176
Benvenuti, Giovanni 93
Bergen, Candace 42, 163
Bergin, Patrick 81
Bewley, Esther L. 68
Bezely, Mr. 24
Bickford, Charles 61, 137
Big Bear 71
Big Bill 45
Big Bow 133
Big Crow 71
Big Mouth 113
*The Big Trail* (1930) 52, 53, 55, 97–99, 155, 168
Big Tree 133
Birch, James E. 143
Bishop, Ben 121
Black Hawk War 64
Black Kettle 79, 84, 112, 113, 124, 192
Blackfoot 36, 73
Blaine, James 138
Blanchard, Andrew 123–124
Blanchard Wagon Train 120, 124
Blanchett, Kate 26
Blawinsky, Charles 140, 141
*Blazing Arrows* (1922) 36
Blinn, Clara 61, 79, 111–113, 115
Blinn, Hubbell 111
Blinn, Richard 111–113
Blinn, Willie 61, 79, 111–113, 115
Blinn-Buttles Wagon Train 111–112
Bloody Point Massacre 90, 126
Blue, Monte 53
Blue Duck 163, 182, 185
Bodine, Charles 120
Boetticher, Bud 31
Boggs, Thomas O. 17, 18
*Bonanza* 6
Bone, Joseph 70, 71
Boone, Albert G. 124
Boone, Daniel "Sandy" 163

231

# Index

Boone, Doc 172
Borgnine, Ernest 129
Botalye 134
Bothwell, William 119
Bouchey, Willis 75
Bourland, James 175
Bowie, Jim 53, 54
Bowler, Matt 70
Box, Ida 57–59, 61
Box, James 56–58, 178
Box, Josephine 57–59, 61
Box, Laura 57, 59
Box, Margaret 57–59, 61
Box, Mary M. 56–59, 61
Boyd, William 6
Boyer, John 96
Bozeman, John M. 96, 103
Bozeman Trail 1, 96, 116, 118, 120, 132, 149
Bradford, Thomas 93
Bradley, James H. 102
Bragg, Bull 138
Bragg, George 175
Bramley, Raymond 146
Brandon, Henry 74, 179
Breckinridge, Hank 155, 156
Brennan, Walter 117
Bretney, Henry C. 127
Brewster, Daniel 78, 79, 81
Brewster, James 33
Bridger, Jim 52, 96, 168
Brimhall family 33
Brings Plenty 105
Bristol, Captain 93
*Broken Arrow* (1950) 144, 146, 170, 195
Brown 140
Brown, Albert E. 150
Brown, Alpha 63, 64
Brown, Dee 8, 195, 196
Brown, James 94
Brown, Johnny Mack 6, 138, 139, 145
Brown, Mrs. 63
Brown, Sergeant 172
Brundage, T.J. 97
Brunson, Captain 57, 61
Brunson, Dan 57, 61
Buck 172
Buck, Daniel 134
*Buffalo Bill and the Indians* (1976) 197–198
Bull Bear 71, 138, 149
Bullwinkle, Charles 92, 94
Buntline, Ned 198
Burleson, Jim 187
Burnall, Colonel 146
Burrell, Edward 153
Burrell, Louisa H. 153
Burrell, Mary 153, 155
Burrell-Foster Wagon Train 153–156
Burrowes, Thomas B. 117
*Bury My Heart at Wounded Knee* 191, 195
Bush, Joe 84
Butterfield, E. 97
Butterfield Trail 1, 31, 170, 185
Buttles, John F. 111
Buttles, Sarah 111

Calamity Jane 134, 136, 137
California Trail 7, 90, 155
Call, Woodrow 182–185
Callery, Terrence 117
Cameron, Rod 6
Cameron, Ruth 98, 99
Cameron family 44
Camp Douglas 164
Camp Floyd 52
Camp Napoleon 176
Camp Rankin 73
Camp Supply 79, 113, 133, 134, 136, 146
Camp Weld 72, 192
Campbell, Hiram H. 118
Cantrell, Empson 38, 39
Canutt, Yakima 156, 173
Carey, Harry 6
Carey, Harry, Jr. 75, 163, 179, 180
Carleton, James H. 30, 31
Carnuel, Jose 18
Carpenter, Louis 138
Carpenter, Milton 51
Carradine, John 172
Carrol, Captain 129
Carrol, Regina 75
Carson, Christopher "Kit" 17, 53, 66, 108, 176, 197
Carson, Jack 48
Carson, Moses 108, 109
Carson, N. 175
Carson, Stephen 119
Carter, Alexander J. 177
Carter, Elijah 175, 176
Casey, P. 171
Cash, Johnny 198
Cassady, A.J. 92, 93
Cassady, Samuel H. 148
Cassidy, Hopalong 5
Cazeau, Mary 116
Cazeau, Peter 116
Cetah 81
Chaffee, Charles 11, 13, 14
Champion, Mat 170
Chandler, Jeff 144, 146, 170
Chapman, Geraldine 198
Chase, Daniel 11
Chase, Elizabeth 11, 14, 15
Chase, Mary 15
Chata 86, 87
Chavez, Helena 129, 130
Chaykin, Maury 199
Cherokee Trail 44
*Cheyenne* 6
*Cheyenne Autumn* (1964) 195
Chickasaw Brown 109
*China 9, Liberty 37* (1978) 198
Chisholm, Jesse 177
Chivington, John M. 191, 192
Chuka 129, 130
*Chuka* (1967) 129–132
Churchill, Henry 172
Churchill, Marguerite 98
Churchill, Ward 194, 195
*Cimarron City* 6
Cimarron Cut-off 17
Cisco 199
Cisco Kid 5
City of Rocks 94, 95, 98
Clark, Dane 129

Clark, Steve 47
Clay, Jason 106
Clegg, Greeley 75
Clegg, Hannah 75
Clegg, Henry 75
Clegg, Ortho 75
Clift, Montgomery 6, 117, 118
Clifton, Isaiah 178
Clint 56
Cochise 109, 146, 170
Cody, Jefferson 31, 32
Cody, William F. "Buffalo Bill" 136, 137, 197, 198
Cole, Osmer F. 149, 150
Cole, Tommy 155
Coleman, Breck 97–99, 168
Collings, Anne 66
Collins, William O. 101
Columbine High School 7
Colter, John 156
Colyer, Vincent 178
*Comanche Station* (1960)\ 31
Comanche Todd 46, 47, 56
*The Comancheros* (1961) 31
Cometsevah 157
Comstock, William 85, 126
Connor, Patrick E. 91, 149, 150
Cooke, William W. 126, 127
Cooke Wagon Train 126
Cooley, D.N. 59, 177
Cooper, Courtney R. 137
Cooper, Gary 6, 52, 53, 136
Cord, Alex 198
Corkle, Jim 48
Corrigan, Ray "Crash" 53
*The Corsican Brothers* 37
Cortez, Jose 18
Costner, Kevin 199
Cotton, Jim 109
Cotton, Joseph 6, 37
Couch 52
Council House fight 26
Coursey, Jim 57
*The Covered Wagon* (1923) 53, 53, 151, 155, 166, 167
*The Cowboys and the Indians* (1949) 195
Cox, Elizabeth 38
Cox, William A. 38
Coy, Walter 42, 179
Crabb, Caroline 114, 196
Crabb, Jack 113, 114, 173, 196
Crawford, James 93
Crawford, John 87
Crawford, Paint 180
Crawford, Samuel 112
Crepin, Henry N. 97
Cressy, Judson 11, 13
Cresta 42, 87, 105, 163
Cristal, Linda 75
Crockett, Davy 5, 53, 54, 156, 193, 197
Crook, George 142
Crow, Jerome E. 122
Crow Wagon Train 120
Crowder, John 140
Cruze, James 166, 167
Cuneo, Lester 36
Cureton, Dennis 180
Curtis, Ken 75

Custard, Amos J. 127–130, 141
Custard Wagon Train 126
Custer, Elizabeth 59, 60, 80, 127
Custer, George A. 42, 56, 59, 60, 79, 80–82, 85, 86, 113–115, 126, 127, 137–139, 142, 154, 180, 191, 192, 196, 197
Custer, Thomas W. 60
Cut Nose 85, 86
Cutter, Jake 31
Cuttings, Private 170

Daguerre, Alejandro 170
Dahl, Arlene 109
Dallas 172, 173
Daly, Lieutenant 129
Damita, Lily 52, 53
*Dances with Wolves* (1990) 114, 191, 199, 200
Daniels, Napoleon H. 116, 117
Danon, Fifi 168
Dante, Michael 144
Darcel, Denise 168
*Daughter of the West* (1949) 195
Davenport, Mr. 73
Daves, Delmer 46, 146
Davis, Nicholas S. 122
Davison, Bruce 23
*Dawn on the Great Divide* (1942) 47, 48, 55, 144
Dean, Clay 87
Dearborn, William H. 118
DeArmond, William 133
DeBuin, Garnett 23
Deets, Josh 183, 184, 188
DeFonde, Baptiste 148
Degen, Sally 66
Degen, Theopolis 65, 66, 67
DeLise, Frank 120
DeMille, Cecil B. 136, 137
Dent, Frederick T. 14
*Devil's Doorway* (1950) 195
Devine, Andy 172
DeVoto, Bernard 199
Dewey, Dellon M. 31
Diggs, William 49
Dilleland, James 149, 150
Dillon, William 117, 118
Dilts, Jefferson 104, 105
Disney, Walt 155, 156
Dixon, Louis 169
Dole, William 130
Donaho, William 22
Doniphan, Tom 196
Donnelly, Peter 141, 142
Donner, Tamsen 152
Donner Party 15, 152
Dorman, Lo 74
Drago, Harry Sinclair 37
Drew, Charles S. 108
Dru, Joanne 117
Drumm, Clayton 198
Drury, James 47
Dry Route, Santa Fe Trail 17, 18, 123
*Duel at Diablo* (1966) 86–88, 105
Dull Knife 149
Dumas, Alexander 37
Dunbar, Lieutenant 199
Dunlap, Rachel 45

Dunlap, Ruth 45
Dunlap, W. 177
Dunlap family 44
Dunlop, O.F. 122
Dunson, Thomas 117
Dupray 53, 55
Durkin, Charlotte "Lottie" 175–178
Durkin, Millie S. 175, 177
Durkin, Milly J. 175–178
Durkin, Owen 177
Dutch, Doc 67
Dutchman 45
Duvall, Robert 182, 183
Dyer, Joel H. 124
Dykstra, Robert R. 7, 194

Earp, Wyatt 5, 197
Easton, Alton R. 122
Eastwood, Clint 125
Eccles, Aimee 113
Edwards, Aaron 42, 179
Edwards, Amos 180
Edwards, Ben 42
Edwards, Debbie 179, 180
Edwards, Edward H. 148
Edwards, Ethan 23, 42, 74, 79, 115, 179, 180
Edwards, Lucy 42, 179
Edwards, Martha 42, 179
Eighteenth U.S. Infantry 116
Eighth U.S. Infantry 143
Elam, Jack 31
Eleventh Kansas Cavalry 127, 128
Eleventh Ohio Cavalry 101, 127
Elliott, Bill 6
Elliott, Joel 113
Elliott, Sam 89
Ellison, James 136
Elm Creek raid 36, 175–178
Emerson, Hope 168
*End of the Rope* (1923) 37
Estes, Ben F. 148
Eubank, Isabelle 72, 73
Eubank, Lucinda 36, 72, 73, 74, 78, 112
Eubank, Willie 72, 73
Evans, John 192

Fagan, Mr. 120–122, 126
Fairbanks, Douglas 6, 74
Fairbanks Wagon Train 50
Fairchild, John B. 36
Fambrough, Major 199
Fancher, Alexander 44–46
Fancher, Kit Carson 47
Fancher, Matt 45
Fancher-Baker Wagon Train 44–47, 126
Faragher, John 8, 27
Farnsworth, Captain 81
Farnsworth, Hiram W. 177
Farr, Felicia 47, 56
Farrell, Tom 109
*A Fate Worse Than Death* 87
Felice 52
Fen 117
Fernandez, Andres 19
Fetterman, William J. 132
Fifteenth Kansas Cavalry 122

Fifth Minnesota Infantry 130
Fifth U.S. Infantry 133, 134, 146, 159
Fifth U.S. Volunteers 148
*Fighting Caravans* (1931) 52, 53, 55, 168
First California Infantry 122
First Colorado Cavalry 72, 124
First Dakota Cavalry 103, 148
First Dragoons 14, 30, 120
First Oregon Cavalry 108
First U.S. Cavalry 83
First U.S. Infantry 143
Fischer, Rudolph 76
Fisk Wagon Train 103–105, 150
Fitzgerald, Gordon 141, 142
Fitzpatrick, Elizabeth Ann 36, 175–178
Fitzpatrick, Thomas 177
Flack, Red 98, 99
Flesher, Nelson 24
Fletcher, Amanda 84–86
Fletcher, Elizabeth 84–86
Fletcher, Jasper 84, 85
Fletcher, Jasper, Jr. 84
Fletcher, John 70
Fletcher, Mary Ann 84
Fletcher, Oscar D. 84
Fletcher, William 69, 84
Flood 37
Floyd, Nathan 118
Floyd Wagon Train 118
Flynn, Errol 6
Fonda, Henry 6, 87, 190, 196, 197
Ford, John 23, 42, 64, 97, 98, 118, 162, 163, 172, 173, 174, 178, 180, 196, 197, 199
Ford, Nathaniel 65
*The Forest Rose* (1912) 74
Forman, Mrs. 165
Forrest, Frederic 163, 182
Forsyth, George A. 137, 138
Fort Abraham Lincoln 59
Fort Apache 94
*Fort Apache* (1948) 87, 196
Fort Arbuckle 31, 113
Fort Bascom 176, 178
Fort Belknap 28, 175, 177, 185
Fort Berthold 103
Fort Boise 40, 41
Fort Bragg 175
Fort Bridger 44, 164
Fort C.F. Smith 116, 132, 141, 142
Fort Chadbourne 28
Fort Clark 169
Fort Clendennon 129, 131
Fort Cobb 112, 113
Fort Concho 86, 87
Fort Connor 149
Fort Dalles 14
Fort Davis 143
Fort Defiance 95, 132
Fort Dilts 104
Fort Dodge 58, 59, 78, 84, 85, 111
Fort Douglas 11
Fort Elliott 178
Fort Fetterman 142
Fort Gibson 113
Fort Griffin 88, 89, 178, 180
Fort Hall 11, 38, 51, 66, 165

# Index

Fort Halleck 84
Fort Hays 81, 137
Fort Kearny 70, 71, 73, 83, 84
Fort Klamath 108
Fort Lancaster 88, 143, 144
Fort Laramie 73, 100, 101, 142, 153–156
Fort Larned 58, 61, 85, 122–124
Fort Leavenworth 16, 59, 61, 120, 122
Fort Lemhi 11
Fort Lyon 111, 192
Fort Mann 122
Fort McKavett 76
Fort Murrah 175
Fort Phantom Hill 28, 30
Fort Phil Kearny 116, 117, 132, 141, 142
Fort Reno 116, 117, 119, 132, 149
Fort Rice 103, 104
Fort Richardson 88, 89, 180, 186
Fort Ridgely 103, 130, 131
Fort Riley 59, 85, 127
Fort Sill 76, 88
Fort Sully 104, 105
Fort Sumner 185, 187, 188
Fort Walla Walla 13, 66
Fort Wallace 126, 127, 137, 138, 157, 158, 172
Fort Worth 182, 183
Fort Yuma 35
Fort Zarah 58, 122, 170, 177
Foster, Dan 106
Foster, Grace 153
Foster, Isaac 153
Fourth U.S. Infantry 41
Fox, George W. 119
Fox, Sallie 64
Francisco 35
Franklin 100, 101
Frazier, Robert 37
Freeland, William 141
Frémont, John C. 66
Friday 192
Frontier Battalion 182
Frontier Regiment 185
Frost, John 31
Fuller, Lance 106

Gable, Clark 6, 98
Gable, Sergeant 95
Gallegos, Raphael 96
Galvanized Yankees 148
Garner, James 86
Garrard, Lewis 120
Garth, Matt 117
Gary, Jim 74–76
Gates, Nancy 31, 32
Gatewood 172
Gay, Will 70
George, Dan 114
Gere, Thomas P. 130
German, Catherine 157–161, 163
German, Joanna 157, 158
German, John 157
German, Julia 157–161, 163
German, Lydia 157
German, Nancy "Addie" 157–161
German, Rebecca J. 157
German, Sophia 157–161

German, Stephen 157, 158
German family 81, 156, 158, 161, 163
Geronimo 199
GI generation 6
Gibbon, John 102
Gibson, Hoot 6, 53
Giddings, Frank 169
Giddings, George H. 143, 169
Gilkeson, Lily 26
Gilkeson, Maggie 26
Gilliam, Cornelius 65
Gish, Lilliam 37, 61
Givens, Emory 140
Gleason, Samuel 11, 14
Glover, Danny 183, 188
Godfrey, John F. 148
*Gone with the Wind* (1939) 98
Gonzales Wagon Train 88
Goodale family 33
Goodnight, Charles 182–188
Goombi 178
Gordon, Jack 169
Gort, Jen 109
Gould, Jane 94, 152
Goulding, Harry 64
Goulding, Mike 64
Gragory, Ena 37
Grange, Ellen 86, 87, 105
Grange, Willard 86, 87
Grant, Bill 57
Grant, Charlie 57
Grant, Honus 42
Grant, Saginaw 82
Grant, Ulysses S. 189
Grattan Massacre 190
Gravelly Ford Massacre 90–91, 126
Gray, Colleen 117
Gray, Isaac 124
Grayson, John "Doc" 155, 156
Green, John 141
Grey Beard 146, 159, 161
Greyeyes, Michael 81
Griffin, Lee 64
Griffin, Stephanie 56
Griffinstein, William 112, 113
Griffith, D.W. 128, 129
Grimes, Karolyn 163
Grinnell, Mr. 35
Groot, Nadine 117
Grover, Cuvier 58
Grundvig, Jensine 86
*Gunsmoke* 6

Hale, Alan 166
Hale, Monte 6
Hale, Owen 85
*The Half Breed* (1916) 74
*Halfbreed* 74
Hall, Porter 137
Haller, Granville O. 41
Hallie 196
Halsey 198
Hamblin, Jacob 44
Hamilton, Billy 150
Hamilton, Buckskin 150, 151
Hamilton, Dran 23
Hammer, Elisha 170, 171
Hancock, Winfield S. 60, 85
Hanger, Charles 84, 85

Hannibal, Mary 153
Hannibal, William 153
Hansbach, Otto 129
Hanu 130
Hardin, John 148
Hardy, Captain 124
Harper, Bull 46
Harrington, Fanny 51, 52
Harrington, George 171
Harrington, Milton 51, 52
Harris, Mr. 21
Harris, Mrs. 21–22, 26
Harris family 20–21
Harrison, Emily 80, 81
Hart, Mr. 28, 29
Hart, William S. 6, 150, 174
Harter, Isaac 153
Hartz, Edward 143, 144
Harvey, Paul 137
Haskell, Alexander 143
Hastings Cut-off 90
Hat Creek Cattle Company 182
Hatfield 172, 198
Hatton, Raymond 47
Hau-tau 89
*Have Gun Will Travel* 6
Hawkins, Deadwood 138, 139
Hawkins, Linda 82
Hawks, Howard 118
Hawley, Patience 168
Haworth, James 178
Hayden, Mr. 120–122
Hayden Wagon Train 120, 126
Hayward, Louis 129
Hazen, William B. 112, 113
Heavy Horn 149
Hedges, Charles E. 148
Hedges, Daniel T. 148
Hedges, Nathaniel D. 148, 149
Hedgpeth, Tom 64
Heek Reel Wagon Train 1
Henderson, Sister 165
Hennessey, Patrick 88
Hepburn, Audrey 36, 61, 62
Hereford Wagon Train 50
Herron, Lee 58
Hesselberger, Gustave A. 58, 59
Hewitt, Christian C. 158
*Hiawatha* (1952) 195
Hickman, Henry 28
Hickok, William B. "Wild Bill" 134, 136, 137, 197
Hicks, Mr. 24
Hiles, John 122
Hill, Alfred 52
Hill, Charley 140, 141
Hine, Robert 8
Hoffman, Dustin 113, 172, 196
Hogan 125
Holden, William 6
Holland, Gladys 56
Holland, J.M. 171
Holliday, Doc 198, 199
Holliman, Earl 163
Holloway, Mrs. 23
Holloway, Sterling 106
Holloway Wagon Train 23
Holmes, Mr. 153
Holt, Tim 6
*Hondo* (1953) 146

## Index

Hopkins, Sandy  47 48
Horn, John  20, 21, 22
Horn, Joseph  20–22
Horn, Sarah A.  20–22, 26, 31
Horn-Harris Wagon Train  20–23, 108
Horseface  31
Houston, Sam  20, 109
*How the West Was Won* (1962)  110, 168, 174, 189–193
Howard, Oliver O.  146, 170
Howe, Marshall S.  11
Howling Wolf  124
Howluck  108
Hoyt, John  86
Huckobey, Thomas  134
Hudelmeyer, Frank  97
Hudspeth Cut-off  49, 91
Huero  95
Huffman, Zeke  57
Hull, Henry  106
Humason, Orlando  40
Humphreys, Major  31
Hungate family  192
Hunter, Andrew J.  91, 92
Hunter, James  169
Hunter, Jeffrey  23, 79, 115, 180
Hurley, Mary  100, 101
Husted, Zach  118
Huston, Angelica  184
Huston, John  36
Hyde, George  86

Ikard, Bose  188
Iliff, Charles  70
Iliff, J.W.  185
*In the Days of the Pilgrims* (1908)  26
Ince, Thomas H.  150
Ingram, Barbara  37
*Into the West*  191–193
Irish Pete  143
Iron Eyes Cody  156, 173
Isaac, Henry  41
*It's a Wonderful Life* (1946)  163
Iverson, Colonel  42

Jackson, Bill  52
Jackson, Marion  154
Jackson, William  168
Jacques, Mrs.  26
James, George  159
Jamison, Walter  53
Jarman, Claude, Jr.  161
Jeffords, Tom  146, 170
Jeffrey's Cut-off  38
Jenkins, Richard W.  170
Jennings, Waylon  198
Jenny  56
Johnson, Ben  163
Johnson, Britt  175–178, 180
Johnson, Dyke  31
Johnson, Jim  175
Johnson, Mary  175, 176
Jolie  56
Jones, Buck  6, 47, 48, 144
Jones, Eliza J.  38
Jones, Elizabeth  64
Jones, Harvey  38–40
Jones, John  131

Jones, Samuel  26
Jones, Shirley  74
Jones, Sister  165
Jones, Tommy Lee  26, 182, 183
Jordan, Dorothy  42, 179
Jorgensen, Brad  179, 180
Jose  64
Juan Jose  30
Jumping Bull  104

Kaquitts, Frank  198
Keene, Tom  6
Kees, Morgan  69
Keith, Ian  98
Kelly, Fanny W.  100–102, 104, 105, 112
Kelly, Jean L.  81
Kelly, Josiah H.  100, 101, 105
Kelly, Michael  70
Kelly, Robert  36
Kelly family  33, 34
Kelly-Larimer Wagon Train  100–102
Kelsey, Abe  61
Kempton, Sister  165
Kendrick, Silas  95
Kennedy, John  190, 193
Kennedy, John K.  92, 93
Kennedy Wagon Train  92–94, 118
Kent, David  74, 75
*Kentucky Rifle* (1956)  106–107
Kerr, Michael  141
Kerrigan, J. Warren  166
Kicking Bird  122
Killdeer Mountain fight  102, 103
Kimble, Susan  68
King, Charles  53
King, Hannah T.  165, 166
King, Mike  168
Kingsbury, Henry P.  136
Kinney, Nathaniel C.  117
Kirby, Alex  47, 48
Kirkendall, Hugh  117, 118
Kirkendall Wagon Train  117
Kirkland, Mariah  39
Kirkland, Moses  38, 39
Kirkland, Nancy P.  38
Kirtland, Thaddeus S.  117
Kishnell, Charles  11, 13
Kleitz, Veronica  129, 130
Kline, Myron  51
Knight, Amelia  152
Knight, Fuzzy  138, 139
Knudsen, Freda  75
Kohler, Fred  52
Kohner, Susan  56
Korn, Adolph  76
Kristofferson, Kris  198
Krug, William  64
Kuhn, Mickey  117

Ladd, Alan  146
Lake, Elizabeth  38
Lake, George  38, 39
Lame Bear  124
Lamme, Samuel C.  17
Lamy, Jean Baptiste  124
Lancaster, Burt  23, 37, 61, 62, 198
Lander's Cut-off  51, 91
Lane, Ben  31

Lane, Diane  163, 182
Lane, Hondo  9, 145–147
*Laramie*  6
Larimer, Frank  100
Larimer, Sarah  100, 101, 105
Larimer, William J.  100, 101
*Last Days of the Sioux Nation*  192
*The Last Train from Gun Hill* (1959)  163
*The Last Wagon* (1956)  46, 56
Lattimer, John  137
Lawson, Lewis  11, 12
Leavenworth, Jesse H.  177
Le Conte, Dr.  33
Lee, Billy  52
Lee, Elliott  17, 18
Lee, John D.  44–46
Lee, Nelson  26
Left Hand  128
Lehmann, Herman  76
Lehmann, Willie  76
Le May, Alan  61, 175, 178, 180
Lewis, Granville  133
Lewis, Nat  140
Libby, Sergeant  143
Lightning, William  81
Lippi, Massimo  92
Lippincott, Henry  113
Little, John  119
Little Arkansas Treaty  58, 61
Little Beaver  17
*Little Big Man* (1970)  42, 60, 113, 114, 173, 191, 196, 198, 199
Little Bighorn fight  102, 127, 142, 154, 190, 191, 192
Little Buffalo  175
Little Crow  130, 131
Little Heart  122
Little Mountain  176
Little Raven (son)  124
Little Robe  123
Little Rock  113
Livingston, Bob  6
Livingston, Henry B.  52
Lockhart, Matilda  25, 26
Logan, Sheriff  37
Lone Eagle  37
*Lone Ranger*  6
Lone Wolf  133, 154, 155
*Lonesome Dove* (1989)  163, 182, 183, 185, 188
Long, Nathan  89
Long Back  160
Lopez  98, 99
Lopez, Marco  130
Loring, Old Jack  57
Lost Bird  61, 62
Love, John  120–122
Lovell, Don G.  149
Loving, John  57
Loving, Oliver  183, 185–188
Lowe, Angie  146
Lowe, Ed  146
Lowe, John  31, 32
Lowe, Johnny  146
Lowe, Nancy  31, 32
Lower Military Road  140, 143, 169
Lucas, Wilfred  128
Luta  82
Lybe, A. Smith  127

Lyden, Robert 42
Lyman, Wyllys 133, 134, 136
Lyman Wagon Train 133–134, 136, 137
Lynde, Isaac 50, 52
Lyons, Cliff 76
Lyons, Dr. 140

Mackenzie, Ranald S. 89, 115
MacLaine, Shirley 125
Madriaga, Elena de la 75, 76
Madrid, Mariano 109
Maggie 90, 91
Mahoney, Sergeant 159
Mallory, Lucy 172
Mamanti 88, 133
*The Man Who Shot Liberty Valence* (1962) 196, 198
Manco Burro Pass 18
Mangas Coloradas 109, 170
Manifest Destiny 189, 191
Mankato 131
Mann, John L. 140
Many Stars 156
Marble, Ann 72
Marble, Danny 70–73
Marble, William 70
Marcy, Randolph 88
Marks, Paula Mitchell 194
Marsh, Mae 75
Marshal Curly 198
Marshall, Jack 149
Marshall, Tully 52, 98, 168
Martin, Dewey 66
Martinez, Joaquin 23
Marvin, Lee 196
Mason, LeRoy 53
Mason, Margaret 138
*The Massacre* (1912) 128
*Massacre* (1956) 129
Massacre Rocks 91, 93
Masters, Rip 94
Masterson, James A. 38, 40
Masterson, Robert 38
Masterson, Valinda C. 38
Masterson, William 42
Masterson family 153
Mateer family 33
Mathews, George 46
Mattes, Merrill 7, 27, 155, 164
Maverick, Mary 26
Maxwell, Lucien 17
May, James 109
Maynard, Ken 6, 154, 155
McAllister, Scott 86, 87
McBride, Charles 94
McBride-Andrews Wagon Train 94, 108
McCabe, Guthrie 74–76
McCall, Jack 137
McCandless, Mary 76
McCandless, Toby 76
McCandless, William 76
McCarthy, Florence 141
McClellan Creek fight 163
McClure, Doug 37, 61
McCoy 175
McCoy, James 133
McCoy, Max 193
McCoy, Tim 6, 37, 200

McCrae, Augustus 182–185
McDonald 140
McDonald, Caroline 177, 178
McDonald, Mahala 177, 178
McDonald, Rebecca 177
McGarry, Edward 91
McGee, Buster 117
McGeever, James 141, 142
McGowan, J.P. 154
McGuire, J. 49
McIntosh 23
McIntyre, John 168
McKim, Robert 150
McKim, Sammy 53
McLaglen, Victor 197
McLaurie, John 58
McMurtry, Larry 182, 183, 185, 188
McNees, Robert 16
McRae, Charles P. 123, 124
McRae, James 171
McRae, Joel 6, 109
Means, John 16
Medicine Water 157, 158
Meek, Donald 172
Meek, Helen Mar 68
Meek, Joe 68
Meriwether, David 30, 31
Meriwether, Raymond 30
Merrill, E.G. 149, 150
Merriweather, Alardyce T. 196
Merton, Guy 150
Meyers, Edward 126, 127
Miles, Nelson A. 133, 136, 160
Miles, Vera 196
Miljan, John 137
Millay, Tess 117
Miller, Henry C. 120
Miller, John 93
Miller family 44
Mills, Anson 170
Mills, Emmitt 170
Mills, John 129
Mills, Mr. 97
Miltimore, Alonzo 51, 52
Miltimore, Catherine D. 51
Miltimore, Charles N. 51, 52
Miltimore, Edwin A. 51, 91
Miltimore, George 51, 52
Miltimore, James 51
Miltimore, Mary Ellen 51, 52
Miltimore, William 51
Miltimore Wagon Train 11, 51, 52
Minimic 84, 85
*The Missing* (2004) 26
Mitchell, Thomas 172
Mitchell family 44
Mix, Tom 6
Mochi 157, 158
Monroe, Daniel 16
Monument Valley 64, 110, 172, 173
Mooers, John 138
Moon, Johnny 37
Moore, Horace 70
Moquetas 45
Morgan, Anna Brewster 36, 61, 78–82, 115
Morgan, Dan 81, 82
Morgan, Henry 189
Morgan, Ira A. 80
Morgan, James S. 78, 80

Morgan, John Hunt 97
Morgan, Roger 110
Mortimer, David 78
Morton, Charlotte 70
Morton, Frank T. 70, 71
Morton, Nancy 70–74, 81, 84, 112
Morton, Samuel T. 70
Morton-Marble Wagon Train 70–71
Mottes, William 93
Mountain Meadows 44–46
Mouseketeers 155
Mousley, Sarah M. 165
Mulligan, Richard 114, 196
Mulligan, Samuel 38–40
Munkres, Robert 8, 9, 27
Munson, Goodsel 11, 13–15
Murdoch, Theodore 11, 13
Murdock, Ken 53
Murdock, Lee 52
Murphy, Audie 37, 61, 144
My Lai Massacre 42, 114
Myers, John 11, 13
Myers, Joseph 11, 13, 14
Myers, Mary 11
Myres, Sandra 8, 27

Naish, J. Carrol 161
*Navaho* (1952) 195
Neely, David A. 38, 40
Neighbors, Robert S. 30, 31
Neilon, Frederick 134
Nelson, Anthony 149
Nelson, Ralph 42, 86
Nelson, Willie 198, 199
Newby, Asher 97
Newman, Paul 198
Newman, Thomas 93
Nineteenth Kansas Cavalry 79, 80, 113
Nineteenth U.S. Infantry 158
Ninth U.S. Cavalry 76
Ninth U.S. Infantry 14
Noble, John T. 40
Nolan, Jeanette 76
Notah 37
Novak, Jane 150
Nye, James 91

Oakley, Annie 198
Oates, Warren 198
Oatman, Charity 33–34
Oatman, Lorenzo 33–36
Oatman, Lucy 33–34, 36
Oatman, Mary Ann 33–35, 63
Oatman, Olive 33–36, 63
Oatman, Roland 33–34
Oatman, Royse 33–34
Oatman, Royse, Jr. 33–34
Oatman Wagon Train 33–34
O'Brien, Cubby 155, 156
O'Brien, George 6, 197
O'Day, Nell 139
Ogden, Peter S. 68
Ogle, Charles 166
O'Hara, Biff 94
Old Lodge Skins 114
Olsen, Wilbur 198
O'Neil, H. 17
Oregon Trail 1, 7, 8, 11, 19, 26, 27,

# Index

31, 66, 70, 83, 90, 91, 94, 96, 100, 127, 140, 155, 157, 166
*The Oregon Trail* (1939) 55, 138, 139, 145
O'Rourke, Michael S. 87
Ortwell, Captain 154
Ottawa 100
*The Outlaw Josey Wales* (1976) 200
*The Outriders* (1950) 109, 174
Overland Trail 8, 11, 83, 142
Owens, Will 109, 110

Pagaeh 51
Page, Geraldine 146
Paget, Debra 146
*The Painted Stallion* (1937) 53–55
Paluzzi, Lucianna 129, 131
Parker, Cynthia Ann 36, 87
Parker, Fess 155, 156
Parker, Pea Eye 183–185
Parker, Quanah 36, 74, 75, 179
Parker's Fort 36, 190
Parson, George 49
Partenheimer, Harold 141, 142
Pate, Michael 146
Patrick, Gail 53
Patterson, John 93
Paul, Thomas 93
Pawley, Martin 23, 79, 115, 180
Pawnee Killer 138
Peacock 172
Pease, Elisha M. 31
Peck, Gregory 6, 110
Peckinpah, Sam 198
Pell, John H. 104
Pendleton, Karen 155, 156
Penn, Arthur 42, 196
Pennington, Jack 109
Peppard, George 168, 189
Perrin, Jack 53
Perry, Harriet 38
Perry, Mary 39
Perry, Walter G. 38–39
Perry-Kirkland Wagon Train 39
Petersen family 68
Phillips, America 109
Phillips, Robert 109
Pierce Wagon Train 50
Pierson, Leo 150
*The Plainsman* (1936) 135–138
Platt, Louise 172
Platt, Private 170
Plummer, Luke 173
Plummer Gang 173
Pocatello 91
Poisal Brothers 85
Poitier, Sidney 86
Pope, John 103
Portell, John 170
Powell, Peter 86
Power, Tyrone 6
Power, Tyrone, Sr. 98
Pratt, Purnell 137
Pratt, Richard H. 192
Prescott family 189
Preston, Robert 110
Priest, Jerry 140
Pringle, Clark 69
Pringle, Virgil K. 153
Promontory Point 157

Prowers, John 192
Purcell, Marty 74–76
Purcell, Steve 74, 76

Quantrill, William 109, 192

Rainey, Ford 75
Rains, Clayborn F. 49
Ramon 129
Rand, A.C. 169
*Rawhide* 6
Rawlings, Zeb 168
Rawlings family 189
Rawlins, Charlie 61
Rawlins, Hagar 61
Rawlins, Zeb 61
Rawze, John 149
Ray, Aldo 67
*The Rebel* 6
Red Cloud 71, 149, 183
Red Hawk 144
*The Red Raiders* (1927) 154, 155
*Red River* (1948) 117–118
Red River War 145, 159
Redding, William 109
Reel, A.H. "Heck" 142
Reese, Benjamin 24
Reese, Perry 24
Regret, Paul 31
Reilly, Hugh 129
Reith, Jacob 11, 13–15
Reith, Joseph 11, 13–15
Remsberg, Jess 86, 87
Renaldo, Duncan 53
Reno, Marcus A. 14
Rettig, Tommy 46, 47
Richardson, John 108
Richardson, Mrs. 164
Ridge 46, 47, 56
*The Rifleman* 6
Riley, Bennet 16, 17
Riley, Glenda 8, 9, 27
Ringo, John 164, 165
Ringo, Martin 164
Ringo, Mary 164
Ringo, Mattie Bell 164
Ringo Kid 172, 173, 198
*Rio Grande* (1950) 42, 144, 161, 162
Riordan, Mrs. 23
Ritter, Tex 6
Rivas, Carlos 61
Riviere, Pascual 17, 18
Robbins, Samuel M. 126
Roberts, Buck 47, 48
Robson, Putnam 153
Rodann, Ziva 163
Roescher, Joe 170
Rogers, Roy 5, 6
Roland, Gilbert 6
Roman Nose 138
Romero, Ned 82
Root, A.L. 51
Roper, Laura 72–74, 81, 84, 112
Rose 74
Rose, L.J. 64
Rose, Leonard 63
Rose, Mrs. 63
Rose-Baley Wagon Train 63–64
*Rose of Cimarron* (1952) 195
Rukeyser, Mrs. 56

Rukeyser, Willie 87
Running Wolf 75, 76
Russell, William H. 120
Rusty 94, 146
Ruysdael, Basil 146
Ryan, Benjamin W. 96

Sage, John 123, 124
Sager, Catherine 65, 66, 68, 69, 164
Sager, Elizabeth M. 65, 69
Sager, Francisco "Frank" 65, 68
Sager, Hannah L. 65, 66, 68
Sager, Henry 65, 66
Sager, John C. 65, 66, 68
Sager, Matilda J. 65, 66, 68
Sager, Naomi 65, 66
Sager, Rosanna (Henrietta Naomi) 65, 66, 69
Sager Wagon Train 65–68
St. Clair, John 109
St. Clair, Mr. 70
Salmi, Albert 61
Sampson, Will 198
San Antonio and San Diego Mail Company 170
Sand Creek Massacre 42, 43, 85, 112, 157, 190–192
Sand Hill 84
Sanford, Ben 140
Santa Fe Trail 1, 7, 8, 16, 19, 33, 63, 111, 120, 122, 123, 124, 150, 176
Satank 122
Satanta 56–59, 61, 122, 133, 134, 176, 178
Savedra, Jose M. 63
Sawyer, Francis 165
Sawyer, Joe 94
Sawyers, James 148–150
Sawyers, Newell M. 148
Sawyers Wagon Train 126, 150
Saxon, John 62
Scar 179, 180
Schaumberg, Charles 11, 13
Schevekendeck, Mrs. William 83
Schlissel, Lillian 8, 9
Schmalsle, William 134
Schroeder, Ernest 143
Schultz, John 38–40
Schultz, Rudolph 38–40
Scott, Jeff 138, 139, 145
Scott, John 154, 155
Scott, Pippa 42, 179
Scott, Randolph 6, 31, 32, 52
Scott, Tim 183–184
*The Searchers* (1956) 23, 42, 74, 79, 115, 175, 178–180
Sears, Charles W. 148
Sebanek, Catherine 198
Sebanek, Matthew 198
Second California Cavalry 150
Second Colorado Cavalry 170
Second Dragoons 11, 30, 52
Second U.S. Cavalry 141
Sera, Marcela 88
Sessions, Patty 153
Setter, Lon 106
*Seven Alone* (1974) 66–68
Seventh Iowa Cavalry 70, 170
Seventh U.S. Cavalry 80, 112, 113, 126, 137, 138, 172, 173

Seventh U.S. Infantry 31, 50, 102
Shackleford, Ted 81
*Shane* (1953) 146
Sharkey, Sister 165
Sharp, Andrew 100, 101
Sharp, Nathaniel 109
Shatner, William 37
Shaw, William 65, 66, 67
Sheehan, Timothy J. 130, 131
Shepard, George 92
Shepherd, Annie 49, 50
Shepherd, Bettie Diggs 49, 50
Shepherd, Ferguson 49
Shepherd, Oliver L. 95, 132
Shepherd, William 49
Shepherd Wagon Train 49, 50, 52, 91
Sheridan, Andrew 58, 59
Sheridan, Phillip H. 113, 137, 161, 197
Sherman, Sylvester 142, 143
Sherman, William T. 59, 88, 113, 138, 178
Shipley, Alexander N. 95
Shockley, William 81
Shoup, George 192
Shrader, James W. 128
Shurly, Edmund R.P. 141, 142
Sibley, Henry H. 30
Silent Generation 6
Silsby, Mr. 24
Simmons, Seneca G. 31
*Sioux Blood* (1929) 37
Sirola, Joseph 130, 131
Sitting Bull 104, 105, 198
Sixth Michigan Cavalry 149
Sixth U.S. Cavalry 133, 146, 159
Sixth U.S. Infantry 16, 127
Skaggs Wagon Train 50
Skillman, Henry 169
Sky Fire 36
Slemmons Wagon Train 123
Sloss, John 119
Slotkin, Richard 195, 196
Smart-Adams Wagon Train 91–94, 118
Smart Wagon Train 152
Smith, A.A. 72
Smith, Andrew J. 14
Smith, Bull 53
Smith, Clinton 76
Smith, Dean 66
Smith, Elizabeth Dixon 153
Smith, Henry C. 128
Smith, Ignatious M. 49
Smith, Jack C. 138
Smith, James 70
Smith, Jane Cox 28
Smith, Jedediah 122, 192
Smith, Jefferson 76
Smith, John S. 120
Smith, Lieutenant 103, 104
Smith, Louis H. 148
Smith, Mary 68
Smith, Mrs. 70, 71
Smith, William 28
Smith Wagon Train 91
Smoky Hill Trail 157
Snow, Marguerite 74
Snyder, Anna 124

Snyder, Henry 11, 13, 15
Snyder, John 124
Snyder Wagon Train 120
Socrates 7
*Soldier Blue* (1970) 42, 43, 86, 87, 105, 163, 191
Sonseeahray 146
Sowwich 51
"Spaghetti Westerns" 190
Spielberg, Steven 193
*Spin & Marty* 156
Spoon, Jake 183
Spotted Cow 97
Spotts, David L. 80
Sprague, Owen A. 177
*Stagecoach* (1939) 64, 98, 172–174
*Stagecoach* (1966) 198
*Stagecoach* (1986) 198
Stanford, James L. 134, 136
Stanley, Louise 138
Stanton, Jeff 144
*Star Trek* 37
Starett, Charles 6
Stebbins, Charles 90, 91
Steele, Bob 6
Stephen 128
Stephen, Jerry 156
Steuart, George H. 83
Stevens, Charles 98
Stewart, George R. 8
Stewart, James 74, 75, 144, 146, 170, 196
Stewart, Roy 52
Stillwell family 24
Stoddard, Ransom 196
*Stolen Women, Captured Hearts* (1997) 81–82
Stollery, David 156
Stone Calf 75, 159–161
Stone Forehead 79
Story, Nelson 183
Stowe, Harriet Beecher 193
Stratton, Royal B. 36
Strauss, Peter 42
Stricklin, Ray 56
Strode, Woody 75
Strong, John 36
Stuart, Clark 53, 55
Stuart Wagon Train 123
Stumbling Bear 186
Suberr, Lorenza 51
*Sugarfoot* 6
Sullivan, Andrew 100, 101
Sullivan, E.A. 93
Sully, Alfred 102–104
Summers, Edwin 128
Summers, Samuel 71
Sun Boy 178
Sunshine 114
Sutter's Mill 190
Sutton, Sarah 153
Swain, Byron 128
Sweeney, Edwin 170
Swenson, Karl 87

Tabbaboo 40
Taliaferro, Hal 53
*The Talisman* (1966) 82
Tall Bull 138
Tamblyn, Russ 189

Tappl, M.O. 93
Tarzan 155
Tate, Michael 8, 9, 27, 83, 84, 86
Tatum, Lawrie 178
Taylor, Alice 177
Taylor, Dorcas 177
Taylor, Ephriam 93
Taylor, I.C. 58, 59, 61, 62, 84
Taylor, James 177
Taylor, Mr. 100, 101
Taylor, Robert 168
Taylor, Rod 129, 131
Taylor, Tobias 106
Taza 170
Teaser, George 93
Temple, Shirley 87
Templeton, George 116, 117
Tenth U.S. Cavalry 138
Terry, Alfred 138
Testi, Fabio 198
Tevis, Peter Joseph de 17, 19
Tharp, James 17, 19
Tharp, Mary 17, 19
Tharp, William 17, 18, 120
Thayer, Julia 55
Thibault, J.J. 170
Third Colorado Cavalry 192
Third U.S. Infantry 58, 95, 132, 172
Thomas, Freeman 170, 171
Thompson, Dan 156
Thompson, Myra 156
Thompson, R.R. 41
Thompson family 33, 36
Thompson Lewis, Susan 36
Thompson Wagon Train 94
Thorp, Bill 98
Thorp, John 65
Thorpe, Jim 138
Throckmorton, James W. 176
Throstle, George 142, 143
Thursday, Owen 87, 196, 197
Thursday, Philadelphia 87
Tingley, Daniel W. 148
Titus, Nathan 52
Tjader, Anton W. 50
Tokalah 81, 82
Toller 86, 87
Tonner, Wesley 153, 154
Tootle-Leach Wagon Train 117
Torrence, Ernest 52, 168
Tosawi 176
Towne, Charles 17, 18
Towne, Smith 17
Towne-Tevis Wagon Train 17–19
Townsend, A.A. 96, 97
Townsend Wagon Train 96–98, 100
Tracey, Doreen 155
Travers, Bill 86
Trent, Lou 130
Trevor, Claire 172
Trimble, Christopher 11, 13–14
Trimble, Elizabeth 11, 14
Trimble, Emeline 11, 13–15
Turner, Frederick Jackson 7, 200
Turner, Janine 81
Twenty-Seventh U.S. Infantry 141
*Two Mules for Sister Sara* (1970) 125

# Index

*Two Rode Together* (1961) 74, 179
Two Socks 199
Tyler, Tom 173
Tyree, Travis 163

Udall, Stuart L. 7, 194
Udell family 63
Ulzana 23
*Ulzana's Raid* (1972) 23, 56, 87
*The Unforgiven* (1960) 36, 61, 62
Union Pacific Railroad 157
Unruh, John 7, 8, 9, 165
Urich, Robert 183
Utley, Robert 192
Utley, William 11, 12
Utter, Abagel 11, 13
Utter, Abby 13
Utter, Charles 13, 14
Utter, Emma 13
Utter, Henry 14
Utter, Mary 13
Utter, Elijah 11–13
Utter, Susan 13, 14
Utter, Wesley 13
Utter–Van Ornum Wagon Train 11–15, 38

Valence Liberty 196
Valinda 56
Valois, Stuart 129, 130
Van Halen, Cleve 110
Van Orden, Debbie 66
Van Ornum, Abigail 11 14
Van Ornum, Alexis 11, 12, 38
Van Ornum, Eliza 11, 14
Van Ornum, Lucinda 11, 14
Van Ornum, Marcus 11
Van Ornum, Minerva 11, 14
Van Ornum, Reuben 11, 14
Van Ornum, Zachias 14
Van Ornum Wagon Train 11–15, 190
Veal's Station 176
Vetri, Victoria 129, 131
Victorio 144
Viet Nam War 42, 114, 190, 195
Vincent 165
Vittorio 146

Wade, Mrs. Noble 73
Wadsworth, William 108, 109
*Wagon Tracks* (1919) 150–151
*Wagon Train* 6
*Wagon Wheels* (1934) 52, 53
Wakefield, Gardner 100, 101
Waldo, David 16, 17
Waldo, William 16, 17
Walker, Captain 94, 96, 98
Walker, John 93, 117
Walker, June 61
Walsh, Raoul 97
Waltermire, Wash 171
Wanger, Walter 64
Ward 153
Ward, Alexander 38–40
Ward, Edward I. 38, 41

Ward, Flora A. 38, 41
Ward, Francis 38, 41
Ward, James 49
Ward, James H. 42
Ward, Margaret R. 38, 41
Ward, Mary E. 38, 40
Ward, Newton J. 38, 40–42
Ward, Robert G. 38–40
Ward, Susan F. 38, 41
Ward, Thomas C. 38, 41
Ward, William M. 38, 40–42
Ward-Masterson Wagon Train 38–41, 43
Ward Wagon Train 11
Warren, A. 97
Washburn, David 150, 151
Washburn, Jane 150
Washita fight 60, 80, 81, 113–115, 190, 191, 192
Wattles, Mrs. 166
Wayne, John 6, 9, 23, 31, 79, 97, 98, 115, 117, 118, 144, 145, 146, 161, 168, 172, 179, 180, 196, 197
Weaver, Dennis 81, 86, 88
Webster, Booker 24–26
Webster, Dolly 24–26
Webster, John 24
Webster, Patsy 24–26
Webster Wagon Train 24
Wellington, Nancy 53
Wellington, Sonny 52
Wellman, William 168
Wells Fargo 141
West, Charles 128
West, Frank 133
West, Robert M. 126, 127
Western Cattle Trail 183
*Westward Ho the Wagons* (1956) 155, 156, 174
*Westward the Women* (1952) 168
Wet Route 124
Wethered, James S. 120
Wharton, Henry W. 83
Wheeler, family 191
Wheeling family 33
White, David 176
White, Elizabeth M. 38, 40
White, Elonzo 176
White, George 38, 41
White, Richard 8
White, Sarah 61, 78–82, 115
White, William 38
White Antelope 192
White Bull 104, 138
*White Comanche* (1968) 37
*White Feather* (1956) 195
White Man Runs Him 154
Whitman, Marcus 65, 68, 156
Whitman, Narcissa 66, 156
Whitman, Roy 168
Whitman, Stuart 31
Whitman Mission 66–68, 190
Whitmore, James 130
Whitney, Chauncey 138
Widmark, Richard 46, 47, 56, 74, 75, 168, 190

Wilcox, Curly 172, 173
Wilcox, W. 171, 172
*Wild Bill Hickok* 6
"Wild West" 6, 7, 9, 194
Wilder family 33, 34
Williford, George 148–150
Wills, Chill 106
Wilson, Bill "One Arm" 185–187
Wilson, Captain 93
Wilson, George 29, 31
Wilson, James 28
Wilson, Jane 28–31
Wilson, John 170
Wilson, Lois 166
Wilson, Meredith 29, 31
Wilson, Mrs. 83
Wilson, Whip 6
Wilson Wagon Train 28–30
Wilstach, Frank J. 137
Windlass Hill 98
Wingate, Jesse 166, 168
Wingate, Molly 166
Wiseman, Joseph 61
Withers, Grant 197
Wolf Robe 160
Wood, Captain 137
Wood, Evan Rachel 26
Wood, John R. 148, 150
Wood, Lana 179
Wood, Loreena 163
Wood, Natalie 180
Woodhull, Sam 166
Woods, Harry 48
Wootton, Dick 19
Wounded Knee Massacre 192
Wright, George 91
Wright, James D. 49, 50
Wright, Joe 50
Wright, Mrs. 49, 50
Wright, Townsend 49
Wrightman, Oscar 153
Wrightman, Silas 153
Wringle, Harry J. 75, 76
Wyatt, Buck 168
Wynkoop, Edward 72, 78, 85, 192

Yani, Rossana 37
Yantis, Alexander S. 38–41, 153
Yellow Hand 137
Yellow Snake 138
York, Gerald 129
York, Jeff 155, 161, 163
York, Kirby 144, 161, 163, 196
Young, Brigham 44
Young, Ewing 17
Yowlache 154

Zachary, Andy 37, 61, 62
Zachary, Ben 37, 61, 62
Zachary, Cash 37, 61, 62
Zachary, Matilda 37, 61
Zachary, Rachel 36, 37, 61, 62
Zachary, William 61
Zamorro 53, 55
Zeke 98, 168
Zimmer, Eugene 109

www.ingramcontent.com/pod-product-compliance
Ingram Content Group UK Ltd.
Pitfield, Milton Keynes, MK11 3LW, UK
UKHW012135070125
453106UK00015B/219